Taste of Home Just Keeps Getting Better!

With **your favorite recipes** from *Taste of Home* magazine, this exciting cookbook features hundreds of all-new dishes shared by **home cooks just like you**.

53

42

16

After more than two decades of publishing family recipes from cooks across the country, *Taste of Home* magazine continues to serve up fresh, delicious dishes that fit today's lifestyles. You'll find all-new favorites right here in this convenient collection.

The 21st edition in our best-selling book series, this *Taste of Home Annual Recipes* cookbook features a full year's worth of specialties from the magazine. And, we've added bonus dishes. It all adds up to 514 recipes!

Here's just a taste of the new features you'll find:

- **More At-a-Glance Recipe Icons**
  Look for these helpful icons next to recipes:
  FAST FIX = Recipes that take 30 minutes or less to fix from start to finish
  EAT SMART = Recipes that are lower in calories, fat and sodium
  SLOW COOKER = Recipes made in a slow cooker
  (5) INGREDIENTS = Recipes that use 5 or fewer ingredients (excluding salt, pepper, water and canola/olive oil)
- **Expert Help From the Taste of Home Pros**
  The "Cooking School" chapter features helpful tips, how-tos and advice to make cooking even easier.
- **More Stories About Cooks Like You**
  Get to know the people behind the recipes with personal photos, stories and quotes.

With 19 big chapters, full-color photos, handy hints and two indexes, *Taste of Home Annual Recipes* has everything you need to share the goodness!

BEST-LOVED RECIPES

Savory main dishes, delectable desserts, festive party starters...they're all here in *Taste of Home Annual Recipes*. Choose from hundreds of memorable specialties such as (from top) summery Corn with Cilantro-Lime Butter, satisfying Black Bean 'n' Pumpkin Chili and refreshing Strawberry Lemonade Smoothie.

45

56

84

177

Taste of Home
Annual Recipes
2014

EDITORIAL
Editor-in-Chief **Catherine Cassidy**
Creative Director **Howard Greenberg**
Editorial Operations Director **Kerri Balliet**

Managing Editor/Print and Digital Books **Mark Hagen**
Associate Creative Director **Edwin Robles Jr.**

Editor **Michelle Rozumalski**
Art Director **Jessie Sharon**
Layout Designers **Catherine Fletcher, Nancy Novak**
Editorial Production Manager **Dena Ahlers**
Copy Chief **Deb Warlaumont Mulvey**
Contributing Copy Editor **Valerie Phillips**
Copy Editors **Mary C. Hanson, Dulcie Shoener**

Chief Food Editor **Karen Berner**
Food Editors **James Schend; Peggy Woodward, RD**
Associate Food Editor **Krista Lanphier**
Associate Editor/Food Content **Annie Rundle**
Recipe Editors **Mary King; Jenni Sharp, RD; Irene Yeh**
Content Operations Manager **Colleen King**
Executive Assistant **Marie Brannon**
Editorial Intern **Devin Mulertt**

Test Kitchen and Food Styling Manager **Sarah Thompson**
Test Cooks **Matthew Hass, Lauren Knoelke**
Food Stylists **Kathryn Conrad (senior),
Shannon Roum, Leah Rekau**
Prep Cooks **Megumi Garcia, Nicole Spohrleder,
Bethany VanOpdorp**

Photography Director **Stephanie Marchese**
Photographers **Dan Roberts, Jim Wieland**
Photographer/Set Stylist **Grace Natoli Sheldon**
Set Stylists **Stacey Genaw, Melissa Haberman,
Dee Dee Jacq**

Business Analyst **Kristy Martin**
Billing Specialist **Mary Ann Koebernik**

Editor, *Taste of Home* **Jeanne Ambrose**
Art Director, *Taste of Home* **Kristin Bowker**

BUSINESS
General Manager, Taste of Home Cooking Schools
Erin Puariea

Vice President, Brand Marketing **Jennifer Smith**
Vice President, Circulation and Continuity Marketing
Dave Fiegel

READER'S DIGEST NORTH AMERICA
Vice President, Business Development and Marketing
Alain Begun
President, Books and Home Entertainment **Harold Clarke**
General Manager, Canada **Philippe Cloutier**
Vice President, Operations **Mitch Cooper**
Chief Operating Officer **Howard Halligan**
Vice President, Chief Sales Officer **Mark Josephson**
Vice President, General Manager, Milwaukee **Frank Quigley**
Vice President, Digital Sales **Steve Sottile**
Vice President, Chief Content Officer **Liz Vaccariello**
Vice President, Global Financial Planning and Analysis
Devin White

THE READER'S DIGEST
ASSOCIATION, INC.
President and Chief Executive Officer **Robert E. Guth**

COVER PHOTOGRAPHY
Photographer **Grace Natoli Sheldon**
Food Stylist **Shannon Roum**
Set Stylist **Stephanie Marchese**

© 2013 Reiman Media Group, Inc.
5400 S. 60th St., Greendale WI 53129

International Standard Book Number (13):
978-1-61765-257-8

International Standard Serial Number: 1094-3463

Component Number: 117400044H00

Contents

PICTURED ON THE COVER Peach-Blueberry
Crumble Tart (p. 201), Scalloped Potatoes au
Gratin (p. 50), Apple Walnut Salad (p. 283)
and Oven Barbecued Chicken (p. 63).

FOR OTHER TASTE OF HOME BOOKS AND PRODUCTS, VISIT
ShopTasteofHome.com

**JANIE BOTTING'S
MARINATED CHICKEN WINGS**
PAGE 17

Appetizers & Beverages

For **holiday parties, snacktime or anytime,** rely on the special munchies and thirst-quenching drinks in this chapter. You'll find dozens of **sized-right refreshments** that are sure to satisfy.

**NOELLE MYERS'
FIVE-CHEESE SPINACH &
ARTICHOKE DIP** *PAGE 6*

**JAMIE KING'S
STRAWBERRY LEMONADE SMOOTHIE**
PAGE 16

**TRINA LINDER-MOBLEY'S
ITALIAN MEATBALL BUNS**
PAGE 7

FAST FIX **Firecracker Mary**

START TO FINISH: 10 MIN.
MAKES: 2 SERVINGS

- 1½ cups tomato juice
- 2 ounces vodka
- 3 tablespoons beef broth
- 2 teaspoons dill pickle juice
- 2 teaspoons stone-ground mustard
- 1 teaspoon lemon juice
- 1 teaspoon lime juice
- ½ teaspoon hot pepper sauce
- ½ teaspoon Worcestershire sauce
- ½ teaspoon prepared horseradish
- ¼ teaspoon garlic powder
- ¼ teaspoon pepper
  Ice cubes

In a small pitcher, mix the first 12 ingredients; serve over ice.

"While cleaning out my fridge, a lot of the ingredients for a Bloody Mary just jumped out at me. I couldn't resist combining them into a spiced-up variation."

—**JIMMY CABABA** WEST ALLIS, WI

FIRECRACKER MARY

FIVE-CHEESE SPINACH & ARTICHOKE DIP

SLOW COOKER

Five-Cheese Spinach & Artichoke Dip

Whenever I'm invited to an event, I receive a request for this slow-cooked dip. Five different cheeses make it a standout.
—**NOELLE MYERS** GRAND FORKS, ND

PREP: 20 MIN. • **COOK:** 2½ HOURS
MAKES: 16 SERVINGS (¼ CUP EACH)

- 1 jar (12 ounces) roasted sweet red peppers
- 1 jar (6½ ounces) marinated quartered artichoke hearts
- 1 package (10 ounces) frozen chopped spinach, thawed and squeezed dry
- 8 ounces fresh mozzarella cheese, cubed
- 1½ cups (6 ounces) shredded Asiago cheese
- 2 packages (3 ounces each) cream cheese, softened and cubed
- 1 cup (4 ounces) crumbled feta cheese
- ⅓ cup shredded provolone cheese
- ⅓ cup minced fresh basil
- ¼ cup finely chopped red onion
- 2 tablespoons mayonnaise
- 2 garlic cloves, minced
  Assorted crackers

1. Drain the red peppers, reserving 1 tablespoon liquid; chop the peppers. Drain the artichokes, reserving 2 tablespoons liquid; coarsely chop artichokes.
2. In a 3-qt. slow cooker coated with cooking spray, combine the spinach, cheeses, basil, red onion, mayonnaise, garlic, artichoke hearts and peppers. Stir in reserved pepper and artichoke liquids. Cook, covered, on high 2 hours. Stir dip; cook, covered, 30-60 minutes longer. Stir before serving; serve with crackers.

Spicy Cheese Crackers

Crisp and flaky with a touch of zip...it's no wonder these little homemade nibbles disappear in a flash. They're great as a Christmastime gift packed alongside a bottle of wine.

—DONNA LINDECAMP MORGANTON, NC

START TO FINISH: 30 MIN.
MAKES: 32 CRACKERS

- 1½ cups (6 ounces) shredded extra-sharp cheddar cheese
- ¾ cup all-purpose flour
- ½ teaspoon kosher salt
- ¼ teaspoon crushed red pepper flakes
- ¼ cup cold butter, cubed
- 1 to 2 tablespoons half-and-half cream

1. Place the cheese, flour, salt and pepper flakes in a food processor; process until blended. Add butter; pulse until butter is the size of peas. While pulsing, add just enough cream to form moist crumbs.

2. On a lightly floured surface, roll dough to ⅛-in. thickness. Cut with a floured 3-in. cookie cutter. Place 2 in. apart on greased baking sheets. Reroll scraps and repeat.

3. Bake at 350° for 13-17 minutes or until golden brown. Remove from pans to wire racks to cool completely. Store in an airtight container.

SPICY CHEESE CRACKERS

ITALIAN MEATBALL BUNS

Italian Meatball Buns

I love preparing special recipes just for my six grandchildren. I tuck Italian meatballs inside frozen dough to create little golden rolls that have a savory surprise.

—TRINA LINDER-MOBLEY CLOVER, SC

PREP: 30 MIN. + RISING • **BAKE:** 15 MIN.
MAKES: 2 DOZEN

- 12 frozen bread dough dinner rolls
- 1 package (12 ounces) frozen fully cooked Italian meatballs, thawed
- 2 tablespoons olive oil
- ¼ cup grated Parmesan cheese
- ¼ cup minced fresh basil
- 1½ cups marinara sauce, warmed

1. Let the dinner roll dough stand at room temperature 25-30 minutes or until softened.

2. Cut each dinner roll in half. Wrap each half around a meatball, enclosing the meatball completely; pinch the dough firmly to seal. Place on greased baking sheets, seam side down. Cover with kitchen towels; let rise in a warm place until almost doubled, about 1½ to 2 hours.

3. Preheat oven to 350°. Bake 12-15 minutes or until golden brown. Brush the tops of the buns with oil; sprinkle with Parmesan cheese and basil. Serve with marinara sauce.

SWEET POTATO CROSTINI

TURKEY-CRANBERRY MINIS

GREEN BEAN CASSEROLE
STUFFED MUSHROOMS

FAST FIX ▶ Sweet Potato Crostini

I turned a sweet potato side dish into an appetizer by spooning it onto slices of a French baguette. Complete with browned mini marshmallows on top, the little toasts are hard to resist.
—**STEVE WESTPHAL** WIND LAKE, WI

START TO FINISH: 30 MIN. • **MAKES:** 2 DOZEN

- 24 **slices French bread baguette (¼ inch thick)**
- ¼ **cup butter, melted**
- 2 **tablespoons sugar**
- ½ **teaspoon ground cinnamon**

TOPPING

- 2 **cups mashed sweet potatoes**
- ¼ **cup chopped pecans**
- 3 **tablespoons packed brown sugar**
- 2 **tablespoons butter, melted**
- 1¼ **cups miniature marshmallows, halved**
  Minced fresh rosemary, optional

1. Place bread in a single layer on ungreased baking sheets; brush with butter. In a small bowl, mix sugar and cinnamon; sprinkle over tops. Bake at 400° for 2-3 minutes or until lightly browned.

2. Meanwhile, in another bowl, mix sweet potatoes, pecans, brown sugar and butter. Spoon onto toasts; top with mini marshmallows, pressing lightly to adhere. Broil 3-4 in. from the heat for 1-2 minutes or until marshmallows are lightly browned. Sprinkle with rosemary if desired.

Turkey-Cranberry Minis

At casual get-togethers during the holiday season, we serve these tiny tarts as fun stand-ins for the traditional turkey and trimmings.
—**NADINE MESCH** MOUNT HEALTHY, OH

PREP: 25 MIN. • **BAKE:** 10MIN. • **MAKES:** 2½ DOZEN

- ⅓ **cup mayonnaise**
- 4 **teaspoons minced fresh parsley**
- 4 **teaspoons honey mustard**
- ½ **teaspoon chopped seeded jalapeno pepper**
- ⅛ **teaspoon pepper**
- 2 **cups cubed cooked turkey breast**
- ⅓ **cup chopped celery**
- ⅓ **cup dried cranberries, chopped**
- ⅓ **cup shredded Swiss cheese**
- ¼ **cup chopped pecans, toasted**
- 30 **frozen miniature phyllo tart shells**

1. In a large bowl, mix the first five ingredients. Add the turkey, celery, dried cranberries, Swiss cheese and pecans; toss to coat.

2. Arrange tart shells on an ungreased baking sheet. Fill with turkey mixture. Bake at 375° for 10-12 minutes or until heated through. Serve warm.

NOTE *To toast nuts, spread in a 15-in. x 10-in. x 1-in. baking pan. Bake at 350° for 5-10 minutes or until lightly browned, stirring occasionally. Or, spread in a dry nonstick skillet and heat over low heat until lightly browned, stirring occasionally.*

Green Bean Casserole Stuffed Mushrooms

Green bean casserole is one of our must-haves for Thanksgiving dinner, but it needed updating. This bite-size variation gets an enthusiastic reaction from everyone who tastes it.

—**KAYTIE PICKETT** JACKSON, MS

PREP: 20 MIN. • **BAKE:** 20 MIN. • **MAKES:** 2½ DOZEN

- 3 turkey bacon strips, diced
- 1½ teaspoons minced garlic
- 1 can (14½ ounces) French-style green beans, drained
- ¾ cup grated Parmesan cheese, divided
- ¼ cup condensed cream of onion soup, undiluted
- ¼ cup water
- ⅛ teaspoon ground nutmeg
- ⅛ teaspoon pepper
- 1 cup dry bread crumbs
- 30 whole baby portobello mushrooms
   Cooking spray
- 1 can (2.8 ounces) French-fried onions

1. In a small skillet, cook bacon over medium heat until crisp. Add the garlic; cook 1 minute longer. Place the green beans, ½ cup Parmesan cheese, cream of onion soup, water, nutmeg, pepper and bacon mixture in a food processor; process until blended. Transfer to a small bowl; fold in the bread crumbs.

2. Remove stems from mushrooms; discard stems or save for another use. Spritz mushroom caps with cooking spray; place in an ungreased 15-in. x 10-in. x 1-in. baking pan, stem side down. Bake at 425° for 10 minutes, turning once.

3. Drain liquid from mushroom caps; fill with green bean mixture. Top with remaining cheese and fried onions. Bake 8-10 minutes longer or until mushrooms are tender and filling is heated through.

 Did you know?

With their large size and meaty texture, portobello mushrooms are well suited for grilling or broiling. Their meaty texture makes them popular in vegetarian burgers and other vegetarian recipes. Baby portobello mushrooms are also known as cremini mushrooms. They can be used instead of white mushrooms for a flavor boost.

FAST FIX ▶ Buffalo Chicken Dip

START TO FINISH: 30 MIN. • **MAKES:** ABOUT 2 CUPS

- 1 package (8 ounces) cream cheese, softened
- 1 can (10 ounces) chunk white chicken, drained
- ½ cup buffalo wing sauce
- ½ cup ranch salad dressing
- 2 cups (8 ounces) shredded Colby-Monterey Jack cheese
   French bread baguette slices, celery ribs or tortilla chips, optional

1. Preheat oven to 350°. Spread cream cheese into an ungreased shallow 1-qt. baking dish. Layer with chicken, wing sauce and salad dressing. Sprinkle with cheese.

2. Bake, uncovered, 20-25 minutes or until cheese is melted. If desired, serve with baguette slices.

"Chicken, ranch dressing, buffalo wing sauce and cheese make a great party dip. Just try it and see!"
—**PEGGY FOSTER** FLORENCE, KY

BUFFALO CHICKEN DIP

50 Shakes *for* 50 States

Start with vanilla ice cream and milk, toss in these **signature state goodies** and blend. Then just **sip and smile!**

Alabama
Coconut Cake
Add coconut extract and sprinkle with toasted coconut.

Alaska
Bear Claw
Add layers of caramel syrup, cashews and grated chocolate.

Arizona
Date
Add chopped dates; serve with two straws.

Arkansas
Natural Banana Pudding
Add banana; garnish with vanilla wafers and sliced bananas.

California
Almond
Sub almond milk for dairy milk; top with whipped cream and toasted sliced almonds.

Colorado
Snowcapped Mountain
Add Sno-Cap candies.

Connecticut
Nutmeg State
Add freshly grated nutmeg.

Delaware
Stars and Stripes
Swirl with pureed strawberries and top with fresh blueberries.

Florida
Key Lime Pie
Add sweetened condensed milk, Key lime juice and grated lime peel.

Georgia
Peach
Add fresh chopped peaches, ground ginger and honey.

Hawaii
Aloha
Add fresh chopped pineapple and macadamia nuts.

Idaho
Potato Chip Crunch
Swirl with chocolate hard-shell ice cream topping. Top with crushed potato chips.

Illinois
Strawberry-Rhubarb
Add strawberry-rhubarb jam.

Indiana
Hoosier Cream Pie
Add a slice of Hoosier pie to the blender.

Iowa
Caramel Corn
Add caramel sauce; sprinkle with caramel corn.

Kansas
Ruby Slipper
Add pomegranate juice and fresh raspberries.

Kentucky
Derby Shake
Add Kentucky bourbon, pecans and chocolate chips.

Louisiana
Bananas Foster
Add dark rum, bananas and brown sugar.

Maine
Wild Blueberry
Add wild blueberries; top with additional blueberries.

Maryland
Smith Island Cake
Pour vanilla shake into glass alternately with chocolate syrup, chopped-up fudge candy and crumbled yellow cake.

Massachusetts
Boston Cream Pie
Add vanilla pudding mix; stir in pieces of vanilla cake; top with chocolate syrup.

Michigan
Mackinac Island Fudge
Add fudge pieces; swirl with fudge sauce.

Minnesota
Honeycrisp
Add peeled, chopped Honeycrisp apples.

Mississippi
Mississippi Mud
Use rocky road ice cream; add chocolate milk; swirl with fudge sauce and top with chopped pecans.

Missouri
Ozark Pudding
Add apple pie filling and black walnuts.

Montana
Huckleberry Pie
Add huckleberries and cinnamon; sprinkle with crumbled graham cracker crust.

Nebraska
Kool-Aid
Add Kool-Aid Tropical Punch.

Nevada
Big Winner
Chop and add 100 Grand and PayDay candy bars.

New Hampshire
Whoopie Pie
Use chocolate ice cream; swirl with marshmallow creme.

New Jersey
Saltwater Taffy
Add strawberries and bananas; fold in whipped cream and top with chopped saltwater taffy.

New Mexico
Chocolate Shake with a Kick
Use chocolate ice cream; add ground ancho chili pepper and cinnamon.

New York
New York Cheesecake
Add ready-to-eat cheesecake filling; top with cherry pie filling.

North Carolina
Sweet Potato Pie
Add canned sweet potatoes; sprinkle with cinnamon and nutmeg.

North Dakota
Glorified Rice Whirl-A-Whip
Add prepared rice pudding, fruit cocktail and crushed pineapple; top with mini marshmallows.

Ohio
Buckeye
Use peanut butter cup ice cream; add peanut butter; top with chocolate hard-shell ice cream topping.

Oklahoma
Strawberry Shortcake
Use strawberry ice cream; add strawberries; swirl with strawberry syrup and shortcake pieces.

Oregon
Hazelnut Mocha
Add brewed hazelnut coffee and chocolate syrup. Top with whipped cream and hazelnuts.

Pennsylvania
Hershey's
Use chocolate ice cream; add Hershey's syrup; garnish with grated Hershey's dark chocolate.

Rhode Island
Coffee Milk Shake
Use coffee ice cream; add espresso; garnish with chocolate-covered coffee beans.

South Carolina
Sweet Tea
Add iced tea mix; garnish with lemon.

South Dakota
Apricot Kuchen
Add fresh chopped apricots and custard powder; sprinkle with cinnamon.

Tennessee
Elvis
Add peanut butter and banana; garnish with banana slices and bacon.

Texas
Watermelon
Chop and add watermelon; stir in mini chocolate chips.

Utah
Lime Jell-O
Add lime gelatin powder; garnish with green maraschino cherries.

Vermont
Maple Blast
Add maple syrup; sprinkle with maple candy.

Virginia
Shoofly Pie
Add molasses; dollop with whipped cream.

Washington
Cherry Cream
Use black cherry ice cream; add Jones cream soda and fresh cherries.

West Virginia
Appalachian Stack Cake
Add apple butter and apple pie spice; stir in yellow cake pieces and garnish with dried apples.

Wisconsin
Cranberry Custard
Sub vanilla custard for ice cream; add cranberry sauce.

Wyoming
Cowboy Cookie
Use cookie dough ice cream; stir in mini chocolate chips and sprinkle with pecan granola and coconut.

GARLICKY HERBED SHRIMP

MUSHROOM
PALMIERS

SMOKED SALMON BITES

WARM FIG & BRIE CRISPS

Garlicky Herbed Shrimp

I love shrimp, garlic and herbs. Cook 'em all in butter and what could be better?

—DAVE LEVIN VAN NUYS, CA

START TO FINISH: 25 MIN.
MAKES: ABOUT 3 DOZEN

- 2 **pounds uncooked jumbo shrimp, peeled and deveined**
- 5 **garlic cloves, minced**
- 2 **green onions, chopped**
- ½ **teaspoon garlic powder**
- ½ **teaspoon ground mustard**
- ¼ **teaspoon seasoned salt**
- ¼ **teaspoon crushed red pepper flakes**
- ⅛ **teaspoon pepper**
- ½ **cup butter, divided**
- ¼ **cup lemon juice**
- 2 **tablespoons minced fresh parsley**
- 1 **tablespoon minced fresh tarragon**

1. In a large bowl, combine the first eight ingredients; toss to combine. In a large skillet, heat ¼ cup butter over medium-high heat. Add half of shrimp mixture; cook and stir for 4-5 minutes or until shrimp turns pink. Transfer to a clean bowl.

2. Repeat with the remaining butter and shrimp mixture. Return cooked shrimp to pan. Stir in the lemon juice; heat through. Stir in herbs.

Mushroom Palmiers

While working at a small-town museum in West Texas years ago, I came across this popular recipe. It's still a big hit at parties, and using convenient frozen puff pastry reduces my time in the kitchen.

—JUDY LOCK PANHANDLE, TX

PREP: 20 MIN. + COOLING
BAKE: 15 MIN./BATCH • **MAKES:** 4 DOZEN

- 2 **tablespoons butter**
- ¾ **pound fresh mushrooms, finely chopped**
- 1 **small onion, finely chopped**
- 1 **teaspoon minced fresh thyme or ¼ teaspoon dried thyme**
- ¾ **teaspoon lemon juice**
- ¾ **teaspoon hot pepper sauce**
- ¼ **teaspoon salt**
- 1 **package (17.3 ounces) frozen puff pastry, thawed**
- 1 **egg**
- 2 **teaspoons water**

1. In a large skillet, heat butter over medium heat. Add mushrooms and onion; cook and stir until tender. Stir in thyme, lemon juice, hot pepper sauce and salt. Cool completely.

2. Unfold one sheet of puff pastry. Spread half of the mushroom mixture to within ½ in. of the edges of sheet. Roll up the left and right sides toward the center, jelly-roll style, until rolls meet in the middle. Cut into 24 slices. Repeat with the remaining puff pastry and mushrooms.

3. Place on greased baking sheets. In a small bowl, whisk the egg and water; brush over pastries. Bake at 400° for 15-20 minutes or until golden brown. Serve warm or at room temperature.

Warm Fig & Brie Crisps

These crisps are not only distinctive, but also fun to adapt to suit our mood. We sometimes substitute toasted slices of baguette and a different cheese.

—HANNAH BUTLER RHODESDALE, MD

START TO FINISH: 30 MIN.
MAKES: ABOUT 3½ DOZEN

- 1 **package (6 ounces) baked pita chips or 1 package (5¼ ounces) melba rounds**
- ½ **cup fig or peach preserves**
- 1 **round (8 ounces) Brie cheese, thinly sliced**
- ¼ **cup honey**

1. Arrange pita chips on two foil-lined baking sheets. Spread with preserves; top with Brie cheese. Drizzle each with ¼ teaspoon honey.

2. Broil 3-4 in. from the heat for 3-4 minutes or until heated through. Cool for 5 minutes before serving. Refrigerate leftovers.

Smoked Salmon Bites

Here's a great no-cook option. Because smoked salmon is one of my favorite ingredients, it plays a starring role.

—THOMAS FAGLON SOMERSET, NJ

START TO FINISH: 20 MIN.
MAKES: 2 DOZEN

- 6 **radishes or 24 assorted crackers**
- ½ **cup plain Greek yogurt**
- 4 **ounces smoked salmon or lox, cut into bite-size pieces**
- 3 **tablespoons drained capers**
- 3 **tablespoons finely chopped red onion**

1. Cut each radish crosswise into 4 slices; arrange on a serving platter. Spoon ½ teaspoon plain yogurt over each slice; top with the salmon and remaining yogurt.

2. Sprinkle half of the appetizers with capers; sprinkle remaining appetizers with onion. Refrigerate leftovers.

Bubbly Champagne Punch

My golden punch takes just a few minutes to stir together. With orange slices and cranberries, it suits the Christmas season but goes over well year-round.

—ANITA GEOGHAGAN WOODSTOCK, GA

PREP: 10 MIN. + FREEZING
MAKES: 16 SERVINGS (¾ CUP)

- 3 **orange slices, halved**
  Fresh or frozen cranberries
- 2½ **cups unsweetened pineapple juice**
- 1½ **cups ginger ale**
- 2 **bottles (750 milliliters each) brut Champagne, chilled**
- 1 **bottle (375 milliliters) sweet white wine, chilled**
- 1 **can (12 ounces) frozen lemonade concentrate, thawed**

1. Line the bottom of a 4½-cup ring mold with the orange slices and cranberries. Combine pineapple juice and ginger ale; pour over fruit. Freeze until solid.

2. Just before serving, unmold ice ring into a punch bowl. Gently stir in the remaining ingredients.

BUBBLY CHAMPAGNE PUNCH

Chocolate Eggnog

I love Christmas so much that I decorate in October. I don't care for traditional eggnog, but it's always so popular during the holiday season that I came up with a chocolaty version even I like!

—**DEBBIE HOLCOMBE** BRUNSWICK, GA

PREP: 15 MIN. • **COOK:** 15 MIN. + CHILLING
MAKES: 12 SERVINGS (⅔ CUP EACH)

- 6 eggs
- ⅔ cup sugar
- 4 cups 2% chocolate milk, divided
- 3 cups chocolate ice cream
- 1 teaspoon vanilla extract
- ½ teaspoon ground nutmeg
- 1 cup heavy whipping cream
  Optional toppings: whipped cream, ground nutmeg and/or chocolate curls

1. In a small heavy saucepan, whisk eggs and sugar until blended; stir in 2 cups chocolate milk. Cook and stir over medium heat for 12-15 minutes or until mixture is just thick enough to coat a spoon and a thermometer reads at least 160°. Do not allow to boil. Immediately transfer to a large bowl.
2. Stir in the ice cream, vanilla and nutmeg until blended. Add remaining chocolate milk. In a small bowl, beat the heavy whipping cream until soft peaks form; stir into eggnog mixture. Transfer to a pitcher.
3. Refrigerate, covered, until cold. Stir just before serving. If desired, serve with toppings.

SPARKLING CRANBERRY KISS

CHOCOLATE EGGNOG

"My four-ingredient punch recipe is easy to double, triple—even quadruple. I love the tartness of the cranberry juice. Add orange slices for a festive look."
—**SHANNON ARTHUR** LUCASVILLE, OH

⑤ INGREDIENTS FAST FIX

Sparkling Cranberry Kiss

START TO FINISH: 5 MIN.
MAKES: 12 SERVINGS

- 6 cups cranberry juice
- 1½ cups orange juice
- 3 cups ginger ale
  Ice cubes
  Orange slices, optional

In a pitcher, combine cranberry and orange juices. Just before serving, stir in ginger ale; serve over ice. If desired, serve with orange slices.

⑤INGREDIENTS FAST FIX
Ginger Cardamom Tea

START TO FINISH: 25 MIN.
MAKES: 4 SERVINGS

- 2 **cups water**
- 4 **teaspoons honey**
- 1 **tablespoon minced fresh gingerroot**
- ½ **teaspoon ground cardamom**
- 6 **individual tea bags**
- 1½ **cups fat-free milk**

1. In a small saucepan, combine the water, honey, ginger and cardamom; bring to a boil. Reduce heat; simmer 10 minutes.

2. Pour over tea bags in a 2-cup glass measuring cup. Steep 3-5 minutes according to taste. Strain tea back into saucepan, discarding ginger and tea bags. Stir in milk; heat through.

"When the weather starts to turn cold, I flavor my tea with fresh ginger and cardamom for a warm, spicy treat. It really hits the spot after a long fall afternoon spent in the yard raking leaves."
—TRISHA KRUSE EAGLE, ID

GINGER CARDAMOM TEA

Hot Cider Punch

This hot beverage has been a favorite in our family for more than 20 years and has made many appearances at get-togethers. For an extra-special touch, dress it up with clove-studded orange wedges.
—ANITA BELL HERMITAGE, TN

PREP: 5 MIN. • **COOK:** 30 MIN.
MAKES: 12 SERVINGS

- 3½ **cups apple cider or juice**
- 2 **tablespoons sugar**
- 1 **cinnamon stick (3 inches)**
- ½ **teaspoon ground nutmeg**
- 1 **teaspoon whole cloves**
- 1 **medium orange, cut into wedges**
- 3 **cups orange juice**
- 3 **cups unsweetened pineapple juice**

1. In a large saucepan, combine the apple cider, sugar, cinnamon stick and nutmeg; bring to a boil. Reduce heat; simmer, covered, for 20 minutes.

2. Meanwhile, insert cloves into the orange wedges; add to cider mixture. Stir in orange and pineapple juices; heat through. Discard cinnamon stick. Serve warm.

STRAWBERRY LEMONADE SMOOTHIE

1 teaspoon cayenne pepper
½ teaspoon garlic powder
½ teaspoon chili powder
¼ teaspoon salt
4 cups mixed nuts

1. In a large bowl, mix the first six ingredients. Add nuts; toss to coat. Spread onto a 15-in. x 10-in. x 1-in. baking pan.
2. Bake at 300° for 35-40 minutes or until nuts are lightly toasted and appear dry, stirring occasionally. Serve warm or at room temperature. Store in an airtight container.

(5) INGREDIENTS FAST FIX

Brie in Puff Pastry

Here's a rich, elegant appetizer for special occasions. Your guests will never guess how simple it is to prepare!
—**MARION LOWERY** MEDFORD, OR

START TO FINISH: 30 MIN. • **MAKES:** 8-10 SERVINGS

1 sheet frozen puff pastry, thawed
¼ cup apricot jam
1 round (13.2 ounces) Brie cheese
1 egg
1 tablespoon water
  Apple slices

1. Roll the sheet of puff pastry into a 14-in. square. Spread the apricot jam into a 4½-in. circle in the center of pastry; place Brie cheese over jam. Fold pastry around cheese; trim the excess dough. Pinch the edges to seal. Place seam side down on ungreased baking sheet. Beat the egg and water; brush over pastry.
2. Cut the trimmed pastry pieces into decorative shapes and place on top; brush with egg mixture if desired. Bake at 400° for 20-25 minutes or until puffed and golden brown. Serve warm with apple slices.

BRIE IN PUFF PASTRY

(5) INGREDIENTS FAST FIX

Strawberry Lemonade Smoothie

We love the blend of sweetness and tangy citrus in this refreshing smoothie. It's so easy to throw together, I often find myself fixing one as a breakfast treat or midday snack.
—**JAMIE KING** DULUTH, MN

START TO FINISH: 5 MIN. • **MAKES:** 4 SERVINGS

2 cups lemonade
¾ cup (6 ounces) lemon yogurt
½ teaspoon vanilla extract
2 cups frozen unsweetened strawberries

Place all ingredients in a blender; cover and process 15 seconds or until blended. Serve immediately.

Fancy Roasted Nuts

My kitchen is a busy place during the holiday season, but I always take time to make a batch of spicy roasted nuts. They go over big with friends, family—everyone who tries them.
—**VALERIE BELLEY** ST. LOUIS, MO

PREP: 5 MIN. • **BAKE:** 35 MIN. • **MAKES:** 4 CUPS

¼ cup sugar
2 tablespoons olive oil

LOADED BAKED POTATO DIP

![SLOW COOKER]

Marinated Chicken Wings

These nicely flavored chicken wings go into the slow cooker and come out moist and tender. I've brought them to countless parties and always get lots of compliments.

—**JANIE BOTTING** SULTAN, WA

PREP: 5 MIN. + MARINATING • **COOK:** 3 HOURS
MAKES: 20 SERVINGS

- 20 whole chicken wings (about 4 pounds)
- 1 cup soy sauce
- ¼ cup white wine or reduced-sodium chicken broth
- ¼ cup canola oil
- 1 tablespoon sugar
- 2 garlic cloves, minced
- 1 teaspoon ground ginger

1. Cut chicken wings into three sections; discard wing tips. Place wings in a large resealable plastic bag. In a small bowl, whisk remaining ingredients until blended. Add to chicken; seal bag and turn to coat. Refrigerate overnight.
2. Transfer chicken and marinade to a 5-qt. slow cooker. Cook, covered, on low 3-4 hours or until chicken is tender. Using tongs, remove wings to a serving plate.
NOTE *Uncooked chicken wing sections (wingettes) may be substituted for whole chicken wings.*

FAST FIX ▶ Loaded Baked Potato Dip

I never thought of using waffle-cut fries as dippers until a friend of mine did it at a baby shower. They're ideal for my cheesy bacon and chive dip, which tastes just like a baked potato topping.

—**BETSY KING** DULUTH, MN

START TO FINISH: 10 MIN. • **MAKES:** 2½ CUPS

- 2 cups (16 ounces) reduced-fat sour cream
- 2 cups (8 ounces) shredded reduced-fat cheddar cheese
- 8 center-cut bacon or turkey bacon strips, chopped and cooked
- ⅓ cup minced fresh chives
- 2 teaspoons Louisiana-style hot sauce
  Hot cooked waffle-cut fries

In a small bowl, mix the first five ingredients until blended; refrigerate until serving. Serve with waffle fries.

Crate Solution

I use a clean milk crate to transport my slow cooker to parties. I line the crate with a towel, take the cover off the slow cooker and put foil over it. I set the cooker in the crate with my serving utensil. The crate keeps the pot from tipping and catches any drips. And when I leave, I don't have to look for my lid!

—**HELEN PHILLIPS** HORSEHEADS, NY

MARINATED CHICKEN WINGS

ANNE KEEDY'S
MINTED FRESH FRUIT SALAD
PAGE 20

Salads & Dressings

How refreshing—salad bowls bursting with creative combinations of veggies, fruits, pasta and more. Whether you want a scrumptious **side dish or a main course**, look here for sensational selections!

ANGELA LEINENBACH'S HERO PASTA SALAD
PAGE 23

DEVON DELANEY'S CHILI-RUBBED STEAK & BREAD SALAD *PAGE 26*

DARLENE BRENDEN'S LAYERED BROCCOLI SALAD
PAGE 28

EAT SMART FAST FIX ▸ Minted Fresh Fruit Salad

Here's a colorful fruit medley that allows for substitutions such as peaches, plums, watermelon, oranges or grapefruit, depending on availability.
—**ANNE KEEDY** LEBANON, CT

START TO FINISH: 25 MIN.
MAKES: 24 SERVINGS (¾ CUP EACH)

- 1 medium cantaloupe, peeled, seeded and cubed
- 1 pound fresh strawberries, halved
- 1 fresh pineapple, peeled and cubed
- 2 large Granny Smith apples, cubed
- 2 cups seedless red or green grapes
- ½ cup dried cranberries
- ¾ cup orange juice
- ⅓ cup lemon juice
- 2 tablespoons minced fresh mint
- 1 teaspoon ground cinnamon
- ½ cup flaked coconut, optional

In a large bowl, combine the first six ingredients. In a small bowl, whisk orange juice, lemon juice, mint and cinnamon. Drizzle over fruit; toss lightly to coat. If desired, top with coconut before serving.

PER SERVING *54 cal., trace fat (trace sat. fat), 0 chol., 3 mg sodium, 14 g carb., 2 g fiber, 1 g pro.* **Diabetic Exchange:** *1 fruit.*

GRILLED VEGETABLE ORZO SALAD

MINTED FRESH FRUIT SALAD

EAT SMART Grilled Vegetable Orzo Salad

In-season vegetables make great additions to this grilled specialty. It's the perfect contribution to summer picnics.
—**DANIELLE MILLER** WESTFIELD, IN

PREP: 35 MIN. • **GRILL:** 10 MIN.
MAKES: 8 SERVINGS

- 1¼ cups uncooked orzo pasta
- ½ pound fresh asparagus, trimmed
- 1 medium zucchini, cut lengthwise into ½-inch slices
- 1 medium sweet yellow or red pepper, halved
- 1 large portobello mushroom, stem removed
- ½ medium red onion, halved

DRESSING

- ⅓ cup olive oil
- ¼ cup balsamic vinegar
- 3 tablespoons lemon juice
- 4 garlic cloves, minced
- 1 teaspoon lemon-pepper seasoning

SALAD

- 1 cup grape tomatoes, halved
- 1 tablespoon minced fresh parsley
- 1 tablespoon minced fresh basil
- ½ teaspoon salt
- ¼ teaspoon pepper
- 1 cup (4 ounces) crumbled feta cheese

1. Cook orzo pasta according to the package directions. Place vegetables in a large bowl. In a small bowl, whisk the dressing ingredients. Add to the vegetables and toss to coat.

2. Remove vegetables, reserving the dressing. Grill the mushroom, pepper and onion, covered, over medium heat 5-10 minutes or until tender, turning occasionally. Grill the asparagus and zucchini, uncovered, 3-4 minutes or until the desired doneness, turning occasionally.

3. When cool enough to handle, cut the vegetables into bite-size pieces. In a large bowl, combine the cooked orzo, grilled vegetables, tomatoes, parsley, basil, salt, pepper and reserved dressing; toss to combine. Serve at room temperature or refrigerate until cold. Just before serving, stir in cheese.

PER SERVING *260 cal., 12 g fat (3 g sat. fat), 8 mg chol., 352 mg sodium, 30 g carb., 2 g fiber, 8 g pro.* **Diabetic Exchanges:** *2 fat, 1½ starch, 1 vegetable.*

Shrimp Salad with Peaches

My husband is a meat-and-potatoes man. But when I tossed together spicy marinated shrimp, greens, peaches and cheese for dinner one night, he was pleasantly surprised.

—GILDA LESTER MILLSBORO, DE

PREP: 25 MIN. • **GRILL:** 10 MIN.
MAKES: 4 SERVINGS

- ¾ pound uncooked large shrimp
- ½ cup hoisin sauce
- 6 tablespoons olive oil, divided
- ¼ cup lemon juice, divided
- 1 teaspoon hot pepper sauce
- ½ teaspoon ground cumin
- 4 medium peaches, halved
- ¼ teaspoon salt
- 8 cups fresh arugula
- ½ cup fresh cilantro leaves
- ½ cup crumbled goat cheese
- 1 medium lemon, quartered

1. Peel and devein the shrimp, leaving the tails on. In a large resealable plastic bag, combine the hoisin sauce, 2 tablespoons oil, 2 tablespoons lemon juice, hot sauce and cumin. Add the shrimp; seal the bag and turn to coat. Refrigerate for up to 30 minutes. Drain and discard marinade.

2. Thread the shrimp on four metal or soaked wooden skewers. Moisten a paper towel with cooking oil; using long-handled tongs, lightly coat the grill rack. Brush peach halves with 1 tablespoon oil.

3. Grill shrimp and peaches, covered, over medium heat or broil 4 in. from the heat for 6-8 minutes or until shrimp turn pink, turning once.

4. In a large bowl, combine salt with the remaining oil and lemon juice. Add the arugula and cilantro; toss to coat. Divide among four plates. Top with the peaches, shrimp and cheese. Squeeze lemon over salads.

FREEZER SLAW

EAT SMART Freezer Slaw

This unusual but convenient make-ahead coleslaw from my mother can be frozen for up to 3 months. Just thaw it overnight in the refrigerator before serving.

—ALICE CAMPBELL DICKINSON, ND

PREP: 30 MIN. + FREEZING
COOK: 10 MIN. + COOLING
MAKES: 18 SERVINGS (¾ CUP EACH)

- 2 medium heads cabbage, shredded (about 16 cups)
- 2 teaspoons salt
- 2 cups sugar
- 2 cups water
- 2 cups cider vinegar
- 2 teaspoons celery seed
- 2 teaspoons mustard seed
- 2 medium sweet red peppers, chopped
- 2 medium carrots, shredded

1. Place cabbage in a very large bowl; toss with salt. Let stand 1 hour.

2. Meanwhile, in a large saucepan, combine sugar, water, cider vinegar, celery seed and mustard seed. Bring to a boil, stirring to dissolve the sugar. Cook 1 minute. Remove from heat; cool slightly.

3. Drain excess liquid from cabbage, if necessary. Add red peppers and carrots to cabbage. Add dressing; toss to coat. Cool completely. Transfer to freezer containers. Freeze, covered, up to 3 months.

4. To serve, thaw coleslaw overnight in refrigerator. Stir before serving.

PER SERVING *126 cal., trace fat (trace sat. fat), 0 chol., 287 mg sodium, 30 g carb., 3 g fiber, 2 g pro.*

EAT SMART Garden Bow Tie Salad

For family gatherings and church potlucks, I took what was originally a vegetable dish and added pasta. If you like, toss in sliced mushrooms and diced tomatoes before serving.
—**BARBARA BURKS** HUNTSVILLE, AL

PREP: 30 MIN. + CHILLING • **COOK:** 10 MIN.
MAKES: 24 SERVINGS (¾ CUP EACH)

- 1 medium cucumber
- 1 medium yellow summer squash
- 1 medium zucchini
- 1 medium sweet red pepper
- 1 medium green pepper
- 4 cups fresh broccoli florets
- 3 cups fresh cauliflowerets
- 1 small red onion, finely chopped
- 2 packages Italian salad dressing mix
- 4½ cups uncooked bow tie pasta
- ¼ cup olive oil
- ¼ cup red wine vinegar
- ¾ teaspoon salt
- ½ teaspoon pepper

1. Wash the first five ingredients but do not dry; chop and transfer to a large bowl. Add remaining vegetables. Sprinkle with the dry dressing mix; toss to coat. Refrigerate, covered, 4-6 hours or overnight.

2. Cook pasta according to package directions. Drain; rinse with cold water. Add to vegetable mixture. In a small bowl, whisk remaining ingredients. Add to salad; toss to coat.

PER SERVING *89 cal., 3 g fat (trace sat. fat), 0 chol., 296 mg sodium, 14 g carb., 2 g fiber, 3 g pro.* **Diabetic Exchanges:** *1 vegetable, ½ starch, ½ fat.*

CRISP & SPICY CUCUMBER SALAD

Crisp & Spicy Cucumber Salad

Sweet-hot Asian flavors from rice vinegar, sesame oil and cayenne pepper will tingle your taste buds. Just try it and see!
—**ALIVIA DOCKERY** PARKER, CO

PREP: 25 MIN. + MARINATING • **MAKES:** 6 SERVINGS

- 2 small English cucumbers, thinly sliced
- 2 medium carrots, thinly sliced
- 1 large sweet red pepper, julienned
- ½ medium red onion, thinly sliced
- 2 green onions, sliced
- ½ serrano or jalapeno pepper, seeded and thinly sliced, optional

MARINADE
- ⅓ cup sugar
- ⅓ cup rice vinegar
- ⅓ cup water
- 1 teaspoon each salt, garlic powder and pepper
- 1 teaspoon sesame oil
- 1 teaspoon reduced-sodium soy sauce
- 1 small garlic clove, minced
- ½ teaspoon minced fresh gingerroot
- ¼ teaspoon cayenne pepper, optional
  Optional toppings: minced fresh cilantro, chopped peanuts and additional sliced green onion

1. In a large bowl, combine the first six ingredients. In a small bowl, mix marinade ingredients, stirring to dissolve sugar. Pour over vegetables; toss to combine. Refrigerate, covered, 30 minutes or overnight.

2. Serve with a slotted spoon. If desired, sprinkle with toppings.

NOTE *Wear disposable gloves when cutting hot peppers; the oils can burn skin. Avoid touching your face.*

GARDEN BOW TIE SALAD

Hero Pasta Salad

Savor the taste of a traditional hero sandwich in a salad bowl. For even more variety in your mix of ingredients, include some kalamata olives, peppers or yellow tomatoes.

—ANGELA LEINENBACH MECHANICSVILLE, VA

PREP: 35 MIN. • **MAKES:** 4 SERVINGS

- 3 tablespoons olive oil
- 3 tablespoons balsamic vinegar
- 2 small garlic cloves, minced
- ⅛ teaspoon salt
- ⅛ teaspoon pepper

SALAD

- 2 cups uncooked spiral pasta
- 1 small red onion, halved and thinly sliced
- ¾ cup sliced pepperoncini
- 4 ounces cubed provolone cheese
- 2 ounces thinly sliced deli ham, cut into strips (⅔ cup)
- 2 ounces thinly sliced hard salami, cut into strips (⅔ cup)
- 5 cups shredded lettuce
- 1 large tomato, coarsely chopped
- ¾ cup cherry tomatoes, halved

1. In a small bowl, whisk the first five ingredients until blended. Cook pasta according to the package directions. Drain pasta; rinse with cold water.

2. In a large bowl, combine onion, pepperoncini, cheese, meats and pasta. Just before serving, add the lettuce and tomatoes. Drizzle with dressing; toss to coat.

HOMEMADE ANTIPASTO SALAD

Homemade Antipasto Salad

PREP: 1 HOUR + CHILLING • **MAKES:** 50 SERVINGS (¾ CUP EACH)

- 2 packages (1 pound each) spiral pasta
- 4 cups chopped green peppers
- 4 cups chopped seeded tomatoes
- 3 cups chopped onions
- 2 cans (15 ounces each) garbanzo beans or chickpeas, rinsed and drained
- 1 pound thinly sliced Genoa salami, julienned
- 1 pound sliced pepperoni, julienned
- ½ pound provolone cheese, cubed
- 1 cup pitted ripe olives, halved

DRESSING

- 1 cup red wine vinegar
- ½ cup sugar
- 2 tablespoons dried oregano
- 2 teaspoons salt
- 1 teaspoon pepper
- 1½ cups olive oil

1. Cook pasta according to the package directions. Drain; rinse with cold water. In several large bowls, combine pasta, green peppers, tomatoes, onions, beans, salami, pepperoni, cheese and olives.

2. Place the vinegar, sugar, oregano, salt and pepper in a blender. While processing, gradually add oil in a steady stream. Pour over pasta salad; toss to coat. Refrigerate, covered, 4 hours or overnight.

HERO PASTA SALAD

Sunny Strawberry & Cantaloupe Salad

My children ask me to make this speedy recipe all the time. The cantaloupe, berries and cheese are so yummy together.

—AYSHA SCHURMAN AMMON, ID

START TO FINISH: 15 MIN.
MAKES: 4 SERVINGS

- 1 cup sliced fresh strawberries
- 1 cup cubed cantaloupe
- ½ cup (about 2 ounces) cubed part-skim mozzarella cheese
- 2 tablespoons raspberry vinaigrette
- ½ cup fresh raspberries
- 1 tablespoon sunflower kernels
  Thinly sliced fresh mint leaves, optional

In a large bowl, combine strawberries, cantaloupe and mozzarella cheese. Drizzle with vinaigrette and toss to coat. Just before serving, gently stir in the raspberries; top with sunflower kernels. If desired, sprinkle with mint.

PER SERVING *105 cal., 2 g fat (trace sat. fat), 4 chol., 113 mg sodium, 10 g carb., 2 g fiber, 3 g pro.* **Diabetic Exchanges:** *½ fruit, 1½ fat.*

"I think oven roasting is a great way to prepare root veggies because it brings out their subtle sweetness. Serving them over endive with a homemade dressing in My Underground Vegetable Salad is a mouthwatering bonus!" —PETER HALFERTY CORPUS CHRISTI, TX

MY UNDERGROUND VEGETABLE SALAD

SUNNY STRAWBERRY & CANTALOUPE SALAD

My Underground Vegetable Salad

PREP: 20 MIN. • **BAKE:** 40 MIN.
MAKES: 8 SERVINGS

- 1 pound medium fresh mushrooms, halved
- 8 small carrots, peeled and halved lengthwise
- 2 cups cubed peeled celery root (about ½ pound)
- 2 cups cubed peeled rutabaga (about 1 medium)
- 2 cups cubed peeled sweet potatoes (about 1 medium)
- 2 tablespoons olive oil
- ¼ teaspoon salt
- 2 cups cherry tomatoes, halved
- 8 cups torn curly endive

VINAIGRETTE
- 3 tablespoons apple cider or juice
- 2 tablespoons lemon juice
- 2 tablespoons cider vinegar
- 1 teaspoon stone-ground mustard
- 1 teaspoon grated lemon peel
- ½ teaspoon fennel seed, crushed
- ¼ teaspoon salt
- ¼ teaspoon pepper
- ½ cup olive oil

1. Preheat oven to 400°. In a large bowl, combine the first five ingredients. Add oil and salt; toss to coat. Transfer to a greased shallow roasting pan. Roast 30-35 minutes or until vegetables are tender, stirring occasionally. Add the tomatoes; bake 10 minutes longer.

2. Place endive in a large bowl. In a small bowl, whisk the first eight vinaigrette ingredients. Gradually whisk in the oil until blended. Pour over the endive; toss to coat. Divide endive among eight plates; top with roasted vegetables.

PER SERVING *261 cal., 18 g fat (trace sat. fat), 0 chol., 261 mg sodium, 24 g carb., 7 g fiber, 4 g pro.*

FAST FIX ▸ Makeover Spinach Salad Dressing

Here's a lightened-up favorite you won't want to miss. Store-bought versions just can't compare! Drizzle it over a bowlful of leafy greens...or use it to jazz up the usual chicken salad or coleslaw.

—**CINDY HARNISH** WEXFORD, PA

START TO FINISH: 5 MIN.
MAKES: 1⅓ CUPS

- ⅓ cup sugar
- 1 small onion, finely chopped
- ¼ cup cider vinegar
- ¼ cup unsweetened applesauce
- 2 tablespoons water
- 2 tablespoons canola oil
- 4 teaspoons prepared mustard
- 1 teaspoon salt
- ½ teaspoon coarsely ground pepper
  Fresh spinach leaves

Combine the first nine ingredients in a blender or food processor; cover and process until smooth. Serve over fresh spinach. Store leftover dressing in the refrigerator.

(5)INGREDIENTS FAST FIX ▸ Pear & Blue Cheese Salad

Toss together a restaurant-worthy dish in a mere 10 minutes with only a handful of ingredients—pears, blue cheese, glazed pecans, romaine and balsamic vinaigrette. After one taste, you'll be glad you did!

—**TASTE OF HOME TEST KITCHEN**

START TO FINISH: 10 MIN.
MAKES: 10 SERVINGS

- 12 cups torn romaine
- ⅔ cup balsamic vinaigrette
- 2 medium pears, sliced
- ⅔ cup crumbled blue cheese
- ⅔ cup glazed pecans

Place romaine in a large bowl. Drizzle with the balsamic vinaigrette; toss to coat. Top with pears, blue cheese and pecans. Serve immediately.

? Did you know?

Fresh corn is best eaten the same day you buy it. As soon as it is picked, the sugar begins to convert to starch, reducing its sweetness.

Fresh Corn & Arugula Salad

PREP: 20 MIN. • **GRILL:** 10 MIN. + COOLING
MAKES: 6 SERVINGS

BASIL VINAIGRETTE
- ½ cup olive oil
- ¼ cup balsamic vinegar
- 3 tablespoons minced fresh basil
- 1 teaspoon chopped shallot
- 1 teaspoon minced fresh rosemary
- 1 teaspoon lemon juice
- ¼ teaspoon salt
- ¼ teaspoon pepper

SALAD
- 2 ears fresh corn, husked
- 1 teaspoon olive oil
- 8 cups fresh arugula or baby spinach
- 4 plum tomatoes, quartered
- ¼ cup pecan halves, toasted
- ¼ cup shaved Parmesan cheese

1. In a small bowl, whisk vinaigrette ingredients until blended.

2. Brush corn with oil; grill, covered, over medium heat or broil 4 in. from heat 8-10 minutes or until the corn is crisp-tender and browned, turning occasionally. When cool enough to handle, cut corn off cobs and place in a large bowl.

3. Add the arugula, tomatoes and pecans to corn. Drizzle with half of the vinaigrette; toss to coat. Top with the cheese; serve immediately. Cover and refrigerate remaining vinaigrette for later use.

NOTE *To toast nuts, spread in a 15-in. x 10-in. x 1-in. baking pan. Bake at 350° for 5-10 minutes or until lightly browned, stirring occasionally. Or, spread in a dry nonstick skillet and heat over low heat until lightly browned, stirring occasionally.*

"In my family, this fresh-tasting combo is known as 'Aunt Pammy's Salad.' It's wonderful during the height of summer when just-picked sweet corn is plentiful."
—**PAMELA DAMM** SOUTH BELOIT, IL

FRESH CORN & ARUGULA SALAD

CHILI-RUBBED STEAK & BREAD SALAD

Chili-Rubbed Steak & Bread Salad

In our house, grilled steak is always a popular entree. I decided to serve it with a ranch-inspired bread salad that combines a variety of flavors and textures—creamy, crunchy, fresh and tangy.
—**DEVON DELANEY** WESTPORT, CT

PREP: 35 MIN. + STANDING • **GRILL:** 15 MIN. • **MAKES:** 6 SERVINGS

- 2 **teaspoons chili powder**
- 2 **teaspoons brown sugar**
- ½ **teaspoon salt**
- ½ **teaspoon pepper**
- 1 **beef top sirloin steak (1 inch thick and 1¼ pounds)**
- 2 **cups cubed multigrain bread**
- 2 **tablespoons olive oil**
- 1 **cup ranch salad dressing**
- 2 **tablespoons finely grated horseradish**
- 1 **tablespoon prepared mustard**
- 3 **large tomatoes, cut into 1-inch pieces**
- 1 **medium cucumber, cut into 1-inch pieces**
- 1 **small red onion, halved and thinly sliced**

1. Mix chili powder, brown sugar, salt and pepper; rub over steak. Let stand 15 minutes.
2. Meanwhile, toss bread cubes with oil. In a large skillet, toast bread over medium heat 8-10 minutes or until crisp and lightly browned, stirring frequently. In a small bowl, whisk salad dressing, horseradish and mustard.
3. Grill steak, covered, over medium heat or broil 4 in. from heat 6-8 minutes on each side or until meat reaches desired doneness (for medium-rare, a thermometer should read 145°; medium, 160°; well-done, 170°). Let stand 5 minutes.
4. In a large bowl, combine tomatoes, cucumber, onion and toasted bread. Add ½ cup dressing mixture; toss to coat. Slice steak; serve with salad and remaining dressing.

Roasted Butternut Squash & Rice Salad

We have end-of-season picnics for my son's flag football team. This recipe makes enough for plenty of hungry boys and their families.
—**DOLORES DEIFEL** MUNDELEIN, IL

PREP: 10 MIN. • **COOK:** 25 MIN. + COOLING
MAKES: 12 SERVINGS (¾ CUP EACH)

- 3 **tablespoons brown sugar**
- 3 **tablespoons balsamic vinegar**
- 2 **tablespoons olive oil**
- 1 **tablespoon kosher salt**
- 1 **medium butternut squash (2½ to 3 pounds), peeled and cut into ¾-inch cubes**
- 2 **cups uncooked jasmine rice**
- 2 **large sweet red peppers, cut into ½-inch pieces**
- 1 **cup pine nuts, toasted**
- 6 **green onions, thinly sliced**
- 3 **tablespoons snipped fresh dill**
- 3 **tablespoons coarsely chopped fresh parsley**

DRESSING
- ½ **cup olive oil**
- 3 **tablespoons red wine vinegar**
- 1 **teaspoon kosher salt**
- ¼ **teaspoon pepper**

1. In a large bowl, combine brown sugar, balsamic vinegar, oil and salt. Add butternut squash; toss to coat. Transfer to a greased, foil-lined 15-in. x 10-in. x 1-in. baking pan. Bake at 425° for 25-30 minutes or until tender, stirring occasionally. Cool completely.
2. Meanwhile, cook rice according to package directions. Remove from the heat; cool completely.
3. In a large bowl, combine red peppers, pine nuts, green onions, dill, parsley, squash and rice. In a small bowl, whisk the dressing ingredients. Pour over salad; toss to coat. Serve at room temperature. Cover and refrigerate leftovers.
NOTE *To toast nuts, spread in a 15-in. x 10-in. x 1-in. baking pan. Bake at 350° for 5-10 minutes or until lightly browned, stirring occasionally. Or, spread in a dry nonstick skillet and heat over low heat until lightly browned, stirring occasionally.*

ROASTED BUTTERNUT SQUASH & RICE SALAD

WATERMELON SHARK

Glazed Fruit Medley

A simple orange dressing really complements the strawberries, honeydew, green grapes and bananas in my fruit medley. Try it when you have guests for breakfast or brunch.

—KAREN BOURNE MAGRATH, AB

PREP: 20 MIN. + CHILLING • **MAKES:** 10 SERVINGS

- 2 **cups orange juice**
- 1 **cup sugar**
- 2 **tablespoons cornstarch**
- 3 **cups cubed honeydew**
- 3 **medium firm bananas, sliced**
- 2 **cups green grapes**
- 2 **cups halved fresh strawberries**

1. In a small saucepan, mix the juice, sugar and cornstarch until smooth. Bring to a boil, stirring constantly; cook and stir for 2 minutes or until thickened. Transfer to a small bowl; cool slightly. Refrigerate, covered, for at least 2 hours.
2. Just before serving, combine the fruit in a large serving bowl. Drizzle with juice mixture; toss gently to coat.

GLAZED FRUIT MEDLEY

EAT SMART Watermelon Shark

Take a bite out of summertime boredom with this kid-friendly food project. It's wholesome, easy and fun!
—TASTE OF HOME TEST KITCHEN

PREP: 1 HOUR • **MAKES:** 32 SERVINGS

- 1 **large watermelon**
- 2 **cups seedless red grapes**
- 1 **medium cantaloupe, peeled, seeded and cubed**
- 2 **cups fresh blueberries**
- 2 **medium oranges**
- 1 **jar (12 ounces) pineapple preserves**

1. Using a large sharp knife, cut off one end of watermelon so watermelon stands at an angle. Using a razor blade or small knife, score an opening for the mouth. With knife, cut out and remove mouth. Cut out triangles for teeth; remove rind from teeth.
2. For the shark fin, cut a triangle from the removed rind; attach to the shark with toothpicks. For the eyes, attach two grapes with toothpicks.
3. Remove fruit from inside watermelon; cut into cubes. In a large bowl, combine watermelon, cantaloupe, blueberries and remaining grapes. Finely grate peel from oranges and squeeze juice. In a small bowl, mix preserves, orange juice and peel; add to fruit and toss gently.
4. Stand shark on a platter. Fill opening with some of the fruit mixture. Serve with remaining fruit.
PER SERVING *129 cal., 1 g fat (trace sat. fat), 0 chol., 7 mg sodium, 30 g carb., 2 g fiber, 2 g pro.* **Diabetic Exchanges:** *1½ fruit, ½ starch.*

FAST FIX ▶ Sunflower Noodle Coleslaw

My coleslaw features both sunflower oil and sunflower kernels. Using a packaged mix means I can have a big bowlful ready to serve in only 15 minutes.
—EILEEN HERMAN BRINSMADE, ND

START TO FINISH: 15 MIN.
MAKES: 10 SERVINGS

- 1 package (3 ounces) chicken ramen noodles
- 1 package (14 ounces) coleslaw mix
- ½ cup unsalted sunflower kernels
- ¼ cup chopped green pepper
- ⅓ cup sunflower oil
- ¼ cup white vinegar
- 3 tablespoons sugar
- 1 tablespoon poppy seeds
- ¾ teaspoon pepper

1. Break the noodles into small pieces. In a large bowl, combine the noodles, coleslaw mix, sunflower kernels and green pepper.
2. In a small bowl, whisk the oil, vinegar, sugar, poppy seeds, pepper and contents of seasoning packet. Pour over the salad and toss to coat. Chill until serving.

LAYERED BROCCOLI SALAD

"Layered Broccoli Salad is a simple but popular contribution to luncheons and other get-togethers. The crisp florets and bacon contrast nicely with the dried cranberries." —DARLENE BRENDEN SALEM, OR

SUNFLOWER NOODLE COLESLAW

FAST FIX
Layered Broccoli Salad

START TO FINISH: 20 MIN.
MAKES: 8 SERVINGS

- 6 cups chopped fresh broccoli florets
- 1 small red onion, thinly sliced
- ⅔ cup dried cranberries
- ½ cup plain yogurt
- 2 tablespoons mayonnaise
- 2 tablespoons honey
- 2 tablespoons cider vinegar
- 1½ cups (6 ounces) shredded cheddar cheese
- ¼ cup sunflower kernels
- 2 bacon strips, cooked and crumbled

In a large glass bowl, layer broccoli, onion and cranberries. Combine the yogurt, mayonnaise, honey and cider vinegar; drizzle over salad. Sprinkle with cheddar cheese, sunflower kernels and bacon.

⑤ INGREDIENTS FAST FIX
Beets & Greens Salad

Like to carve pumpkins? Save the seeds and use them for this fall favorite.
—TASTE OF HOME TEST KITCHEN

START TO FINISH: 10 MIN.
MAKES: 10 SERVINGS

- 12 cups spring mix salad greens
- ⅔ cup champagne vinaigrette
- 3 cooked beets, sliced
- ⅔ cup crumbled goat cheese
- ¼ cup salted pumpkin seeds or pepitas

Place the salad greens in a large bowl. Drizzle with vinaigrette; toss to coat. Top with beets, cheese and pumpkin seeds. Serve immediately.

Sweet Potato & Chickpea Salad

With filling chunks of sweet potatoes and chickpeas, this colorful and satisfying dish can make a light meal all by itself.

—BRENDA GLEASON HARTLAND, WI

PREP: 15 MIN. • **BAKE:** 20 MIN.
MAKES: 8 SERVINGS

- 2 medium sweet potatoes (about 1 pound), peeled and cubed
- 1 tablespoon olive oil
- ½ teaspoon salt
- ¼ teaspoon pepper
- 1 can (15 ounces) garbanzo beans or chickpeas, rinsed and drained

DRESSING
- 2 tablespoons seasoned rice vinegar
- 4 teaspoons olive oil
- 1 tablespoon minced fresh gingerroot
- 1 garlic clove, minced
- ¼ teaspoon salt
- ¼ teaspoon pepper

SALAD
- 4 cups spring mix salad greens
- ¼ cup crumbled feta cheese

1. In a large bowl, combine the sweet potatoes, oil, salt and pepper; toss to coat. Transfer to a 15-in. x 10-in. x 1-in. baking pan coated with cooking spray. Roast at 425° for 20-25 minutes or until tender, stirring once.

2. In a large bowl, combine garbanzo beans and sweet potatoes. In a small bowl, whisk the dressing ingredients. Add to the sweet potato mixture; toss to coat. Serve over salad greens; top with feta cheese.

Removing Melon Rinds

Trying to remove the rind from wedges of cantaloupe or slices of watermelon using a standard knife can be challenging. I've discovered that the best tool for the job is one meant for a totally different purpose—a curved grapefruit knife. It lets me cut off the rind cleanly and easily.

—RUTH M. MILFORD, NH

"Here's a savory way to enhance nearly any summer menu. Keep the recipe in mind when your garden vegetables and herbs are ready to harvest and enjoy."

—CAROLYN KUMPE EL DORADO, CA

SUMMERTIME TOMATO-MELON SALAD

FAST FIX Summertime Tomato-Melon Salad

START TO FINISH: 30 MIN.
MAKES: 12 SERVINGS (¾ CUP EACH)

- 4 cups small baby heirloom tomatoes, halved
- 1 English cucumber, peeled and cubed
- 2 cups cubed cantaloupe
- 1 package (8 ounces) feta cheese, cubed
- 1 medium ripe avocado, peeled and cubed
- 1 bunch watercress, coarsely chopped
- ½ cup fresh basil leaves, coarsely chopped
- ¼ cup chopped red onion

CORIANDER-LIME VINAIGRETTE
- 1 teaspoon coriander seeds
- ⅓ cup canola oil
- 3 tablespoons lime juice
- 2 tablespoons rice vinegar
- 1 tablespoon honey
- 1 tablespoon grated lime peel
- ½ teaspoon salt
- ¼ teaspoon pepper

1. In a large bowl, combine tomatoes, cucumber, cantaloupe, feta cheese, avocado, watercress, basil and onion.

2. In a dry small skillet over medium heat, toast the coriander seeds until aromatic, about 2-3 minutes. Cool. Transfer to a spice grinder or a mortar and pestle; coarsely grind.

3. In a small bowl, whisk the oil, lime juice, vinegar, honey, peel, salt, pepper and coriander. Pour over the tomato mixture and gently toss to coat.

SPICY GAZPACHO SALAD

"Cool, classic gazpacho soup becomes a delicious fork food when I add romaine lettuce. If you like, change the heat level by adjusting the amount of hot sauce."
—DONNA MARIE RYAN TOPSFIELD, MA

Grilled Potato Salad with Balsamic Dressing

A Texas-size family reunion demands a substantial dish like this one. It disappears quickly at all of our get-togethers.
—ELAINE SWEET DALLAS, TX

PREP: 35 MIN. **GRILL:** 10 MIN.
MAKES: 12 SERVINGS

- 6 medium red potatoes (about 1½ pounds), quartered
- 2¼ teaspoons canola oil
- 3 cups fresh baby spinach
- 1 cup fresh or frozen corn, thawed
- ½ medium sweet red pepper, julienned
- ½ poblano pepper, seeded and julienned
- ½ medium red onion, thinly sliced
- 3 green onions, chopped
- 6 bacon strips, diced
- 3 garlic cloves, minced
- 2 shallots, minced
- ½ cup balsamic vinegar
- 2 tablespoons stone-ground mustard
- 1 teaspoon pepper
- 2 hard-cooked eggs, coarsely chopped
- ¼ cup sunflower kernels

1. Place the red potatoes in a large saucepan; cover with water. Bring to a boil. Reduce heat; cover and cook for 8-10 minutes or until crisp-tender. Drain; toss potatoes with oil.

2. Place potatoes in a grill wok or basket. Grill, covered, over medium heat for 8-12 minutes or until golden brown, stirring frequently. Transfer to a large salad bowl; add spinach, corn, peppers and onions. Set aside.

3. In a large skillet, cook bacon over medium heat until partially cooked but not crisp. Add garlic and shallots; cook for 1-2 minutes or until tender. Stir in balsamic vinegar, mustard and pepper. Bring to a gentle boil; cook and stir for 2-3 minutes or until slightly thickened.

4. Drizzle over the potato mixture and gently toss to coat. Sprinkle with the eggs and sunflower kernels. Serve immediately.

NOTE *Wear disposable gloves when cutting hot peppers; the oils can burn skin. Avoid touching your face.*

Spicy Gazpacho Salad

PREP: 25 MIN. + CHILLING
MAKES: 10 SERVINGS

- 3 cups chopped and seeded tomatoes
- 1 medium cucumber, seeded and chopped
- 1 medium green pepper, chopped
- 4 green onions, chopped
- 1 celery rib, thinly sliced
- 1 tomatillo, husk removed, seeded and chopped
- ½ cup red wine vinaigrette
- 2 tablespoons lemon juice
- 2 tablespoons Worcestershire sauce
- 2 garlic cloves, minced
- 1 teaspoon coarsely ground pepper
- 1 teaspoon hot pepper sauce
- ½ teaspoon kosher salt
- 1 bunch romaine, torn

1. In a large bowl, combine the first six ingredients. In a small bowl, whisk the red wine vinaigrette, lemon juice, Worcestershire sauce, garlic, pepper, pepper sauce and salt. Pour over the tomato mixture; toss to coat. Cover and refrigerate for 4 hours.

2. Just before serving, place romaine in a large serving bowl. Top with the vegetable mixture and toss to combine.

Smoky Spanish Potato Salad

PREP: 1 HOUR + COOLING
MAKES: 8 SERVINGS

- 1¾ pounds red potatoes (about 7 medium)
- 2 tablespoons olive oil
- 1 teaspoon smoked Spanish paprika
- ½ teaspoon salt
- 1 jar (6 ounces) marinated quartered artichoke hearts
- 1 cup (8 ounces) sour cream
- ¼ cup mayonnaise
- 1 celery rib, thinly sliced
- 2 tablespoons capers, drained
- 2 green onions, sliced
- 3 tablespoons minced fresh basil

1. Scrub potatoes; cut into 1-in. pieces. Place in a large bowl; drizzle with oil and sprinkle with paprika and salt. Toss to coat. Transfer to a greased 15-in. x 10-in. x 1-in. baking pan. Bake at 425° for 35-40 minutes or until tender, stirring occasionally. Cool.
2. Drain the artichokes, reserving 2 tablespoons marinade; place artichokes and potatoes in a large bowl. In another bowl, combine the sour cream, mayonnaise, celery, capers, onions, basil and reserved marinade. Pour over potato mixture and toss to coat. Chill until serving.

"I created Smoky Spanish Potato Salad for red potatoes, but I've discovered that it works well with fingerlings and Yukon Golds, too. Give it a try for your next barbecue." —HELEN CONWELL PORTLAND, OR

SMOKY SPANISH POTATO SALAD

BLACK BEAN-MANGO SALAD

FAST FIX ▶ Black Bean-Mango Salad

Here's a lively way to complement grilled beef, chicken or fish. Plus, the recipe couldn't be much simpler—just combine the ingredients, refrigerate and enjoy!
—**DONNA HOLLON** PORT ORCHARD, WA

START TO FINISH: 25 MIN.
MAKES: 4 SERVINGS

- 2 medium mangoes, peeled and cubed
- 1 cup canned black beans, rinsed and drained
- ¼ cup finely chopped sweet red pepper
- 2 tablespoons finely chopped red onion
- 2 tablespoons minced fresh cilantro
- 2 tablespoons orange juice
- 1 tablespoon finely chopped jalapeno pepper
- 1 tablespoon lime juice
- ⅛ teaspoon ground cumin
  Dash salt

In a small bowl, combine all ingredients. Refrigerate until serving.
NOTE *Wear disposable gloves when cutting hot peppers; the oils can burn skin. Avoid touching your face.*

SHARI MEISSNER'S WHITE CHILI
PAGE 37

Soups & Sandwiches

Here's **comfort food** at its best—the classic combo of a steaming bowl of soup and piled-high sandwich. With these recipes, you can treat your family to a **heartwarming lunch or dinner** anytime.

RACHEL KUNKEL'S BBQ CHICKEN SLIDERS
PAGE 34

KAREN LEMAY'S CHICKEN POTPIE SOUP
PAGE 44

IVY ABBADESSA'S MEDITERRANEAN VEGETABLE PITAS *PAGE 34*

EAT SMART Mediterranean Vegetable Pitas

Craving a fast and healthy meal? This one packs tomato, cucumber, onion and olives. Add a touch of cayenne for a kick.

—IVY ABBADESSA LOXAHATCHEE, FL

PREP: 20 MIN. + MARINATING
MAKES: 4 SERVINGS

- ¼ **cup olive oil**
- 2 **tablespoons balsamic vinegar**
- 2 **teaspoons grated lemon peel**
- 2 **teaspoons minced fresh oregano or ½ teaspoon dried oregano**
- ½ **teaspoon garlic powder**
- ½ **teaspoon pepper**
- ⅛ **teaspoon cayenne pepper, optional**
- 1 **large tomato, chopped**
- 1 **cup chopped seeded cucumber**
- ½ **cup chopped red onion**
- 1 **can (2¼ ounces) sliced ripe olives, drained**
- 2 **cups torn romaine**
- 8 **whole wheat pita pocket halves**
- ½ **cup crumbled feta cheese**

1. In a large bowl, whisk the first six ingredients until blended; if desired, stir in cayenne pepper. Add tomato, cucumber, onion and olives; toss to coat. Refrigerate until serving.
2. To serve, add lettuce to vegetables; toss to combine. Spoon into the pita halves; sprinkle with cheese.
PER SERVING *354 cal., 19 g fat (4 g sat. fat), 8 mg chol., 580 mg sodium, 39 g carb., 7 g fiber, 9 g pro.*

MEDITERRANEAN VEGETABLE PITAS

"When fixing my sliders, I brine the chicken overnight. That step results in especially good flavor and makes the meat melt-in-your-mouth tender."

—RACHEL KUNKEL SCHELL CITY, MO

SLOW COOKER BBQ Chicken Sliders

PREP: 25 MIN. + BRINING • **COOK:** 4 HOURS
MAKES: 8 SERVINGS (2 SLIDERS EACH)

BRINE
- 1½ **quarts water**
- ¼ **cup packed brown sugar**
- 2 **tablespoons salt**
- 1 **tablespoon liquid smoke**
- 2 **garlic cloves, minced**
- ½ **teaspoon dried thyme**

CHICKEN
- 2 **pounds boneless skinless chicken breast halves**
- ⅓ **cup liquid smoke**
- 1½ **cups hickory smoke-flavored barbecue sauce**
- 16 **slider buns or dinner rolls, split and warmed**

1. In a large bowl, mix the brine ingredients, stirring to dissolve brown sugar. Reserve 1 cup brine for cooking chicken; cover and refrigerate.
2. Place chicken in a large resealable bag; add the remaining brine. Seal bag, pressing out as much air as possible; turn to coat chicken. Place in a large bowl; refrigerate 18-24 hours, turning occasionally.
3. Remove chicken from brine and transfer to a 3-qt. slow cooker; discard brine in bag. Add reserved 1 cup brine and ⅓ cup liquid smoke to chicken. Cook, covered, on low 4-5 hours or until chicken is tender.
4. Remove the chicken; cool slightly. Discard cooking juices. Shred chicken with two forks and return to the slow cooker. Stir in barbecue sauce; heat through. Serve on buns.

EAT SMART Chicken and Dumpling Soup

Like a security blanket for the soul, this dumpling-filled soup is a true classic. My husband isn't very fond of leftovers, but he enjoys this so much, he says he could eat it every day of the week.

—MORGAN BYERS BERKLEY, MI

PREP: 25 MIN. • **COOK:** 40 MIN.
MAKES: 4 SERVINGS

- ¾ **pound boneless skinless chicken breasts, cut into 1-inch cubes**
- ¼ **teaspoon salt**
- ⅛ **teaspoon pepper**
- 2 **teaspoons olive oil**
- ¼ **cup all-purpose flour**
- 4 **cups reduced-sodium chicken broth, divided**
- 1 **cup water**
- 2 **cups frozen French-cut green beans**
- 1½ **cups sliced onions**
- 1 **cup shredded carrots**
- ¼ **teaspoon dried marjoram**
- ⅔ **cup reduced-fat biscuit/baking mix**
- ⅓ **cup cornmeal**
- ¼ **cup shredded reduced-fat cheddar cheese**
- ⅓ **cup fat-free milk**

1. Sprinkle the chicken with salt and pepper. In a large nonstick skillet, heat oil over medium-high heat. Add chicken; cook and stir until no longer pink. Remove from heat.
2. In a large saucepan, whisk the flour and ½ cup chicken broth until smooth. Stir in water and remaining broth. Add beans, onions, carrots and marjoram. Bring to a boil. Reduce heat; simmer, uncovered, 10 minutes. Add chicken; return to a simmer.
3. Meanwhile, in a small bowl, mix biscuit mix, cornmeal and cheese. Stir in the milk just until moistened. Drop the batter in 12 portions on top of the simmering soup. Reduce heat to low; cover and cook 15 minutes or until a toothpick inserted into the center of dumpling comes out clean.

PER SERVING *353 cal., 8 g fat (2 g sat. fat), 52 mg chol., 1,111 mg sodium, 44 g carb., 5 g fiber, 28 g pro.* **Diabetic Exchanges:** *3 lean meat, 2 starch, 2 vegetable, 1 fat.*

"For me, football, cool weather and chili just seem to go together. Whether we're cheering on the local team on a Friday night or watching an Oklahoma Sooners game on a Saturday afternoon, my Spicy Touchdown Chili scores big." —CHRIS NEAL QUAPAW, OK

SPICY TOUCHDOWN CHILI

SLOW COOKER
Spicy Touchdown Chili

PREP: 30 MIN. • **COOK:** 4 HOURS
MAKES: 12 SERVINGS (3 QUARTS)

- 1 **pound ground beef**
- 1 **pound bulk pork sausage**
- 2 **cans (16 ounces each) kidney beans, rinsed and drained**
- 2 **cans (15 ounces each) pinto beans, rinsed and drained**
- 2 **cans (10 ounces each) diced tomatoes with mild green chilies, undrained**
- 1 **can (14½ ounces) diced tomatoes with onions, undrained**
- 1 **can (12 ounces) beer**
- 6 **bacon strips, cooked and crumbled**
- 1 **small onion, chopped**
- ¼ **cup chili powder**
- ¼ **cup chopped pickled jalapeno slices**
- 2 **teaspoons ground cumin**
- 2 **garlic cloves, minced**
- 1 **teaspoon dried basil**
- ¾ **teaspoon cayenne pepper**

1. In a large skillet, cook the beef over medium heat 6-8 minutes or until no longer pink, breaking into crumbles; drain. Transfer to a 6-qt. slow cooker. Repeat with sausage.
2. Stir in remaining ingredients. Cook, covered, on low 4-5 hours.

 ## Did you know?

One of the advantages of using a slow cooker is that it uses very little electricity because of its low wattage. But don't peek! Every time you lift the lid during cooking, steam is lost and you add 15 to 30 minutes to the cooking time of your recipe.

TURKEY WILD RICE SOUP

Turkey Wild Rice Soup

Two Minnesota favorites, turkey and wild rice, are the stars of this sensational soup. Be prepared to serve seconds!
—**TERRI HOLMGREN** SWANVILLE, MN

PREP: 10 MIN. • **COOK:** 35 MIN.
MAKES: 12 SERVINGS (ABOUT 3 QUARTS)

- ½ cup butter, cubed
- 2 carrots, finely chopped
- 2 celery ribs, finely chopped
- 1 medium onion, chopped
- ½ cup all-purpose flour
- 4 cups chicken or turkey broth
- 2 cups cooked wild rice
- 2 cups cubed cooked turkey
- 2 cups half-and-half cream
- 1 teaspoon dried parsley flakes
- ½ teaspoon salt
- ¼ teaspoon pepper

1. In a Dutch oven, heat butter over medium-high heat. Add the carrots, celery and onion; cook and stir until tender.
2. Stir in flour until blended; cook until bubbly. Gradually whisk in broth. Bring to a boil, stirring constantly; cook and stir for 1-2 minutes or until thickened. Stir in the remaining ingredients; return to a boil. Reduce the heat; simmer for 20 minutes, stirring occasionally.

Baked Lasagna in a Bun

Here's a real family-pleaser. I tuck the lasagna ingredients into hollowed-out buns, then round out the meal with a crisp salad.
—**CINDY MORELOCK** AFTON, TN

PREP: 20 MIN. • **BAKE:** 25 MIN. • **MAKES:** 8 SERVINGS

- 8 submarine or hoagie buns (8 inches)
- 1 pound ground beef
- 1 cup spaghetti sauce
- 1 tablespoon garlic powder
- 1 tablespoon Italian seasoning
- 1 cup ricotta cheese
- ¼ cup grated Parmesan cheese
- 1 cup (4 ounces) shredded cheddar cheese, divided
- 1 cup (4 ounces) shredded part-skim mozzarella cheese, divided

1. Preheat oven to 350°. Make a 2-in.-wide V-shaped cut in the center of each bun to within 1 inch of bottom. Remove the cut portion and save for another use. Place buns on an ungreased baking sheet.
2. In a large skillet, cook the beef over medium heat 6-8 minutes or until no longer pink, breaking into crumbles; drain. Stir in the spaghetti sauce, garlic powder and Italian seasoning; heat through.
3. Meanwhile, in a small bowl, mix the ricotta cheese, Parmesan cheese and half of the cheddar and mozzarella cheeses. Spoon the meat sauce into buns; top with ricotta mixture. Cover loosely with foil.
4. Bake 20 minutes. Sprinkle tops with remaining cheddar and mozzarella cheeses; bake, uncovered, 3-5 minutes or until cheese is melted.

BAKED LASAGNA IN A BUN

WHITE CHILI

 SLOW COOKER White Chili

White chili may be a little different from what you're used to, but it's guaranteed to warm up everyone on a cold night. My version gets a bit of Mexican flair from cilantro and cumin.
—**SHARI MEISSNER** CHESTER, MT

PREP: 20 MIN. • **COOK:** 6 HOURS • **MAKES:** 8 SERVINGS (2 QUARTS)

- 1 tablespoon olive oil
- 3 medium onions, chopped
- 2 garlic cloves, minced
- 4 cups cubed cooked chicken or turkey
- 2 cans (15 ounces each) white kidney or cannellini beans, rinsed and drained
- 1 can (15 ounces) garbanzo beans or chickpeas, rinsed and drained
- 2 cups chicken broth
- 1 can (4 ounces) chopped green chilies
- 2 teaspoons ground cumin
- ½ teaspoon dried oregano
- ¼ teaspoon cayenne pepper
- ¼ teaspoon salt
- ¼ cup minced fresh cilantro
  Optional toppings: corn chips, shredded Monterey Jack cheese and sour cream

1. In a large skillet, heat oil over medium-high heat. Add the onions; cook and stir until tender. Add the garlic; cook 1 minute longer.

2. Transfer to a 3-qt. slow cooker. Stir in chicken, beans, broth, chilies and dry seasonings.

3. Cook, covered, on low 6-8 hours or until heated through. Stir in cilantro. If desired, serve with corn chips, cheese and sour cream.

Beef & Mushroom Braised Stew

Every spring, my family members head to our woods to collect morel mushrooms. Then it's time to stock up on this wonderfully hearty, beefy stew. We love a big helping spooned over hot mashed potatoes. If you can't find morels, prepare the recipe using button mushrooms or baby portobellos instead.
—**AMY WERTHEIM** ATLANTA, IL

PREP: 35 MIN. • **BAKE:** 1½ HOURS • **MAKES:** 6 SERVINGS

- 1 boneless beef chuck roast (2 to 3 pounds), cut into 1-inch cubes
- ¼ teaspoon salt
- ¼ teaspoon pepper
- 3 tablespoons olive oil
- 1 pound sliced fresh mushrooms
- 2 medium onions, sliced
- 2 garlic cloves, minced
- 1 carton (32 ounces) beef broth
- 1 cup dry red wine or additional beef broth
- ½ cup brandy
- 1 tablespoon tomato paste
- ¼ teaspoon each dried parsley flakes, rosemary, sage leaves, tarragon and thyme
- 3 tablespoons all-purpose flour
- 3 tablespoons water
  Hot mashed potatoes

1. Preheat oven to 325°. Sprinkle beef with salt and pepper. In an ovenproof Dutch oven, heat oil over medium heat; brown beef in batches. Remove from pan.

2. In same pan, add mushrooms and onions; cook and stir until tender. Add garlic; cook 1 minute longer. Stir in broth, wine, brandy, tomato paste and herbs. Return beef to pan. Bring to a boil.

3. Bake, covered, 1 hour. In a small bowl, mix the flour and water until smooth; gradually stir into stew. Bake, covered, 30 minutes longer or until sauce is thickened and beef is tender. Skim fat. Serve with mashed potatoes.

BEEF & MUSHROOM BRAISED STEW

FAST FIX › Simple Tomato Soup

I came up with this recipe on a day when we had bad weather. Now my husband, Mic, and my daughter, Liz, often ask me to stir up a pot. Every time I send along some with my daughter for her school lunch, I include extra for her friend.

—**LANAEE O'NEILL** CHICO, CA

START TO FINISH: 30 MIN.
MAKES: 8 SERVINGS (2 QUARTS)

- 2 **cans (14.5 ounces each) diced tomatoes with basil, oregano and garlic, undrained**
- ¼ **cup butter**
- ½ **cup finely chopped red onion**
- 2 **garlic cloves, minced**
- 6 **tablespoons all-purpose flour**
- 1 **carton (48 ounces) chicken broth Grated Parmesan cheese, optional**

1. Place the tomatoes with juices in a blender; cover and process until pureed. In a large saucepan, heat the butter over medium-high heat. Add onion; cook and stir until tender. Add garlic; cook 1 minute longer.

2. Remove from the heat; stir in the flour until smooth. Cook for 1 minute. Gradually whisk in the chicken broth. Add the pureed tomatoes; bring to a boil over medium heat, stirring occasionally. Reduce heat and simmer for 20-25 minutes to allow the flavors to blend. If desired, sprinkle with Parmesan cheese.

EAT SMART FAST FIX › Mustache Tortilla Cutouts

Put a tortilla mustache on a bowl of soup, and get ready for laughs! It's one of my favorite ways to enliven mealtime for children. Change things up with different shapes, such as bow ties or top hats.

—**SHANNON ROUM** WAUKESHA, WI

START TO FINISH: 25 MIN.
MAKES: 8 SERVINGS

- 4 **flour or sun-dried tomato tortillas (8 inches)**
- 2 **tablespoons butter, melted**
- ½ **teaspoon dried basil**
- ½ **teaspoon dried thyme**
- ¼ **teaspoon seasoned salt**
- ¼ **teaspoon garlic powder**
- ⅛ **teaspoon pepper**

SIMPLE TOMATO SOUP
MUSTACHE TORTILLA CUTOUTS

Using kitchen shears, cut out two mustaches from each tortilla; discard scraps. Brush both sides of mustaches with butter; place on an ungreased baking sheet. Combine seasonings; sprinkle over mustaches. Bake at 400° for 5-7 minutes or until crisp.

PER SERVING *99 cal., 4 g fat (2 g sat. fat), 8 mg chol., 192 mg sodium, 13 g carb., trace fiber, 2 g pro.* **Diabetic Exchanges:** *1 starch, ½ fat.*

top tip

Giggles from Garnishes

Want other kid-friendly ideas for topping off soup? Little ones will love fun garnishes such as goldfish crackers, wagon wheel pasta, pepperoni and cheese slices cut with a cookie cutter.

🍲 SLOW COOKER Pumpkin Harvest Beef Stew

PREP: 25 MIN. • **COOK:** 6½ HOURS
MAKES: 6 SERVINGS

- 1 tablespoon canola oil
- 1 beef top round steak (1½ pounds), cut into 1-inch cubes
- 1½ cups cubed peeled pie pumpkin or sweet potatoes
- 3 small red potatoes, peeled and cubed
- 1 cup cubed acorn squash
- 1 medium onion, chopped
- 2 cans (14½ ounces each) reduced-sodium beef broth
- 1 can (14½ ounces) diced tomatoes, undrained
- 2 bay leaves
- 2 garlic cloves, minced
- 2 teaspoons reduced-sodium beef bouillon granules
- ½ teaspoon chili powder
- ½ teaspoon pepper
- ¼ teaspoon ground allspice
- ¼ teaspoon ground cloves
- ¼ cup water
- 3 tablespoons all-purpose flour

1. In a large skillet, heat the oil over medium-high heat. Brown the beef in batches; remove with a slotted spoon to a 4- or 5-qt. slow cooker. Add the pumpkin, red potatoes, acorn squash and onion. Stir in the beef broth, tomatoes and seasonings. Cover and cook on low for 6-8 hours or until the meat is tender.

2. Remove bay leaves. In a small bowl, mix the water and flour until smooth; gradually stir into the stew. Cover and cook on high for 30 minutes or until the liquid is thickened.

🍲 SLOW COOKER Slow-Cooked Reuben Brats

Sauerkraut gives my brats a flavor boost, but it's the combination of chili sauce and cheese that puts them over the top.
—ALANA SIMMONS JOHNSTOWN, PA

PREP: 30 MIN. • **COOK:** 7¼ HOURS
MAKES: 10 SERVINGS

- 10 uncooked bratwurst links
- 3 cans (12 ounces each) light beer or nonalcoholic beer
- 1 large sweet onion, sliced
- 1 can (14 ounces) sauerkraut, rinsed and well drained
- ¾ cup mayonnaise
- ¼ cup chili sauce
- 2 tablespoons ketchup
- 1 tablespoon finely chopped onion
- 2 teaspoons sweet pickle relish
- 1 garlic clove, minced
- ⅛ teaspoon pepper
- 10 hoagie buns, split
- 10 slices Swiss cheese

1. In a large skillet, brown bratwurst in batches; drain. In a 5-qt. slow cooker, combine beer, sliced onion and sauerkraut; top with bratwurst. Cook, covered, on low 7-9 hours or until sausages are cooked through.

2. Preheat oven to 350°. In a small bowl, mix the mayonnaise, chili sauce, ketchup, chopped onion, pickle relish, garlic and pepper until blended. Spread over the cut sides of buns; top with Swiss cheese, bratwurst and sauerkraut mixture. Place on an ungreased baking sheet. Bake 8-10 minutes or until cheese is melted.

SLOW-COOKED REUBEN BRATS

Tastes of America

Celebrate the flavors of the U.S. with foods inspired by regional specialties. From Tex-Mex Sloppy Joes to Philly Cheesesteaks, these favorites have one thing in common—they're delicious!

FAST FIX ▶ Tex-Mex Sloppy Joes

Sloppy joes appeal to adults and children alike. I deviated from the traditional recipe by adding a little Southwestern spiciness.
—**GERALDINE SAUCIER** ALBUQUERQUE, NM

START TO FINISH: 30 MIN. • **MAKES:** 6 SERVINGS

- 1 pound ground beef
- 1 small onion, chopped
- 2 garlic cloves, minced
- 1 cup ketchup
- 1 can (4 ounces) chopped green chilies
- ½ cup beef broth
- ¼ cup chili sauce
- 1 teaspoon chili powder
- ½ teaspoon ground cumin
- ¼ teaspoon crushed red pepper flakes
- ¼ teaspoon salt
- ¼ teaspoon coarsely ground pepper
- 6 hamburger buns, split
- 2 tablespoons butter, softened

1. In a large skillet, cook beef and onion over medium heat for 6-8 minutes or until beef is no longer pink, breaking up beef into crumbles; drain. Add the garlic; cook 1-2 minutes longer. Stir in the ketchup, chilies, broth, chili sauce and seasonings. Bring to a boil. Reduce heat; simmer, uncovered, for 15 minutes, stirring occasionally.

2. Meanwhile, spread cut sides of buns with butter. Place on baking sheets, buttered side up. Broil 4 in. from the heat for 1-2 minutes or until toasted. Serve beef mixture in buns.

TEX-MEX SLOPPY JOES

"I grew up in northern New Jersey, where hot dogs with grilled potatoes were born. It's a combo you'll love."
—**SUZANNE BANFIELD** BASKING RIDGE, NJ

JERSEY-STYLE HOT DOGS

Jersey-Style Hot Dogs

PREP: 20 MIN. • **GRILL:** 40 MIN.
MAKES: 12 SERVINGS (10 CUPS POTATO MIXTURE)

- 6 medium Yukon Gold potatoes (about 3 pounds), halved and thinly sliced
- 3 large sweet red peppers, thinly sliced
- 3 large onions, peeled, halved and thinly sliced
- ⅓ cup olive oil
- 6 garlic cloves, minced
- 3 teaspoons salt
- 1½ teaspoons pepper
- 12 bun-length beef hot dogs
- 12 hot dog buns, split

1. In a large bowl, combine the potatoes, red peppers and onions. In a small bowl, mix the oil, garlic, salt and pepper; add to potato mixture and toss to coat.

2. Transfer to two 13-in. x 9-in. disposable foil pans; cover with foil. Place the pans on grill rack over medium heat; cook, covered, 30-35 minutes or until potatoes are tender. Remove from heat.

3. Grill hot dogs, covered, over medium heat 7-9 minutes or until heated through, turning occasionally. Place buns on grill, cut side down; grill until lightly toasted. Place the hot dogs and potato mixture in buns. Serve with the remaining potato mixture.

Philly Cheesesteaks

PREP: 30 MIN. + FREEZING • **BROIL:** 5 MIN. • **MAKES:** 4 SERVINGS

- 1 beef top sirloin steak (1½ pounds)
- 3 tablespoons butter, divided
- 4 medium onions, halved and sliced
- 2 small green peppers, cut into thin strips
- 2 small sweet red peppers, cut into thin strips
- 1 teaspoon hot pepper sauce
- 4 submarine buns, split and toasted
- ¾ teaspoon salt
- ½ teaspoon pepper
- 8 slices cheddar cheese

1. Freeze the steak 1 hour until firm but not frozen.

2. In a large skillet, heat 2 tablespoons butter over medium heat. Add onions, peppers and pepper sauce; cook and stir 5 minutes or until tender; remove and keep warm.

3. Place bun bottoms on a baking sheet, cut side up. Remove steak from freezer; cut into thin slices. Sprinkle with salt and pepper. In same skillet, heat remaining butter over medium-high heat. Add beef in batches; cook and stir 1-2 minutes or until meat is no longer pink. Remove from pan.

4. Layer the bun bottoms with meat, onion mixture and cheese. Broil 4 in. from heat for 2-3 minutes or until the cheese is melted. Replace tops.

"Steak of any kind goes over big in our house. Philly Cheesesteaks are a satisfying choice for dinner and a fantastic alternative to the usual burgers."
—**SUSAN SEYMOUR** VALANTIE, NY

PHILLY CHEESESTEAKS

CINCINNATI-STYLE CHILI

SLOW COOKER EAT SMART

Cincinnati-Style Chili

My husband had this type of chili when visiting a friend in Ohio and was thrilled when I made it at home.
—**TARI AMBLER** SHOREWOOD, IL

PREP: 35 MIN. • **COOK:** 6 HOURS • **MAKES:** 10 SERVINGS (1½ QUARTS)

- 2 pounds extra-lean ground turkey
- 2 medium onions, finely chopped
- 4 garlic cloves, minced
- 2 cans (8 ounces each) no-salt-added tomato sauce
- 1 can (14½ ounces) reduced-sodium beef broth
- 2 tablespoons cider vinegar
- ½ ounce unsweetened chocolate, chopped
- 3 tablespoons chili powder
- 1 bay leaf
- 2 teaspoons Worcestershire sauce
- 1 teaspoon ground cumin
- ¾ teaspoon salt
- ¾ teaspoon ground cinnamon
- ¼ teaspoon ground allspice
- ⅛ teaspoon ground cloves
- ⅛ teaspoon cayenne pepper
- 1 package (16 ounces) whole wheat spaghetti

TOPPINGS
- 1 can (16 ounces) kidney beans, rinsed and drained
- 1¼ cups (5 ounces each) shredded reduced-fat cheddar cheese
- 1 medium onion, chopped

1. In a nonstick Dutch oven coated with cooking spray, cook turkey, onions and garlic until turkey is no longer pink. Transfer to a 3-qt. slow cooker.

2. In a large bowl, combine tomato sauce, broth, vinegar, chocolate and seasonings; pour over turkey mixture. Cook, covered, on low 6-8 hours.

3. Cook spaghetti according to package directions; drain. Remove bay leaf from chili. Serve chili over spaghetti; top servings with beans, cheese and onion.

PER SERVING *388 cal., 6 g fat (3 g sat. fat), 47 mg chol., 523 mg sodium, 52 g carb., 10 g fiber, 37 g pro.*

Acorn Squash & Pear Soup

My family loves a side dish that features stuffed acorn squash. I decided to blend the same flavors into a creamy soup. It's true comfort food.

—HEATHER ROTUNDA ST. CLOUD, MN

PREP: 20 MIN. • **BAKE:** 1¼ HOURS
MAKES: 10 SERVINGS (2½ QUARTS)

- 2 medium acorn squash, peeled and cut into ¾-inch cubes
- 4 medium firm pears, peeled and coarsely chopped
- 3 celery ribs, thinly sliced
- 1 large onion, finely chopped
- 2 tablespoons butter, melted
- 1 teaspoon dried thyme
- 1 teaspoon salt
- ½ teaspoon dried sage leaves
- ½ teaspoon pepper
- 1 carton (48 ounces) chicken broth

1. In a large bowl, combine the first nine ingredients; toss to coat. Transfer to a greased shallow roasting pan. Roast at 375° for 1¼ hours or until squash is tender, stirring occasionally.
2. Cool slightly. In a food processor, process squash mixture with the broth in batches until smooth. Transfer to a Dutch oven; heat through, stirring occasionally.

ACORN SQUASH & PEAR SOUP

BLACK BEAN 'N' PUMPKIN CHILI

SLOW COOKER EAT SMART
Black Bean 'n' Pumpkin Chili

We can't get enough of this slow-cooked chili, especially on cold autumn and winter days. I've found that it freezes well—and that the leftovers taste even better!

—DEBORAH VLIET HOLLAND, MI

PREP: 20 MIN. • **COOK:** 4 HOURS
MAKES: 10 SERVINGS (2½ QUARTS)

- 2 tablespoons olive oil
- 1 medium onion, chopped
- 1 medium sweet yellow pepper, chopped
- 3 garlic cloves, minced
- 2 cans (15 ounces each) black beans, rinsed and drained
- 1 can (15 ounces) solid-pack pumpkin
- 1 can (14½ ounces) diced tomatoes, undrained
- 3 cups chicken broth
- 2½ cups cubed cooked turkey
- 2 teaspoons dried parsley flakes
- 2 teaspoons chili powder
- 1½ teaspoons ground cumin
- 1½ teaspoons dried oregano
- ½ teaspoon salt
- Optional toppings: cubed avocado and thinly sliced green onions

1. In a large skillet, heat the oil over medium-high heat. Add onion and pepper; cook and stir until tender. Add garlic; cook 1 minute longer.
2. Transfer to a 5-qt. slow cooker; stir in the remaining ingredients. Cook, covered, on low 4-5 hours. If desired, top with avocado and green onions.
PER SERVING *192 cal., 5 g fat (1 g sat. fat), 28 mg chol., 658 mg sodium, 21 g carb., 7 g fiber, 16 g pro.* **Diabetic Exchanges:** *2 lean meat, 1½ starch, ½ fat.*

Creamy Cauliflower Soup with Artichoke Hearts & Bacon

When I was recovering from surgery, my oldest son, a chef, cooked my meals. He fixed a cream of cauliflower recipe using on-hand ingredients. I was so touched that he came to care for me, and this delicious creation reminds me of that time.

—**MILDRED LYNN CARUSO** BRIGHTON, TN

START TO FINISH: 30 MIN.
MAKES: 6 SERVINGS

- 1 **large head cauliflower, broken into florets**
- 2 **cans (14½ ounces each) chicken broth**
- ½ **cup heavy whipping cream**
- ½ **teaspoon ground nutmeg**
- ½ **teaspoon salt**
- ⅛ **teaspoon pepper**
- 1 **can (14 ounces) water-packed artichoke hearts, rinsed, drained and coarsely chopped**
- ⅓ **cup shredded Asiago cheese or Parmesan cheese**
- 6 **pieces bacon strips, cooked and crumbled**

1. In a large saucepan, combine the cauliflower and chicken broth; bring to a boil. Reduce heat; cover and simmer for 10-15 minutes or until cauliflower is tender.

2. Cool slightly. In a blender, process soup in batches until smooth. Return all to the pan. Stir in heavy whipping cream, nutmeg, salt and pepper; heat through. Serve with artichoke hearts, cheese and bacon.

CREAMY CAULIFLOWER SOUP WITH ARTICHOKE HEARTS & BACON

Classic French Onion Soup

Enjoy this the way my granddaughter, Becky, does—in a French onion soup bowl complete with garlic toast and gobs of melted cheese on top. She prefers Swiss, but it's also good with Gruyere.

—**LOU SANSEVERO** FERRON, UT

PREP: 20 MIN. • **COOK:** 2 HOURS
MAKES: 12 SERVINGS

- 5 **tablespoons olive oil, divided**
- 1 **tablespoon butter**
- 8 **cups thinly sliced onions (about 3 pounds)**
- 3 **garlic cloves, minced**
- ½ **cup port wine**
- 2 **cartons (32 ounces each) beef broth**
- ½ **teaspoon pepper**
- ¼ **teaspoon salt**
- 24 **slices French bread baguette (½ inch thick)**
- 2 **large garlic cloves, peeled and halved**
- ¾ **cup shredded Gruyere or Swiss cheese**

1. In a Dutch oven, heat 2 tablespoons oil and butter over medium heat. Add onions; cook and stir for 10-13 minutes or until softened. Reduce the heat to medium-low; cook for 30-40 minutes or until deep golden brown, stirring occasionally. Add minced garlic; cook 2 minutes longer.

2. Stir in the wine. Bring to a boil; cook until liquid is reduced by half. Add the beef broth, pepper and salt; return to a boil. Reduce heat; simmer for 1 hour, stirring occasionally.

3. Meanwhile, place the baguette slices on a baking sheet; brush both sides with remaining oil. Bake at 400° for 3-5 minutes on each side or until toasted. Rub toasts with halved garlic.

4. To serve, place twelve 8-oz. broiler-safe bowls or ramekins on baking sheets. Place two toasts in each. Ladle with soup; top with cheese. Broil 4-in. from heat until cheese is melted.

Biscuit Bowl Chili

Kids love helping to make these biscuit bowls almost as much as they love eating them. For a different meal another time, bake the yummy little cups as directed and stuff them with popular taco fixings—or even your favorite sloppy joe filling.

—**CASSY RAY** PARKERSBURG, WV

PREP: 20 MIN. • **COOK:** 30 MIN. • **MAKES:** 8 SERVINGS

- 1 tube (16.3 ounces) large refrigerated flaky biscuits
- 2 teaspoons cornmeal
- 1 pound lean ground beef (90% lean)
- ½ cup chopped onion
- 1 can (16 ounces) kidney beans, rinsed and drained
- 1 can (11½ ounces) V8 juice
- 1 cup ketchup
- 2 teaspoons chili powder
- ½ teaspoon salt
- ¼ to ½ teaspoon cayenne pepper
- ¼ teaspoon crushed red pepper flakes
- ¼ teaspoon pepper
- ½ cup shredded cheddar cheese

1. Preheat oven to 350°. Place two muffin tins upside down; spray the bottoms and sides of eight alternating muffin cups. On a work surface, roll or press the biscuits into 4-in. circles. Sprinkle both sides with cornmeal, pressing lightly to adhere. Place biscuits over greased muffin cups, shaping biscuits around cups.

2. Bake 11-13 minutes or until lightly browned. Carefully remove biscuit bowls from pans; cool on a wire rack.

3. Meanwhile, in a large skillet, cook beef and onion over medium heat 6-8 minutes or until beef is no longer pink; drain. Stir in beans, V8 juice, ketchup and seasonings. Bring to a boil. Reduce heat; simmer, covered, 10 minutes. Serve in biscuit bowls; top with cheese.

BISCUIT BOWL CHILI

CHICKEN POTPIE SOUP

Chicken Potpie Soup

My grandmother hand-wrote a cookbook. She supplied the best pie crust, and I came up with this recipe.

—**KAREN LEMAY** PEARLAND, TX

PREP: 20 MIN. + CHILLING • **COOK:** 20 MIN. • **MAKES:** 6 SERVINGS

- 2 cups all-purpose flour
- 1¼ teaspoons salt
- ⅔ cup shortening
- 5 to 6 tablespoons 2% milk

SOUP

- 2 tablespoons butter
- 1 cup cubed peeled potatoes
- 1 cup chopped sweet onion
- 2 celery ribs, chopped
- 2 medium carrots, chopped
- ½ cup all-purpose flour
- ½ teaspoon salt
- ¼ teaspoon pepper
- 3 cans (14½ ounces each) chicken broth
- 2 cups shredded cooked chicken
- 1 cup frozen petite peas
- 1 cup frozen corn

1. In a large bowl, mix flour and salt; cut in shortening until crumbly. Gradually add the milk, tossing with a fork until dough holds together when pressed. Shape into a disk; wrap in plastic wrap. Refrigerate for 30 minutes or overnight.

2. On a lightly floured surface, roll the dough to ⅛-in. thickness. Using a floured 2½-in. heart-shaped or round cutter, cut 18 shapes. Place 1 in. apart on ungreased baking sheets. Bake at 425° for 8-11 minutes or until golden brown. Cool on a wire rack.

3. For soup, in a Dutch oven, heat butter over medium-high heat. Add the potatoes, onion, celery and carrots; cook and stir for 5-7 minutes or until onion is tender.

4. Stir in the flour, salt and pepper until blended; gradually whisk in broth. Bring to a boil, stirring occasionally. Reduce heat; simmer, uncovered, for 8-10 minutes or until potatoes are tender. Stir in the remaining ingredients; heat through. Serve with pastries.

(5) INGREDIENTS FAST FIX ▶ Roasted Tomato Soup with Fresh Basil

PREP: 40 MIN. • **COOK:** 5 MIN. • **MAKES:** 6 SERVINGS

- 3½ **pounds tomatoes (about 11 medium), halved**
- 1 **small onion, quartered**
- 2 **garlic cloves, peeled and halved**
- 2 **tablespoons olive oil**
- 2 **tablespoons fresh thyme leaves**
- 1 **teaspoon salt**
- ¼ **teaspoon pepper**
- 12 **fresh basil leaves**
   Julienned fresh basil leaves, optional

1. Preheat oven to 400°. Place the tomatoes, onion and garlic in a greased 15-in. x 10-in. x 1-in. baking pan; drizzle with the oil. Sprinkle with the thyme, salt and pepper; toss to coat. Roast 25-30 minutes or until tender, stirring once. Cool slightly.

2. Process tomato mixture and basil leaves in batches in a blender until smooth. Transfer to a large saucepan; heat through. If desired, top with julienned basil.

"Roasting brings out the tomato flavor in my soup, and the slightly chunky texture adds homemade appeal. I top off each bowl with extra basil." —**MARIE FORTE** RARITAN, NJ

Eggs Benedict Burgers

To feed my daughter's hungry cowboy friends after a rodeo, I jazzed up leftover burgers with fried eggs, hollandaise sauce, mustard and bacon. They were a huge hit!

—**BONNIE GEAVARAS-BOOTZ** SCOTTSDALE, AZ

PREP: 25 MIN. • **GRILL:** 10 MIN. • **MAKES:** 4 SERVINGS

- 1½ **pounds ground beef**
- ½ **teaspoon salt**
- ¼ **teaspoon pepper**
- 4 **hamburger buns, split**
- 1 **envelope hollandaise sauce mix**
- 1½ **teaspoons stone-ground mustard**
- 4 **eggs**
- 4 **lettuce leaves**
- 4 **slices tomato**
- 6 **bacon strips, halved and cooked**

1. In a large bowl, combine beef, salt and pepper, mixing lightly but thoroughly. Shape into four ½-in.-thick patties.

2. Grill burgers, covered, over medium heat 4-6 minutes on each side or until a thermometer reads 160°. Grill buns, cut side down, until toasted. Meanwhile, prepare the sauce mix according to package directions using milk; stir in mustard. Keep warm.

3. Heat a large nonstick skillet coated with cooking spray over medium-high heat. Break eggs, one at a time, into pan; reduce heat to low. Cook until desired doneness, turning after whites are set if desired.

4. Serve lettuce, tomato and burgers on buns; top with bacon, eggs and sauce. Replace tops.

ROASTED TOMATO SOUP WITH FRESH BASIL

GAIL PRATHER'S ROASTED BRUSSELS SPROUTS WITH HAZELNUTS *PAGE 51*

Side Dishes & Condiments

Round out your menu with any of the special accompaniments in this chapter. No matter what your main course may be, these sensational plate fillers just might **steal the spotlight!**

**HEIDI FLEEK'S
EASY SLOW COOKER MAC &
CHEESE** *PAGE 49*

**LYNN IRELAND'S
SLOW-COOKED RANCH POTATOES**
PAGE 50

**TINA BLACKMAN'S
DR PEPPER BBQ SAUCE**
PAGE 56

BASIL CORN & TOMATO BAKE

⟨5⟩INGREDIENTS FAST FIX ▶
Smoky Cauliflower

Smoked Spanish paprika gives a simple side of roasted cauliflower extra color and depth of flavor. Try it and see!

—JULIETTE MULHOLLAND CORVALLIS, OR

START TO FINISH: 30 MIN.
MAKES: 8 SERVINGS

- 1 large head cauliflower, broken into 1-inch florets (about 9 cups)
- 2 tablespoons olive oil
- 1 teaspoon smoked paprika
- ¾ teaspoon salt
- 2 garlic cloves, minced
- 2 tablespoons minced fresh parsley

1. Place cauliflower in a large bowl. Combine the oil, paprika and salt. Drizzle over cauliflower; toss to coat. Transfer to a 15-in. x 10-in. x 1-in. baking pan. Bake, uncovered, at 450° for 10 minutes.

2. Stir in garlic. Bake 10-15 minutes longer or until the cauliflower is tender and lightly browned, stirring occasionally. Sprinkle with parsley.

SMOKY CAULIFLOWER

EAT SMART Basil Corn & Tomato Bake

This cheese-topped baked dish is one of my favorites when sweet corn is in season.
—ERIN CHILCOAT CENTRAL ISLIP, NY

PREP: 30 MIN. • **BAKE:** 45 MIN. + STANDING
MAKES: 10 SERVINGS

- 2 teaspoons olive oil
- 1 medium onion, chopped
- 2 eggs
- 1 can (10¾ ounces) reduced-fat reduced-sodium condensed cream of celery soup, undiluted
- 4 cups fresh or frozen corn
- 1 small zucchini, chopped
- 1 medium tomato, seeded and chopped
- ¾ cup soft whole wheat bread crumbs
- ⅓ cup minced fresh basil
- ½ teaspoon salt
- ½ cup shredded part-skim mozzarella cheese
  Additional minced fresh basil, optional

1. Preheat oven to 350°. In a small skillet, heat oil over medium heat. Add onion; cook and stir until tender. In a large bowl, whisk eggs and condensed soup until blended. Stir in vegetables, bread crumbs, basil, salt and onion. Transfer mixture to an 11-in. x 7-in. baking dish coated with cooking spray.

2. Bake, uncovered, 40-45 minutes or until bubbly. Sprinkle with cheese. Bake 5-10 minutes longer or until the cheese is melted. Let stand 10 minutes before serving. If desired, sprinkle with additional basil.

PER SERVING *131 cal., 4 g fat (1 g sat. fat), 47 mg chol., 299 mg sodium, 20 g carb., 3 g fiber, 6 g pro.* **Diabetic Exchanges:** *1 starch, ½ fat.*

NOTE *To make soft bread crumbs, tear bread into pieces and place in a food processor or blender. Cover and pulse until crumbs form. One slice of bread yields ½ to ¾ cup crumbs.*

Herbed Potato Dumplings

I think of myself as a "tinkerer" in the kitchen. It's fun to take a recipe, change ingredients and make the final result my own. For a twist on traditional dumplings, I used shredded potatoes.
—**SHAWN ASIALA** DEL RAY BEACH, FL

PREP: 20 MIN. • **COOK:** 30 MIN.
MAKES: 6 SERVINGS

- 1 egg, lightly beaten
- ¾ cup seasoned dry bread crumbs
- 1 tablespoon all-purpose flour
- 1 tablespoon minced fresh parsley
- 1 tablespoon minced chives
- 1½ teaspoons minced fresh thyme or ½ teaspoon dried thyme
- ½ teaspoon salt
- ½ teaspoon pepper
- 2½ cups finely shredded uncooked potatoes
  Additional all-purpose flour

1. In a large bowl, mix the first eight ingredients. Stir in potatoes. Shape into 1½-in. balls; dust with flour.
2. Drop the dumplings on top of the simmering soup or stew of your choice. Reduce heat to low; cover and cook 30 minutes or until dumplings are cooked through. Serve immediately.

---

(5)INGREDIENTS FAST FIX
Lemony Green Beans

Want special but quick green beans for dinner? Chicken broth, oil, seasoning and lemon wedges are all you need.
—**JENNIFER TARANTINO** RUTHERFORD, NJ

START TO FINISH: 20 MIN.
MAKES: 6 SERVINGS

- ¼ cup chicken broth
- 2 tablespoons olive oil
- 1½ pounds fresh green beans, trimmed
- ¾ teaspoon lemon-pepper seasoning
  Lemon wedges

In a large skillet, heat chicken broth and oil over medium-high heat. Add the green beans; cook and stir until crisp-tender. Sprinkle with lemon-pepper. Serve with lemon wedges.

EASY SLOW COOKER MAC & CHEESE

"My son always cheers, 'You're the best mom in the world!' when I surprise him with my slow-cooked mac and cheese. It doesn't get much better than that!"
—**HEIDI FLEEK** HAMBURG, PA

SLOW COOKER **Easy Slow Cooker Mac & Cheese**

PREP: 25 MIN. • **COOK:** 1 HOUR
MAKES: 8 SERVINGS

- 2 cups uncooked elbow macaroni
- 1 can (10¾ ounces) condensed cheddar cheese soup, undiluted
- 1 cup 2% milk
- ½ cup sour cream
- ¼ cup butter, cubed
- ½ teaspoon onion powder
- ¼ teaspoon white pepper
- ⅛ teaspoon salt
- 1 cup (4 ounces) shredded cheddar cheese
- 1 cup (4 ounces) shredded fontina cheese
- 1 cup (4 ounces) shredded provolone cheese

1. Cook the macaroni according to the package directions for al dente. Meanwhile, in a large saucepan, combine the soup, milk, sour cream, butter and seasonings; cook and stir over medium-low heat until blended. Stir in cheeses until melted.
2. Drain pasta; transfer to a greased 3-qt. slow cooker. Stir in the cheese mixture. Cook, covered, on low 1-2 hours or until heated through.

Scalloped Potatoes au Gratin

I found I could reduce the time needed to prepare scalloped potatoes by simmering them on top of the stove in an ovenproof skillet, then slipping the skillet into the oven to finish them with a brown crust.
—**LILY JULOW** GAINESVILLE, FL

PREP: 35 MIN. • **BAKE:** 15 MIN. + CHILLING
MAKES: 2 SERVINGS

- 2 **cups thinly sliced peeled potatoes (about 2 large)**
- 2 **teaspoons all-purpose flour**
  Dash each salt, pepper and ground nutmeg
- 2 **teaspoons butter**
- ⅔ **to 1 cup half-and-half cream**
- ⅓ **cup shredded Gouda cheese**

1. Place half of the potatoes in a greased small ovenproof skillet; sprinkle with 1 teaspoon flour. Repeat layers. Sprinkle with salt, pepper and nutmeg. Dot with butter.
2. Add enough half-and-half cream to fill the skillet about three-fourths full. Bring to a boil over medium-high heat. Reduce heat; simmer, uncovered, for 15-20 minutes or until most of the liquid is absorbed.
3. Carefully place the skillet in the oven. Bake, uncovered, at 350° for 10-15 minutes or until bubbly and the potatoes are tender. Sprinkle with the cheese; bake 5 minutes longer or until cheese is melted.

SCALLOPED POTATOES AU GRATIN

SLOW-COOKED RANCH POTATOES

SLOW COOKER

Slow-Cooked Ranch Potatoes

Even after seven years, my family still asks for this yummy bacon-sprinkled dish.
—**LYNN IRELAND** LEBANON, WI

PREP: 15 MIN. • **COOK:** 7 HOURS
MAKES: 10 SERVINGS

- 6 **bacon strips, chopped**
- 2½ **pounds small red potatoes, cubed**
- 1 **package (8 ounces) cream cheese, softened**
- 1 **can (10¾ ounces) condensed cream of potato soup, undiluted**
- ¼ **cup 2% milk**
- 1 **envelope buttermilk ranch salad dressing mix**
- 3 **tablespoons thinly sliced green onions**

1. In a large skillet, cook the bacon over medium heat until crisp, stirring occasionally. Remove with a slotted spoon; drain on paper towels. Drain drippings, reserving 1 tablespoon.
2. Place the potatoes in a 3-qt. slow cooker. In a bowl, beat cream cheese, soup, milk, dressing mix and reserved drippings until blended; stir into the potatoes. Sprinkle with bacon.
3. Cook, covered, on low 7-8 hours or until potatoes are tender. Top with green onions.

Did you know?

Green onions, which are also referred to as scallions, are immature onions that were harvested before the bulb had time to develop.

FAST FIX ▶ Carrot Fritters

Crispy and mild-flavored, these fun finger foods always get snatched up. Plus, any leftovers reheat well for a snack the next day. To keep them warm until the entire recipe is cooked, place the drained fritters on an ovenproof platter, cover it loosely with foil and place it in a 200° oven.
—**SUSAN WITT** FAIRBURY, NE

START TO FINISH: 30 MIN.
MAKES: 20 FRITTERS

- 1 cup all-purpose flour
- 1 teaspoon salt
- 1 teaspoon baking powder
- 2 eggs
- ½ cup milk
- 1 teaspoon canola oil
- 3 cups shredded carrots
  Oil for deep-fat frying

1. In a large bowl, combine the flour, salt and baking powder. Combine the eggs, milk and oil; add to the dry ingredients just until moistened. Fold in carrots.

2. In an electric skillet, heat ¼ in. of oil to 375°. Drop the batter by 2 tablespoonfuls into hot oil; press lightly to flatten. Fry until golden brown, about 1-2 minutes on each side. Drain on paper towels.

CARROT FRITTERS

"I love the combination of ingredients in my Roasted Brussels Sprouts with Hazelnuts. It's nice enough for a holiday yet easy enough for a busy weeknight."
—**GAIL PRATHER** HASTINGS, NE

ROASTED BRUSSELS SPROUTS WITH HAZELNUTS

⑤ INGREDIENTS FAST FIX
Roasted Brussels Sprouts with Hazelnuts

START TO FINISH: 20 MIN.
MAKES: 4 SERVINGS

- 3 tablespoons butter
- ½ to 1 teaspoon pepper
- ½ teaspoon salt
- 1½ pounds fresh Brussels sprouts, trimmed and quartered
- ⅓ cup chopped hazelnuts

1. Preheat oven to 450°. In a small heavy saucepan, melt butter over medium heat. Heat 2-3 minutes or until golden brown, stirring constantly. Remove from heat; stir in the pepper and salt.

2. Place the Brussels sprouts and hazelnuts in a 15-in. x 10-in. x 1-in. baking pan coated with cooking spray. Drizzle with the butter mixture; toss to coat. Roast 10-15 minutes or until the Brussels sprouts are tender, stirring occasionally.

BLACK-EYED PEAS WITH BACON

Swiss Cheese Potatoes

You'll often find a dish like this one in German-Swiss restaurants, but it's really easy to make your own at home.

—**WOLFGANG HANAU** WEST PALM BEACH, FL

PREP: 30 MIN. • **BROIL:** 5 MIN. • **MAKES:** 12 SERVINGS (¾ CUP EACH)

- 8 large potatoes, peeled and cubed (about 4 pounds)
- 1½ teaspoons salt, divided
- 2 cups chopped celery
- ¾ cup chopped onion
- 1½ cups (6 ounces) shredded Swiss cheese, divided
- ⅔ cup 2% milk
- 3 tablespoons butter
- ¼ teaspoon pepper

1. Place the potatoes and 1 teaspoon salt in a Dutch oven; add water to cover. Bring to a boil. Reduce the heat; cook, uncovered, for 10 minutes. Add celery and onion; cook 10-15 minutes longer or until vegetables are tender. Drain; transfer to a large bowl.

2. Mash potato mixture, gradually adding ¾ cup cheese, milk, butter, pepper and remaining salt. Transfer to a greased 8-in. square baking pan; sprinkle with remaining cheese. Broil 3-4 in. from the heat for 5-8 minutes or until cheese is lightly browned.

Black-Eyed Peas with Bacon

A real Southern favorite, black-eyed peas are traditionally served on New Year's Day to bring good luck. But if you eat them only on Jan. 1, you're missing out! I think my mom's recipe featuring bacon, garlic and thyme just can't be beat.

—**RUBY WILLIAMS** BOGALUSA, LA

PREP: 10 MIN. + SOAKING • **COOK:** 35 MIN. • **MAKES:** 8 SERVINGS

- 1 pound dried black-eyed peas, rinsed and sorted
- ½ pound bacon, cooked and crumbled
- 1 tablespoon butter
- 1 large onion, chopped
- 1 garlic clove, minced
- ½ teaspoon dried thyme
  Salt to taste
  Additional cooked and crumbled bacon, optional

1. Place peas and bacon in a large Dutch oven; add water to cover. Bring to a boil; boil for 2 minutes. Remove from the heat; let soak, covered, for 1 hour. Do not drain.

2. In a skillet, heat butter over medium-high heat. Add the onion; cook and stir until tender. Add garlic; cook 1 minute longer. Stir in thyme and salt.

3. Add to pea mixture; return to the heat. Cook, covered, over medium heat for 30 minutes or until peas are tender, stirring occasionally. If desired, top with additional crumbled bacon.

SWISS CHEESE POTATOES

> "I created a lime butter especially for grilled corn and love to add the fresh cilantro from my garden."
>
> —**ANDREA REYNOLDS** ROCKY RIVER, OH

CORN WITH CILANTRO-LIME BUTTER

Corn with Cilantro-Lime Butter

PREP: 15 MIN. + CHILLING • **GRILL:** 15 MIN. • **MAKES:** 12 SERVINGS

- ½ cup butter, softened
- ¼ cup minced fresh cilantro
- 1 tablespoon lime juice
- 1½ teaspoons grated lime peel
- 12 medium ears sweet corn, husks removed
   Grated cotija cheese, optional

1. In a small bowl, mix the butter, cilantro, lime juice and lime peel. Shape into a log; wrap in plastic wrap. Refrigerate 30 minutes or until firm. Wrap each ear of corn with a piece of heavy-duty foil (about 14 in. square).

2. Grill corn, covered, over medium heat 15-20 minutes or until tender, turning occasionally. Meanwhile, cut lime butter into 12 slices. Remove corn from grill. Carefully open foil, allowing steam to escape. Serve corn with butter and, if desired, cheese.

---

⑤ INGREDIENTS FAST FIX

Coconut Acorn Squash

Sometimes acorn squash can be too bland, so I decided to dress it up with a tropical mix of purchased mango chutney, butter and coconut. It really makes the squash flavor pop. To save time in the kitchen, I do the cooking in the microwave.

—**DEIRDRE COX** KANSAS CITY, KS

START TO FINISH: 20 MIN. • **MAKES:** 4 SERVINGS

- 2 small acorn squash
- ¼ cup mango chutney
- ¼ cup flaked coconut
- 3 tablespoons butter, melted
- ¼ teaspoon salt
- ⅛ teaspoon pepper

1. Cut each squash in half; remove and discard seeds. Place squash in a microwave-safe dish, cut side down. Microwave, covered, on high for 10-12 minutes or until tender.

2. Turn the squash cut side up. Mix the chutney, coconut and melted butter; spoon into the centers of the squash. Sprinkle with salt and pepper. Microwave, covered, on high for 2-3 minutes or until heated through.

NOTE *This recipe was tested in a 1,100-watt microwave.*

COCONUT ACORN SQUASH

FAST FIX ▶ Texas-Style BBQ Sauce

Here's a barbecue sauce that has all the right "Texas-style" ingredients: ketchup, brown sugar, mustard, lemon juice, chili powder and Worcestershire sauce.

—**SANDY KLOCINSKI** SUMMERVILLE, SC

START TO FINISH: 25 MIN.
MAKES: 1¾ CUPS

- 1 **tablespoon butter**
- 1 **small onion, chopped**
- 2 **garlic cloves, minced**
- 1 **cup ketchup**
- ¼ **cup packed brown sugar**
- ¼ **cup lemon juice**
- 2 **tablespoons apple cider vinegar**
- 2 **tablespoons tomato paste**
- 1 **tablespoon yellow mustard**
- 1 **tablespoon Worcestershire sauce**
- 2 **teaspoons chili powder**

In a large saucepan, heat butter over medium heat. Add onion; cook and stir 2-3 minutes or until tender. Add garlic; cook 1 minute longer. Stir in remaining ingredients; bring to a boil. Reduce heat; simmer, uncovered, 15-20 minutes to allow flavors to blend.

TEXAS-STYLE BBQ SAUCE

APPLE & PECAN STUFFED SWEET POTATOES

Apple & Pecan Stuffed Sweet Potatoes

We first made these for a beef cook-off that my sister-in-law entered. Our beef didn't win, but we won best side dish!

—**JENNIFER KUEHN** AVON, IL

PREP: 30 MIN. • **BAKE:** 1 HOUR + COOLING
MAKES: 6 SERVINGS

- 6 **medium sweet potatoes (about 8 ounces each)**
- ½ **cup butter, cubed**
- ¼ **cup packed brown sugar**
- ½ **teaspoon grated orange peel**
- 1 **medium apple, chopped**
- ¼ **cup chopped pecans**

1. Scrub and pierce potatoes with a fork. Place on a foil-lined 15-in. x 10-in. x 1-in. baking pan. Bake at 400° for 45-60 minutes or until tender.

2. When cool enough to handle, cut off a thin slice from the top of each potato; discard. Scoop out pulp, leaving ¼-in.-thick shells; transfer to a large bowl. Mash pulp with butter, adding brown sugar and orange peel. Fold in apple and pecans.

3. Spoon into potato shells. Return to baking pan. Bake 15-20 minutes longer or until heated through.

Savory Glazed Pearl Onions

I fixed glazed pearl onions on a whim one Christmas when we craved a vegetable other than our usual Brussels sprouts. The recipe proved to be a keeper.

—**ERIKA SZYMANSKI** PULLMAN, WA

PREP: 15 MIN. • **COOK:** 40 MIN.
MAKES: 12 SERVINGS

- 1 **tablespoon olive oil**
- 4 **cups frozen pearl onions (about 1½ pounds), thawed**
- 1½ **cups dry red wine**
- ⅓ **cup balsamic vinegar**
- 1 **tablespoon packed brown sugar**
- 1½ **teaspoons dried thyme**
- ¾ **teaspoon salt**
- ¾ **teaspoon white pepper**

1. In a large skillet, heat oil over medium heat. Add onions; cook and stir for 9-11 minutes or until lightly browned. Stir in the remaining ingredients; bring to a boil. Reduce heat; simmer, covered, for 20-25 minutes or until onions are tender.

2. Uncover; simmer for 8-10 minutes or until onions are glazed, stirring occasionally. Serve warm or at room temperature.

FAST FIX ▸ Cranberry Honey Butter

Looking for an edible holiday gift for a friend or family member? Skip the usual bottle of wine or plate of cookies and whip up a jar of this irresistible treat.

—**ARISA CUPP** WARREN, OR

START TO FINISH: 10 MIN.
MAKES: 24 SERVINGS

- 1 **cup butter, softened**
- ⅓ **cup finely chopped dried cranberries**
- ¼ **cup honey**
- 2 **teaspoons grated orange peel**
- ⅛ **teaspoon kosher salt**

In a small bowl, beat all ingredients until blended. Store, covered, in the refrigerator for up to 2 weeks.

🥘 SLOW COOKER
Green Beans with Bacon and Tomatoes

Bacon brings mouthwatering flavor to everything, and slow-cooked veggies are no exception. If you prefer, substitute garlic salt for the seasoned salt.

—**CATHY BELL** JOPLIN, MO

PREP: 15 MIN. • **COOK:** 4½ HOURS
MAKES: 12 SERVINGS (¾ CUP)

- 1 **package (14 ounces) thick-sliced bacon strips, chopped**
- 1 **large red onion, chopped**
- 2 **packages (16 ounces each) frozen cut green beans**
- 1 **can (28 ounces) petite diced tomatoes, undrained**
- ¼ **cup packed brown sugar**
- 1 **tablespoon seasoned pepper**
- ½ **teaspoon seasoned salt**
- 1 **can (16 ounces) red beans, rinsed and drained**

1. In a large skillet, cook bacon over medium heat until partially cooked but not crisp, stirring occasionally. Remove with a slotted spoon; drain on paper towels. Discard drippings, reserving 2 tablespoons. Add onion to drippings; cook and stir over medium-high heat until tender.

2. In a 4- or 5-qt. slow cooker, combine green beans, tomatoes, brown sugar, pepper, salt, bacon and onion. Cook, covered, on low 4 hours. Stir in red beans. Cook 30 minutes longer or until heated through.

🍲 SLOW COOKER Sweet & Spicy Beans

We can't get enough of these sweet and savory beans. They make a satisfying side dish, but you could also serve them as a hearty snack with tortilla or corn chips for dipping.

—SONDRA POPE MOORESVILLE, NC

PREP: 10 MIN. • **COOK:** 5 HOURS
MAKES: 12 SERVINGS (⅔ CUP EACH)

- 1 can (16 ounces) kidney beans, rinsed and drained
- 1 can (15¼ ounces) whole kernel corn, drained
- 1 can (15 ounces) garbanzo beans or chickpeas, rinsed and drained
- 1 can (15 ounces) black beans, rinsed and drained
- 1 can (15 ounces) chili with beans
- 1 cup barbecue sauce
- 1 cup salsa
- ⅓ cup packed brown sugar
- ¼ teaspoon hot pepper sauce
  Chopped green onions, optional

In a 4- or 5-qt. slow cooker, combine the first nine ingredients. Cover and cook on low for 5-6 hours. Top with green onions if desired.

SWEET & SPICY BEANS

top tip

Secret of the Sauce

For best results when grilling with a barbecue sauce, make sure your grill is at the proper temperature before placing the food on the grill rack. Then wait to brush on thick or sweet sauces until the last 10 to 15 minutes of cooking; baste and turn every few minutes to prevent burning.

DR PEPPER BBQ SAUCE

Dr Pepper BBQ Sauce

Our family is stationed in Italy with my husband, Lt. William Robert Blackman. He grew up in Tennessee and I'm from Texas, so the food that really says "home" to us is a good old-fashioned barbecue. I have my own sauce recipe that features Dr Pepper, orange juice, mustard and brown sugar. We enjoy it over sliced brisket and reminisce about special meals with loved ones.

—TINA BLACKMAN NAPLES, ITALY

PREP: 5 MIN. • **COOK:** 35 MIN. • **MAKES:** 1 CUP

- 1 can (12 ounces) Dr Pepper
- 1 cup crushed tomatoes
- ¼ cup packed brown sugar
- 2 tablespoons spicy brown mustard
- 1 tablespoon orange juice
- 1 tablespoon Worcestershire sauce
- 1 garlic clove, minced
- ¼ teaspoon salt
- ⅛ teaspoon pepper

In a small saucepan, combine all ingredients; bring to a boil. Reduce the heat; simmer, uncovered, 30-35 minutes or until slightly thickened, stirring occasionally. Refrigerate leftovers.

Tomato Pie

PREP: 50 MIN. + CHILLING • **BAKE:** 30 MIN. • **MAKES:** 8 SERVINGS

- 1 cup plus 2 tablespoons all-purpose flour
- ¼ teaspoon salt
- ½ cup cold butter, cubed
- 2 to 3 tablespoons ice water

FILLING

- ¾ cup mayonnaise
- ½ cup shredded cheddar cheese
- ⅓ cup thinly sliced green onions
- 1 tablespoon minced fresh oregano
- ½ teaspoon ground coriander
- ¼ teaspoon salt
- ¼ teaspoon pepper
- 10 medium tomatoes (1¾ pounds), cut into ¼-inch slices
- 4 bacon strips, cooked and crumbled

1. In a large bowl, mix flour and salt; cut in butter until crumbly. Gradually add ice water, tossing with a fork until dough holds together when pressed. Shape into a disk; wrap in plastic wrap. Refrigerate 30 minutes or overnight.

2. Preheat oven to 350°. On a lightly floured surface, roll dough to a ⅛-in.-thick circle; transfer to a 9-in. pie plate. Trim pastry to ½ in. beyond rim of plate; flute edge. Line unpricked pastry with a double thickness of foil. Fill with pie weights, dried beans or uncooked rice.

3. Bake 20-25 minutes or until bottom is lightly browned. Remove foil and weights; bake 5-10 minutes longer or until light brown. Cool on a wire rack.

4. In a bowl, mix mayonnaise, cheese, green onions and seasonings. Arrange one-third of the tomatoes in crust; spread with one-third of the mayonnaise mixture. Repeat layers twice. Bake 25 minutes. Top with bacon; bake 5-10 minutes longer or until filling is bubbly. Let stand 10 minutes.

"For Tomato Pie, choose tomatoes that are firm but not too ripe so the results aren't too juicy."
—**LOIS MORGAN** EDISTO BEACH, SC

TOMATO PIE

OH-SO-GOOD CREAMY MASHED POTATOES

Oh-So-Good Creamy Mashed Potatoes

I like to use Yukon Gold spuds for my mashed potatoes because of their buttery flavor and low moisture content.
—**BRITTANY JACKSON** SEYMOUR, WI

PREP: 20 MIN. • **COOK:** 25 MIN.
MAKES: 18 SERVINGS (¾ CUP EACH)

- 8 large Yukon Gold potatoes, peeled and quartered (about 6 pounds)
- 2 teaspoons salt
- 2½ cups 2% milk
- ½ cup butter, cubed
- 3 teaspoons garlic salt
- 1 teaspoon pepper
- ¼ cup sour cream
  Additional 2% milk, optional
  Chopped fresh parsley

1. Place potatoes and salt in a stockpot; add water to cover. Bring to a boil. Reduce heat; cook, uncovered, for 20-25 minutes or until potatoes are tender. Meanwhile, in a large saucepan, heat milk, butter, garlic salt and pepper over medium heat until butter is melted.

2. Drain the potatoes, then shake over low heat for 1-2 minutes to dry. Mash the potatoes with a potato masher or beat with a mixer; gradually add the milk mixture. Stir in the sour cream. Stir in additional milk to thin if desired. Sprinkle with parsley.

DIANE HIGGINS'
20 CLOVES OF GARLIC
ROAST CHICKEN PAGE 66

Main Dishes

From a **special tenderloin roast** for your family's holiday feast to an **easy pasta casserole** that's perfect for weeknights, these winning entrees give you mouthwatering choices for every menu.

PATTI LAVELL'S SPAGHETTI PIE CASSEROLE
PAGE 67

MELISSA HASS' CAROLINA CRAB BOIL
PAGE 71

MARY KANDELL'S EASY & ELEGANT TENDERLOIN ROAST PAGE 72

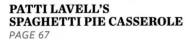

Garlic Beef Enchiladas

Enchiladas are typically prepared with corn tortillas, but we prefer flour tortillas in this saucy beef casserole.

—JENNIFER STANDRIDGE DALLAS, GA

PREP: 30 MIN. • **BAKE:** 40 MIN.
MAKES: 5 SERVINGS

- 1 pound ground beef
- 1 medium onion, chopped
- 2 tablespoons all-purpose flour
- 1 tablespoon chili powder
- 1 teaspoon salt
- 1 teaspoon garlic powder
- ½ teaspoon ground cumin
- ¼ teaspoon rubbed sage
- 1 can (14½ ounces) stewed tomatoes, cut up

SAUCE

- ⅓ cup butter
- 4 to 6 garlic cloves, minced
- ½ cup all-purpose flour
- 1 can (14½ ounces) beef broth
- 1 can (15 ounces) tomato sauce
- 1 to 2 tablespoons chili powder
- 1 to 2 teaspoons ground cumin
- 1 to 2 teaspoons rubbed sage
- ½ teaspoon salt
- 10 flour tortillas (6 inches), warmed
- 2 cups (8 ounces) shredded Colby-Monterey Jack cheese, divided

1. In a large skillet, cook the beef and onion over medium heat 6-8 minutes or until the beef is no longer pink, breaking up beef into crumbles; drain. Stir in the flour and seasonings. Stir in tomatoes; bring to a boil. Reduce heat; simmer, covered, 15 minutes.

2. Preheat oven to 350°. In a saucepan, heat butter over medium-high heat. Add the garlic; cook and stir 1 minute or until tender. Stir in the flour until blended; gradually whisk in the beef broth. Bring to a boil; cook and stir 2 minutes or until thickened. Stir in the tomato sauce and seasonings; heat through.

3. Pour 1½ cups sauce into an ungreased 13-in. x 9-in. baking dish. Place about ¼ cup beef mixture off center on each flour tortilla; top with 1-2 tablespoons cheese. Roll up and place over sauce, seam side down. Top with remaining sauce.

4. Bake, covered, 30-35 minutes or until heated through. Sprinkle with remaining cheese. Bake, uncovered, 10-15 minutes longer or until cheese is melted.

SUMMER VEGETABLE COBBLER

GARLIC BEEF ENCHILADAS

Summer Vegetable Cobbler

Turn your garden produce into vegetarian comfort food. If you like, use crookneck or pattypan squash in place of the zucchini.

—ELISABETH LARSEN
PLEASANT GROVE, UT

PREP: 40 MIN. • **BAKE:** 25 MIN.
MAKES: 4 SERVINGS

- 2 tablespoons butter
- 3 small zucchini, sliced
- 1 small sweet red pepper, finely chopped
- 1 small onion, finely chopped
- 2 garlic cloves, minced
- 2 tablespoons all-purpose flour
- 1 cup 2% milk
- ½ teaspoon salt
- ¼ teaspoon pepper

BISCUIT TOPPING

- 1 cup all-purpose flour
- 1 teaspoon baking powder
- ½ teaspoon salt
- 3 tablespoons cold butter
- ¼ cup shredded Parmesan cheese
- 3 tablespoons minced fresh basil
- ⅔ cup 2% milk

1. Preheat oven to 400°. In a large skillet, heat butter over medium-high heat. Add zucchini, red pepper and onion; cook and stir 10-12 minutes or until zucchini is crisp-tender. Add garlic; cook 1 minute longer.

2. In a small bowl, whisk flour, milk, salt and pepper; stir into pan. Bring to a boil, stirring constantly; cook and stir 2-3 minutes or until sauce is thickened. Spoon into a greased 8-in.-square baking dish.

3. For the topping, in a small bowl, whisk the flour, baking powder and salt. Cut in the butter until the mixture resembles coarse crumbs. Stir in the cheese and basil. Add milk; stir just until moistened. Drop by rounded tablespoonfuls over the filling. Bake 25-30 minutes or until filling is bubbly and biscuits are golden brown.

Chicken Burritos

This south-of-the-border recipe makes two big pans, giving you one delicious dinner to enjoy today and one to save in the freezer for a more time-crunched night. Keep the cheesy burritos in mind for your next potluck, too.

—SONYA NIGHTINGALE BURLEY, ID

PREP: 20 MIN. • **BAKE:** 35 MIN.
MAKES: 2 CASSEROLES (6 SERVINGS EACH)

- 6 tablespoons butter
- 1 large onion, chopped
- ¼ cup chopped green pepper
- ½ cup all-purpose flour
- 3 cups chicken broth
- 1 can (10 ounces) diced tomatoes and green chilies, undrained
- 1 teaspoon ground cumin
- 1 teaspoon chili powder
- ½ teaspoon garlic powder
- ½ teaspoon salt
- 2 tablespoons chopped jalapeno pepper, optional
- 1 can (15 ounces) chili with beans
- 1 package (8 ounces) cream cheese, cubed
- 8 cups cubed cooked chicken
- 24 flour tortillas (6 inches), warmed
- 6 cups (24 ounces) shredded Colby-Monterey Jack cheese
  Salsa, optional

1. Preheat oven to 350°. In a large skillet, heat butter over medium-high heat. Add onion and pepper; cook and stir until tender. Stir in the flour until blended; gradually stir in the chicken broth. Bring to a boil; cook and stir 2 minutes. Reduce the heat; stir in the tomatoes, seasonings and, if desired, jalapeno. Cook 5 minutes. Stir in chili and cream cheese until cream cheese is melted. Stir in chicken.

2. Spoon about ½ cup filling across the center of each tortilla; sprinkle each with ¼ cup Colby-Monterey Jack cheese. Fold bottom and sides over filling and roll up. Place in two greased 13-in. x 9-in. baking dishes.

3. Bake, covered, 35-40 minutes or until heated through. If desired, serve with salsa.

FREEZE OPTION *Cool unbaked casseroles; cover and freeze. To use, partially thaw in the refrigerator overnight. Remove from refrigerator 30 minutes before baking. Preheat oven to 350°. Cover casserole with foil; bake as directed, increasing covered time to 50-55 minutes or until heated through and a thermometer inserted into center reads 160°.*

NOTE *Wear disposable gloves when cutting hot peppers; the oils can burn skin. Avoid touching your face.*

Family Quilt Pizza

PREP: 30 MIN. • **BAKE:** 20 MIN.
MAKES: 6 SERVINGS

- 1 tube (13.8 ounces) refrigerated pizza crust
- 1 can (8 ounces) pizza sauce
- 4 cups (16 ounces) shredded part-skim mozzarella cheese
- 2 ounces sliced deli ham, cut into ½-in. strips

"Quilt pizzas are so much fun to create. My family and friends get involved, and they come up with the most clever toppings and designs. Every pie looks different!"
—MARIE LOUISE LUDWIG PHOENIXVILLE, PA

Optional toppings: slices of sweet peppers, tomatoes, fully cooked sausage, mushrooms, ripe olives, pineapple, pepperoni, yellow summer squash and red onion; broccoli florets; crumbled feta cheese; and minced fresh basil and chives

1. Preheat oven to 425°. Unroll pizza crust and press to fit into a greased 15-in. x 10-in. x 1-in. pan, pinching edges to form a rim. Bake 8-10 minutes or until edges are lightly browned.

2. Spread crust with sauce; top with mozzarella cheese. Using ham strips, outline 12 quilt sections. Arrange toppings of your choice in each section to create a patchwork design. Bake 10-15 minutes or until crust is golden brown and cheese is melted.

FAMILY QUILT PIZZA

CHICKEN SALAD-STUFFED PEPPERS

Chicken Salad-Stuffed Peppers

We love this entree because it combines the refreshing taste of summer bell peppers with creamy chicken salad.
—**MARY MARLOWE LEVERETTE** COLUMBIA, SC

PREP: 30 MIN. • **BAKE:** 15 MIN. • **MAKES:** 4 SERVINGS

    4 green onions, finely chopped
    ½ cup mayonnaise
    2 tablespoons lemon juice
    ½ teaspoon dried tarragon
    ½ teaspoon pepper
    ¼ teaspoon salt
    2 cups finely chopped rotisserie chicken
    ½ cup shredded Monterey Jack cheese
    1 celery rib, finely chopped
    4 medium sweet red peppers
       Crushed potato chips, optional

1. Preheat oven to 350°. In a small bowl, mix the first six ingredients. Add chicken, cheese and celery; toss to coat.
2. Cut peppers lengthwise in half; remove seeds. In a Dutch oven, cook peppers in boiling water 3-4 minutes or until crisp-tender; drain.
3. Place in a greased 13-in. x 9-in. baking dish. Fill with chicken mixture. If desired, sprinkle with chips. Bake, uncovered, 15-20 minutes or until filling is heated through.

Standing Rib Roast

PREP: 5 MIN. • **BAKE:** 2¼ HOURS + STANDING • **MAKES:** 10 SERVINGS

    1   tablespoon lemon-pepper seasoning
    1   tablespoon paprika
    1½   teaspoons garlic salt
    1   teaspoon dried rosemary, crushed
    ½   teaspoon cayenne pepper
    1   bone-in beef rib roast (6 to 7 pounds)
    2   cups beef stock

1. In a small bowl, mix the first five ingredients; rub over roast. Place roast in a shallow roasting pan, fat side up. Roast at 325° for 2¼ to 2¾ hours or until meat reaches desired doneness (for medium-rare, a thermometer should read 145°; medium, 160°; well-done, 170°).
2. Remove the roast from oven; tent with foil. Let stand for 15 minutes before carving.
3. Meanwhile, pour drippings and loosened browned bits from roasting pan into a small saucepan; skim fat. Add beef stock to drippings; bring to a boil. Serve with roast.

"I often serve slices of tender Standing Rib Roast for special occasions. If you like, use the seasoning blend on a different beef roast. Either way, you'll have a mouthwatering main course."
—**LUCY MEYRING** WALDEN, CO

STANDING RIB ROAST

KANSAS CITY-STYLE RIBS

Kansas City-Style Ribs

Over the years, our family-favorite rib recipe has continuously evolved. I think it's reached the point of near perfection.
—**LINDA SCHEND** KENOSHA, WI

PREP: 1 HOUR + CHILLING • **GRILL:** 1 HOUR 25 MIN.
MAKES: 12 SERVINGS

- 1⅓ cups packed brown sugar
- 2 teaspoons each garlic powder, onion powder and smoked paprika
- 1¼ teaspoons each ground cumin, coarsely ground pepper and cayenne pepper
- 12 bone-in country-style pork ribs (about 7 pounds)

SAUCE

- 2 tablespoons canola oil
- 1 medium onion, finely chopped
- 1 cup tomato sauce
- ⅓ cup dark brown sugar
- ¼ cup ketchup
- ¼ cup molasses
- 1 tablespoon apple cider vinegar
- 2 teaspoons Worcestershire sauce
- 1 teaspoon salt
- 1 teaspoon ground mustard
- ¼ teaspoon smoked paprika
- ¼ teaspoon cayenne pepper

1. In a small bowl, mix the brown sugar and seasonings; sprinkle over the ribs. Refrigerate, covered, at least 1 hour.
2. For sauce, in a large saucepan, heat oil over medium heat. Add onion; cook and stir 5-6 minutes or until tender. Stir in remaining ingredients; bring to a boil, stirring occasionally. Remove from heat.

3. Wrap ribs in a large piece of heavy-duty foil; seal edges of foil. Grill, covered, over indirect medium heat 1¼ to 1¾ hours or until ribs are tender.
4. Carefully remove ribs from foil. Place ribs over direct medium heat; baste with some of the sauce. Grill, covered, 8-10 minutes or until browned, turning and basting occasionally with remaining sauce.

Oven Barbecued Chicken

During my married life on a dairy farm, this saucy dish was always a popular dinner choice after Sunday church.
—**ESTHER SHANK** HARRISONBURG, VA

PREP: 25 MIN. • **BAKE:** 45 MIN. • **MAKES:** 8 SERVINGS

- 2 tablespoons canola oil
- 1 broiler/fryer chicken (3 to 4 pounds), cut up
- 3 tablespoons butter
- ⅓ cup chopped onion
- ¾ cup ketchup
- ½ cup water
- ⅓ cup cider vinegar
- 3 tablespoons brown sugar
- 1 tablespoon Worcestershire sauce
- 2 teaspoons prepared mustard
- ¼ teaspoon salt
- ⅛ teaspoon pepper

1. Preheat oven to 350°. In a large skillet, heat oil over medium heat. Brown chicken on both sides. Remove to paper towels to drain.
2. Meanwhile, in a small saucepan, heat the butter over medium-high heat. Add onion; cook and stir until tender. Stir in the remaining ingredients. Bring to a boil. Reduce heat; simmer, uncovered, 15 minutes.
3. Place chicken in an ungreased 13-in. x 9-in. baking dish. Pour sauce over chicken. Bake, uncovered, 45-60 minutes or until chicken juices run clear, basting occasionally.

OVEN BARBECUED CHICKEN

Roasted Kielbasa & Vegetables

I combine hearty kielbasa, sweet potatoes, onion, carrots and squash in the oven for a home-style dinner we all enjoy.
—**MARIETTA SLATER** JUSTIN, TX

PREP: 20 MIN. • **BAKE:** 40 MIN. • **MAKES:** 6 SERVINGS

- 3 medium sweet potatoes, peeled and cut into 1-inch pieces
- 1 large sweet onion, cut into 1-inch pieces
- 4 medium carrots, cut into 1-inch pieces
- 2 tablespoons olive oil
- 1 pound smoked kielbasa or Polish sausage, halved and cut into 1-inch pieces
- 1 medium yellow summer squash, cut into 1-inch pieces
- 1 medium zucchini, cut into 1-inch pieces
- ¼ teaspoon salt
- ¼ teaspoon pepper
  Dijon mustard, optional

1. Preheat oven to 400°. Divide the sweet potatoes, sweet onion and carrots between two greased 15-in. x 10-in. x 1-in. baking pans. Drizzle with oil; toss to coat. Roast 25 minutes, stirring occasionally.

2. Add the kielbasa, squash and zucchini to pans; sprinkle with salt and pepper. Roast 15-20 minutes longer or until vegetables are tender. Transfer to a serving bowl; toss to combine. If desired, serve with mustard.

ROASTED KIELBASA & VEGETABLES

"With fresh cilantro in the sauce, these steaks are part of our favorite summer grilling menu."
—**LYNNE KEAST** MONTE SERENO, CA

GRILLED STEAKS WITH CILANTRO SAUCE

Grilled Steaks with Cilantro Sauce

PREP: 25 MIN. • **GRILL:** 15 MIN. • **MAKES:** 8 SERVINGS (3 CUPS SAUCE)

- 2 cups fresh parsley leaves
- 2 cups fresh cilantro leaves
- 1 cup fresh mint leaves
- 8 garlic cloves, chopped
- 1¾ teaspoons kosher salt, divided
- ½ teaspoon plus ¾ teaspoon freshly ground pepper, divided
- 2 cups olive oil
- ⅔ cup red wine vinegar
- 2 tablespoons lemon juice
- ½ teaspoon crushed red pepper flakes
- 4 pounds beef flat iron steaks or top sirloin steaks (1 inch thick)

1. Place the herbs, garlic, 1 teaspoon salt and ½ teaspoon pepper in a food processor; pulse until herbs are chopped. Gradually add oil, vinegar, lemon juice and pepper flakes, processing just until blended.

2. Sprinkle the steaks with the remaining salt and pepper. Grill, covered, over medium heat or broil 4 in. from the heat 6-8 minutes on each side or until the meat reaches desired doneness (for medium-rare, a thermometer should read 145°; medium, 160°; well-done, 170°). Cut the steaks into ¼-in. slices; serve with sauce.

Paprika Chicken Thighs

PREP: 15 MIN. • **BAKE:** 50 MIN. • **MAKES:** 8 SERVINGS

- ¼ cup butter
- 3 tablespoons all-purpose flour
- 2 tablespoons paprika
- 1 teaspoon poultry seasoning
- 8 bone-in chicken thighs, skin removed
- ½ teaspoon salt
- ½ teaspoon pepper
- 1 can (10¾ ounces) condensed cream of mushroom soup, undiluted
- 1 cup 2% milk
- 8 ounces sliced fresh mushrooms
- 2 tablespoons minced fresh parsley
  Hot cooked rice, optional

1. In a small saucepan, melt the butter over medium heat. Remove from the heat; stir in the flour, paprika and poultry seasoning. Sprinkle the chicken with salt and pepper; place in an ungreased 13-in. x 9-in. baking dish. Spread butter mixture over chicken.

2. In a bowl, whisk the soup and milk; stir in mushrooms. Pour over chicken. Bake, covered, at 350° for 35 minutes. Uncover; bake 15-20 minutes longer or until a thermometer inserted into chicken reads 180°. Sprinkle with parsley. If desired, serve with rice.

"The gravy in my Paprika Chicken Thighs recipe is perfect over rice, grits or mashed potatoes."
—**JUDY ARMSTRONG** PRAIRIEVILLE, PA

PAPRIKA CHICKEN THIGHS

TACO CORN BREAD CASSEROLE

Taco Corn Bread Casserole

A whole can of chilies adds fire to this beefy casserole. Reduce the amount if your family prefers a milder flavor.
—**LISA PAUL** TERRE HAUTE, IN

PREP: 15 MIN. • **BAKE:** 1 HOUR • **MAKES:** 8 SERVINGS

- 2 pounds ground beef
- 2 envelopes taco seasoning
- 2 cans (14½ ounces each) diced tomatoes, drained
- 1 cup water
- 1 cup cooked rice
- 1 can (4 ounces) chopped green chilies
- 2 packages (8½ ounces each) corn bread/muffin mix
- 1 can (8¾ ounces) whole kernel corn, drained
- 1 cup (8 ounces) sour cream
- 2 cups corn chips
- 2 cups (8 ounces) shredded Mexican or cheddar cheese, divided
- 1 can (2¼ ounces) sliced ripe olives, drained
  Shredded lettuce and chopped tomatoes, optional

1. Preheat oven to 400°. In a Dutch oven, cook the beef over medium heat 8-10 minutes or until no longer pink, breaking into crumbles; drain. Stir in the taco seasoning. Add tomatoes, water, rice and green chilies; heat through, stirring occasionally.

2. Meanwhile, prepare the corn bread mix according to the package directions; stir in the corn. Pour half of the batter into a greased 13-in. x 9-in. baking dish. Layer with half of the meat mixture, all the sour cream, half of the corn chips and 1 cup cheese. Top with the remaining batter, remaining meat mixture, olives and remaining corn chips.

3. Bake, uncovered, 55-60 minutes or until the corn bread is cooked through. Sprinkle with remaining cheese; bake 3-5 minutes longer or until the cheese is melted. If desired, serve with lettuce and chopped tomatoes.

Asian Chicken Thighs

A thick, tangy sauce coats this golden chicken. Serve it over long-grain rice or with ramen noodle slaw.

—**DAVE FARRINGTON** MIDWEST CITY, OK

PREP: 15 MIN. • **COOK:** 50 MIN.
MAKES: 5 SERVINGS

- 5 **teaspoons olive oil**
- 5 **bone-in chicken thighs (about 1¾ pounds), skin removed**
- ⅓ **cup water**
- ¼ **cup packed brown sugar**
- 2 **tablespoons orange juice**
- 2 **tablespoons reduced-sodium soy sauce**
- 2 **tablespoons ketchup**
- 1 **tablespoon white vinegar**
- 4 **garlic cloves, minced**
- ½ **teaspoon crushed red pepper flakes**
- ¼ **teaspoon Chinese five-spice powder**
- 2 **teaspoons cornstarch**
- 2 **tablespoons cold water**
  Sliced green onions
  Hot cooked rice, optional

1. In a large skillet, heat the oil over medium heat. Add the chicken; cook 8-10 minutes on each side or until no longer pink. In a small bowl, whisk the water, brown sugar, orange juice, soy sauce, ketchup, vinegar, garlic, red pepper flakes and five-spice powder. Pour over chicken. Bring to a boil. Reduce heat; simmer, uncovered, 30-35 minutes or until chicken is tender, turning chicken occasionally.
2. In a bowl, mix cornstarch and cold water until smooth; stir into pan. Bring to a boil; cook and stir 1 minute or until sauce is thickened. Sprinkle with green onions. If desired, serve with rice.
PER SERVING *292 cal., 14 g fat (3 g sat. fat), 87 mg chol., 396 mg sodium, 15 g carb., 25 g pro.* **Diabetic Exchanges:** *3 lean meat, 1 starch, 1 fat.*

PIZZA-STYLE MANICOTTI

Pizza-Style Manicotti

Stuff manicotti shells with popular pizza toppings, and you'll have an Italian dinner that appeals to children and adults alike. A green salad is the perfect side dish.

—**JUDY ARMSTRONG** PRAIRIEVILLE, LA

PREP: 20 MIN. • **BAKE:** 25 MIN.
MAKES: 4 SERVINGS

- 8 **uncooked manicotti shells**
- 1 **jar (24 ounces) spaghetti sauce**
- 8 **slices deli ham (about 6 ounces)**
- 8 **fresh basil leaves**
- 8 **pieces string cheese**
- 24 **slices pepperoni**
- 1 **can (2¼ ounces) sliced ripe olives, drained**
- 1 **cup shredded Parmesan cheese**

1. Cook manicotti according to the package directions for al dente; drain. Preheat oven to 350°.
2. Pour 1 cup spaghetti sauce into a 13-in. x 9-in. baking dish. On a short side of each ham slice, layer one basil leaf, one piece string cheese and three slices pepperoni; roll up. Insert into manicotti shells; arrange in a single layer in baking dish.
3. Pour the remaining spaghetti sauce over the top. Sprinkle with the ripe olives and Parmesan cheese. Bake, uncovered, 25-30 minutes or until heated through.

20 Cloves of Garlic Roast Chicken

The garlic tucked into my chicken mellows to a subtle seasoning as it roasts.

—**DIANE HIGGINS** TAMPA, FL

PREP: 10 MIN.
BAKE: 1¼ HOURS + STANDING
MAKES: 4 SERVINGS

- 20 **garlic cloves, peeled, divided**
- 1 **broiler/fryer chicken (3 to 4 pounds)**
- 4 **lemon wedges**
- 8 **fresh thyme sprigs, cut in half**
- 2 **tablespoons butter, softened**
- ½ **teaspoon kosher salt**
- ⅛ **teaspoon freshly ground pepper**

1. Cut 12 garlic cloves in half. Place the chicken on a cutting board. Tuck wings under chicken. With a sharp paring knife, cut 24 small slits in thighs, breasts and drumsticks. Fill each with a halved clove. Place lemon, thyme and remaining whole cloves in chicken cavity. Tie drumsticks together.
2. Transfer chicken to a rack in a shallow roasting pan, breast side up. Rub skin with butter; sprinkle with salt and pepper.
3. Roast, uncovered, at 350° for 1¼ to 1½ hours or until a thermometer inserted in thigh reaches 180°. Remove chicken from oven; tent with foil. Let stand for 15 minutes before carving.

Spaghetti Pie Casserole

My family can't get enough of this beefy pasta casserole. It's true comfort food!

—PATTI LAVELL ISLAMORADA, FL

PREP: 30 MIN. • **BAKE:** 25 MIN.
MAKES: 8 SERVINGS

- 1 package (8 ounces) spaghetti
- 1 pound ground beef
- 1 small onion, chopped
- 2 garlic cloves, minced
- 1 jar (14 ounces) spaghetti sauce
- ½ teaspoon salt
- ¼ teaspoon pepper
- 3 ounces reduced-fat cream cheese
- 1 cup (8 ounces) reduced-fat sour cream
- 3 green onions, chopped
- 1½ cups (6 ounces each) shredded cheddar-Monterey Jack cheese

1. Cook the spaghetti according to the package directions; drain. Meanwhile, in a large skillet, cook ground beef, onion and garlic over medium heat for 6-8 minutes or until beef is no longer pink, breaking up beef into crumbles; drain. Stir in spaghetti sauce, salt and pepper; bring to a boil. Reduce heat; simmer, uncovered, for 20 minutes, stirring occasionally.

2. In a small bowl, mix cream cheese and sour cream until blended; stir in green onions. In a greased 11-in. x 7-in. baking dish, layer the spaghetti, cream cheese mixture and meat mixture. Top with shredded cheese.

3. Bake, covered, at 350° for 25 minutes. Uncover; bake 5-10 minutes longer or until cheese is bubbly.

SPAGHETTI PIE CASSEROLE

BACON & CHEESE MEAT LOAF

Bacon & Cheese Meat Loaf

To persuade my son to eat meat loaf, we tried flavoring it with crumbled bacon and blue cheese. It worked!

—LILA ALLEN FALLON, NV

PREP: 30 MIN. • **BAKE:** 1¼ HOURS
MAKES: 1 LOAF (8 SERVINGS)

- 1 teaspoon canola oil
- ½ cup shredded carrot
- ½ cup finely chopped onion
- 1 cup soft bread crumbs
- ½ pound bacon strips, cooked and crumbled
- 2 eggs, lightly beaten
- 4 teaspoons Worcestershire sauce
- 2 teaspoons garlic powder
- 2 teaspoons pepper
- 1 teaspoon salt
- 2 pounds ground beef

TOPPING

- ¾ cup crumbled blue cheese
- 2 tablespoons minced fresh sage
- 2 tablespoons minced fresh chives

1. In a skillet, heat oil over medium-high heat. Add carrot and onion; cook and stir until tender. Cool slightly.

2. In a large bowl, combine the bread crumbs, bacon, eggs, Worcestershire sauce, spices and carrot mixture. Add beef; mix lightly but thoroughly.

3. Shape the mixture into an 8-in. x 4-in. loaf in an ungreased 13-in. x 9-in. baking dish. Bake, uncovered, at 350° for 1¼ to 1½ hours or until a thermometer reads 160°.

4. In a bowl, combine the topping ingredients; mix well. Pat onto meat loaf; let stand for 10 minutes before serving. Remove to a platter.

EAT SMART Popcorn & Pretzel Chicken Tenders

Popcorn and pretzels are two of our favorite snacks. My daughter thought of turning them into a coating for chicken.
—SUZANNE CLARK PHOENIX, AZ

PREP: 25 MIN. + MARINATING
BAKE: 20 MIN.
MAKES: 6 SERVINGS (1 CUP SAUCE)

- 1½ pounds chicken tenderloins
- 1 cup buttermilk
- 2 teaspoons garlic powder
- 1 teaspoon salt
- 1 teaspoon onion powder
- ½ teaspoon pepper
- ¾ cup fat-free plain Greek yogurt
- ¼ cup peach preserves
- 1 tablespoon prepared mustard
- 4 cups miniature pretzels, crushed
- 2 cups air-popped popcorn, crushed
  Cooking spray

1. In a large bowl, combine the first six ingredients; toss to coat. Refrigerate, covered, at least 30 minutes. In a small bowl, mix the yogurt, preserves and mustard; refrigerate until serving.
2. Preheat oven to 400°. In a large shallow dish, combine the crushed pretzels and popcorn. Remove the chicken from marinade, discarding marinade. Dip both sides of chicken into the pretzel mixture, patting to help the coating adhere. Place on a parchment paper-lined baking sheet; spritz with cooking spray.
3. Bake 20-25 minutes or until coating is golden brown and chicken is no longer pink. Serve with sauce.
PER SERVING *296 cal., 3 g fat (.078 g sat. fat), 67 mg chol., 636 mg sodium, 36 g carb., 2 trace fiber, 33 g pro.* **Diabetic Exchanges:** *3 lean meat, 2 starch.*

POPCORN & PRETZEL CHICKEN TENDERS

FIVE-CHEESE JUMBO SHELLS

"Recipes that include five different types of cheese usually aren't considered 'light.' But this meatless entree featuring onion, mushrooms and zucchini is a delicious exception. The stuffed pasta shells also freeze beautifully, so leftovers—if you have any—are a cinch to save for dinner on another night when you're short on time." —LISA RENSHAW KANSAS CITY, MO

EAT SMART Five-Cheese Jumbo Shells

PREP: 45 MIN. • **BAKE:** 50 MIN. + STANDING
MAKES: 8 SERVINGS

- 24 uncooked jumbo pasta shells
- 1 tablespoon olive oil
- 1 medium zucchini, shredded and squeezed dry
- ½ pound baby portobello mushrooms, chopped
- 1 medium onion, finely chopped
- 2 cups reduced-fat ricotta cheese
- ½ cup shredded part-skim mozzarella cheese
- ½ cup shredded provolone cheese
- ½ cup grated Romano cheese
- 1 egg, lightly beaten
- 1 teaspoon Italian seasoning
- ½ teaspoon crushed red pepper flakes
- 1 jar (24 ounces) meatless spaghetti sauce
- ¼ cup grated Parmesan cheese

1. Preheat oven to 350°. Cook shells according to package directions for al dente; drain.
2. In a large skillet, heat the oil over medium-high heat. Add vegetables; cook and stir until tender. Remove from heat. In a bowl, combine ricotta, mozzarella, provolone and Romano cheeses; stir in the egg, seasonings and vegetables.
3. Spread 1 cup sauce in a 13-in. x 9-in. baking dish coated with cooking spray. Fill the pasta shells with the cheese mixture; place in baking dish. Top with the remaining sauce. Sprinkle with Parmesan cheese.
4. Bake, covered, 40 minutes. Bake, uncovered, 10 minutes longer or until cheese is melted. Let stand 10 minutes before serving.
PER SERVING *298 cal., 9 g fat (5 g sat. fat), 55 mg chol., 642 mg sodium, 36 g carb., 3 trace fiber, 18 g pro.* **Diabetic Exchanges:** *2 lean meat, 2 starch, .5 fat.*

Homey Mac & Cheese

Here's a dish I like to call "My Grandson's Mac & Cheese." Zachary has served in the military in Iraq and Afghanistan, and I've been privileged to make his favorite casserole for him for more than 20 years.
—**ALICE BEARDSELL** OSPREY, FL

PREP: 20 MIN. • **BAKE:** 25 MIN.
MAKES: 8 SERVINGS

- 2½ cups uncooked elbow macaroni
- ¼ cup butter, cubed
- ¼ cup all-purpose flour
- ½ teaspoon salt
- ¼ teaspoon pepper
- 3 cups 2% milk
- 5 cups (20 ounces) shredded sharp cheddar cheese, divided
- 2 tablespoons Worcestershire sauce
- ½ teaspoon paprika

1. Preheat oven to 350°. Cook the macaroni according to the package directions for al dente.
2. Meanwhile, in a large saucepan, heat butter over medium heat. Stir in the flour, salt and pepper until smooth; gradually whisk in the milk. Bring to a boil, stirring constantly; cook and stir 2-3 minutes or until thickened.
3. Reduce heat. Stir in 3 cups cheddar cheese and Worcestershire sauce until cheese is melted.
4. Drain macaroni; stir into sauce. Transfer to a greased 11-in. x 7-in. baking dish. Bake, uncovered, for 20 minutes. Top with the remaining cheddar cheese; sprinkle with paprika. Bake 5-10 minutes longer or until bubbly and cheese is melted.

Cottage Pie

I use two pounds of ground turkey—one is the light kind, the other is dark—for this savory, English-style meat pie. If you like, substitute beef or lamb.
—**JANE LEEVES** LOS ANGELES, CA

PREP: 30 MIN. • **BAKE:** 20 MIN.
MAKES: 6 SERVINGS

- 2 pounds ground turkey
- 2 large carrots, finely chopped
- 2 celery ribs, finely chopped
- 1 large onion, finely chopped
- 2 garlic cloves, minced
- 2 tablespoons all-purpose flour
- 1 tablespoon minced fresh sage
- 1 tablespoon minced fresh thyme
- 2 teaspoons minced fresh rosemary
- 2 teaspoons Worcestershire sauce
- 1½ teaspoons salt
- ¼ teaspoon pepper
- ½ cup chicken broth
- 1 cup frozen peas
- 2½ cups mashed potatoes (with added milk and butter), warmed
- ½ cup shredded cheddar cheese, optional

1. In a Dutch oven, cook the first five ingredients over medium heat until the turkey is no longer pink and the vegetables are tender, breaking up meat into crumbles; drain.
2. Stir in flour, herbs, Worcestershire sauce, salt and pepper until blended. Add chicken broth; cook and stir for 1-2 minutes or until broth is absorbed. Stir in peas; heat through.
3. Transfer to a greased 9-in. deep-dish pie plate. Top with mashed potatoes; if desired, sprinkle with cheddar cheese. Bake at 400° for 20-25 minutes or until filling is bubbly.

🍲 SLOW COOKER (5) INGREDIENTS
Sweet and Savory Ribs

PREP: 10 MIN. • **COOK:** 8 HOURS
MAKES: 8 SERVINGS

- 1 large onion, chopped
- 4 pounds boneless country-style pork ribs
- 1 bottle (18 ounces) honey barbecue sauce
- ⅓ cup maple syrup
- ¼ cup spicy brown mustard
- ½ teaspoon salt
- ¼ teaspoon pepper

Place the onion in a 5-qt. slow cooker. Top with the ribs. In a small bowl, combine the remaining ingredients; pour over ribs. Cook, covered, on low 8-9 hours or until meat is tender.

SWEET AND SAVORY RIBS

"My husband and I love barbecued ribs. We let our slow cooker do the work while we're gone during the day. By the time we get home, the tender pork is ready to devour." —**KANDY BINGHAM** GREEN RIVER, WY

Fresh from the Sea

What's the catch of the day? These main dishes featuring tuna, catfish, salmon and crab. From the first mouthwatering bite to the last, your family and friends will be hooked!

PRETZEL-CRUSTED CATFISH BITES

Maple Teriyaki Salmon Fillets

Maple syrup and apple juice create a mildly sweet marinade for my salmon. Broiled or grilled, it glazes nicely when basted.
—**KATHY SCHRECENGOST** OSWEGO, NY

PREP: 10 MIN. + MARINATING • **GRILL:** 10 MIN. • **MAKES:** 4 SERVINGS

- ⅓ **cup apple juice**
- ⅓ **cup maple syrup**
- 3 **tablespoons reduced-sodium soy sauce**
- 2 **tablespoons finely chopped onion**
- 2 **garlic cloves, minced**
- 4 **salmon fillets (6 ounces each)**

1. In a small bowl, whisk the first five ingredients until blended. Remove ½ cup for basting; cover and refrigerate. Pour remaining marinade into a large resealable plastic bag. Add salmon; seal bag and turn to coat. Refrigerate 1-3 hours.
2. Drain salmon, discarding marinade in bag. Moisten a paper towel with cooking oil; using long-handled tongs, rub on grill rack to coat lightly. Place salmon on grill rack, skin side down. Grill, covered, over medium heat or broil 4 in. from heat 10-12 minutes or until fish flakes easily with a fork, basting frequently during the last 4 minutes.
PER SERVING *349 cal., 16 g fat (3 g sat. fat), 85 mg chol., 512 mg sodium, 20 g carb., trace fiber, 30 g pro.* **Diabetic Exchanges:** *5 lean meat, 1 starch.*

MAPLE TERIYAKI SALMON FILLETS

Pretzel-Crusted Catfish Bites

I'm not a big fish eater, but when I sampled a pretzel coating for catfish, I fell in love. The little fried bites are great served with an herb rice pilaf and corn muffins spread with butter and honey.
—**KELLY WILLIAMS** FORKED RIVER, NJ

PREP: 25 MIN. • **COOK:** 5 MIN./BATCH • **MAKES:** 4 SERVINGS

- 1½ **pounds catfish fillets, cut into 1-inch pieces**
- ½ **teaspoon salt**
- ½ **teaspoon pepper**
- 2 **eggs**
- ⅓ **cup Dijon mustard**
- 2 **tablespoons 2% milk**
- ½ **cup all-purpose flour**
- 4 **cups honey mustard miniature pretzels, finely crushed**
  Oil for frying
  Lemon wedges, optional

1. Sprinkle the catfish fillets with salt and pepper. In a shallow bowl, whisk the eggs, mustard and milk. Place the flour and crushed miniature pretzels in separate shallow bowls. Dip the fish in the flour to coat all sides; shake off excess. Dip in the egg mixture, then in the pretzels, patting to help the coating adhere.
2. Heat ¼ in. of oil to 375° in an electric skillet. Fry fish, a few pieces at a time, 1-2 minutes on each side or until fish flakes easily with a fork. Drain on paper towels. If desired, serve with lemon wedges.

Carolina Crab Boil

Everyone enjoys digging into this combo of sausage, crab legs, corn, potatoes and more. Utensils are strictly optional!
—**MELISSA HASS** GILBERT, SC

PREP: 15 MIN. • **COOK:** 35 MIN. • **MAKES:** 4 SERVINGS

- 2 teaspoons canola oil
- 1 package (14 ounces) smoked turkey sausage, cut into ½-inch slices
- 2 cartons (32 ounces each) reduced-sodium chicken broth
- 4 cups water
- 1 can (12 ounces) light beer or 1½ cups additional reduced-sodium chicken broth
- ¼ cup seafood seasoning
- 5 bay leaves
- 4 medium ears sweet corn, cut into 2-inch pieces
- 1 pound fingerling potatoes
- 1 medium red onion, quartered
- 2 pounds cooked snow crab legs
  Pepper to taste

1. In a stockpot, heat oil over medium-high heat; brown the sausage. Stir in the chicken broth, water, beer, seafood seasoning and bay leaves. Add vegetables; bring to a boil. Reduce heat; simmer, uncovered, 20-25 minutes or until potatoes are tender.
2. Add the crab; heat through. Drain; remove bay leaves. Transfer to a serving bowl; season with pepper.

CAROLINA CRAB BOIL

BROCCOLI TUNA CASSEROLE

EAT SMART Broccoli Tuna Casserole

When I was in the Navy, a co-worker's wife shared her tuna casserole recipe. It still brings back fond memories of that time.
—**YVONNE COOK** HASKINS, OH

PREP: 35 MIN. • **BAKE:** 1 HOUR • **MAKES:** 8 SERVINGS

- 5 cups uncooked whole wheat egg noodles
- 1 teaspoon butter
- ¼ cup chopped onion
- ¼ cup cornstarch
- 2 cups fat-free milk
- 1 teaspoon dried basil
- 1 teaspoon dried thyme
- ¾ teaspoon salt
- ½ teaspoon pepper
- 1 cup reduced-sodium chicken broth
- 1 cup (4 ounces) shredded Monterey Jack cheese, divided
- 4 cups frozen broccoli florets, thawed
- 2 pouches (6.4 ounces each) albacore white tuna in water
- ⅓ cup panko (Japanese) bread crumbs
- 1 tablespoon butter, melted

1. Preheat oven to 350°. Cook the egg noodles according to the package directions; drain. Transfer to a shallow 3-qt. or 13-in. x 9-in. baking dish coated with cooking spray.
2. Meanwhile, in a large nonstick skillet coated with cooking spray, heat butter over medium-high heat. Add onion; cook and stir until tender. In a small bowl, whisk cornstarch, milk and seasonings until smooth; stir into pan. Stir in broth. Bring to a boil; cook and stir 2 minutes or until thickened. Stir in ¾ cup cheese until melted; stir in broccoli and tuna.
3. Spoon over noodles; mix well. Sprinkle with remaining cheese. Toss bread crumbs with melted butter; sprinkle over casserole. Bake, covered, 45 minutes. Bake, uncovered, 15-20 minutes longer or until cheese is melted.
PER SERVING 271 cal., 8 g fat (4 g sat. fat), 38 mg chol., 601 mg sodium, 30 g carb., 4 g fiber, 22 g pro. **Diabetic Exchanges:** 2 lean meat, 2 starch, ½ fat.

(5) INGREDIENTS
Easy & Elegant Tenderloin Roast

PREP: 10 MIN. • **BAKE:** 50 MIN. + STANDING
MAKES: 12 SERVINGS

- 1 **beef tenderloin roast (5 pounds)**
- 2 **tablespoons olive oil**
- 4 **garlic cloves, minced**
- 2 **teaspoons sea salt**
- 1½ **teaspoons coarsely ground pepper**

1. Place the roast on a rack in a shallow roasting pan. In a small bowl, mix the oil, garlic, salt and pepper; rub over roast.

2. Roast at 425° for 50-70 minutes or until meat reaches desired doneness (for medium-rare, a thermometer should read 145°; medium, 160°; well-done, 170°). Remove from oven; tent with foil. Let stand 15 minutes before slicing.

EASY & ELEGANT TENDERLOIN ROAST

BRUSCHETTA CHICKEN

EAT SMART
Bruschetta Chicken

Colorful and delicious, this entree is deceptively easy to fix. It's also a great option when you want a healthier meal.
—**CAROLIN CATTOI-DEMKIW**
LETHBRIDGE, AB

PREP: 10 MIN. • **BAKE:** 30 MIN.
MAKES: 4 SERVINGS

- ½ **cup all-purpose flour**
- ½ **cup egg substitute**
- 4 **boneless skinless chicken breast halves (4 ounces each)**
- ¼ **cup grated Parmesan cheese**
- ¼ **cup dry bread crumbs**
- 1 **tablespoon butter, melted**
- 2 **large tomatoes, seeded and chopped**
- 3 **tablespoons minced fresh basil**
- 1 **tablespoon olive oil**
- 2 **garlic cloves, minced**
- ½ **teaspoon salt**
- ¼ **teaspoon pepper**

1. Preheat oven to 375°. Place the flour and egg substitute in separate shallow bowls. Dip the chicken in the flour, then in egg substitute; place in a greased 13-in. x 9-in. baking dish. In a small bowl, mix cheese, bread crumbs and butter; sprinkle over chicken.

2. Loosely cover the baking dish with foil. Bake 20 minutes. Uncover; bake 5-10 minutes longer or until a thermometer reads 165°.

3. Meanwhile, in a small bowl, toss the tomatoes with the remaining ingredients. Spoon over chicken; bake 3-5 minutes or until tomato mixture is heated through.

PER SERVING *316 cal., 11 g fat (4 g sat. fat), 75 mg chol., 563 mg sodium, 22 g carb., 2 g fiber, 31 g pro.* **Diabetic Exchanges:** *3 lean meat, 1½ fat, 1 starch, 1 vegetable.*

? Did you know?

When a recipe calls for grated Parmesan cheese, it makes no difference whether you grate your own or purchase a package of grated cheese from the supermarket. If you decide to buy a chunk of Parmesan cheese and grate it yourself, make sure to use the finest section on your grating tool. You could also use a blender or food processor in place of a grater. Simply cut the chunk of cheese into 1-inch cubes, then process 1 cup of cubes at a time on high until they are finely grated.

FAST FIX ▶ Sweet Barbecued Pork Chops

This recipe is one of my all-time favorites. I often prepare a big batch, then freeze half for another time. When I pull out the tangy chops later and prepare them for company, no one ever guesses that the fresh-tasting entree had been frozen.

—SUSAN HOLDERMAN FOSTORIA, OH

START TO FINISH: 25 MIN.
MAKES: 8 SERVINGS

- 2 **tablespoons canola oil**
- 8 **boneless pork loin chops (¾ inch thick and 8 ounces each)**
- ½ **cup packed brown sugar**
- ½ **cup chopped sweet onion**
- ½ **cup each ketchup, barbecue sauce, French salad dressing and honey**

1. In a large skillet, heat the oil over medium heat. In batches, brown the pork chops 2-3 minutes on each side. Return all to pan.

2. In a small bowl, mix the remaining ingredients; pour over chops. Bring to a boil. Reduce heat; simmer, covered, 4-5 minutes or until a thermometer reads 145°. Let stand 5 minutes before serving.

FREEZE OPTION *Place the pork chops in freezer containers; top with sauce. Cool and freeze. To use, partially thaw in the refrigerator overnight. Heat through in a covered saucepan, gently stirring sauce and adding a little water if necessary.*

Stuffed Chicken Breasts with Cranberry Quinoa

Every year, I travel to Peru on a medical mission trip and was introduced to quinoa there. I tried using it in place of the rice in my stuffed chicken dinner, and we fell in love with it.

—JOYCE MOYNIHAN LAKEVILLE, MN

PREP: 45 MIN. • **BAKE:** 30 MIN.
MAKES: 6 SERVINGS

- 2 **cups chicken broth**
- 1 **cup quinoa, rinsed**
- 1 **fresh thyme sprig**
- 1 **tablespoon olive oil**
- 8 **green onions, chopped**
- 1 **celery rib, chopped**
- ⅔ **cup dried cranberries**
- ⅔ **cup chopped dried apricots**
- 3 **tablespoons lemon juice**
- 2½ **teaspoons grated lemon peel**
- ½ **teaspoon salt**

CHICKEN
- ¾ **cup dry sherry**
- ¼ **cup water**
- 3 **tablespoons red wine vinegar**
- 1 **tablespoon brown sugar**
- 2 **teaspoons cornstarch**
- ¼ **teaspoon ground ginger**
- 1 **large tart apple, peeled and chopped**
- ½ **cup dried cranberries**
- ⅓ **cup chopped walnuts**
- ½ **cup apricot preserves**
- 2 **tablespoons butter**
- 6 **boneless skinless chicken breast halves (6 ounces each)**
- 1 **tablespoon olive oil**

1. In a small saucepan, bring chicken broth to a boil. Add the quinoa and thyme. Reduce heat; cover and simmer for 12-15 minutes or until the liquid is absorbed. Remove from the heat; fluff with a fork. Discard thyme.

2. In a large skillet, heat the oil over medium heat. Add the green onions and celery; cook and stir until tender. Add the cooked quinoa. Stir in the dried fruits, lemon juice, lemon peel and salt.

3. In a large saucepan, mix the first six chicken ingredients until smooth. Bring to a boil; cook and stir until slightly thickened. Add the apple, dried cranberries and walnuts. Stir in preserves and butter until melted.

4. Cut a pocket horizontally in the thickest part of each chicken breast. Fill each with 2-3 tablespoons quinoa mixture; secure with toothpicks. Place remaining quinoa mixture in a greased 1-qt. baking dish; cover with foil. In a large skillet, heat the oil over medium-high heat. Carefully brown the stuffed chicken on both sides. Transfer to a greased 13-in. x 9-in. baking dish; pour apple mixture over top.

5. Bake the chicken and quinoa at 350° for 20-25 minutes or until a thermometer inserted into chicken reads 170° and quinoa is heated through. Serve chicken with quinoa. Discard toothpicks before serving.

STUFFED CHICKEN BREASTS WITH CRANBERRY QUINOA

GARLIC PORK ROAST

Garlic Pork Roast

With 11 children to cook for, Mom usually served fuss-free foods. But on New Year's Day, she treated us to this special roast.

—RUBY WILLIAMS BOGALUSA, LA

PREP: 10 MIN. • **BAKE:** 1 HOUR 30 MIN. + STANDING
MAKES: 8 SERVINGS

1	bone-in pork loin roast (5 pounds)
½	medium green pepper, finely chopped
½	cup thinly sliced green onions
½	cup chopped celery
8	garlic cloves, minced
1	teaspoon salt
¼	teaspoon cayenne pepper

1. Preheat oven to 350°. With a sharp knife, cut a deep pocket between each rib on the meaty side of the roast. In a bowl, mix the green pepper, green onions, celery and garlic; stuff into the pockets. Sprinkle salt and cayenne pepper over the roast.

2. Place roast in a shallow roasting pan, stuffing side up. Roast 1½ to 1¾ hours or until a thermometer inserted into pork reads 145°. Remove roast from oven; tent with foil. Let stand 15 minutes before carving.

Hearty Beef & Cabbage Pockets

I discovered a recipe for beef and cabbage pockets many years ago. After a bit of experimenting, I hit on the version I like best. Your own homemade dough can be substituted for the frozen whole wheat dinner rolls. Or, use a 48-ounce package of frozen bread dough cut into 24 pieces.

—ELAINE CLARK WELLINGTON, KS

PREP: 1 HOUR + RISING • **BAKE:** 15 MIN. • **MAKES:** 2 DOZEN

24	frozen dough Texas-size whole wheat dinner rolls, thawed
1½	pounds lean ground beef (90% lean)
½	pound reduced-fat bulk pork sausage
1	large onion, chopped
1	pound carrots, grated
2	cans (4 ounces each) chopped green chilies
2	tablespoons prepared mustard
½	teaspoon salt
½	teaspoon pepper
1	small head cabbage, shredded
2	egg whites
2	teaspoons water
	Caraway seeds

1. Let dough stand at room temperature 30-40 minutes or until softened. In a Dutch oven, cook beef, sausage and onion over medium heat 12-15 minutes or until the meat is no longer pink, breaking meat into crumbles; drain. Stir in carrots, chilies, mustard, salt and pepper. Add cabbage in batches; cook and stir until tender.

2. On a lightly floured surface, press or roll each dinner roll into a 5-in. circle. Top with a heaping ⅓ cup filling; bring edges of dough up over filling and pinch to seal.

3. Place on baking sheets coated with cooking spray, seam side down. Cover with kitchen towels; let rise in a warm place until almost doubled, about 45 minutes. Preheat oven to 350°.

4. Whisk egg whites and water; brush over tops. Sprinkle with seeds. Bake 15-20 minutes or until golden brown.

PER SERVING *239 cal., 7 g fat (2 g sat. fat), 24 mg chol., 379 mg sodium, 33 g carb., 2 g fiber, 12 g pro.* **Diabetic Exchanges:** *1 lean meat, 2 starch.*

HEARTY BEEF & CABBAGE POCKETS

MOM'S SWEDISH MEATBALLS

Mom's Swedish Meatballs

My mother often prepared her traditional Swedish meatballs for family dinners and potluck suppers. The aroma of the meat as it browns is wonderful. Add to that the sweet scent of onions caramelizing, and everyone's mouth starts watering!

—MARYBETH MANK MESQUITE, TX

PREP: 30 MIN. • **COOK:** 40 MIN. • **MAKES:** 6 SERVINGS

- ¾ cup seasoned bread crumbs
- 1 medium onion, chopped
- 2 eggs, lightly beaten
- ⅓ cup minced fresh parsley
- 1 teaspoon coarsely ground pepper
- ¾ teaspoon salt
- 2 pounds ground beef

GRAVY
- ½ cup all-purpose flour
- 2¾ cups 2% milk
- 2 cans (10½ ounces each) condensed beef consomme, undiluted
- 1 tablespoon Worcestershire sauce
- 1 teaspoon coarsely ground pepper
- ¾ teaspoon salt

NOODLES
- 1 package (16 ounces) egg noodles
- ¼ cup butter, cubed
- ¼ cup minced fresh parsley

1. In a large bowl, combine the first six ingredients. Add the beef; mix lightly but thoroughly. Shape into 1½-in. meatballs (about 36). In a large skillet, brown meatballs in batches. Using a slotted spoon, remove to paper towels to drain, reserving drippings in pan.

2. For gravy, stir flour into drippings; cook and stir until light brown (do not burn). Gradually whisk in milk until smooth. Stir in the consomme, Worcestershire sauce, pepper and salt. Bring to a boil; cook and stir for 2 minutes or until thickened.

3. Return the meatballs to the pan. Cook, uncovered, 15-20 minutes longer or until the meatballs are cooked through, stirring occasionally.

4. Meanwhile, cook noodles according to the package directions. Drain; toss with butter. Serve with meatball mixture; sprinkle with parsley.

FAST FIX ▶ Pizza-Flavored Pasta Sauce

For a sure hit at dinnertime, jazz up jarred spaghetti sauce with popular pizza ingredients. Complete the meal with your favorite pasta, garlic bread and a mixed green salad.

—ANGELINA FALZARANO MIDLOTHIAN, TX

START TO FINISH: 25 MIN. • **MAKES:** 9 SERVINGS (2¼ QUARTS)

- 1 pound bulk Italian sausage
- ½ pound sliced fresh mushrooms
- 2 packages (3½ ounces each) sliced pepperoni
- ¾ cup chopped green pepper
- ½ cup chopped onion
- 7 cups meatless spaghetti sauce
- 1 can (2¼ ounces) sliced ripe olives, drained
- 2 tablespoons Italian seasoning
  Hot cooked pasta

1. In a large skillet, cook sausage, mushrooms, pepperoni, pepper and onion over medium heat until sausage is no longer pink, breaking up sausage into crumbles; drain. Stir in spaghetti sauce, olives and Italian seasoning.

2. Bring to a boil. Reduce the heat; simmer, uncovered, 10-12 minutes or until heated through. Serve over pasta.

FREEZE OPTION *Freeze cooled sauce in freezer containers. To use, partially thaw in refrigerator overnight. Heat through in a saucepan, stirring occasionally.*

PIZZA-FLAVORED PASTA SAUCE

Chicken Potpie

Loaded with a savory filling, this potpie is classic comfort food. The recipe makes two, so you can serve one right away and save the other for a busier night.
—**KAREN JOHNSON** BAKERSFIELD, CA

PREP: 40 MIN. • **BAKE:** 35 MIN. + STANDING
MAKES: 2 POTPIES (8 SERVINGS EACH)

- 2 cups diced peeled potatoes
- 1¾ cups sliced carrots
- 1 cup butter, cubed
- ⅔ cup chopped onion
- 1 cup all-purpose flour
- 1¾ teaspoons salt
- 1 teaspoon dried thyme
- ¾ teaspoon pepper
- 3 cups chicken broth
- 1½ cups milk
- 4 cups cubed cooked chicken
- 1 cup frozen peas
- 1 cup frozen corn
- 2 packages (14.1 ounces each) refrigerated pie pastry

1. Preheat oven to 425°. Place the potatoes and carrots in a large saucepan; add water to cover. Bring to a boil. Reduce the heat; cook, covered, 8-10 minutes or until vegetables are crisp-tender; drain.
2. In a large skillet, heat butter over medium-high heat. Add onion; cook and stir until tender. Stir in flour and seasonings until blended. Gradually stir in chicken broth and milk. Bring to a boil, stirring constantly; cook and stir 2 minutes or until thickened. Stir in the chicken, peas, corn and potato mixture; remove from heat.
3. Unroll a pastry sheet into each of two 9-in. pie plates; trim even with rims. Add chicken mixture. Unroll remaining pastry; place over filling. Trim, seal and flute edges. Cut slits in tops.
4. Bake 35-40 minutes or until crust is lightly browned. Let stand 15 minutes before cutting.

FREEZE OPTION *Cover and freeze unbaked pies. To use, remove from freezer 30 minutes before baking (do not thaw). Preheat oven to 425°. Place pies on baking sheets; cover edges loosely with foil. Bake 30 minutes. Reduce oven setting to 350°; bake 70-80 minutes longer or until crust is golden brown and a thermometer inserted into center reads 165°.*

Herbed Beer Can Chicken

One of our July Fourth traditions is to grill chickens that stand up on a can of beer. It's always a fun conversation piece.
—**KAREN BARROS** BRISTOL, RI

CHICKEN POTPIE

PREP: 15 MIN.
GRILL: 1¼ HOURS + STANDING
MAKES: 4 SERVINGS

- 2 tablespoons canola oil
- 1 tablespoon minced fresh tarragon or 1 teaspoon dried tarragon
- 1 tablespoon minced fresh basil or 1 teaspoon dried basil
- 2 teaspoons minced fresh parsley
- 1 teaspoon garlic powder
- ½ teaspoon salt
- ¼ teaspoon pepper
- 3 garlic cloves, minced, divided
- 1 broiler/fryer chicken (3 to 4 pounds)
- 1 can (12 ounces) beer
- 1 fresh rosemary sprig

1. In a small bowl, combine the first seven ingredients; stir in half of the minced garlic. Rub the mixture over the outside and inside of the chicken. Tuck wings under chicken.
2. Prepare the grill for indirect heat. Completely cover all sides of an 8- or 9-in. round baking pan with foil. Place a beer-can chicken rack in the pan. Remove ⅓ cup beer from the can; save for another use. Using a can opener, make additional large holes in the top of the can. Insert rosemary sprig and remaining garlic into can. Add beer can to rack.
3. Place chicken vertically onto rack. Place pan on grill rack. Grill, covered, over indirect medium heat 1¼ to 1½ hours or until a thermometer inserted into thigh reads 180°.
4. Remove the pan from the grill; tent the chicken with foil. Let stand 15 minutes. Carefully remove the chicken from the rack.

HERBED BEER CAN CHICKEN

Beef & Spinach Lo Mein

I discovered this dish at an international luncheon and just had to try it at home. The beefy lo mein is quick, easy and a hit with everyone who likes stir-fry.

—DENISE PATTERSON BAINBRIDGE, OH

START TO FINISH: 30 MIN.
MAKES: 5 SERVINGS

- ¼ cup hoisin sauce
- 2 tablespoons soy sauce
- 1 tablespoon water
- 2 teaspoons sesame oil
- 2 garlic cloves, minced
- ¼ teaspoon crushed red pepper flakes
- 1 pound beef top round steak, thinly sliced
- 6 ounces uncooked spaghetti
- 4 teaspoons canola oil, divided
- 1 can (8 ounces) sliced water chestnuts, drained
- 2 green onions, sliced
- 1 package (10 ounces) fresh spinach, coarsely chopped
- 1 red chili pepper, seeded and thinly sliced

1. In a small bowl, mix the first six ingredients. Remove ¼ cup mixture to a large bowl; add beef and toss to coat. Marinate at room temperature 10 minutes.

2. Cook the spaghetti according to the package directions. Meanwhile, in a large skillet, heat 1½ teaspoons canola oil until hot. Add half of the beef mixture; stir-fry 1-2 minutes or until no longer pink. Remove from the pan. Repeat with an additional 1½ teaspoons oil and remaining beef mixture.

3. Stir-fry the water chestnuts and green onions in remaining canola oil 30 seconds. Stir in the spinach and remaining hoisin mixture; cook until spinach is wilted. Return beef to pan; heat through.

4. Drain the spaghetti; add to the beef mixture and toss to combine. Sprinkle with chili pepper.

NOTE *Wear disposable gloves when cutting hot peppers; the oils can burn skin. Avoid touching your face.*

Pizza Macaroni & Cheese

My grandmother made pizza-flavored macaroni and cheese for us once when she came to visit, and I never forgot how good it was. I knew my kids would enjoy it just as much as I did!

—JULI MEYERS HINESVILLE, GA

PREP: 30 MIN. • **BAKE:** 25 MIN.
MAKES: 12 SERVINGS

- 2 packages (14 ounces each) deluxe macaroni and cheese dinner mix
- ½ cup sour cream
- 1 can (14½ ounces) petite diced tomatoes, drained
- 1 can (15 ounces) pizza sauce
- 1 small green pepper, chopped
- 1 small sweet red pepper, chopped
- 2 cups (8 ounces) shredded Italian cheese blend
- 2 ounces sliced pepperoni

1. Preheat oven to 350°. Cook the macaroni according to the package directions for al dente. Drain; return to pan. Stir in the contents of cheese packets and sour cream. Transfer to a greased 13-in. x 9-in. baking dish.

2. In a small bowl, combine tomatoes and pizza sauce; spread over top. Top with peppers, cheese and pepperoni. Bake, uncovered, 25-30 minutes or until bubbly.

PIZZA MACARONI & CHEESE

SARA EICHENLAUB'S
CRANBERRY ORANGE MUFFINS
PAGE 84

Breads, Rolls & Muffins

Golden goodies warm from the oven—**what could be better?**
Choose scrumptious loaves, biscuits, coffee cakes, breadsticks or
any of the other **fresh-baked sensations** in this chapter!

**MARIE RIZZIO'S
GARLIC BREAD SPIRALS**
PAGE 82

**HEATHER DETERDING'S
CHOCOLATE MONKEY BREAD**
PAGE 85

**KAY DALY'S
SAVORY PARTY BREAD**
PAGE 90

Eggnog Bread

This rich loaf is a Christmas tradition at my home here in the foothills of the Blue Ridge Mountains. Red and green candied cherries give each slice a festive look.

—**RUTH BICKEL** HICKORY, NC

PREP: 15 MIN. • **BAKE:** 70 MIN.
MAKES: 1 LOAF (16 SLICES)

- 2 eggs
- ¾ cup sugar
- ¼ cup butter, melted
- 2¼ cups all-purpose flour
- 2 teaspoons baking powder
- 1 teaspoon salt
- 1 cup eggnog
- ½ cup chopped pecans
- ½ cup raisins
- ½ cup chopped red and green candied cherries

1. In a large bowl, beat eggs, sugar and butter until well blended. In another bowl, mix the flour, baking powder and salt; add to the egg mixture alternately with the eggnog, beating just until blended. Fold in the pecans, raisins and cherries.

2. Transfer to a greased 8-in. x 4-in. loaf pan. Bake at 350° for 70 minutes or until a toothpick inserted into center comes out clean. Cool in the pan for 10 minutes before removing to a wire rack to cool.

NOTE *This recipe was tested with commercially prepared eggnog.*

"Mom often served her savory Herb & Sun-Dried Tomato Muffins in place of bread or buns. Now I do the same thing when I'm making soup or chili."
—**ELIZABETH KING** DULUTH, MN

HERB & SUN-DRIED TOMATO MUFFINS

EGGNOG BREAD

Herb & Sun-Dried Tomato Muffins

PREP: 15 MIN. • **BAKE:** 20 MIN.
MAKES: 1 DOZEN

- 2 cups all-purpose flour
- 2 teaspoons baking powder
- 1 teaspoon snipped fresh dill or ¼ teaspoon dill weed
- 1 teaspoon minced fresh thyme or ¼ teaspoon dried thyme
- ½ teaspoon baking soda
- ½ teaspoon salt
- ½ teaspoon pepper
- 1 egg
- 1¼ cups 2% milk
- ¼ cup olive oil
- ½ cup shredded cheddar cheese
- ½ cup oil-packed sun-dried tomatoes, finely chopped

1. In a large bowl, mix the first seven ingredients. In another bowl, whisk the egg, milk and oil. Add to flour mixture; stir just until moistened. Fold in cheese and tomatoes.

2. Fill greased muffin cups three-fourths full. Bake at 375° for 18-20 minutes or until a toothpick inserted into center comes out clean. Cool for 5 minutes before removing from pan to a wire rack. Serve warm.

Cherry-Pecan Cocoa Bread

This nutty, cherry-dotted treat boasts a mild cocoa flavor no one can seem to resist. Enjoy it for breakfast, afternoon snacktime...any time at all. A tall glass of milk is the perfect accompaniment.

—**MARGARET BEYERSDORF** KISSIMMEE, FL

PREP: 10 MIN. • **BAKE:** 3 HOURS
MAKES: 1 LOAF (1½ POUNDS, 16 SLICES)

- ⅔ **cup warm whole milk (70° to 80°)**
- ⅓ **cup water (70° to 80°)**
- 5 **tablespoons butter, softened**
- ⅓ **cup packed brown sugar**
- 1 **teaspoon salt**
- 3 **cups bread flour**
- 5 **tablespoons baking cocoa**
- 2¼ **teaspoons active dry yeast**
- ½ **cup chopped pecans**
- ½ **cup dried cherries**

1. In bread machine pan, place the first eight ingredients in the order suggested by the manufacturer. Select basic bread setting. Choose crust color and loaf size if available.

2. Check the dough after 5 minutes of mixing; add 1 to 2 tablespoons of water or flour if needed. Just before the final kneading (your bread machine may audibly signal this), add the pecans and cherries. Bake according to bread machine directions.

CHERRY-PECAN COCOA BREAD

BANANA BEIGNET BITES

FAST FIX

Banana Beignet Bites

When I was a little girl, my grandmother took me into the kitchen one day and taught me how to prepare her signature banana beignets. I didn't have to wait long to sample one of our creations—they're ready to eat in just 30 minutes.

—**AMY DOWNING** SOUTH RIDING, VA

START TO FINISH: 30 MIN.
MAKES: ABOUT 3 DOZEN

- ¾ **cup sugar**
- ¼ **cup packed brown sugar**
- 1½ **teaspoons ground cinnamon**

BEIGNETS
- 2 **cups cake flour**
- ¾ **cup sugar**
- 2½ **teaspoons baking powder**
- ½ **teaspoon ground cinnamon**
- 1 **teaspoon salt**
- 1 **egg**
- 1 **cup mashed ripe bananas (about 3 medium)**
- ½ **cup whole milk**
- 2 **tablespoons canola oil**
  Oil for deep-fat frying

1. In a small bowl, mix sugars and cinnamon until blended. In a large bowl, whisk the first five beignet ingredients. In another bowl, whisk egg, bananas, milk and 2 tablespoons oil until blended. Add to flour mixture; stir just until moistened.

2. In an electric skillet or deep fryer, heat oil to 375°. Drop tablespoonfuls of batter, a few at a time, into the hot oil. Fry about 45-60 seconds on each side or until golden brown. Drain on paper towels. Roll in sugar mixture while warm.

? Did you know?

French in origin, a beignet (pronounced ben-YAY) is often enjoyed as a dessert. Similar to doughnuts or fritters, it starts with a basic sweet dough, sometimes filled with fruit, that is deep-fried and sprinkled with sugar.

SWEDISH PUFF COFFEE CAKE

FAST FIX **Garlic Bread Spirals**

Take advantage of refrigerated French loaf dough to get these savory spirals on the table fast. You'll have a terrific addition to your dinner menu in less than half an hour.
—MARIE RIZZIO INTERLOCHEN, MI

START TO FINISH: 25 MIN. • **MAKES:** 1 DOZEN

- ¼ cup butter, melted
- 2 green onions, finely chopped
- 3 tablespoons grated Parmesan cheese
- 2 tablespoons minced fresh parsley
- 3 garlic cloves, minced
- 1 tube (11 ounces) refrigerated crusty French loaf

1. In a small bowl, mix the first five ingredients. Unroll the French loaf dough; spread the butter mixture to within ½ in. of the edges. Roll up jelly-roll style, starting with a long side. Cut into 12 slices; place in greased muffin cups, cut side down.
2. Bake at 400° for 10-12 minutes or until golden brown.

Swedish Puff Coffee Cake

Some of my most treasured childhood memories involve waking up to the heavenly scent of a Swedish coffee cake baking in the oven. Now I fondly recall those times when I make my own.
—MARY SHENK DEKALB, IL

PREP: 35 MIN. • **BAKE:** 30 MIN. + COOLING • **MAKES:** 12 SERVINGS

- 1 cup all-purpose flour
- ½ cup cold butter, cubed
- 2 tablespoons ice water

TOPPING
- 1 cup water
- ½ cup butter
- 1 teaspoon almond extract
- 1 cup all-purpose flour
- 3 eggs

GLAZE
- 1 cup confectioners' sugar
- 2 tablespoons butter, softened
- 1 tablespoon 2% milk
- 1 teaspoon almond extract
- 1 cup flaked coconut

1. Preheat oven to 375°. Place flour in a small bowl; cut in butter until crumbly. Gradually add ice water, tossing with a fork until the dough holds together when pressed. On an ungreased baking sheet, press dough into a 10-in. circle.
2. For topping, in a large saucepan, bring water and butter to a rolling boil. Remove from heat; stir in extract. Add flour all at once and beat until blended. Cook over medium heat until mixture pulls away from sides of pan and forms a ball, stirring vigorously. Remove from heat; let stand 5 minutes.
3. Add eggs, one at a time, beating well after each addition until smooth. Continue beating until mixture is smooth and shiny; spread over pastry.
4. Bake 30-35 minutes or until lightly browned. Cover loosely with foil during the last 5 minutes if needed to prevent overbrowning. Remove from the pan to a wire rack to cool completely.
5. For the glaze, in a small bowl, beat confectioners' sugar, butter, milk and extract until smooth. Spread over the top; sprinkle with coconut.

GARLIC BREAD SPIRALS

Zucchini Nut Bread

This zucchini bread is lighter and fluffier than most. It's a great way to use the harvest from your vegetable garden.
—**KEVIN BRUCKERHOFF** COLUMBIA, MO

PREP: 15 MIN. • **BAKE:** 55 MIN. + COOLING
MAKES: 2 LOAVES (12 SLICES EACH)

- 2 **cups sugar**
- 1 **cup canola oil**
- 3 **eggs**
- 2 **teaspoons vanilla extract**
- 3 **cups all-purpose flour**
- 1 **teaspoon salt**
- 1 **teaspoon baking soda**
- 1 **teaspoon grated lemon peel**
- 1 **teaspoon ground cinnamon**
- ¼ **teaspoon baking powder**
- 2 **cups shredded zucchini (about 2 medium)**
- ½ **cup chopped walnuts or pecans**

1. Preheat oven to 350°. Grease two 8-in. x 4-in. loaf pans. In a large bowl, beat sugar, oil, eggs and vanilla until well blended. In another bowl, whisk flour, salt, baking soda, lemon peel, cinnamon and baking powder; gradually beat into sugar mixture, mixing just until moistened. Stir in the zucchini and walnuts.

2. Transfer to prepared pans. Bake 55-65 minutes or until a toothpick inserted into the center comes out clean. Cool 10 minutes before removing from pans to wire racks to cool.

MINI ZUCCHINI LOAVES *Transfer batter to four greased 5¾-in. x 3-in. x 2-in. loaf pans. Bake at 350° for 35-40 minutes or until a toothpick inserted near the center comes out clean. Cool as directed.*

CHOCOLATE ZUCCHINI BREAD *Omit lemon peel and nuts. Reduce flour to 2¾ cups. Add ⅓ cup baking cocoa to flour mixture. Stir in 1 cup semisweet chocolate chips with the zucchini. Bake as directed.*

ZUCCHINI APPLE BREAD *Omit peel. Reduce sugar to 1 cup and add 1 cup brown sugar. Add ¼ teaspoon ground nutmeg with cinnamon. Reduce zucchini to 1½ cups. Add 1 cup grated peeled tart apple with zucchini and nuts. Bake as directed.*

ZUCCHINI NUT BREAD

BREAKFAST-IN-A-MUFFIN

Breakfast-in-a-Muffin

I can never seem to get out of bed early enough to fix a good breakfast. My solution is to prepare egg- and sausage-stuffed muffins in advance, then heat them in the microwave for 30 seconds just before heading out the door.
—**SARA SANDERS** FOUNTAIN CITY, IN

PREP: 20 MIN. • **BAKE:** 15 MIN. • **MAKES:** 1 DOZEN

- ⅓ **pound bulk Italian sausage**
- 3 **eggs**
- ⅛ **teaspoon seasoned salt**
- ⅛ **teaspoon pepper**
- 1 **package (8½ ounces) corn bread/muffin mix**
- ¾ **cup shredded cheddar cheese, divided**

1. Preheat oven to 400°. In a skillet, cook the sausage over medium heat 4-5 minutes or until no longer pink, breaking into crumbles. Remove to paper towels to drain.

2. In a small bowl, whisk eggs, seasoned salt and pepper. Pour into the same pan; cook and stir over medium heat until the eggs are thickened and no liquid egg remains. Remove from heat.

3. In a large bowl, prepare the corn muffin mix according to the package directions. Fold in the sausage, scrambled eggs and ½ cup cheddar cheese. Fill paper-lined muffin cups two-thirds full.

4. Bake 10 minutes. Sprinkle with the remaining cheese; bake 5 minutes longer or until a toothpick inserted into the center comes out clean. Cool 5 minutes before removing from pan. Serve warm.

JUMBO BLUEBERRY MUFFINS

Jumbo Blueberry Muffins

Michigan is one of the top states when it comes to blueberry production. I like to use those little blue gems in a variety of recipes, including this jumbo version of a classic.

—JACKIE HANNAHS BRETHREN, MI

PREP: 15 MIN. • **BAKE:** 20 MIN. • **MAKES:** 8 JUMBO MUFFINS

- ½ cup butter, softened
- 1 cup sugar
- 2 eggs
- ½ cup buttermilk
- 1 teaspoon vanilla extract
- 2 cups all-purpose flour
- 2 teaspoons baking powder
- ¼ teaspoon salt
- 2 cups fresh or frozen blueberries

TOPPING
- 3 tablespoons sugar
- ⅛ teaspoon ground cinnamon
- ⅛ teaspoon ground nutmeg

1. Preheat oven to 400°. In a large bowl, cream butter and sugar until light and fluffy. Add eggs, one at a time, beating well after each addition. Beat in buttermilk and vanilla. In another bowl, whisk flour, baking powder and salt. Add to creamed mixture; stir just until moistened. Fold in berries.
2. Fill greased or paper-lined jumbo muffin cups two-thirds full. Mix the topping ingredients; sprinkle over tops. Bake 20-25 minutes or until a toothpick inserted into center comes out clean. Cool 5 minutes before removing from pan to a wire rack. Serve warm.
FOR STANDARD-SIZE MUFFINS *Make muffin batter as directed; fill greased or paper-lined standard muffin cups two-thirds full. Bake in a preheated 400° oven for 15-20 minutes or until a toothpick comes out clean. Yield: about 16 standard muffins.*

FAST FIX ▶ Cranberry Orange Muffins

My 30-minute muffins are made with whole wheat flour and have a splash of orange flavor. They're so simple to fix, my husband and I have one for breakfast almost every morning.
—SARA EICHENLAUB BURLINGTON, ON

START TO FINISH: 30 MIN. • **MAKES:** 1 DOZEN

- 2 cups whole wheat flour
- ⅓ cup sugar
- 2 teaspoons baking powder
- ½ teaspoon baking soda
- ¼ teaspoon salt
- 1½ cups orange juice
- ¼ cup canola oil
- 1 egg
- 1 cup fresh or frozen cranberries, halved

1. In a large bowl, combine the flour, sugar, baking powder, baking soda and salt. In another bowl, combine the orange juice, oil and egg; stir into the dry ingredients just until moistened. Fold in cranberries.
2. Coat muffin cups with cooking spray or use paper liners; fill three-fourths full with batter. Bake at 400° for 15-20 minutes or until a toothpick inserted near the center comes out clean. Cool for 5 minutes before removing from pans to wire racks. Serve warm.

CRANBERRY ORANGE MUFFINS

Almond & Cranberry Coconut Bread

This yummy quick bread is great any time of year, but the ruby red cranberries lend every slice extra appeal for Christmas.

—**ROSEMARY JOHNSON** IRONDALE, AL

PREP: 20 MIN. • **BAKE:** 1 HOUR + COOLING
MAKES: 2 LOAVES (16 SLICES EACH)

- 2 **cups flaked coconut**
- 1 **cup slivered almonds**
- 1 **cup butter, softened**
- 1 **cup sugar**
- 4 **eggs**
- 1 **cup (8 ounces) vanilla yogurt**
- 1 **teaspoon almond extract**
- 4½ **cups all-purpose flour**
- 3 **teaspoons baking powder**
- ½ **teaspoon salt**
- ½ **teaspoon baking soda**
- 1 **can (15 ounces) cream of coconut**
- 1 **cup dried cranberries**

1. Place coconut and almonds in an ungreased 15-in. x 10-in. x 1-in. pan. Bake at 350° for 10-15 minutes or until lightly toasted, stirring occasionally. Cool.
2. In a large bowl, cream butter and sugar until light and fluffy. Add the eggs, one at a time, beating well after each addition. Beat in yogurt and extract until blended. Combine the flour, baking powder, salt and baking soda. Add to the creamed mixture alternately with the cream of coconut, beating well after each addition. Fold in the cranberries, coconut and almonds.
3. Transfer to two greased and floured 9-in. x 5-in. loaf pans. Bake at 350° for 60-70 minutes or until a toothpick inserted near the center comes out clean. Cool for 10 minutes before removing from pans to wire racks to cool completely.

ALMOND & CRANBERRY COCONUT BREAD

CHOCOLATE MONKEY BREAD

Chocolate Monkey Bread

Here's a special treat we indulge in during the holiday season. With lots of chocolate, the pull-apart loaf is impossible to resist!

—**HEATHER DETERDING** ODENTON, MD

PREP: 20 MIN. • **BAKE:** 40 MIN. • **MAKES:** 16 SERVINGS

- 1 **cup packed brown sugar**
- ¾ **cup butter, cubed**
- 2 **cans (16.3 ounces each) large refrigerated buttermilk biscuits**
- 64 **milk chocolate kisses**
- ½ **cup sugar**
- 2 **teaspoons ground cinnamon**

1. In a small saucepan, combine brown sugar and butter. Cook and stir over medium-low heat for 10-12 minutes or until sugar is melted; set aside.
2. Cut each biscuit into quarters. Shape each piece around a chocolate kiss; pinch seams to seal. In a large resealable plastic bag, combine the sugar and cinnamon. Add biscuits, a few pieces at a time, and shake to coat.
3. Spoon ¼ cup caramel into a well-greased 10-in. fluted tube pan. Arrange a third of the biscuits in pan and drizzle with ¼ cup caramel. Repeat layers twice.
4. Bake, uncovered, at 350° for 40-45 minutes or until golden brown. Cover loosely with foil if biscuits brown too quickly. Immediately invert onto a serving plate. Let stand for 10 minutes before serving.

FAST FIX ▶ Herbed Cheese Sticks

We love the seasoned breadsticks served at our local pizza parlor when they're hot and gooey, right from the oven. Now we can enjoy the same finger-licking treat without ever leaving the house!

—HEATHER BATES ATHENS, ME

START TO FINISH: 30 MIN.
MAKES: 16 CHEESE STICKS

1 package (6½ ounces) pizza crust mix
1½ teaspoons garlic powder
1 tablespoon olive oil
1 cup (4 ounces) shredded part-skim mozzarella cheese
¼ cup shredded Parmesan cheese
1 teaspoon Italian seasoning
 Pizza sauce

1. Preheat oven to 450°. Mix pizza dough according to the package directions, adding garlic powder to dry mix. Cover; let rest 5 minutes.
2. Knead dough 4-5 times or until easy to handle. On a greased baking sheet, press dough into an 8-in. square. Brush the top with oil; sprinkle with cheeses and Italian seasoning.
3. Bake 6-8 minutes or until cheese is lightly browned. Cut in half; cut each half crosswise into eight strips. Serve with pizza sauce.

GRANDMA'S ROSEMARY DINNER ROLLS

"My grandmother (I called her Baba) made her dinner rolls in a coal oven. How she regulated the temperature is beyond me! She always used part of the dough to shape extras for the neighbors to bake at home. My mom and aunts delivered the unbaked goodies." —CHARLOTTE HENDERSHOT HUDSON, PA

HERBED CHEESE STICKS

Grandma's Rosemary Dinner Rolls

PREP: 35 MIN. + RISING • **BAKE:** 20 MIN.
MAKES: 1 DOZEN

1 package (¼ ounce) active dry yeast
¼ cup warm water (110° to 115°)
3 cups bread flour
2 tablespoons sugar
1 tablespoon minced fresh rosemary, divided
¾ teaspoon salt
⅔ cup warm 2% milk (110° to 115°)
1 egg
¼ to ⅓ cup canola oil
EGG WASH
1 egg yolk
2 tablespoons 2% milk

1. In a small bowl, dissolve the yeast in warm water. Place the flour, sugar, 2 teaspoons rosemary and salt in a food processor; pulse until blended. Add the warm milk, egg and yeast mixture; cover and pulse 10 times or until almost blended.
2. While processing, gradually add oil just until the dough pulls away from the sides and begins to form a ball. Process 2 minutes longer to knead dough (dough will be very soft).
3. Transfer dough to a greased bowl, turning once to grease the top. Cover with plastic wrap and let rise in a warm place until doubled, about 1 hour.
4. Punch down the dough. Turn onto a lightly floured surface; divide and shape into 12 balls. Roll each into a 15-in. rope. Starting at one end, loosely wrap dough around itself to form a coil. Tuck end under; pinch to seal.
5. Place 2 in. apart on greased baking sheets. Cover and let rise until doubled, about 30 minutes.
6. For egg wash, in a small bowl, whisk the egg yolk and milk; brush over rolls. Sprinkle with the remaining rosemary. Bake at 350° for 18-22 minutes or until golden brown. Remove from pans to wire racks; serve warm.

EAT SMART | Favorite Banana Chip Muffins

My chocolate-dotted muffins are one of the first things my husband, U.S. Army Lt. Col. John Duda Jr., craves when he gets home from deployment. I make sure to have the overripe bananas and other ingredients all ready to go!

—KIMBERLY DUDA SANFORD, NC

PREP: 20 MIN. • **BAKE:** 20 MIN.
MAKES: 1 DOZEN

- 1½ cups all-purpose flour
- ⅔ cup sugar
- 1 teaspoon baking soda
- ¼ teaspoon ground cinnamon
- ⅛ teaspoon salt
- 1 egg
- 1⅓ cups mashed ripe bananas (about 3 medium)
- ⅓ cup butter, melted
- 1 teaspoon vanilla extract
- ½ cup semisweet chocolate chips

1. Preheat oven to 375°. In a large bowl, whisk flour, sugar, baking soda, cinnamon and salt. In another bowl, whisk egg, bananas, melted butter and vanilla until blended. Add to the flour mixture; stir just until moistened. Fold in chocolate chips.

2. Fill greased or paper-lined muffin cups three-fourths full. Bake 17-20 minutes or until a toothpick inserted into the center comes out clean. Cool 5 minutes before removing from pan to a wire rack. Serve warm.

PER SERVING *207 cal., 8 g fat (5 g sat. fat), 31 mg chol., 172 mg sodium, 33 g carb., 2 g fiber, 3 g pro.* **Diabetic Exchanges:** *2 starch, 1½ fat.*

Did you know?

Yeast is a microorganism that becomes activated when it is combined with warm water and sugar. It consumes the sugars in sweeteners and flours, and it produces carbon dioxide gas that helps give bread its light and airy texture. There are several different types of yeast, which are all handled differently. Always check the expiration date on the package before using yeast and discard it if it is past the date.

Overnight Cherry Danish

With cherry-filled centers, these Danish absolutely melt in your mouth. I love the convenience of being able to start the prep work the night before. They also store well, unfrosted, in the freezer.

—LEANN SAUDER TREMONT, IL

PREP: 1½ HOURS + CHILLING
BAKE: 15 MIN. + COOLING
MAKES: 3 DOZEN

- 2 packages (¼ ounce each) active dry yeast
- ½ cup warm 2% milk (110° to 115°)
- 6 cups all-purpose flour
- ⅓ cup sugar
- 2 teaspoons salt
- 1 cup cold butter, cubed
- 1½ cups warm half-and-half cream (70° to 80°)
- 6 egg yolks
- 1 can (21 ounces) cherry pie filling

ICING
- 3 cups confectioners' sugar
- 2 tablespoons butter, softened
- ¼ teaspoon vanilla extract
  Dash salt
- 4 to 5 tablespoons half-and-half cream

1. In a small bowl, dissolve the yeast in warm milk. In a large bowl, combine flour, sugar and salt. Cut in butter until crumbly. Add the yeast mixture, cream and egg yolks; stir until mixture forms a soft dough (the dough will be sticky). Refrigerate, covered, overnight.

2. Punch down the dough. Turn onto a lightly floured surface; divide into four portions. Roll each into an 18-in. x 4-in. rectangle; cut into 4-in. x 1-in. strips.

3. Place two strips side by side; twist together. Shape into a ring and pinch the ends together. Place 2 in. apart on greased baking sheets. Repeat with the remaining strips. Cover with kitchen towels; let rise in a warm place until doubled, about 45 minutes.

4. Preheat oven to 350°. Using the end of a wooden spoon handle, make a ½-in.-deep indentation in the center of each Danish. Fill each with about 1 tablespoon pie filling. Bake 14-16 minutes or until lightly browned. Remove from pans to wire racks to cool.

5. For the icing, in a bowl, beat the confectioners' sugar, butter, vanilla, salt and enough half-and-half cream to reach the desired consistency. Drizzle over Danish.

OVERNIGHT CHERRY DANISH

Jumbo Jalapeno Cheddar Rolls

When I want to bring a little excitement to mealtime, I fill a big basket with my jumbo rolls. The jalapeno flavor is mild, but everyone enjoys the zippy taste.
—**LINDA FOREMAN** LOCUST GROVE, OK

PREP: 35 MIN. + RISING • **BAKE:** 20 MIN.
MAKES: 1 DOZEN

- 2 packages (¼ ounce each) active dry yeast
- 2 tablespoons sugar
- 2 cups warm milk (110° to 115°)
- 2 eggs
- 2 teaspoons salt
- 6½ to 7½ cups all-purpose flour
- 2 cups (8 ounces) shredded cheddar cheese
- ¼ cup chopped seeded jalapeno pepper

EGG WASH
- 1 egg
- 2 teaspoons water

1. In a large bowl, dissolve yeast and sugar in warm milk. Add the eggs, salt and 4 cups flour. Beat on medium speed for 3 minutes. Add cheese and jalapeno. Stir in enough remaining flour to form a firm dough.

2. Turn dough onto a floured surface; knead until smooth and elastic, about 6-8 minutes. Place in a greased bowl, turning once to grease the top. Cover and let rise in a warm place until doubled, about 1 hour.

3. Punch dough down. Turn onto a lightly floured surface; divide into 12 pieces. Shape each into a roll. Place 3-in. apart on lightly greased baking sheets. Cover and let rise until doubled, about 30 minutes.

4. Combine egg and water; brush over rolls. Bake at 375° for 16-20 minutes or until golden brown. Remove from pans to wire racks. Serve warm.
NOTE *Wear disposable gloves when cutting hot peppers; the oils can burn skin. Avoid touching your face.*

Sun-Dried Tomato Focaccia

Accented with sun-dried tomatoes and red onion, this colorful focaccia looks inviting and doesn't disappoint when you take a bite. I love the fact that my bread machine does much of the work for me.
—**KATHY KATZ** OCALA, FL

PREP: 1 HOUR 40 MIN. + RISING
BAKE: 20 MIN.
MAKES: 2 LOAVES (8 SERVINGS EACH)

- ¼ cup chopped sun-dried tomatoes (not packed in oil)
- ½ cup boiling water
- 1¼ cups warm V8 juice (70° to 80°)
- 2 tablespoons olive oil
- ¼ cup grated Parmesan cheese
- 1 tablespoon dried parsley flakes
- 2 teaspoons sugar
- 1 teaspoon salt
- 1 teaspoon dried basil
- ½ teaspoon garlic powder
- 2 cups whole wheat flour
- 1½ cups all-purpose flour
- 2 teaspoons active dry yeast

TOPPING
- 2 tablespoons slivered sun-dried tomatoes (not packed in oil)
- ¼ cup boiling water
- 12 thin slices red onion, halved
- 1 tablespoon olive oil

1. In a small bowl, combine chopped sun-dried tomatoes and boiling water. Let stand for 5 minutes; drain.

2. In bread machine pan, place the V8 juice, oil, softened tomatoes, cheese, parsley, sugar, salt, basil, garlic powder, flours and yeast in the order suggested by the manufacturer. Select the dough setting (check dough after 5 minutes of mixing; add 1 to 2 tablespoons of water or flour if needed).

3. In a small bowl, combine slivered tomatoes and boiling water. Let stand for 5 minutes; drain and pat dry with paper towels.

4. When the cycle is completed, turn dough onto a lightly floured surface. Punch down. Divide in half; roll each portion into a 9-in. circle. Transfer to two greased 9-in. round baking pans.

5. Using the end of a wooden spoon handle, make ¼-in. indentations in dough. Arrange tomato slivers and onion slices over dough; press down lightly. Cover and let rise in a warm place until doubled, about 30 minutes. Brush with oil. Bake at 375° for 20-25 minutes or until golden brown. Remove to wire racks.

SUN-DRIED TOMATO FOCACCIA

Majestic Cinnamon Rolls

Want a special treat for your breakfast or brunch? These large goodies are bursting with cinnamon and smothered with a velvety caramel topping.

—BETTE LU LERWICK ALBIN, WY

PREP: 40 MIN. + RISING • **BAKE:** 35 MIN.
MAKES: 1 DOZEN

- 1 **tablespoon active dry yeast**
- ⅓ **cup sugar, divided**
- ¾ **cup warm water (110° to 115°)**
- ¾ **cup warm 2% milk (110° to 115°)**
- 2 **eggs**
- 3 **tablespoons butter, melted**
- 1½ **teaspoons salt**
- 4½ **to 5 cups all-purpose flour**

FILLING
- 1½ **cups packed brown sugar**
- ½ **cup butter, melted**
- 2 **tablespoons ground cinnamon**

TOPPING
- 1½ **cups packed brown sugar**
- ¾ **cup butter, melted**
- 3 **tablespoons half-and-half cream**

1. In a large bowl, dissolve yeast and 1 tablespoon sugar in warm water. Add the milk, eggs, butter, salt, remaining sugar and 2 cups flour. Beat until smooth. Stir in enough remaining flour to form a soft dough (the dough will be sticky).

2. Turn dough onto a floured surface; knead until smooth and elastic, about 6-8 minutes. Place in a greased bowl, turning once to grease the top. Cover and let rise in a warm place until doubled, about 1 hour.

3. Punch dough down. On a lightly floured surface, roll into an 18-in. x 12-in. rectangle. In a small bowl, combine the brown sugar, butter and cinnamon; spread over rectangle to within ½ in. of edges. Roll up jelly-roll style, starting with a long side; pinch seam to seal. Cut into 1½-in. slices.

4. In a small bowl, combine the brown sugar, butter and cream; pour into a greased 13-in. x 9-in. baking dish. Place the rolls, cut side down, in the brown sugar mixture.

5. Cover and let rise in a warm place until doubled, about 30 minutes. Bake at 350° for 35-40 minutes or until golden brown. Cool in dish for 5 minutes; invert onto a serving platter. Serve warm.

UPSIDE-DOWN ONION BREAD

Upside-Down Onion Bread

Try a rich, savory loaf loaded with sharp cheddar cheese, crumbled bacon and chopped sweet onion. The thick wedges are fantastic served alongside a main course—or even used for sandwiches.

—MARY MARLOWE LEVERETTE COLUMBIA, SC

PREP: 1 HOUR • **BAKE:** 30 MIN.
MAKES: 1 LOAF (10 WEDGES)

- 1 **large sweet onion, chopped**
- 1 **tablespoon olive oil**
- 1 **tablespoon butter**
- ¾ **teaspoon minced fresh thyme**
- 3 **cups all-purpose flour**
- 3 **teaspoons baking powder**
- 3 **teaspoons sugar**
- 1 **teaspoon salt**
- 1 **teaspoon pepper**
- 1 **cup cold butter**
- 1 **cup heavy whipping cream**
- 1½ **cups (6 ounces) shredded sharp cheddar cheese**
- ½ **cup crumbled cooked bacon**

1. In a large skillet over low heat, cook the sweet onion in oil and butter for 50 minutes or until golden brown, stirring occasionally. Transfer to a greased 9-in. deep-dish pie plate; sprinkle with thyme.

2. In a large bowl, combine the flour, baking powder, sugar, salt and pepper. Cut in butter until mixture resembles coarse crumbs. Stir in cream just until moistened. Fold in cheese and bacon. Turn onto a lightly floured surface; knead 8-10 times. Pat or roll into a 9-in. circle. Carefully place over onions.

3. Bake at 400° for 30-35 minutes or until golden brown. Immediately invert onto a large serving platter. Cool slightly; serve warm.

Savory Party Bread

It's impossible to stop nibbling on warm pieces of this cheesy, oniony snack. The easy loaf fans out for a fun presentation. Want to get a jump on the prep work? Slice and fill the bread a day in advance. Right before guests arrive, add the butter, onions and poppy seeds, then bake.

—**KAY DALY** RALEIGH, NC

START TO FINISH: 30 MIN.
MAKES: 8 SERVINGS

- 1 **unsliced round loaf sourdough bread (1 pound)**
- 1 **pound Monterey Jack cheese**
- ½ **cup butter, melted**
- ½ **cup chopped green onions**
- 2 **to 3 teaspoons poppy seeds**

1. Preheat oven to 350°. Cut the sourdough bread crosswise into 1-in. slices to within ½ in. of the bottom of the loaf. Repeat cuts in the opposite direction. Cut cheese into ¼-in. slices; cut the slices into small pieces. Place cheese in cuts.

2. In a small bowl, mix the butter, green onions and poppy seeds; drizzle over the bread. Wrap in foil; place on a baking sheet. Bake 15 minutes. Unwrap; bake 10 minutes longer or until cheese is melted.

SAVORY PARTY BREAD

"My mother's Butter Nut Twists recipe was first published in *Taste of Home* magazine years ago. She always smiled when I told her about the phone calls I got from women around the country saying how much they loved it. It's wonderful that her special treat is enjoyed by families from coast to coast."

—**JOYCE HALLISEY** MOUNT GILEAD, NC

BUTTER NUT TWISTS

Butter Nut Twists

PREP: 30 MIN. + CHILLING • **BAKE:** 15 MIN.
MAKES: 6 DOZEN

- 2 **packages (¼ ounce each) active dry yeast**
- ¼ **cup warm water (110° to 115°)**
- 4 **cups all-purpose flour**
- ⅓ **cup sugar**
- ½ **teaspoon salt**
- 1 **cup cold butter, cubed**
- ¾ **cup buttermilk**
- 2 **eggs, lightly beaten**

FILLING

- 2 **cups ground walnuts (8 ounces)**
- 1 **cup flaked coconut**
- ⅓ **cup sugar**
- 4½ **teaspoons butter, melted**

1. In a small bowl, dissolve yeast in warm water. In a large bowl, mix the flour, sugar and salt. Cut in the butter until crumbly. Add the buttermilk, eggs and yeast mixture; stir to form a soft dough. Cover with plastic wrap; refrigerate overnight.

2. In another bowl, mix the filling ingredients. Punch down the dough; divide into three portions. On a sugared surface, roll one portion into a 12-in. x 9-in. rectangle. Sprinkle ⅓ cup filling lengthwise down one half of the dough. Fold dough in half over filling, forming a 12-in. x 4½-in. rectangle; pat down to press filling into dough. Seal the edges.

3. Sprinkle an additional ⅓ cup filling down one half of the folded dough. Fold in half again, forming a 12-in. x 2¼-in. rectangle. Press to form a 12-in. x 4-in. rectangle. Cut into twenty-four ½-in. slices. Repeat with the remaining dough and additional filling. Twist each slice one time and roll in the remaining filling; place 2 in. apart on greased baking sheets.

4. Bake at 350° for 15-18 minutes or until golden brown. Remove from pans to wire racks; serve warm or at room temperature.

Sour Cream-Pumpkin Coffee Cake

A spiced pumpkin filling is the yummy surprise inside my tender, streusel-topped coffee cake. It lends seasonal flavor to any fall breakfast or brunch.

—**RACHEL DODD** AVONDALE, AZ

PREP: 30 MIN. • **BAKE:** 45 MIN. + COOLING
MAKES: 15 SERVINGS

- 1 cup packed brown sugar
- ¼ cup all-purpose flour
- 2 teaspoons pumpkin pie spice
- ⅓ cup cold butter
- 1 cup chopped pecans

BATTER

- ½ cup butter, softened
- ¾ cup sugar
- 3 eggs
- 1 teaspoon vanilla extract
- 2 cups all-purpose flour
- 1 teaspoon baking powder
- 1 teaspoon baking soda
- 1 cup (8 ounces) sour cream

FILLING

- 1 can (15 ounces) solid-pack pumpkin
- 1 egg, lightly beaten
- ⅓ cup sugar
- 1 teaspoon pumpkin pie spice

1. In a small bowl, combine the brown sugar, flour and pumpkin pie spice. Cut in butter until crumbly. Stir in pecans; set aside.

2. In a large bowl, cream butter and sugar until light and fluffy. Beat in the eggs, one at a time. Stir in the vanilla. Combine the flour, baking powder and baking soda; add to creamed mixture alternately with sour cream.

3. Spread half of batter into a greased 13-in. x 9-in. baking dish. Sprinkle with half of the streusel. Combine the pumpkin, egg, sugar and pumpkin pie spice; drop by tablespoonfuls over streusel and spread evenly. Top with the remaining batter. Sprinkle with the remaining streusel.

4. Bake at 325° for 45-50 minutes or until a toothpick inserted near the center comes out clean. Cool on a wire rack.

FAST FIX
Buttery Apple Biscuits

START TO FINISH: 30 MIN.
MAKES: 6 BISCUITS

- 1 cup self-rising flour
- 1½ teaspoons sugar
  Pinch salt
- 3 tablespoons cold butter
- 1 egg, lightly beaten
- 2 tablespoons fat-free milk
- 1 tablespoon molasses
- ½ cup chopped peeled tart apple

1. In a small bowl, combine the flour, sugar and salt. Cut in the butter until mixture resembles coarse crumbs.

Combine the egg, milk and molasses; stir into the flour mixture just until moistened. Stir in the apple. Turn the dough onto a lightly floured surface; knead 8-10 times.

2. Pat or roll out to ½-in. thickness; cut with a floured 2½-in. biscuit cutter. Place 2 in. apart on a baking sheet coated with cooking spray. Bake at 425° for 6-8 minutes or until golden brown. Serve warm.

NOTE *As a substitute for 1 cup of self-rising flour, place 1½ teaspoons baking powder and ½ teaspoon salt in a measuring cup. Add all-purpose flour to measure 1 cup.*

"What better way to start the morning than with home-style biscuits made with apple and molasses? Fix a double batch and freeze half for busier days."
—**ATHENA RUSSELL** FLORENCE, SC

BUTTERY APPLE BISCUITS

top tip

Glaze from the Microwave

While visiting my mother-in-law, I learned how to make a quick glaze. Simply spoon the desired amount of store-bought vanilla frosting out of its can and place the frosting in a microwave-safe measuring cup. Warm it in the microwave, stirring frequently, until it reaches the right consistency. Then drizzle it over coffee cake, cinnamon buns—whatever!
—**RACHEL LOVE** WILMORE, KY

JACKIE RUCKWARDT'S
LOADED-UP PRETZEL
COOKIES *PAGE 95*

Cookies, Bars & Candies

How do you make **sweet tooths smile**? It's easy! Just pack your cookie jars, gift tins, treat platters and candy dishes with any of the **family-favorite goodies** in this chapter.

**JEANNIE GALLANT'S
MARVELOUS MAPLE FUDGE**
PAGE 96

**JOANN BELACK'S
CHOCOLATE-COVERED ALMOND
BUTTER BRICKLE** PAGE 96

**MILDRED KELLER'S
BAKE-SALE LEMON BARS**
PAGE 104

Chocolate Chai Snickerdoodles

I used to think snickerdoodles could never be improved—until I tasted these!

—KATIE WOLLGAST FLORISSANT, MO

PREP: 30 MIN. • **BAKE:** 10 MIN./BATCH
MAKES: ABOUT 3 DOZEN

- 2¼ cups sugar
- 1 teaspoon each ground ginger, cardamom and cinnamon
- ½ teaspoon ground allspice
- ¼ teaspoon white pepper
- 1 cup butter, softened
- 2 eggs
- 2 teaspoons vanilla extract
- 2¼ cups all-purpose flour
- ½ cup baking cocoa
- 2 teaspoons cream of tartar
- 1½ teaspoons baking powder
- ½ teaspoon salt

1. Preheat oven to 350°. In a large bowl, combine sugar and spices. Remove ½ cup sugar mixture to a shallow dish.

2. Add butter to remaining sugar mixture; beat until light and fluffy. Beat in the eggs and vanilla. In another bowl, whisk flour, baking cocoa, cream of tartar, baking powder and salt; gradually beat into creamed mixture.

3. Shape dough into 1½-in. balls. Roll in reserved sugar mixture; place 2 in. apart on ungreased baking sheets. Flatten slightly with bottom of a glass. Bake 10-12 minutes or until edges are firm. Remove to wire racks to cool.

CHOCOLATE CHAI SNICKERDOODLES

BLACKBERRY CHEESECAKE BARS

Blackberry Cheesecake Bars

Refrigerated dough makes a quick and easy crust for bars. I top it with a lemony cheesecake layer, spreadable fruit and beautiful fresh blackberries.

—TERRI CRANDALL GARDNERVILLE, NV

PREP: 30 MIN. • **BAKE:** 20 MIN. + COOLING
MAKES: 12 SERVINGS

- 1 tube (16½ ounces) refrigerated sugar cookie dough
- 1½ cups ricotta cheese
- 1 carton (8 ounces) mascarpone cheese
- ½ cup sugar
- 2 eggs, lightly beaten
- 3 teaspoons vanilla extract
- 2 teaspoons grated lemon peel
- 1 teaspoon lemon juice
- 1 teaspoon orange juice
- 1 tablespoon amaretto, optional
- 1 cup seedless blackberry spreadable fruit
- 2⅔ cups fresh blackberries

1. Preheat oven to 375°. Let cookie dough stand at room temperature for 5 minutes to soften. Press onto the bottom and 1 in. up the sides of a greased 13-in. x 9-in. baking dish. Bake 12-15 minutes or until golden brown. Cool on a wire rack.

2. Meanwhile, in a large bowl, beat ricotta cheese, mascarpone cheese and sugar until blended. Add eggs; beat on low speed just until combined. Stir in the vanilla, lemon peel, citrus juices and, if desired, amaretto. Pour into the crust.

3. Bake 20-25 minutes or until the center is almost set. Cool 1 hour on a wire rack.

4. Place the spreadable fruit in a small microwave-safe bowl; microwave on high for 30-45 seconds or until melted. Spread over cheesecake layer; top with blackberries. Refrigerate until serving.

Pistachio-Cranberry Rugelach

For the Christmas season, I dressed up traditional rugelach with pistachios, dried cranberries and white icing. The cookies are rich and not too sweet.

—**DEBORAH HINOJOSA** SARATOGA, CA

PREP: 30 MIN. + CHILLING
BAKE: 20 MIN./BATCH + COOLING
MAKES: 4 DOZEN

- 1 cup butter, softened
- 1 package (8 ounces) cream cheese, softened
- 1 teaspoon salt
- ¼ cup heavy whipping cream
- 2½ cups all-purpose flour
- 1 cup dried cranberries, coarsely chopped
- 1 cup finely chopped pistachios
- ¼ cup sugar
- 1¼ teaspoons ground cinnamon
- ¼ cup butter, melted
- 1⅓ cups confectioners' sugar
- ½ teaspoon vanilla extract
- 1 to 2 tablespoons water

1. In a large bowl, cream the softened butter, cream cheese and salt until blended; beat in the cream. Gradually beat in the flour.

2. Divide dough into four portions. Shape each into a disk; wrap in plastic wrap. Refrigerate for 30 minutes or until easy to handle. In a small bowl, combine the cranberries, pistachios, sugar and cinnamon; set aside.

3. Working with one portion of the dough at a time, roll each into a 12-in. circle on a lightly floured surface. Brush with one fourth of the melted butter. Sprinkle with one fourth of the cranberry mixture, pressing lightly to adhere. Cut dough into 12 wedges. Roll up wedges from the wide ends; place 2 in. apart on greased baking sheets, point side down.

4. Bake at 325° for 20-25 minutes or until bottoms are browned. Remove from the pans to wire racks to cool completely.

5. In a small bowl, mix confectioners' sugar, vanilla and enough water to reach the desired consistency. Drizzle over cookies.

ORANGE & LEMON WAFER COOKIES

Loaded-Up Pretzel Cookies

Packed with coconut, M&M's and pretzels, these chunky goodies will keep friends and family coming back for more.

—**JACKIE RUCKWARDT** COTTAGE GROVE, OR

PREP: 20 MIN. • **BAKE:** 15 MIN./BATCH
MAKES: 2 DOZEN

- 1 cup butter, softened
- 1 cup sugar
- 1 cup packed brown sugar
- 2 eggs
- 2 teaspoons vanilla extract
- 2½ cups all-purpose flour
- 1 teaspoon baking powder
- 1 teaspoon baking soda
- 1 teaspoon salt
- 2 cups miniature pretzels, broken
- 1½ cups flaked coconut
- 1½ cups milk chocolate M&M's

1. Preheat oven to 350°. In a large bowl, cream the butter and sugars until light and fluffy. Beat in eggs and vanilla. In another bowl, whisk flour, baking powder, baking soda and salt; gradually beat into creamed mixture. Stir in remaining ingredients.

2. Shape ¼ cupfuls of dough into balls; place 3 in. apart on ungreased baking sheets. Bake 12-14 minutes or until golden brown. Remove from the pans to wire racks to cool.

Orange & Lemon Wafer Cookies

Here's the perfect treat to pair with your afternoon cup of coffee or tea. The citrus flavor is wonderfully refreshing.

—**PATRICIA SWART** GALLOWAY, NJ

PREP: 25 MIN. • **BAKE:** 10 MIN./BATCH
MAKES: ABOUT 4 DOZEN

- ½ cup unsalted butter, softened
- ¾ cup sugar
- 1 egg
- 2 teaspoons grated orange peel
- 1 teaspoon grated lemon peel
- 1 teaspoon vanilla extract
- 1 teaspoon orange extract
- 1 cup all-purpose flour
- 5 teaspoons cornstarch
- ¼ teaspoon baking soda
- ¼ teaspoon salt
  Thin orange or lemon peel strips, optional

1. In a mixing bowl, cream the butter and sugar until light and fluffy. Beat in the egg, orange peel, lemon peel and extracts. In another bowl, mix the flour, cornstarch, baking soda and salt; gradually beat into creamed mixture.

2. Drop by rounded teaspoonfuls 2 in. apart onto parchment paper-lined baking sheets. If desired, top with orange peel strips.

3. Bake at 350° for 6-8 minutes or until edges are golden brown. Remove from pans to wire racks to cool.

MARVELOUS MAPLE FUDGE

Marvelous Maple Fudge

Want to break away from the same old fudge recipe? Add a bit of maple flavoring for a distinctive taste treat.

—JEANNIE GALLANT CHARLOTTETOWN, PE

PREP: 10 MIN. • **COOK:** 20 MIN. + COOLING
MAKES: 1¾ POUNDS (64 PIECES)

- 1 **teaspoon plus 1 cup butter, divided**
- 2 **cups packed brown sugar**
- 1 **can (5 ounces) evaporated milk**
- 1 **teaspoon maple flavoring**
- ½ **teaspoon vanilla extract**
- ⅛ **teaspoon salt**
- 2 **cups confectioners' sugar**

1. Line an 8-in. square pan with foil; grease the foil with 1 teaspoon butter.

2. Cube remaining butter. In a large saucepan, combine the cubed butter, brown sugar and milk. Bring to a full boil over medium heat, stirring constantly. Cook 10 minutes, stirring frequently. Remove from heat.

3. Stir in the maple flavoring, vanilla and salt. Add the confectioners' sugar; beat on medium speed 2 minutes or until smooth. Immediately spread into the prepared pan. Cool completely.

4. Using foil, lift fudge out of pan. Remove foil; cut into 1-in. squares. Store in an airtight container.

Chocolate-Covered Almond Butter Brickle

I love this soft brittle because the texture is delightfully different, and the flavors remind me of one of my favorite candy bars.

—JOANN BELACK BRADENTON, FL

PREP: 10 MIN. • **COOK:** 20 MIN. + CHILLING
MAKES: ABOUT 1¾ POUNDS

- 1½ **teaspoons plus 2 tablespoons unsalted butter, divided**
- 1 **cup crunchy almond butter**
- ½ **teaspoon baking soda**
- 1 **teaspoon plus 2 tablespoons water, divided**

- ¾ **cup sugar**
- ¾ **cup light corn syrup**
- 1 **teaspoon almond extract**
- 1 **cup 60% cacao bittersweet chocolate baking chips**
- ⅓ **cup chopped almonds, toasted**
- ¾ **cup flaked coconut**

1. Grease a 15-in. x 10-in. x 1-in. pan with 1½ teaspoons butter. Place almond butter in a microwave-safe bowl; microwave, covered, at 50% power for 30-60 seconds or until softened, stirring once. In a small bowl, dissolve the baking soda in 1 teaspoon water. Set aside almond butter and baking soda mixture.

2. In a large heavy saucepan, combine the sugar, corn syrup and 2 tablespoons water. Bring to a boil over medium heat, stirring constantly. Using a pastry brush dipped in water, wash down the sides of the pan to eliminate sugar crystals. Cook until a candy thermometer reads 240° (soft-ball stage), stirring occasionally, about 10 minutes. Add the remaining butter; cook until candy thermometer reads 300° (hard-crack stage), stirring frequently, about 5 minutes longer.

3. Remove from the heat; stir in the softened almond butter, almond extract and dissolved baking soda. (Candy will foam.) Immediately pour into prepared pan. Spread to ¼-inch thickness.

4. Sprinkle with chocolate chips; let stand until chocolate begins to melt. Spread evenly; sprinkle with the almonds and coconut, pressing slightly to adhere. Cool slightly. Refrigerate for 1 hour or until chocolate is set.

5. Break candy into pieces. Store between layers of waxed paper in an airtight container.

NOTE *To toast nuts, spread in a 15-in. x 10-in. x 1-in. baking pan. Bake at 350° for 5-10 minutes or until lightly browned, stirring occasionally. Or, spread in a dry nonstick skillet and heat over low heat until lightly browned, stirring occasionally.*

CHOCOLATE-COVERED ALMOND BUTTER BRICKLE

PUMPKIN CREAM CHEESE BARS

Very Chocolate Chip Brownies

These rich brownies get a double dose of chocolate. Semisweet chips dot each one—and melted chips are mixed into the batter!
—**JAN MOCK** DILLON, MT

PREP: 15 MIN. • **BAKE:** 35 MIN. + COOLING • **MAKES:** 3 DOZEN

1½ cups sugar
⅔ cup butter, cubed
¼ cup water
4 cups (24 ounces) semisweet chocolate chips, divided
4 eggs
2 teaspoons vanilla extract
1½ cups all-purpose flour
½ teaspoon baking soda
½ teaspoon salt
  Confectioners' sugar

1. In a large heavy saucepan, combine the sugar, butter and water; bring to a boil, stirring constantly. Remove from the heat; stir in 2 cups semisweet chocolate chips until melted. Cool slightly.

2. In a large bowl, beat eggs and vanilla; stir in chocolate mixture. In another bowl, mix the flour, baking soda and salt; gradually add to chocolate mixture, mixing well. Stir in remaining chocolate chips.

3. Spread into a greased 13-in. x 9-in. baking pan. Bake at 325° for 35-40 minutes or until a toothpick inserted into the center comes out clean. Cool completely in the pan on a wire rack.

4. Sprinkle with confectioners' sugar. Cut into bars. Store in an airtight container.

"Pumpkin Cream Cheese Bars always go over big. When I brought them to a church function, there was barely a crumb left on the platter! Everyone likes the smooth filling, spices and crumbly pecan topping." —**KIM CHAMBERS** LAURELTON, NY

Pumpkin Cream Cheese Bars

PREP: 25 MIN. • **BAKE:** 35 MIN. + COOLING • **MAKES:** 2 DOZEN

1⅓ cups all-purpose flour
¾ cup sugar, divided
½ cup packed brown sugar
¾ cup cold butter, cubed
1 cup old-fashioned oats
½ cup chopped pecans
1 package (8 ounces) cream cheese, softened, cubed
2 teaspoons ground cinnamon
1 teaspoon ground allspice
1 teaspoon ground cardamom
1 can (15 ounces) solid-pack pumpkin
1 teaspoon vanilla extract
3 eggs, lightly beaten

1. Preheat oven to 350°. In a small bowl, mix flour, ¼ cup sugar and brown sugar; cut in butter until crumbly. Stir in oats and pecans. Reserve 1 cup for topping.

2. Press the remaining crumb mixture onto bottom of a greased 13-in. x 9-in. baking pan. Bake 15 minutes.

3. In a small bowl, beat cream cheese, spices and remaining sugar until smooth. Beat in pumpkin and vanilla. Add eggs; beat on low speed just until blended. Pour over warm crust; sprinkle with reserved crumb mixture.

4. Bake 20-25 minutes or until a knife inserted near the center comes out clean and filling is set. Cool on a wire rack. Serve or refrigerate, covered, within 2 hours. Cut into bars.

VERY CHOCOLATE CHIP BROWNIES

(5)INGREDIENTS
Snow-Puffed Meringues

I turn feather-light meringues into sandwich cookies by adding a layer of Nutella hazelnut spread between them. If you prefer, skip that step and simply dust the top of each baked treat with cocoa.

—LORRAINE CALAND SHUNIAH, ON

PREP: 20 MIN. • **BAKE:** 45 MIN. + COOLING
MAKES: ABOUT 3 DOZEN

- 4 egg whites
- ½ teaspoon vanilla extract
- ¼ teaspoon salt
- ½ cup sugar
- 1 cup confectioners' sugar
- ⅓ cup Nutella

1. Place the egg whites in a large bowl; let stand at room temperature for 30 minutes.

2. Add the vanilla and salt to the egg whites; beat on medium speed until foamy. Gradually add sugar, 1 tablespoon at a time, beating on high after each addition until the sugar is dissolved. Continue beating until stiff glossy peaks form. Fold in the confectioners' sugar.

3. Cut a small hole in the tip of a pastry bag or in a corner of a food-safe plastic bag; insert a #96 star tip. Transfer the meringue to the bag. Pipe 1½-in.-diameter cookies 2 in. apart onto parchment paper-lined baking sheets.

4. Bake at 225° for 45-50 minutes or until firm to the touch. Turn the oven off (do not open the oven door); leave the meringues in oven for 1½ hours. Remove from oven; cool completely on baking sheets.

5. Remove the meringues from paper. Spread Nutella on the bottoms of half of the cookies; cover with remaining cookies. Store in airtight containers at room temperature.

Watermelon Slice Cookies

When I made these "melons" for an event, a neighbor of mine was so impressed that she froze one to show friends!

—SUE ANN BENHAM VALPARAISO, IN

PREP: 25 MIN. + CHILLING
BAKE: 10 MIN./BATCH
MAKES: ABOUT 3 DOZEN

- ¾ cup butter, softened
- ¾ cup sugar
- 1 egg
- ½ teaspoon almond extract
- 2 cups all-purpose flour
- ¼ teaspoon baking powder
- ⅛ teaspoon salt
  Red and green gel food coloring
- ⅓ cup miniature semisweet chocolate chips or raisins, chopped
- 1 teaspoon sesame seeds, optional

1. In a large bowl, cream the butter and sugar until light and fluffy. Beat in the egg and extract. In another bowl, whisk flour, baking powder and salt; gradually beat into creamed mixture. Reserve 1 cup dough.

2. Tint the remaining dough red; shape into a 3½-in.-long roll. Wrap in plastic wrap. Tint ⅓ cup of reserved dough green; wrap in plastic wrap. Wrap the remaining plain dough. Refrigerate 2 hours or until firm.

3. On a lightly floured surface, roll the plain dough into an 8½-in. x 3½-in. rectangle. Unwrap the red dough and place on a short end of the plain dough; roll up.

4. Roll green dough into a 10-in. x 3½-in. rectangle. Place the red and plain roll on a short end of the green dough; roll up. Wrap in plastic wrap; refrigerate overnight.

5. Preheat oven to 350°. Unwrap and cut the dough into ³⁄₁₆-in. slices (just less than ¼ in.). Place 2 in. apart on ungreased baking sheets. Lightly press chocolate chips and sesame seeds if desired into red dough to resemble watermelon seeds.

6. Bake 9-11 minutes or until firm. Immediately cut the cookies in half. Remove to wire racks to cool.

WATERMELON SLICE COOKIES

Raspberry Linzer Bars

Want something extra-special that will appeal to adults and kids alike? Look here! Raspberry preserves, lemon, cinnamon and almonds make a sophisticated but yummy combination.

—HOLLY CAIN ST. PETERSBURG, FL

PREP: 15 MIN. • **BAKE:** 35 MIN. + COOLING
MAKES: 18 BARS

- 1⅓ cups butter, softened
- ¾ cup sugar
- 1 egg
- 1 teaspoon grated lemon peel
- 2½ cups all-purpose flour
- 2 cups ground almonds
- 1 teaspoon ground cinnamon
- 1 cup seedless raspberry preserves
  Confectioners' sugar, optional

1. In a large bowl, cream the butter and sugar until light and fluffy. Beat in the egg and lemon peel. In another bowl, mix the flour, ground almonds and cinnamon; gradually beat into the creamed mixture.

2. Press 2 cups of the dough onto the bottom of a greased 13-in. x 9-in. baking pan. Spread with raspberry preserves. Crumble remaining dough over preserves.

3. Bake at 350° for 35-40 minutes or until lightly browned. Cool completely on a wire rack.

4. Sprinkle with confectioners' sugar if desired; cut into bars.

Mackinac Fudge

A lady at my parents' church gave me this recipe—a version of the famous fudge named for Michigan's Mackinac Island. I sometimes pipe a bit of decorating icing on each piece for a festive presentation during the Christmas season.

—KRISTEN EKHOFF AKRON, IN

PREP: 5 MIN. • **COOK:** 25 MIN. + CHILLING
MAKES: 3 POUNDS (117 PIECES)

- 2 teaspoons plus 1 cup butter, divided
- 4 cups sugar
- 1 cup 2% milk
- 25 large marshmallows
- 1 package (11½ ounces) milk chocolate chips
- 2 cups (12 ounces) semisweet chocolate chips
- 2 ounces unsweetened chocolate, chopped
- 1 teaspoon vanilla extract
  Decorating icing and sprinkles, optional

1. Line a 13-in. x 9-in. pan with foil; grease the foil with 2 teaspoons butter.

2. In a large heavy saucepan, combine the sugar, milk and remaining butter. Bring to a rapid boil over medium heat, stirring constantly. Cook, without stirring, for 2 minutes. Remove from the heat.

3. Stir in marshmallows until melted. Add all chocolate; stir until melted. Stir in vanilla. Immediately spread into prepared pan; cool for 1 hour.

4. Score into 1-in. squares. Refrigerate, covered, for 3 hours or until firm. Using the foil, lift out fudge. Remove foil; cut fudge. Store between layers of waxed paper in airtight containers. Decorate as desired.

MACKINAC FUDGE

Cheers for Cherries

Whether tart or sweet, ruby-red cherries make tongue-tingling additions to cookies, candies, bars and other treats. Take your pick of the guaranteed-to-please goodies here.

CANDIED FRUITCAKE SQUARES

Candied Fruitcake Squares

Even people who say they don't care for traditional versions of fruitcake can't resist sampling one of these chunky, colorful bars. After that first bite, I hear raves—and then watch the squares disappear!

—**NANCY JOHNSON** LAVERNE, OK

PREP: 30 MIN. • **BAKE:** 35 MIN. + COOLING • **MAKES:** ABOUT 5 DOZEN

- ½ cup all-purpose flour
- ½ teaspoon baking powder
- ¼ teaspoon salt
- 1¼ cups chopped dates
- ¾ cup chopped candied pineapple
- ¾ cup chopped red candied cherries
- 1 egg
- ¼ cup packed light brown sugar
- ½ teaspoon vanilla extract
- 2 cups pecan halves

1. Line an 8-in. square baking dish with parchment paper, letting ends extend up sides of pan; grease and set aside.
2. In a large bowl, mix the flour, baking powder and salt. Add the dates, pineapple and cherries; toss to coat. In a small bowl, whisk the egg, brown sugar and vanilla until blended; stir into fruit mixture. Stir in pecans. Press firmly into prepared baking dish.

3. Bake at 325° for 35-40 minutes or until a toothpick inserted into center comes out clean and top is golden. Cool in pan for 10 minutes. Using parchment paper, transfer to a wire rack. Remove paper; cool fruitcake completely.
4. Using a serrated knife, cut into 1-in. squares. Store in an airtight container.

Lime Shortbread with Dried Cherries

My slice-and-bake recipe also works well with dried cranberries and orange zest in place of the cherries and lime.

—**ABIGAIL BOSTWICK** TOMAHAWK, WI

PREP: 25 MIN. + CHILLING • **BAKE:** 10 MIN./BATCH
MAKES: ABOUT 5 DOZEN

- 1 cup butter, softened
- ¾ cup confectioners' sugar
- 1 tablespoon grated lime peel
- 2 teaspoons vanilla extract
- ½ teaspoon almond extract
- 2 cups all-purpose flour
- ¼ teaspoon baking powder
- ⅛ teaspoon salt
- ½ cup chopped dried cherries

1. In a large bowl, cream butter and confectioners' sugar until blended. Beat in the lime peel and extracts. In another bowl, mix flour, baking powder and salt; gradually beat into creamed mixture. Stir in cherries.
2. Divide dough in half; shape each into a 7-in.-long roll. Wrap in plastic wrap; refrigerate 3-4 hours or until firm.
3. Preheat oven to 350°. Unwrap and cut dough crosswise into ¼-in. slices. Place 2 in. apart on ungreased baking sheets. Bake 9-11 minutes or until edges are golden brown. Remove from pans to wire racks to cool.

LIME SHORTBREAD WITH DRIED CHERRIES

CHEWY GOOD OATMEAL COOKIES

1. Preheat oven to 350°. In a large bowl, cream butter and sugars until light and fluffy. Beat in the eggs, honey and vanilla. In another bowl, mix the oats, flour, baking soda, salt and cinnamon; gradually beat into creamed mixture. Stir in the remaining ingredients.

2. Drop dough by rounded tablespoonfuls 2 in. apart onto greased baking sheets. Bake 10-12 minutes or until golden brown. Cool on pan 2 minutes; remove to wire racks to cool.

(5) INGREDIENTS

Chocolate Rum-Soaked Cherries

I adore chocolate-covered cherries and make this homemade version to give loved ones at Christmastime. For even more holiday cheer, include cola and a mini bottle of rum with your gift.
—**CATHERINE SCHULTZ** RACINE, WI

PREP: 15 MIN. + SOAKING • **COOK:** 5 MIN. • **MAKES:** 2½ DOZEN

- 1 jar (10 ounces) maraschino cherries (with stems), drained
- ½ cup rum or brandy
- 4 ounces bittersweet chocolate, chopped
- 1 teaspoon shortening

1. Place the cherries in a bowl; cover with rum. Refrigerate, covered, overnight. Drain and pat dry.

2. In a microwave, melt the chocolate and shortening; stir until smooth. Holding the stems, dip the cherries in the chocolate mixture; allow excess to drip off. Place on waxed paper; let stand until set.

CHOCOLATE RUM-SOAKED CHERRIES

Chewy Good Oatmeal Cookies

Here's a wonderful oatmeal cookie loaded with all of my favorites, including white chocolate chips and crunchy macadamia nuts.
—**SANDY HARZ** GRAND HAVEN, MI

PREP: 20 MIN. • **BAKE:** 10 MIN. /BATCH • **MAKES:** 3½ DOZEN

- 1 cup butter, softened
- 1 cup packed brown sugar
- ½ cup sugar
- 2 eggs
- 1 tablespoon honey
- 2 teaspoons vanilla extract
- 2½ cups quick-cooking oats
- 1½ cups all-purpose flour
- 1 teaspoon baking soda
- ½ teaspoon salt
- ½ teaspoon ground cinnamon
- 1⅓ cups dried cherries
- 1 cup white baking chips
- 1 cup (4 ounces) chopped macadamia nuts

Maple-Glazed Cinnamon Chip Bars

Cinnamon chips and a maple glaze give these bars fabulous flavor and a pretty look. When I bake them, the aroma in the kitchen reminds me of Christmas.
—**LYNDI PILCH** SPRINGFIELD, MO

PREP: 20 MIN. • **BAKE:** 20 MIN.
MAKES: 2 DOZEN

- 1 **cup butter, softened**
- 2 **cups packed brown sugar**
- 2 **eggs**
- 2 **teaspoons vanilla extract**
- 2⅔ **cups all-purpose flour**
- 2 **teaspoons baking powder**
- 1 **teaspoon salt**
- ¾ **cup cinnamon baking chips**
- 1 **tablespoon cinnamon-sugar**

GLAZE
- ½ **cup confectioners' sugar**
- 3 **tablespoons maple syrup**
- ½ **teaspoon vanilla extract**

1. In a large bowl, cream butter and brown sugar until well blended. Beat in eggs and vanilla. In another bowl, mix the flour, baking powder and salt; gradually beat into creamed mixture. Stir in cinnamon chips.
2. Spread into a greased 13-in. x 9-in. baking pan. Sprinkle with cinnamon-sugar. Bake at 350° for 20-25 minutes or until golden brown and a toothpick inserted into center comes out clean. Cool completely in pan on a wire rack.
3. In a small bowl, mix all glaze ingredients until smooth; drizzle glaze over the top. Cut into bars. Store in an airtight container.

SCHOOLHOUSE PEANUT BRITTLE

MAPLE-GLAZED CINNAMON CHIP BARS

Schoolhouse Peanut Brittle

I've been making brittle for years. I prefer it thin, which means spreading it quickly. If you want it thicker, you can add a few seconds to your spreading window!
—**BESS KUZMA** DENVER, CO

PREP: 5 MIN. • **COOK:** 50 MIN. + COOLING
MAKES: 2¾ POUNDS

- 3 **cups sugar**
- 2 **cups water**
- ¾ **cup light corn syrup**
- ¾ **cup dark corn syrup**
- 2 **cups Spanish or cocktail peanuts**
- 2 **tablespoons butter, cubed**
- 1 **tablespoon baking soda**
- 1 **teaspoon vanilla extract**

1. Line three 15-in. x 10-in. x 1-in. pans with parchment paper. (Do not spray or grease.)
2. In a large heavy saucepan, combine the sugar, water and corn syrups.

Bring to a boil, stirring constantly to dissolve sugar. Using a pastry brush dipped in water, wash down the sides of the pan to eliminate sugar crystals. Cook, without stirring, over medium heat until a candy thermometer reads 260° (hard-ball stage).
3. Stir in the peanuts and butter; cook to 300° (hard-crack stage), about 9 minutes longer, stirring frequently.
4. Remove from the heat; stir in the baking soda and vanilla. (The mixture will foam.) Immediately pour into the prepared pans, spreading as thin as possible. Cool completely.
5. Break the brittle into pieces. Store between layers of waxed paper in airtight containers.
NOTE *We recommend that you test your candy thermometer before each use by bringing water to a boil; the thermometer should read 212°. Adjust your recipe temperature up or down based on your test.*

Honey-Pecan Squares

When we left Texas to move north, one of our neighbors gave me pecans from his trees. I'm happy to send him batches of my nutty, honey-sweetened squares.

—LORRAINE CALAND SHUNIAH, ON

PREP: 15 MIN. • **BAKE:** 30 MIN.
MAKES: 2 DOZEN

- 1 cup unsalted butter, softened
- ¾ cup packed dark brown sugar
- ½ teaspoon salt
- 3 cups all-purpose flour

FILLING
- ½ cup unsalted butter, cubed
- ½ cup packed dark brown sugar
- ⅓ cup honey
- 2 tablespoons sugar
- 2 tablespoons heavy whipping cream
- ¼ teaspoon salt
- 2 cups chopped pecans, toasted
- ½ teaspoon maple flavoring or vanilla extract

1. Preheat oven to 350°. Line a 13-in. x 9-in. baking pan with parchment paper, letting ends extend up sides of pan. In a large bowl, cream the butter, brown sugar and salt until light and fluffy. Gradually beat in the flour. Press into prepared pan. Bake 16-20 minutes or until lightly browned.
2. In a small saucepan, combine the first six filling ingredients; bring to a boil. Cook 1 minute. Remove from the heat; stir in nuts and maple flavoring. Pour over crust.
3. Bake 10-15 minutes or until bubbly. Cool in pan on a wire rack. Lifting with parchment paper, transfer to a cutting board; cut into bars.

NOTE *To toast nuts, spread in a 15-in. x 10-in. x 1-in. baking pan. Bake at 350° for 5-10 minutes or until lightly browned, stirring occasionally. Or, spread in a dry nonstick skillet and heat over low heat until lightly browned, stirring occasionally.*

? Did you know?

The difference between dark brown sugar and light brown sugar is that the dark variety has more molasses and a more intense flavor.

⑤ INGREDIENTS
Grandma's Divinity

PREP: 5 MIN. • **COOK:** 40 MIN. + STANDING
MAKES: 1½ POUNDS (60 PIECES)

- 2 egg whites
- 3 cups sugar
- ⅔ cup water
- ½ cup light corn syrup
- 1 teaspoon vanilla extract
- 1 cup chopped pecans

1. Place the egg whites in the bowl of a stand mixer; let stand at room temperature for 30 minutes. Meanwhile, line three 15-in. x 10-in. x 1-in. pans with waxed paper.
2. In a large heavy saucepan, combine the sugar, water and light corn syrup; bring to a boil, stirring constantly to dissolve sugar. Cook, without stirring, over medium heat until a candy thermometer reads 252° (hard-ball stage). Just before the temperature is reached, beat egg whites on medium speed until stiff peaks form.
3. Slowly add the hot sugar mixture in a thin stream over egg whites, beating constantly and scraping the sides of the bowl occasionally. Add the vanilla. Beat until the candy holds its shape, about 5-6 minutes. (Do not overmix or the candy will get stiff and crumbly.) Immediately fold in pecans.
4. Quickly drop mixture by heaping teaspoonfuls onto prepared pans. Let stand at room temperature until dry to the touch. Store between waxed paper in an airtight container at room temperature.

NOTE *We recommend that you test your candy thermometer before each use by bringing water to a boil; the thermometer should read 212°. Adjust your recipe temperature up or down based on your test.*

"These snowy white puffs of divinity hold a special place in my heart. They bring back wonderful memories of my grandmother and me when I was a young girl, and of her with my son and me when he was little." **—ANNE CLAYBORNE** WALLAND, TN

GRANDMA'S DIVINITY

Bake-Sale Lemon Bars

My cousin Bernice, a farmer's wife famous for cooking up feasts, gave me her recipe for tangy lemon bars. Am I glad she did!

—MILDRED KELLER ROCKFORD, IL

PREP: 10 MIN. • **BAKE:** 40 MIN. + COOLING
MAKES: 4 DOZEN

- ¾ cup butter, softened
- ⅔ cup confectioners' sugar
- 1½ cups plus 3 tablespoons all-purpose flour, divided
- 3 eggs, lightly beaten
- 1½ cups sugar
- ¼ cup lemon juice
  Additional confectioners' sugar

1. Preheat oven to 350°. In a large bowl, beat butter and confectioners' sugar until blended. Gradually beat in 1½ cups flour. Press onto the bottom of a greased 13-in. x 9-in. pan. Bake 18-20 minutes or until golden brown.

2. Meanwhile, in a small bowl, whisk eggs, sugar, lemon juice and remaining flour until frothy; pour over hot crust.

3. Bake 20-25 minutes longer or until topping is set and lightly browned. Cool completely on a wire rack. Dust with additional confectioners' sugar. Cut into bars. Refrigerate leftovers.

CREAMY ORANGE CARAMELS

BAKE-SALE LEMON BARS

Creamy Orange Caramels

I try making a new candy each Christmas. Last year, I started with my usual caramels and added a splash of orange extract for fun. I think buttered rum extract is next!

—SHELLY BEVINGTON-FISHER

HERMISTON, OR

PREP: 10 MIN. • **COOK:** 30 MIN.+ STANDING
MAKES: ABOUT 2½ POUNDS (80 PIECES)

- 1 teaspoon plus 1 cup butter, divided
- 2 cups sugar
- 1 cup light corn syrup
- 1 can (14 ounces) sweetened condensed milk
- 1 teaspoon orange extract
- 1 teaspoon vanilla extract

1. Line an 11-in. x 7-in. dish with foil; grease foil with 1 teaspoon butter.

2. In a large heavy saucepan, combine the sugar, corn syrup and remaining butter. Bring to a boil over medium heat, stirring constantly. Reduce heat to medium-low; boil gently, without stirring, for 4 minutes.

3. Remove from the heat; gradually stir in milk. Cook and stir until a candy thermometer reads 244°(firm-ball stage). Remove from the heat; stir in extracts. Immediately pour into the prepared dish (do not scrape the saucepan). Let stand until firm.

4. Using foil, lift out candy; remove foil. Using a buttered knife, cut caramel into 1-in. x ¾-in. pieces. Wrap individually in waxed paper; twist ends.

NOTE *We recommend that you test your candy thermometer before each use by bringing water to a boil; the thermometer should read 212°. Adjust your recipe temperature up or down based on your test.*

Chocolate-Drizzled Baklava

These little diamond-shaped pastries turn Old World baklava into easy-to-eat bars.

—**JESSE ZIPURSKY** SAN RAMON, CA

PREP: 1 HOUR • **BAKE:** 30 MIN. + STANDING
MAKES: 3 DOZEN

- 1⅔ cups finely chopped pecans
- 1⅔ cups finely chopped walnuts
- ½ cup sugar
- 1½ teaspoons ground cinnamon
- ½ teaspoon ground allspice
- ½ teaspoon ground cloves
- 1 cup butter, melted
- 24 sheets phyllo dough (14-inch x 9-inch size)

SYRUP
- 1 cup water
- 1 cup honey
- ½ cup sugar
- 1 teaspoon ground cinnamon
- 1 teaspoon vanilla extract

DRIZZLE
- 1 cup (6 ounces) dark chocolate chips
- 1 teaspoon shortening

1. Preheat oven to 350°. In a large bowl, mix the first six ingredients. Brush a 13-in. x 9-in. baking pan with some of the butter. Unroll the phyllo dough; trim to fit into pan.

2. Layer six sheets of phyllo dough in the prepared pan, brushing each with butter. Keep remaining phyllo dough covered with plastic wrap and a damp towel to prevent it from drying out. Sprinkle with a third of nut mixture. Repeat the layers twice. Top with the remaining phyllo sheets, brushing each with butter.

3. Using a sharp knife, cut into 1½-in. diamond shapes. Bake 30-35 minutes or until golden brown.

4. Meanwhile, in a saucepan, combine water, honey, sugar and cinnamon; bring to a boil. Reduce heat; simmer, uncovered, 10 minutes. Stir in vanilla.

5. Pour over the warm baklava. Cool completely in the pan on a wire rack. Cover and let stand for several hours or overnight.

6. In a microwave, melt the dark chocolate chips and shortening; stir until smooth. Drizzle over baklava; let stand until set.

Apricot Pinwheel Cookies

My grandmother always baked her pretty apricot pinwheels to serve during the holiday season. If you like, mix pecans and a bit of hazelnut liqueur into the filling.

—**ROBERT LOGAN** CLAYTON, CA

PREP: 45 MIN. + CHILLING
BAKE: 10 MIN./BATCH
MAKES: ABOUT 5 DOZEN

- ½ cup butter, softened
- ¾ cup sugar, divided
- ½ cup packed brown sugar
- 1 egg
- 1 teaspoon vanilla extract
- 2 cups all-purpose flour
- ¼ teaspoon baking soda
- ⅛ teaspoon salt
- 1½ cups finely chopped dried apricots or dates
- ⅔ cup water
- 1 tablespoon hazelnut liqueur, optional
- 1 cup finely chopped pecans, optional

1. In a large bowl, cream the butter, ½ cup sugar and brown sugar until light and fluffy. Beat in egg and vanilla. In another bowl, mix the flour, baking soda and salt; gradually beat into the creamed mixture. Divide dough in half. Shape each half into a thick rectangle; wrap in plastic wrap. Refrigerate until firm or overnight.

2. In a small saucepan, combine the apricots, water, remaining sugar and, if desired, liqueur; bring to a boil, stirring occasionally. Reduce heat to medium; cook until liquid is almost evaporated, about 5 minutes. Stir in pecans if desired; cool completely.

3. On a floured surface, roll each portion of dough into a 12-in. x 9-in. rectangle. Evenly spread half of the apricot mixture over each rectangle to within ½-in. of edges. Roll up jelly-roll style, starting with a long side; wrap in plastic wrap. Refrigerate for 2 hours or until firm.

4. Unwrap and cut into ¼-in. slices. Place 1 in. apart on greased baking sheets. Bake at 350° for 9-12 minutes or until golden brown. Remove from pans to wire racks to cool.

APRICOT PINWHEEL COOKIES

EDWINA GADSBY'S
CARAMELIZED APPLE
HAND PIES *PAGE 115*

Cakes & Pies

A **luscious homemade dessert** makes any meal extra special. Whether you choose a treat such as Cherry Cola Cake or Macadamia Key Lime Pie, you'll enjoy a **little slice of heaven**.

**CHERI MASON'S
CHERRY COLA CAKE**
PAGE 111

**PEGGY LINTON'S
CHOCOLATE ZUCCHINI CAKE**
PAGE 120

**KALLEE KRONG-MCCREERY'S
CITRUS SOUR CREAM PIE**
PAGE 119

Bananas & Cream Pound Cake

My creamy, layered banana dessert got me a date with my future husband. When he sampled a piece at a church event, he enjoyed it so much that he went back for seconds. The rest is history!

—**COURTNEY FARNON** CARTERSVILLE, GA

PREP: 20 MIN. • **BAKE:** 40 MIN. + CHILLING
MAKES: 15 SERVINGS

- ½ **cup butter, softened**
- 1½ **cups sugar**
- 3 **eggs**
- 1 **teaspoon vanilla extract**
- 1½ **cups all-purpose flour**
- ¼ **teaspoon salt**
- ⅛ **teaspoon baking soda**
- ½ **cup buttermilk**

LAYERS
- 2 **cups 2% milk**
- 1 **package (3.4 ounces) instant French vanilla pudding mix**
- 1 **package (8 ounces) cream cheese, softened**
- ½ **cup sweetened condensed milk**
- 1 **package (12 ounces) frozen whipped topping, thawed, divided**
- 5 **medium ripe bananas**

1. In a large bowl, cream butter and sugar until light and fluffy. Add eggs, one at a time, beating well after each addition. Beat in vanilla. In another bowl, mix flour, salt and baking soda; add to creamed mixture alternately with the buttermilk, beating after each addition just until combined.

BANANAS & CREAM POUND CAKE

2. Transfer to a greased and floured 9-in. x 5-in. loaf pan. Bake at 325° for 40-45 minutes or until a toothpick inserted into the center comes out clean. Cool in the pan for 10 minutes before removing to a wire rack to cool completely.

3. In a small bowl, whisk the milk and vanilla pudding mix for 2 minutes. Let stand for 2 minutes. Meanwhile, in a large bowl, beat the cream cheese and condensed milk until smooth; fold in vanilla pudding. Fold in 3½ cups whipped topping.

4. Cut cake into eight slices; arrange on bottom of an ungreased 13-in. x 9-in. dish, trimming to fit as necessary. Slice the bananas; arrange over cake. Spread pudding mixture over the top. Refrigerate, covered, for 3 hours. Serve with remaining whipped topping.

Mrs. Thompson's Carrot Cake

I received this recipe from the mother of a patient I cared for. It was, and still is, the best carrot cake I've ever tasted. My family members agree and always request it.

—**BECKY WACHOB** KELLY, WY

PREP: 30 MIN. • **BAKE:** 35 MIN.
MAKES: 15 SERVINGS

MRS. THOMPSON'S CARROT CAKE

- 3 **cups shredded carrots**
- 1 **can (20 ounces) crushed pineapple, well-drained**
- 2 **cups sugar**
- 1 **cup canola oil**
- 4 **eggs**
- 2 **cups all-purpose flour**
- 2 **teaspoons baking soda**
- 2 **teaspoons ground cinnamon**

FROSTING
- 1 **package (8 ounces) cream cheese, softened**
- ¼ **cup butter, softened**
- 2 **teaspoons vanilla extract**
- 3¾ **cups confectioners' sugar**

1. In a large bowl, beat the first five ingredients until well blended. In another bowl, mix the flour, baking soda and cinnamon; gradually beat into carrot mixture.

2. Transfer to a greased 13-in. x 9-in. baking pan. Bake at 350° for 35-40 minutes or until a toothpick inserted into the center comes out clean. Cool completely in pan on a wire rack.

3. For the frosting, in a large bowl, beat the cream cheese, butter and vanilla until blended. Gradually beat in confectioners' sugar until smooth. Spread over the cake. Cover and refrigerate leftovers.

Very Vanilla Cupcakes

These goodies will appeal to anyone who likes vanilla. I put that ingredient in both the batter and the frosting.

—**MICHELLE DORSEY** WILMINGTON, DE

PREP: 15 MIN. • **BAKE:** 20 MIN. + COOLING
MAKES: 2 DOZEN

- ¾ **cup unsalted butter, softened**
- 1½ **cups sugar**
- 3 **eggs**
- 1½ **teaspoons vanilla extract**
- 2⅓ **cups cake flour**
- 2½ **teaspoons baking powder**
- ½ **teaspoon salt**
- ¾ **cup whole milk**

FROSTING

- 1 **cup unsalted butter, softened**
- 3 **teaspoons clear vanilla extract**
- 2½ **cups confectioners' sugar**
  Paste food coloring, optional
  Colored sprinkles and nonpareils

1. In a large bowl, cream butter and sugar until light and fluffy. Add eggs, one at a time, beating well after each addition. Beat in vanilla. In another bowl, mix the flour, baking powder and salt; add to creamed mixture alternately with milk, beating well after each addition.

2. Fill paper-lined muffin cups two-thirds full. Bake at 350° for 18-22 minutes or until a toothpick inserted into the center comes out clean. Cool in pans for 10 minutes. Remove to wire racks to cool completely.

3. For the frosting, in a small bowl, beat butter and vanilla until blended. Gradually beat in the confectioners' sugar until smooth. If desired, tint with food coloring. Frost cupcakes. Decorate as desired.

VERY VANILLA CUPCAKES

TART CHERRY LATTICE PIE

Tart Cherry Lattice Pie

Whenever my mom is invited to a party or potluck, she's asked to bring one of her homemade double-crust fruit pies. In the summer, she makes them with fresh tart cherries. I love a just-baked slice topped with a scoop of vanilla ice cream.

—**PAMELA EATON** MONCLOVA, OH

PREP: 20 MIN. • **BAKE:** 40 MIN. + COOLING
MAKES: 8 SERVINGS

- 1⅓ **cups sugar**
- ⅓ **cup all-purpose flour**
- 4 **cups fresh or frozen pitted tart cherries, thawed and drained**
- ¼ **teaspoon almond extract**
  Pastry for double-crust pie (9 inches)
- 2 **tablespoons butter, cut into small pieces**

1. Preheat oven to 400°. In a large bowl, combine the sugar and flour; stir in the cherries and extract.

2. On a lightly floured surface, roll one half of pastry dough to a ⅛-in.-thick circle; transfer to a 9-in. pie plate. Trim pastry to ½ in. beyond rim of plate. Add filling; dot with butter.

3. Roll the remaining dough to a ⅛-in.-thick circle; cut into 1½-in.-wide strips. Arrange over filling in a lattice pattern. Trim and seal strips to the edge of bottom pastry; flute edge. Cover edge loosely with foil.

4. Bake 40-50 minutes or until crust is golden brown and filling is bubbly. Remove foil. Cool on a wire rack.

PASTRY FOR DOUBLE-CRUST PIE (9 INCHES) *Combine 2½ cups all-purpose flour and ½ tsp. salt; cut in 1 cup cold butter until crumbly. Gradually add ⅓ to ⅔ cup ice water, tossing with a fork until dough holds together when pressed. Wrap in plastic wrap and refrigerate 1 hour.*

STICKY TOFFEE PUDDING WITH BUTTERSCOTCH SAUCE

Sticky Toffee Pudding with Butterscotch Sauce

Sticky toffee pudding is a traditional dessert in Britain. I love the fact that I can prepare my own version at home.
—**AGNES WARD** STRATFORD, ON

PREP: 30 MIN. + COOLING • **BAKE:** 30 MIN.
MAKES: 15 SERVINGS (2½ CUPS SAUCE)

- 2 cups coarsely chopped pitted dates (about 12 ounces)
- 2½ cups water
- 2 teaspoons baking soda
- 1⅔ cups sugar
- ½ cup butter, softened
- 4 eggs
- 2 teaspoons vanilla extract
- 3¼ cups all-purpose flour
- 2 teaspoons baking powder

BUTTERSCOTCH SAUCE

- 7 tablespoons butter, cubed
- 2¼ cups packed brown sugar
- 1 cup half-and-half cream
- 1 tablespoon brandy
- ¼ teaspoon vanilla extract
  Whipped cream, optional

1. In a saucepan, combine the dates and water; bring to a boil. Remove from the heat; stir in the baking soda. Cool to lukewarm.
2. In a large bowl, cream sugar and butter until light and fluffy. Add the eggs, one at a time, beating well after each addition. Beat in the vanilla. In another bowl, mix flour and baking powder; gradually add to creamed mixture. Stir in date mixture.
3. Transfer to a greased 13-in. x 9-in. baking pan. Bake at 350° for 30-40 minutes or until a toothpick inserted in the center comes out clean. Cool slightly in pan on a wire rack.
4. Meanwhile, in a small saucepan, melt the butter; add the brown sugar and cream. Bring to a boil over medium heat, stirring constantly. Remove from the heat. Stir in brandy and vanilla. Serve warm with warm cake. If desired, top with whipped cream.

Perfect Rhubarb Pie

Tangy rhubarb takes center stage in this tongue-tingling pie, which has just the right balance of sweet and tart.
—**ELLEN BENNINGER** GREENVILLE, PA

PREP: 20 MIN. + STANDING • **BAKE:** 55 MIN. • **MAKES:** 8 SERVINGS

- 4 cups sliced fresh or frozen rhubarb, thawed
- 4 cups boiling water
- 1½ cups sugar
- 3 tablespoons all-purpose flour
- 1 teaspoon quick-cooking tapioca
- 1 egg
- 2 teaspoons cold water
  Pastry for double-crust pie (9 inches)
- 1 tablespoon butter

1. Place rhubarb in a colander; pour the boiling water over rhubarb and allow to drain. In a large bowl, mix the sugar, flour and tapioca. Add drained rhubarb; toss to coat. Let stand 15 minutes. In a small bowl, whisk egg and cold water; stir into rhubarb mixture.
2. On a lightly floured surface, roll one half of dough to a ⅛-in.-thick circle; transfer to a 9-in. pie plate. Trim pastry even with rim. Add filling; dot with butter. Roll remaining dough to a ⅛-in.-thick circle. Place over filling. Trim, seal and flute edge. Cut slits in top. Bake at 400° for 15 minutes.
3. Reduce oven setting to 350°. Bake 40-50 minutes longer or until crust is golden brown and filling is bubbly. Cool on a wire rack.
NOTE *If using frozen rhubarb, measure rhubarb while still frozen, then thaw completely. Drain in a colander, but do not press liquid out.*
PASTRY FOR DOUBLE-CRUST PIE (9 INCHES) *Combine 2½ cups all-purpose flour and ½ tsp. salt; cut in 1 cup cold butter until crumbly. Gradually add ⅓ to ⅔ cup ice water, tossing with a fork until dough holds together when pressed. Wrap in plastic wrap and refrigerate 1 hour.*

PERFECT RHUBARB PIE

CHERRY COLA CAKE

"What makes chocolate cake even better? Cherry cola, marshmallows and a luscious pink frosting. No one will be able to resist!"

—CHERI MASON HARMONY, NC

Cherry Cola Cake

PREP: 30 MIN. • **BAKE:** 25 MIN. + COOLING • **MAKES:** 12 SERVINGS

- 1½ cups miniature marshmallows
- 2 cups all-purpose flour
- 2 cups sugar
- 1 teaspoon baking soda
- 1 cup butter, cubed
- 1 cup cherry-flavored cola
- 3 tablespoons baking cocoa
- 2 eggs
- ½ cup buttermilk
- 1 teaspoon vanilla extract

FROSTING
- ¾ cup butter, softened
- 1 cup confectioners' sugar
- 1 jar (7 ounces) marshmallow creme
- 2 tablespoons frozen cherry-pomegranate juice concentrate, thawed
- Fresh sweet cherries with stems

1. Preheat oven to 350°. Line bottoms of two greased 9-in. round baking pans with parchment paper; grease paper. Divide marshmallows between pans.

2. In a large bowl, whisk flour, sugar and baking soda. In a small saucepan, combine butter, cola and cocoa; bring just to a boil, stirring occasionally. Add to flour mixture, stirring just until moistened.

3. In a small bowl, whisk eggs, buttermilk and vanilla until blended; add to flour mixture, whisking constantly. Pour into prepared pans, dividing batter evenly. (Marshmallows will float to the top.)

4. Bake 25-30 minutes or until a toothpick inserted in the center comes out clean. Cool in the pans 10 minutes before removing to wire racks; remove paper. Cool completely.

5. For the frosting, in a bowl, beat butter and confectioners' sugar until smooth. Beat in marshmallow creme and juice concentrate on low speed just until blended.

6. Place one cake layer on a serving plate; spread top with 1 cup frosting. Top with remaining cake layer; spread with remaining frosting. Decorate with cherries.

NOTE *To frost sides as well as top of cake, double amounts for frosting.*

Macadamia Key Lime Pie

During summer, I whip up this no-bake treat at least four times a month. It's so refreshing, and the shortbread crust adds richness.

—BRYNN LEMAIRE GUEYDAN, LA

PREP: 20 MIN. + CHILLING • **MAKES:** 8 SERVINGS

- 1 cup crushed shortbread cookies
- ½ cup finely chopped macadamia nuts
- ¼ cup sugar
- ⅓ cup butter, melted

FILLING
- 1 package (8 ounces) cream cheese, softened
- 1 can (14 ounces) sweetened condensed milk
- ½ cup Key lime juice or lime juice
- 1 cup heavy whipping cream
- ¼ cup coarsely chopped macadamia nuts

1. In a small bowl, mix cookie crumbs, macadamia nuts and sugar; stir in butter. Press onto the bottom and up the sides of a greased 9-in. pie plate. Refrigerate 30 minutes.

2. In a large bowl, beat the cream cheese until smooth. Beat in the milk and lime juice until blended. Transfer to crust. Refrigerate, covered, at least 4 hours.

3. In a small bowl, beat cream until soft peaks form; spoon or pipe onto pie. Top with macadamia nuts.

MACADAMIA KEY LIME PIE

SUNSHINE CAKE

Decorate a Window Box

Sunshine Cake (recipe below) calls for simply frosting the cake and inserting plain lollipops into the top. But you can easily make this cake look like a flowery window box as shown in the photo. Here's how!

Box Press cookies against sides of cake. Tie two shoestring licorice pieces together to make a longer strand. Wrap and tie strands around window box.

Flowers Cut Fruit Roll-Ups with flower-shaped cutters. Sandwich cutouts around a lollipop, moistening edges with water.

Stems & Leaves Insert straws into cake. Top with lollipop flowers. Cut leaves from green licorice and place them in the cake.

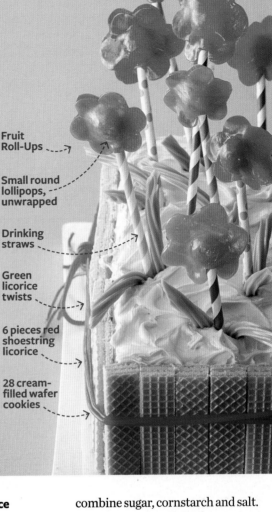

Fruit Roll-Ups

Small round lollipops, unwrapped

Drinking straws

Green licorice twists

6 pieces red shoestring licorice

28 cream-filled wafer cookies

Sunshine Cake

PREP: 1 HOUR + CHILLING
BAKE: 25 MIN. + COOLING
MAKES: 16 SERVINGS

- 1 cup butter, softened
- 1⅔ cups sugar
- 4 eggs
- 1½ teaspoons vanilla extract
- 1½ teaspoons each grated lemon, orange and lime peel
- 2¾ cups all-purpose flour
- 3 teaspoons baking powder
- ¾ teaspoon salt
- 1 cup 2% milk

FILLING
- ½ cup sugar
- ¼ cup cornstarch
- ¼ teaspoon salt
- ¾ cup water
- 2 egg yolks
- 2 tablespoons butter
- ⅓ cup lemon juice

FROSTING
- ½ cup butter, softened
- 3¾ cups confectioners' sugar
- ¼ cup light corn syrup
- 3 tablespoons orange juice
- 1 teaspoon vanilla extract
- ½ teaspoon grated orange peel
  Dash salt
- 3 drops yellow food coloring
- 1 drop red food coloring
  Assorted lollipops, unwrapped

1. Preheat oven to 350°. Line bottom of a greased 15-in. x 10-in. x 1-in. jelly-roll pan with parchment paper; grease paper.

2. In a large bowl, cream butter and sugar until light and fluffy. Add eggs, one at a time, beating well after each addition. Beat in the vanilla and citrus peels. In another bowl, whisk the flour, baking powder and salt; add to the creamed mixture alternately with the milk, beating well after each addition.

3. Transfer to the prepared pan. Bake 25-30 minutes or until a toothpick inserted into the center comes out clean. Cool in pan 5 minutes before removing to a wire rack; remove the parchment paper. Cool completely.

4. For the filling, in a small saucepan, combine sugar, cornstarch and salt. Whisk in the water. Cook and stir over medium heat until thickened and bubbly. Remove from heat.

5. In a small bowl, whisk a small amount of the hot mixture into the egg yolks; return all to the pan, whisking constantly. Bring to a gentle boil; cook and stir 2 minutes. Remove from heat. Stir in the butter. Gently stir in the lemon juice. Press plastic wrap onto the surface of the filling; cool slightly. Refrigerate until cold.

6. For the frosting, in a large bowl, cream the butter until fluffy. Beat in the confectioners' sugar, corn syrup, orange juice, vanilla, orange peel and salt until smooth. Tint orange with yellow and red food coloring.

7. Trim the edges of the cake; cut crosswise into thirds. Place one cake layer on a serving plate; spread with half of the filling. Repeat layers. Top with the remaining cake layer. Frost the top and sides of cake with frosting. Insert lollipops into the top for flowers. Refrigerate leftovers.

"If you like fresh peaches, you're going to love this upside-down cake spiced with cinnamon and ginger. The crunchy pecans make it even better." —**JEANETTE NELSON** SOPHIA, WV

Peach Praline Upside-Down Cake

PREP: 25 MIN. • **BAKE:** 25 MIN. + COOLING • **MAKES:** 8 SERVINGS

- 4 **eggs, separated**
- ¼ **cup butter, cubed**
- ⅔ **cup packed brown sugar**
- 1 **teaspoon ground cinnamon**
- ½ **teaspoon ground ginger**
- 3 **medium peaches, peeled and sliced (2 cups)**
- ½ **cup chopped pecans**
- 1 **cup cake flour**
- 1 **teaspoon baking powder**
- ¼ **teaspoon salt**
- 1 **cup sugar**
- ¼ **cup 2% milk**
- 2 **tablespoons butter, melted**
- 1 **teaspoon vanilla extract**
  Whipped cream and toasted pecan halves, optional

1. Place the egg whites in a large bowl; let stand at room temperature 30 minutes. Meanwhile, preheat oven to 375°.
2. In a 10-in. ovenproof skillet, melt butter over medium heat. Stir in brown sugar, cinnamon and ginger. Remove from heat. Arrange peaches in a single layer over brown sugar mixture; sprinkle with chopped pecans.

PEACH PRALINE UPSIDE-DOWN CAKE

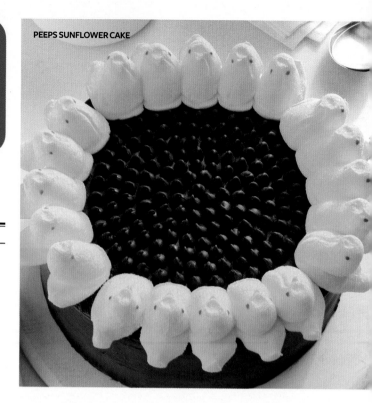

PEEPS SUNFLOWER CAKE

3. In a bowl, whisk flour, baking powder and salt. In a bowl, beat egg yolks until slightly thickened. Gradually add sugar, beating on high speed until thick and lemon-colored. Beat in milk, melted butter and vanilla. Fold in flour mixture.
4. With clean beaters, beat the egg whites on medium until stiff but not dry; gradually fold into batter. Pour batter into skillet. Bake 22-27 minutes or until a toothpick inserted into center comes out clean.
5. Cool 10 minutes before inverting onto a serving plate. Serve warm with whipped cream and pecan halves if desired.

Peeps Sunflower Cake

For a dessert that resembles a sunflower, I line up yellow Peeps candies for the flower petals and fill in the center with chocolate chips for the seeds. It's fun to create—and eat!
—**BETHANY ELEDGE** CLEVELAND, TN

PREP: 15 MIN. • **BAKE:** 30 MIN. + COOLING • **MAKES:** 12 SERVINGS

- 1 **package yellow cake mix (regular size)**
- 2 **cans (16 ounces each) chocolate frosting**
- 19 **to 20 yellow chick Peeps candies**
- 1½ **cups semisweet chocolate chips**

1. Prepare and bake the cake mix according to the package directions, using two parchment paper-lined and greased 9-in. round baking pans. Cool in pans 10 minutes before removing to wire racks; remove paper. Cool completely.
2. If the cake layers have rounded tops, trim with a long serrated knife to make level. Spread frosting between the layers and over top and sides of cake.
3. For petals, arrange Peeps around edge of cake, curving slightly and being careful not to separate the chicks. For sunflower seeds, arrange chocolate chips in center of cake.

⑤ INGREDIENTS
Lemon-Berry Ice Cream Pie

PREP: 15 MIN. + FREEZING • **MAKES:** 8 SERVINGS

- 1 **pint strawberry ice cream, softened**
- 1 **graham cracker crust (9 inches)**
- 1 **cup lemon curd**
- 2 **cups frozen whipped topping, thawed**
- 1 **pint fresh strawberries, halved**

1. Spoon the ice cream into the pie crust; freeze 2 hours or until firm.

2. Spread the lemon curd over ice cream; top with whipped topping. Freeze, covered, 4 hours or until firm.

3. Remove from freezer 10 minutes before serving. Serve with strawberries.

"Here's a cool, refreshing treat you can make ahead and freeze. Just fill a crumb crust with lemon curd, ice cream, strawberries and whipped topping." —ROXANNE CHAN ALBANY, CA

CARAMELIZED APPLE HAND PIES

Caramelized Apple Hand Pies

Caramelized apples are tucked inside these hand-held pies. Each one is an individual serving—so no one will expect you to share!
—**EDWINA GADSBY** HAYDEN, ID

PREP: 25 MIN. + COOLING • **BAKE:** 20 MIN. • **MAKES:** 8 SERVINGS

- 2 **tablespoons unsalted butter**
- 3 **medium apples, peeled and finely chopped**
- ⅓ **cup packed brown sugar**
- ½ **teaspoon cornstarch**
- ⅛ **teaspoon ground cinnamon**
- 1 **teaspoon lemon juice**
- ½ **teaspoon vanilla extract**
- 1 **package (14.1 ounces) refrigerated pie pastry**

TOPPING
- ¼ **cup coarse sugar**
- 1 **teaspoon ground cinnamon**
- 3 **tablespoons unsalted butter, melted**
  Vanilla ice cream, optional

1. In a large skillet, heat the butter over medium heat. Add the apples; cook and stir 5 minutes. Mix the brown sugar, cornstarch and cinnamon; add to apples. Cook and stir 7-8 minutes longer or until apples begin to soften and caramelize. Remove from heat; stir in the lemon juice and vanilla. Cool completely.

2. Preheat oven to 400°. On a lightly floured surface, unroll pastry sheets. Roll to ⅛-in. thickness; cut four 5-in. circles from each sheet. Place about 3 tablespoons filling on one half of each circle. Moisten pastry edges with water. Fold pastry over the filling. Press edges with a fork to seal or, if desired, pinch edges to seal and flute.

3. Transfer to greased baking sheets. Prick tops of pastry with a fork. Bake 20-25 minutes or until golden brown. Remove from pans to wire racks.

4. For topping, mix sugar and cinnamon. Brush pies with melted butter; sprinkle with cinnamon-sugar. Serve warm or at room temperature. If desired, top with ice cream.

LEMON-BERRY ICE CREAM PIE

Bourbon Chocolate-Pecan Pie

To make this dessert without the bourbon, simply substitute three tablespoons of melted butter. You could also lighten up the recipe by omitting the chocolate.

—**SARAH VARNER** SANTA RITA, GU

PREP: 20 MIN. • **BAKE:** 50 MIN.
MAKES: 10 SERVINGS

- **Pastry for single-crust pie (9 inches)**
- ½ **cup miniature semisweet chocolate chips**
- 4 **eggs, lightly beaten**
- 1 **cup corn syrup**
- ½ **cup sugar**
- 6 **tablespoons butter, melted**
- ¼ **cup packed brown sugar**
- 3 **tablespoons bourbon**
- 1 **tablespoon all-purpose flour**
- 3 **teaspoons vanilla extract**
- 1½ **cups chopped pecans, divided**

1. Roll out the pastry to fit a 9-in. pie plate. Transfer pastry to pie plate. Trim pastry to ½ in. beyond edge of plate; flute edges. Sprinkle chocolate chips into pastry shell. Set aside.
2. In a large bowl, whisk eggs, corn syrup, sugar, butter, brown sugar, bourbon, flour and vanilla until smooth. Stir in 1 cup pecans. Pour into the pastry shell; sprinkle with the remaining pecans.
3. Bake at 350° for 50-60 minutes or until set. Cool on a wire rack. Store leftovers in the refrigerator.

BOURBON CHOCOLATE-PECAN PIE

CHOCOLATE & PEANUT BUTTER PUDDING PIE WITH BANANAS

Chocolate & Peanut Butter Pudding Pie with Bananas

Here's my tribute to Elvis, my favorite entertainer, and to Hershey, Pennsylvania, the town where I was born.

—**PENNY HAWKINS** MEBANE, NC

PREP: 25 MIN. + CHILLING • **BAKE:** 10 MIN.
MAKES: 8 SERVINGS

- 1 **cup chocolate wafer crumbs (about 20 wafers)**
- ¼ **cup butter, melted**
- 2 **medium firm bananas**
- ¾ **cup creamy peanut butter**
- 2 **ounces semisweet chocolate, chopped**
- 2 **cups cold 2% milk**
- 2 **packages (3.4 ounces each) instant vanilla pudding mix**
- 2 **cups whipped topping, divided**
- 2 **tablespoons chopped salted peanuts**
- **Peanut butter cups, optional**

1. In a small bowl, mix the chocolate wafer crumbs and butter; press onto the bottom and up the sides of an ungreased 9-in. pie plate. Bake at 350° for 8-10 minutes or until set. Cool completely on a wire rack.
2. Slice the bananas; arrange on the bottom of crust. In a microwave-safe bowl, combine the peanut butter and chocolate; microwave on high for 1 to 1½ minutes or until blended and smooth, stirring every 30 seconds. Spoon over bananas.
3. In a large bowl, whisk the milk and vanilla pudding mix for 2 minutes. Let stand for 2 minutes or until soft-set. Fold in 1 cup whipped topping; spread over the chocolate mixture. Pipe the remaining whipped topping over the edge. Refrigerate, covered, for at least 3 hours.
4. Sprinkle with peanuts just before serving. If desired, serve with cut-up peanut butter cups.

Hot Fudge Cake

Top off a wonderful meal with an equally wonderful dessert—a warm, chocolaty, fudgy cake. It's rich but not too sweet.

—VERA REID LARAMIE, WY

PREP: 20 MIN. • **BAKE:** 35 MIN.
MAKES: 9 SERVINGS

- 1 cup all-purpose flour
- ¾ cup sugar
- 6 tablespoons baking cocoa, divided
- 2 teaspoons baking powder
- ¼ teaspoon salt
- ½ cup 2% milk
- 2 tablespoons canola oil
- 1 teaspoon vanilla extract
- 1 cup packed brown sugar
- 1¾ cups hot water
  Ice cream or whipped cream, optional

1. Preheat oven to 350°. In a large bowl, whisk flour, sugar, 2 tablespoons cocoa, baking powder and salt. In another bowl, whisk milk, oil and vanilla until blended. Add to flour mixture; stir just until moistened.

2. Transfer to an ungreased 9-in.-square baking pan. In a small bowl, mix brown sugar and remaining cocoa; sprinkle over batter. Pour hot water over all; do not stir.

3. Bake 35-40 minutes. Serve warm. If desired, top with ice cream.

HOT FUDGE CAKE

GINGER PUMPKIN PIE WITH STREUSEL

Ginger Pumpkin Pie with Streusel

Want to dress up ordinary pumpkin pie for the holidays? Give it a buttery, sugary streusel topping of crushed gingersnap cookies and chopped pecans.

—KAREN MOORE JACKSONVILLE, FL

PREP: 30 MIN. • **BAKE:** 65 MIN. + COOLING
MAKES: 8 SERVINGS

- Pastry for single-crust pie (9 inches)
- 1 can (15 ounces) solid-pack pumpkin
- 1 cup evaporated milk
- 2 eggs, lightly beaten
- ½ cup packed brown sugar
- 2 teaspoons grated fresh gingerroot
- 1 teaspoon pumpkin pie spice
- ¼ teaspoon salt

GINGERSNAP STREUSEL

- ½ cup crushed gingersnap cookies
- ¼ cup chopped pecans
- 2 tablespoons all-purpose flour
- 2 tablespoons brown sugar
- 2 tablespoons butter, softened

1. Roll out the pastry to fit a 9-in. pie plate. Transfer the pastry to pie plate. Trim pastry to 1 in. beyond the edge of plate; flute the edges. Place plate on a baking sheet.

2. In large bowl, combine pumpkin, milk, eggs, brown sugar, ginger, pie spice and salt. Pour into crust. Cover edges loosely with foil. Bake at 425° for 15 minutes. Reduce heat to 350°; bake for 15 minutes.

3. Meanwhile, in a small bowl, combine the cookie crumbs, pecans, flour and brown sugar. Cut in butter until coarse crumbs form. Sprinkle over pie. Bake 35-45 minutes longer or until knife inserted near the center comes out clean. Cool completely on a wire rack. Store in the refrigerator.

LEMON CHESS PIE WITH BERRY SAUCE

Lemon Chess Pie with Berry Sauce

This dessert is one of those old-fashioned, classic Southern favorites. It just makes everyone feel good!

—**APRIL HEATON** BRANSON, MO

PREP: 45 MIN. + CHILLING • **BAKE:** 35 MIN. + CHILLING
MAKES: 8 SERVINGS (1½ CUPS SAUCE)

- 1 cup all-purpose flour
- ½ cup flaked coconut
- ¼ teaspoon salt
- ⅓ cup cold butter, cubed
- 3 to 4 tablespoons ice water

FILLING

- 6 eggs
- 1½ cups sugar
- ⅓ cup buttermilk
- ⅓ cup lemon juice
- 3 tablespoons cornmeal
- 2 tablespoons grated lemon peel
- ¼ teaspoon salt
  Dash ground nutmeg
- ½ cup butter, melted

BERRY SAUCE

- ⅔ cup water
- ⅓ cup sugar
- 1 package (12 ounces) frozen unsweetened mixed berries, thawed and drained
- 2 teaspoons lemon juice

1. Place the flour, coconut and salt in a food processor; process until blended. Add the butter; pulse until the mixture is the size of peas. While pulsing, add just enough ice water to form moist crumbs. Shape the dough into a disk; wrap in plastic wrap. Refrigerate for 30 minutes or overnight.

2. On a lightly floured surface, roll dough to a ⅛-in.-thick circle; transfer to a 9-in. pie plate. Trim pastry to ½ in. beyond rim of plate; flute edge. Line unpricked pastry with

a double thickness of foil. Fill with pie weights, dried beans or uncooked rice.

3. Bake at 400° on a lower oven rack for 8 minutes. Remove the foil and pie weights; bake 6-9 minutes longer or until the crust is light brown. Cool on a wire rack. Reduce oven setting to 325°.

4. In a large bowl, whisk the eggs, sugar, buttermilk, lemon juice, cornmeal, lemon peel, salt and nutmeg. Gradually whisk in butter. Pour into crust. Cover edge with foil to prevent overbrowning.

5. Bake at 325° for 35-40 minutes or until a knife inserted near the center comes out clean. Remove foil. Cool on a wire rack. Refrigerate, covered, for 3 hours or until chilled.

6. For the sauce, in a small saucepan, bring water and sugar to a boil. Cook until syrup is reduced to ¼ cup; transfer to a small bowl. Cool completely. Just before serving, stir in berries and lemon juice; serve with pie.

Cranberry Walnut Pie

Here's a wonderful choice for your family feast on Christmas or Thanksgiving. Each sweet-tart slice wows with ruby-red cranberries, crunchy walnuts and a golden lattice crust.

—**DIANE EVERETT** DUNKIRK, NY

PREP: 20 MIN. • **BAKE:** 50 MIN. + COOLING • **MAKES:** 8 SERVINGS

- 1 package (12 ounces) fresh or frozen cranberries, thawed
- 1½ cups packed brown sugar
- 1 cup chopped walnuts
- ¼ cup butter, melted
- 4½ teaspoons all-purpose flour
- 2 teaspoons grated orange peel
  Dash salt
  Pastry for double-crust pie (9 inches)

1. Preheat oven to 375°. Place the cranberries in a food processor; cover and process until finely chopped. Transfer to a large bowl; stir in brown sugar, walnuts, butter, flour, orange peel and salt.

2. Roll out half of the pastry to fit a 9-in. pie plate; transfer pastry to pie plate. Pour filling into crust. Roll out remaining pastry; make a lattice crust. Trim, seal and flute the edges. Cover edges loosely with foil.

3. Bake 30 minutes. Remove foil; bake 20-25 minutes or until filling is bubbly and crust is golden brown. Cool on a wire rack.

top tip

Fuss-Free Foil

If you have trouble keeping strips of foil on the edges of a pie crust while it's baking, skip the strips and try this easy technique: Cut a square of foil that's large enough to cover your pie and cut a circle out of the center. Then simply lay the square on top of your pie and wrap the foil over the edges.

—**LORI H.** SPARKS, NV

> "Refreshing bursts of lemon and orange put sunshine into every bite of Citrus Sour Cream Pie. It's super easy to prepare using the microwave."
>
> —**KALLEE KRONG-MCCREERY** ESCONDIDO, CA

CITRUS SOUR CREAM PIE

Citrus Sour Cream Pie

PREP: 20 MIN. + CHILLING • **MAKES:** 8 SERVINGS

- ⅔ cup sugar
- 3 tablespoons cornstarch
- 2 egg yolks, beaten
- ¾ cup orange juice
- ⅔ cup 2% milk
- 2 tablespoons lemon juice
- 1 cup sour cream
- 1 graham cracker crust (9 inches)

TOPPING
- 1 cup heavy whipping cream
- 2 tablespoons confectioners' sugar
- ¼ teaspoon vanilla extract
  Grated orange peel
  Optional fruit toppings: mandarin oranges, sliced fresh strawberries and sliced kiwifruit

1. In a microwave-safe bowl, combine the sugar and cornstarch. In a bowl, combine the egg yolks, orange juice, milk and lemon juice; stir into sugar mixture until smooth.
2. Microwave on high for 5-7 minutes or just until the mixture reaches 160°, stirring every minute. Cool to room temperature; press plastic wrap onto surface of custard. Refrigerate until chilled.

3. Fold in sour cream; pour filling into crust. Cover and chill for at least 4 hours or overnight.
4. Just before serving, in a large bowl, beat cream until it begins to thicken. Add confectioners' sugar and vanilla; beat until stiff peaks form. Spread over pie. Sprinkle with orange peel; top with fruit if desired.
NOTE *This recipe was tested in a 1,100-watt microwave.*

Lemon-Yogurt Tea Cakes

Tender and tangy, these cupcakes are always popular. Enjoy them for brunch, dinner, snacktime—any time at all!
—**RUTH BURRUS** ZIONSVILLE, IN

PREP: 20 MIN. • **BAKE:** 20 MIN. + COOLING • **MAKES:** ABOUT 1 DOZEN

- 2¼ cups all-purpose flour
- 1 cup sugar
- ¾ teaspoon baking powder
- ½ teaspoon baking soda
- ½ teaspoon salt
- ½ cup cold butter
- 1 cup (8 ounces) fat-free plain yogurt
- 3 egg whites
- 2 tablespoons lemon juice
- 4 teaspoons grated lemon peel
- 1 teaspoon lemon extract

1. In a large bowl, combine the flour, sugar, baking powder, baking soda and salt; cut in butter until mixture resembles coarse crumbs. Whisk the yogurt, egg whites, lemon juice, peel and extract; stir into the crumb mixture just until moistened.
2. Fill greased or paper-lined muffin cups three-fourths full. Bake at 350° for 18-22 minutes or until a toothpick inserted near the center comes out clean. Cool for 10 minutes before removing from the pan to a wire rack to cool completely.

LEMON-YOGURT TEA CAKES

FAST FIX ▶ Raspberry Lemon Layer Cake

START TO FINISH: 25 MIN.
MAKES: 6 SERVINGS

- 1½ cups heavy whipping cream
- 3 tablespoons confectioners' sugar
- 3 tablespoons orange juice
- 1 loaf (10¾ ounces) frozen pound cake, thawed
- 1 jar (10 ounces) lemon curd
- 2½ cups fresh raspberries

1. In a bowl, beat cream until it begins to thicken. Add confectioners' sugar and orange juice; beat until stiff peaks form. Using a long serrated knife, cut cake horizontally into three layers.

2. Place the bottom cake layer on a serving plate; spread with about ⅓ cup lemon curd. Top with 1 cup berries and ⅓ cup cream mixture; repeat layers. Replace the cake top; spread with the remaining lemon curd.

3. Frost the top and sides of cake with the remaining cream mixture. Top with the remaining berries; refrigerate until serving.

"Cooking has been a favorite hobby of mine for a long time. I especially enjoy trying different flavor combinations— as I did with Raspberry Lemon Layer Cake."
—JANICE BAKER LONDON, KY

RASPBERRY LEMON LAYER CAKE

CHOCOLATE ZUCCHINI CAKE

Chocolate Zucchini Cake

As soon as I get some zucchini, I start making this wonderful chocolate dessert. Served with a warm custard sauce, it was a popular menu item at my sister's deli.
—PEGGY LINTON COBOURG, ON

PREP: 20 MIN. • **BAKE:** 55 MIN. + COOLING
MAKES: 16 SERVINGS

- 1¾ cups sugar
- ½ cup canola oil
- ¼ cup butter, softened
- ½ cup buttermilk
- 2 eggs
- 1 teaspoon vanilla extract
- 2½ cups all-purpose flour
- ¼ cup baking cocoa
- 1 teaspoon baking soda
- ½ teaspoon ground cinnamon
- ¼ teaspoon ground cloves
- 2 cups finely shredded zucchini
- ½ cup semisweet chocolate chips
- ½ cup sliced almonds

CUSTARD SAUCE
- ½ cup sugar
- 2 tablespoons all-purpose flour
- 2 tablespoons cornstarch
- 3 cups whole milk
- 3 egg yolks
- 3 tablespoons butter
- ¼ teaspoon almond extract

1. Preheat oven to 325°. Grease and flour a 10-in. plain or fluted tube pan. In another bowl, beat the sugar, oil and butter until well blended. Gradually beat in buttermilk, eggs and vanilla.

2. In another bowl, whisk the flour, cocoa, baking soda, cinnamon and cloves; gradually beat into the sugar mixture. Stir in zucchini, chocolate chips and almonds.

3. Transfer to prepared pan. Bake 55-60 minutes or until a toothpick inserted in the center comes out clean. Cool 10 minutes before removing from pan to a wire rack to cool.

4. For the custard sauce, in a large saucepan, mix the sugar, flour and cornstarch. Whisk in the milk. Cook and stir over medium-high heat until thickened and bubbly. Reduce heat to low; cook and stir 2 minutes longer. Remove from heat.

5. In a small bowl, whisk a small amount of hot mixture into egg yolks; return all to pan, whisking constantly. Bring to a gentle boil; cook and stir 2 minutes. Gently stir in butter and extract. Serve warm with cake. Cover and refrigerate leftover sauce.

NOTE *For easier removal of cakes, use solid shortening to grease plain and fluted tube pans.*

Peanut & Banana Cupcakes

If you want cupcakes that'll wow a crowd, look no further! The little frosted goodies have a nice balance of sweet and salty. Save extras for an afternoon snack.

—MARY ANN LEE CLIFTON PARK, NY

PREP: 25 MIN. • **BAKE:** 20 MIN. + COOLING
MAKES: 1½ DOZEN

- ½ cup butter, softened
- 1 cup sugar
- 2 eggs
- 1¼ cups mashed ripe bananas (2-3 medium)
- ¼ cup buttermilk
- 2 teaspoons vanilla extract
- 2 cups cake flour
- 1½ teaspoons baking powder
- ¼ teaspoon baking soda
- ⅛ teaspoon salt
- 1 cup chopped lightly salted dry roasted peanuts

FROSTING
- 2 cups confectioners' sugar
- 1 cup creamy peanut butter
- ½ cup butter, softened
- 2 teaspoons vanilla extract
- 3 to 4 tablespoons 2% milk
- 1 cup chopped lightly salted dry roasted peanuts

1. In a large bowl, cream the butter and sugar until light and fluffy. Add eggs, one at a time, beating well after each addition. Combine the bananas, buttermilk and vanilla. Combine flour, baking powder, baking soda and salt; gradually add to the creamed mixture alternately with the banana mixture, mixing well after each addition. Stir in peanuts.

2. Fill paper-lined muffin cups two-thirds full. Bake at 350° for 18-22 minutes or until a toothpick inserted near the center comes out clean. Cool for 10 minutes before removing from pans to wire racks to cool completely.

3. In a large bowl, beat confectioners' sugar, peanut butter and butter until fluffy. Beat in the vanilla and enough milk to achieve desired consistency. Pipe frosting over cupcakes. Sprinkle with peanuts. Store in refrigerator.

"I found this recipe many years ago and knew it was special. The caramel icing can be a little tricky because you have to work quickly, but it's so worth it!"
—MARIANN JAMES FERGUSON, MO

CHOCOLATE SPICE CAKE WITH CARAMEL ICING

Chocolate Spice Cake with Caramel Icing

PREP: 30 MIN. • **BAKE:** 30 MIN. + COOLING
MAKES: 12 SERVINGS

- 3 ounces unsweetened chocolate, chopped
- ½ cup butter, softened
- 1 cup sugar
- 1 cup packed brown sugar
- 3 eggs
- 2 cups cake flour
- 3 teaspoons baking powder
- 1 teaspoon ground cinnamon
- ½ teaspoon salt
- ½ teaspoon ground allspice
- ⅛ teaspoon ground cloves
- 1⅓ cups 2% milk

ICING
- 1 cup plus 2 tablespoons packed brown sugar
- ¾ cup heavy whipping cream
- 6 tablespoons butter, cubed
- 1½ cups confectioners' sugar
- ¼ teaspoon vanilla extract
  Caramel popcorn with peanuts, optional

1. Preheat oven to 350°. Line bottoms of two well-greased 9-in. round baking pans with parchment paper; grease paper. In a microwave, melt chocolate; stir until smooth. Cool slightly.

2. In a large bowl, cream the butter and sugars until light and fluffy. Add eggs, one at a time, beating well after each addition. Beat in chocolate. In another bowl, whisk flour, baking powder, cinnamon, salt, allspice and cloves; add to the creamed mixture alternately with milk, beating well after each addition.

3. Transfer the batter to the prepared pans. Bake 30-35 minutes or until a toothpick inserted into center comes out clean. Cool in pans 10 minutes before removing to wire racks; remove paper. Cool completely.

4. In a small saucepan, combine the brown sugar, cream and butter. Bring to a boil over medium heat, stirring occasionally. Cook and stir 3 minutes. Remove from heat; gradually beat in confectioners' sugar and vanilla.

5. Place one cake layer on a serving plate; immediately pour half of the hot icing over cake layer. Top with the remaining cake layer. Pour remaining icing over top of cake. If desired, top with caramel popcorn.

**WENDY PAFFENROTH'S
MAPLE-NUT CHEESECAKE**
PAGE 130

Just Desserts

Save plenty of room for the tempting treats in this chapter. From rich cheesecakes and fluffy cream puffs to layered parfaits and fruity crisps, they just might be the **highlight of your meal**.

BARBARA ESTABROOK'S STRAWBERRY-HAZELNUT MERINGUE SHORTCAKES
PAGE 127

CHRISTINA SMITH'S S'MOREOS
PAGE 134

PRISCILLA GILBERT'S BLUEBERRY-BLACKBERRY RUSTIC TART *PAGE 129*

RASPBERRY SORBET

(5) INGREDIENTS

Raspberry Sorbet

With a bountiful crop of raspberries in the backyard, I'm always on the lookout for new ways to use them. They're especially good in this refreshing sorbet.

—**KAREN BAILEY** GOLDEN, CO

PREP: 5 MIN. + FREEZING
MAKES: 6 SERVINGS

- ¼ cup plus 1½ teaspoons fresh lemon juice
- 3¾ cups fresh or frozen unsweetened raspberries
- 2¼ cups confectioners' sugar

In a blender or food processor, combine all ingredients; cover and process until smooth. Transfer to a freezer container; freeze until firm.

Cranberry-Orange Trifle

When I need a showstopper for a special occasion, I like to whip up a big trifle. Sometimes I give it a tropical twist with toasted coconut between the layers.

—**RAYMONDE BOURGEOIS** SWASTIKA, ON

PREP: 45 MIN. • **COOK:** 15 MIN. + CHILLING
MAKES: 16 SERVINGS (1 CUP EACH)

- 2 packages (12 ounces each) fresh or frozen cranberries
- 1½ cups water
- 1⅓ cups sugar
- 2 teaspoons minced fresh gingerroot
- 4 teaspoons grated orange peel

CUSTARD

- 1 cup sugar
- 2 tablespoons cornstarch
- ¼ teaspoon salt
- 3 cups 2% milk
- 6 egg yolks
- 2 teaspoons vanilla extract

TRIFLE

- 1 loaf (16 ounces) frozen pound cake, thawed and cut into 1-inch cubes
- ¼ cup orange liqueur
- ½ cup slivered almonds, toasted
  Sweetened whipped cream and orange sections

1. In a large saucepan, combine the first five ingredients; bring to a boil, stirring to dissolve sugar. Reduce heat to medium; cook, uncovered, until berries pop and mixture is thickened, about 15 minutes. Remove from the heat; cool completely.

2. For custard, in a large saucepan, mix the sugar, cornstarch and salt. Whisk in milk. Cook and stir over medium-high heat until thickened and bubbly. Reduce heat to low; cook and stir 2 minutes longer. Remove from the heat.

3. In a small bowl, whisk a small amount of the hot milk mixture into the egg yolks; return all to the pan, whisking constantly. Bring to a gentle boil; cook and stir for 2 minutes. Immediately transfer to a clean bowl; stir in vanilla. Cool for 30 minutes. Press waxed paper onto the surface of the filling; refrigerate until cold, about 1 hour.

4. To assemble, place half of the pound cake cubes on the bottom of a 4-qt. trifle bowl or glass bowl; drizzle with 2 tablespoons orange liqueur. Layer with half of the cranberry mixture, ¼ cup slivered almonds and half of the custard. Repeat the layers. Refrigerate, covered, until serving. Top with sweetened whipped cream and orange sections.

NOTE *To toast nuts, spread in a 15x10x1-in. baking pan. Bake at 350° for 5-10 minutes or until lightly browned, stirring occasionally. Or, spread in a dry nonstick skillet and heat over low heat until lightly browned, stirring occasionally.*

CRANBERRY-ORANGE TRIFLE

Rhubarb Fool with Strawberries

A fool is a traditional British dessert that's usually prepared with whipped cream and cooked fruit. My speedier version of that classic features tangy rhubarb and sweet fresh strawberries. Want an extra-special treat? Dunk into your bowlful with lemon shortbread cookies for a crispy contrast.

—CHERYL MILLER FORT COLLINS, CO

PREP: 30 MIN. + CHILLING
MAKES: 6 SERVINGS

- 3 **cups sliced fresh or frozen rhubarb (1-inch pieces)**
- ⅓ **cup sugar**
- ¼ **cup orange juice**
  Dash salt
- 1 **cup heavy whipping cream**
- 2 **cups fresh strawberries, halved**

1. In a large saucepan, combine the rhubarb, sugar, orange juice and salt. Bring to a boil. Reduce heat; simmer, covered, 6-8 minutes or until rhubarb is tender. Cool slightly.

2. Process the rhubarb mixture in a blender until smooth. Transfer to a bowl; refrigerate, covered, until cold.

3. Just before serving, in a large bowl, whip the heavy whipping cream until soft peaks form. Lightly fold in pureed rhubarb and strawberries.

RHUBARB FOOL WITH STRAWBERRIES

Peaches and Cream Torte

I make my peachy torte when I'm craving something cool and fruity. The cream cheese lends zing to the fluffy filling.

—ELVA ROBERTS SUMMERSIDE, PE

PREP: 40 MIN. + CHILLING
MAKES: 12 SERVINGS

- 2 **cups graham cracker crumbs**
- ⅓ **cup packed brown sugar**
- ½ **cup butter, melted**

FILLING

- 1 **can (29 ounces) sliced peaches**
- 1¼ **cups sugar, divided**
- 2 **tablespoons cornstarch**
- 1 **package (8 ounces) cream cheese, softened**
- 2 **cups heavy whipping cream**

1. In a small bowl, combine graham cracker crumbs and brown sugar; stir in butter. Set aside ¼ cup for topping. Press remaining crumb mixture onto the bottom and 1 in. up the sides of a greased 9-in. springform pan.

2. Place the pan on a baking sheet. Bake at 350° for 10 minutes. Cool on a wire rack.

3. Drain the peaches, reserving the syrup in a 2-cup measuring cup. Add enough water to measure 1½ cups. In a large saucepan, combine ¼ cup sugar and cornstarch; stir in the syrup mixture until smooth. Add peaches. Bring to a boil over medium heat; cook and stir for 2 minutes or until thickened. Cool to room temperature, stirring occasionally.

4. Meanwhile, in a large bowl, beat the cream cheese and remaining sugar until smooth. In a small bowl, beat the heavy whipping cream until stiff peaks form; fold into the cream cheese mixture.

5. Spread half of the cream cheese mixture over the crust. Top with half of the peach mixture; repeat the layers. Sprinkle with the reserved crumb mixture. Cover and refrigerate for 8 hours or overnight. Remove the sides of the pan before slicing.

Two-Layered Apple Crisp

I'm blessed to have the opportunity to make this treat for the special ladies at the local homeless shelter. Try using Honeycrisp apples, Golden Delicious or a blend of the two varieties.

—CHAR MORSE WHITEHALL, MI

PREP: 30 MIN. • **BAKE:** 45 MIN.
MAKES: 12 SERVINGS

- ¾ cup butter, softened
- 1½ cups packed brown sugar
- 2 teaspoons ground cinnamon
- ½ teaspoon salt
- 2 cups all-purpose flour
- 2 cups old-fashioned oats

FILLING

- 1 cup sugar
- ¾ cup all-purpose flour
- ¼ cup packed brown sugar
- 1 teaspoon ground cinnamon
- ⅛ teaspoon ground nutmeg
- 3 large Honeycrisp or Golden Delicious apples, peeled and sliced (about 6 cups)
- 3 teaspoons vanilla extract
- 1 tablespoon butter
  Optional toppings: vanilla ice cream, caramel sundae syrup and salted pecans

1. In a large bowl, beat the butter, brown sugar, cinnamon and salt until crumbly. Add the flour and oats; mix well. Press 3 cups oat mixture onto the bottom of a greased 13-in. x 9-in. baking dish.

2. In another bowl, mix the first five filling ingredients. Add apples and

TWO-LAYERED APPLE CRISP

"Apple Bread Pudding with Caramel Sauce is always on my buffet when I put together a brunch. I can't remember where I found the recipe, but I'm glad I did!" **—CLEO GONSKE** REDDING, CA

APPLE BREAD PUDDING WITH CARAMEL SAUCE

vanilla; toss to combine. Spoon over oat layer. Dot with butter; sprinkle with remaining oat mixture.

3. Bake, uncovered, at 350° for 45-50 minutes or until golden brown and apples are tender. If desired, serve with toppings.

Apple Bread Pudding with Caramel Sauce

PREP: 50 MIN. • **BAKE:** 40 MIN.
MAKES: 16 SERVINGS (1¾ CUPS SAUCE)

- ¾ cup butter, cubed
- 4 cups chopped peeled tart apples (about 4 medium)
- 2 cups sugar
- ½ cup raisins
- ½ cup chopped walnuts
- 3 teaspoons ground cinnamon
- 2 teaspoons vanilla extract

BREAD PUDDING

- 6 eggs
- 2½ cups 2% milk
- 1½ cups plus 2 tablespoons sugar, divided
- 1 cup heavy whipping cream
- 1½ teaspoons vanilla extract
  Dash ground nutmeg
- 1 loaf (1 pound) French bread, cut into 1-inch cubes

CARAMEL SAUCE

- 1 cup sugar
- ¼ cup water
- 1 cup heavy whipping cream
- 2 tablespoons butter

1. Preheat oven to 350°. In a large skillet, heat butter over medium heat. Add apples, sugar, raisins, walnuts and cinnamon; bring just to a boil, stirring constantly. Reduce heat; simmer, uncovered, until apples are tender, stirring occasionally. Remove from heat; stir in vanilla.

2. For the bread pudding, in a large bowl, whisk the eggs, milk, 1½ cups sugar, cream, vanilla and nutmeg until blended. Stir in bread cubes and apple mixture. Transfer to a greased 13x9-in. baking dish. Sprinkle with remaining sugar. Bake, uncovered, 40-45 minutes or until a knife inserted near the center comes out clean.

3. For caramel sauce, in a small heavy saucepan, combine sugar and water; stir gently to moisten all the sugar. Cook over medium-low heat, gently swirling pan occasionally, until sugar is dissolved. Cover; bring to a boil over medium-high heat. Cook 1 minute.

4. Uncover pan; continue to boil until syrup turns a medium amber color. Immediately remove from heat and carefully stir in cream and butter. Serve with warm bread pudding.

Raspberry Sugar Cream Tarts

These yummy tarts bring back fond memories of baking with my mom.

—**CATHY BANKS** ENCINITAS, CA

PREP: 30 MIN. • **BAKE:** 15 MIN. + COOLING
MAKES: 3 DOZEN

- ¾ **cup unsalted butter, softened**
- ½ **cup sugar**
- 2 **egg yolks**
- ¾ **teaspoon almond or vanilla extract**
- ⅛ **teaspoon salt**
- 1¾ **cups all-purpose flour**

FILLING

- 3 **tablespoons seedless raspberry spreadable fruit**
- ¾ **cup sugar**
- 3 **tablespoons all-purpose flour**
  Dash salt
- ¾ **cup heavy whipping cream**
- ⅓ **cup half-and-half cream**
- ½ **teaspoon almond or vanilla extract**
  Fresh raspberries, optional

1. In a large bowl, cream butter and sugar until light and fluffy. Beat in the egg yolks, extract and salt. Gradually beat in flour.

2. Shape the dough into ¾-in. balls; place in greased mini-muffin cups. Press evenly onto the bottoms and up the sides of the cups. Bake at 350° for 10-12 minutes or until light brown. Cool in pans on wire racks.

3. Spread ¼ teaspoon spreadable fruit onto the bottom of each crust. In a small bowl, combine the sugar, flour and salt. Whisk in the heavy whipping cream, half-and-half and extract just until blended (mixture will be thin). Spoon 2 teaspoons filling into each crust. Bake 12-14 minutes longer or until filling just begins to bubble.

4. Cool for 10 minutes before removing from pans; cool completely on wire racks. If desired, top with raspberries. Refrigerate leftovers.

---

top tip

How to Hull

I insert a straw into the tip of the strawberry and push it through the other end.
—**NATALIE C.** ROSS, TX

Strawberry-Hazelnut Meringue Shortcakes

PREP: 25 MIN. • **BAKE:** 45 MIN. + COOLING
MAKES: 8 SERVINGS

- 2 **egg whites**
- ½ **cup sugar**
- ¼ **cup finely chopped hazelnuts, toasted**
- 6 **cups fresh strawberries, hulled and sliced**
- 4 **cups low-fat frozen yogurt**

1. Place egg whites in a small bowl; let stand at room temperature 30 minutes.

2. Preheat oven to 250°. Beat the egg whites on medium speed until foamy. Gradually add the sugar, 1 tablespoon at a time, beating on high after each addition until the sugar is dissolved. Continue beating until stiff glossy peaks form.

3. Drop the meringue into eight mounds on a parchment paper-lined baking sheet. With the back of a spoon, shape into 3-in. cups. Sprinkle with the hazelnuts. Bake 45-50 minutes or until set and dry. Turn off oven (do not open oven door); leave meringues in oven 1 hour. Remove from oven; cool completely on baking sheets. Remove meringues from paper.

4. Place 3 cups strawberries in a large bowl; mash slightly. Stir in remaining strawberries. Just before serving, top meringues with frozen yogurt and strawberries.

NOTE *To toast nuts, spread in a 15x10x1-in. baking pan. Bake at 350° for 5-10 minutes or until lightly browned, stirring occasionally. Or, spread in a dry nonstick skillet and heat over low heat until lightly browned, stirring occasionally.*

PER SERVING *212 cal., 4 g fat (1 g sat. fat), 5 mg chol., 74 mg sodium, 40 g carb., 3 g fiber, 7 g pro.*

"Summertime means fresh berries are ripe for the picking. With desserts like my Strawberry-Hazelnut Meringue Shortcakes, I take full advantage."
—**BARBARA ESTABROOK** RHINELANDER, WI

STRAWBERRY-HAZELNUT MERINGUE SHORTCAKES

PEAR GINGERBREAD COBBLER

"A sure sign that the fall season has arrived is when my family starts asking me to make Pear Gingerbread Cobbler. Over the years, it acquired the nickname of 'Autumn in the Oven'—a very appropriate description!"

—**CHERYL PETERMAN** PRESCOTT, AZ

EAT SMART Pear Gingerbread Cobbler

PREP: 25 MIN. • **BAKE:** 20 MIN. • **MAKES:** 8 SERVINGS

- 4 cups sliced peeled fresh pears (about 4 medium)
- ½ cup packed brown sugar
- ½ cup water
- 1 tablespoon orange juice
- ¼ teaspoon ground cinnamon
- 2 tablespoons cornstarch
- 2 tablespoons cold water
- 2 tablespoons finely chopped crystallized ginger

GINGERBREAD LAYER

- ½ cup buttermilk
- ¼ cup sugar
- ¼ cup molasses
- 1 egg
- 2 tablespoons canola oil
- 1 cup all-purpose flour
- ½ teaspoon baking soda
- ½ teaspoon baking powder
- ½ teaspoon ground ginger
- ¼ teaspoon salt
- ¼ teaspoon ground nutmeg

1. Preheat oven to 350°. In a large saucepan, combine the first five ingredients; bring to a boil. Reduce heat; simmer, uncovered, 10 minutes or until pears are tender, stirring occasionally.

2. In a small bowl, mix the cornstarch and cold water until smooth; stir into the pears. Bring to a boil; cook and stir 2 minutes or until thickened. Stir in crystallized ginger. Transfer to a greased 8-in.-square baking dish.

3. In a large bowl, beat the buttermilk, sugar, molasses, egg and oil until the sugar is dissolved. In another bowl, whisk the remaining ingredients; gradually beat into buttermilk mixture. Pour over pear mixture.

4. Bake 20-25 minutes or until the filling is bubbly and a toothpick inserted in center comes out clean.

PER SERVING 277 cal., 5 g fat (1 g sat. fat), 27 mg chol., 215 mg sodium, 58 g carb., 3 g fiber, 3 g pro.

(5) INGREDIENTS Lemon Velvet Dessert

When I first served this citrusy treat, everyone oohed and aahed. No one believed me when I told them how easy it was to prepare.
—**MARIA BARNET** ELKINS PARK, PA

PREP: 15 MIN. + CHILLING • **MAKES:** 8 SERVINGS

- 1 package (8 ounces) cream cheese, softened
- ½ cup lemon curd
- 1 envelope unflavored gelatin
- ½ cup water
- 1 cup heavy whipping cream, whipped
- 1 teaspoon grated lemon peel

1. In a small bowl, beat cream cheese and lemon curd until smooth; set aside.

2. In a small saucepan, sprinkle gelatin over water; let stand for 1 minute. Cook and stir over low heat until the gelatin is completely dissolved, about 2 minutes.

3. Beat gelatin into cream cheese mixture. Fold in whipped cream and lemon peel. Pour into eight dessert cups. Cover and refrigerate for 1 hour or until firm.

LEMON VELVET DESSERT

BAKED CRANBERRY PUDDING

Baked Cranberry Pudding

Here's an old-fashioned dessert that goes over especially well at Christmastime. I top the warm slices with whipped cream.
—**LUCY MEYRING** WALDEN, CO

PREP: 20 MIN. • **BAKE:** 45 MIN. + COOLING • **MAKES:** 10 SERVINGS

- 2 eggs, separated
- 1½ cups all-purpose flour
- 3 tablespoons grated orange peel
- 1 teaspoon baking powder
- 1 teaspoon ground cinnamon
- ½ teaspoon ground nutmeg
- ½ teaspoon cream of tartar, divided
- ⅛ teaspoon salt
- 3 cups coarsely chopped cranberries
- 1 cup packed brown sugar
- ½ cup heavy whipping cream
- ¼ cup butter, melted
- 2 teaspoons vanilla extract

TOPPING
- 1½ cups sugar
- ½ cup orange juice
- 2½ cups whole cranberries
- Thin orange peel strips, optional

1. Place the egg whites in a large bowl; let stand at room temperature for 30 minutes.
2. In a large bowl, mix flour, orange peel, baking powder, cinnamon, nutmeg, ¼ teaspoon cream of tartar and salt. Stir in chopped cranberries. In another bowl, mix brown sugar, cream, butter, vanilla and egg yolks. Add to flour mixture; stir just until moistened. (Batter will be stiff.)
3. Add remaining cream of tartar to egg whites; with clean beaters, beat on medium speed until soft peaks form. Fold into batter. Transfer to a greased 9-in. springform pan. Bake at 350° for 45-50 minutes or until a toothpick inserted in center comes out clean.
4. Meanwhile, for topping, combine sugar and orange juice in a small saucepan; bring to a boil, stirring frequently. Cook 2-3 minutes longer or until sugar is dissolved. Add berries; reduce heat and simmer for 6 to 8 minutes or until berries begin to burst. Remove from the heat; cover and keep warm.
5. When pudding tests done, place springform pan on a 15-in. x 10-in. baking pan. Spoon cranberry mixture over top. Return to the oven; bake 10 minutes longer.

6. Cool for 10 minutes before removing sides of springform pan. Cool for at least 1 hour before serving. If made ahead, pudding can be warmed in a 350° oven for 10 minutes. If desired, top with orange peel strips before serving.

Blueberry-Blackberry Rustic Tart

My dad loved to stop along the side of the road in Maine and pick wild blueberries. Mom would bake them in a cornmeal crust.
—**PRISCILLA GILBERT** INDIAN HARBOUR BEACH, FL

PREP: 20 MIN. + CHILLING • **BAKE:** 55 MIN. • **MAKES:** 8 SERVINGS

- 2 cups all-purpose flour
- ⅓ cup sugar
- ¼ cup yellow cornmeal
- ⅔ cup cold butter, cubed
- ½ cup buttermilk

FILLING
- 4 cups fresh blueberries
- 2 cups fresh blackberries
- ⅔ cup sugar
- ⅓ cup all-purpose flour
- 2 tablespoons lemon juice
- 1 egg, beaten
- 2 tablespoons turbinado (washed raw) sugar or coarse sugar
- Whipped cream, optional

1. In a large bowl, mix flour, sugar and cornmeal; cut in butter until crumbly. Gradually add buttermilk, tossing with a fork until dough holds together when pressed. Shape into a disk; wrap in plastic wrap. Refrigerate 30 minutes or overnight.
2. Preheat oven to 375°. On a lightly floured surface, roll the dough into a 14-in. circle. Transfer to a parchment paper-lined baking sheet.
3. In a large bowl, combine berries, sugar, flour and lemon juice; spoon over pastry to within 2 in. of edges. Fold pastry edge over filling, leaving center uncovered. Brush folded pastry with beaten egg; sprinkle with turbinado sugar.
4. Bake 55-60 minutes or until crust is golden brown and filling is bubbly. Using parchment paper, slide tart onto a wire rack to cool. If desired, serve with whipped cream.

BLUEBERRY-BLACKBERRY RUSTIC TART

Maple-Nut Cheesecake

This maple-flavored cheesecake is a little bit different but oh-so-good. Drizzle chocolate on top for an elegant finish.

—WENDY PAFFENROTH PINE ISLAND, NY

PREP: 45 MIN. • **BAKE:** 45 MIN. + CHILLING
MAKES: 12 SERVINGS

- ¾ cup graham cracker crumbs
- ½ cup finely chopped walnuts
- 3 tablespoons sugar
- ¼ cup butter, melted

FILLING

- 4 packages (8 ounces each) cream cheese, softened
- ¾ cup sugar
- 2 teaspoons maple flavoring
- ½ teaspoon almond extract
- ⅛ teaspoon grated lemon peel
- 3 eggs, lightly beaten
  Melted chocolate, optional

1. Place a greased 9-in. springform pan on a double thickness of heavy-duty foil (about 18 in. square). Wrap foil securely around pan.

2. In a small bowl, mix the graham cracker crumbs, walnuts and sugar; stir in butter. Press onto the bottom and 1 in. up the sides of the prepared pan. Place the pan on a baking sheet. Bake at 325° for 10 minutes. Cool on a wire rack.

3. For the filling, in a large bowl, beat cream cheese and sugar until smooth. Beat in the maple flavoring, extract and lemon peel. Add eggs; beat on low speed just until blended. Pour into the crust. Place springform pan in a larger baking pan; add 1 in. of hot water to the larger pan.

4. Bake for 45-55 minutes or until the center is just set and the top appears dull. Remove the springform pan from the water bath. Cool the cheesecake on a wire rack for 10 minutes. Loosen the sides from the pan with a knife; remove the foil. Cool 1 hour longer. Refrigerate overnight.

5. Remove the rim from the pan. If desired, drizzle the cheesecake with melted chocolate.

CINNAMON-PECAN APPLE DUMPLINGS

MAPLE-NUT CHEESECAKE

Cinnamon-Pecan Apple Dumplings

With crescent dough, dessert dumplings are easy to prepare. I always serve extra sauce—people can't seem to get enough!

—CYNTHIA GONZALES MERCEDES, TX

PREP: 15 MIN. • **BAKE:** 25 MIN.
MAKES: 8 SERVINGS (1 CUP SAUCE)

- 1 tube (8 ounces) refrigerated crescent rolls
- 4 small Granny Smith apples, peeled and halved
- 1 teaspoon sugar
- 1 teaspoon ground cinnamon

ORANGE SAUCE

- ¾ cup orange juice
- ½ cup sugar
- ½ cup butter, cubed
- 2 tablespoons chopped pecans, toasted

1. Unroll crescent dough and separate into eight triangles. Wrap one triangle around each apple half. Place on a greased 15-in. x 10-in. x 1-in. baking pan, flat side down.

2. Combine the sugar and cinnamon; sprinkle over the dumplings. Bake at 350° for 23-28 minutes or until golden brown and apples are tender.

3. For the sauce, in a small saucepan, combine the orange juice and sugar; bring to a boil, stirring occasionally. Cook for 10-12 minutes or until liquid is reduced to about ½ cup, stirring frequently. Remove from the heat; gradually stir in the butter just until blended. Serve sauce warm with warm dumplings; sprinkle with pecans.

NOTE *To toast nuts, spread in a 15x10x1-in. baking pan. Bake at 350° for 5-10 minutes or until lightly browned, stirring occasionally. Or, spread in a dry nonstick skillet and heat over low heat until lightly browned, stirring occasionally.*

Cherry-Chocolate Cream Puffs

Like the combo of chocolate and cherries? You'll like it even more in a cream puff!

—**CHRISTOPHER FUSON** MARYSVILLE, OH

PREP: 30 MIN. + COOLING
BAKE: 30 MIN. + COOLING
MAKES: 10 SERVINGS

- 1 **cup water**
- ⅓ **cup butter, cubed**
- 1 **tablespoon sugar**
- ⅛ **teaspoon salt**
- 1 **cup all-purpose flour**
- 4 **eggs**

FILLING

- 1 **carton (8 ounces) frozen whipped topping, thawed**
- ½ **cup sugar**
- ¼ **cup 2% milk**
- 6 **ounces semisweet chocolate, chopped**
- ¾ **pound fresh or frozen pitted sweet cherries (thawed), coarsely chopped**
- **Confectioners' sugar**

1. Preheat oven to 400°. In a small saucepan, bring water, butter, sugar and salt to a rolling boil. Add flour all at once and beat until blended. Cook over medium heat, stirring vigorously until mixture pulls away from sides of pan and forms a ball. Remove from heat; let stand 5 minutes.

2. Add the eggs, one at a time, beating well after each addition until smooth. Continue beating until the mixture is smooth and shiny.

3. Drop the dough by scant ¼ cupfuls 3 in. apart onto greased baking sheets. Bake 30-35 minutes or until puffed, very firm and golden brown. Remove to wire racks. Split the puffs open. Pull out and discard the soft dough from

CHERRY-CHOCOLATE CREAM PUFFS

inside the tops and bottoms. Cool puffs completely on a wire rack.

4. Let whipped topping stand at room temperature 30 minutes. Meanwhile, in a small saucepan, bring the sugar and milk to a boil over medium heat; cook and stir until sugar is dissolved. Reduce heat to low; stir in chocolate until melted. Transfer to a large bowl. Cool to room temperature, about 25 minutes, stirring occasionally. Fold in whipped topping.

5. Just before serving, fill each cream puff with a heaping tablespoonful of cherries; top with the chocolate filling. Replace tops. Dust with confectioners' sugar. Refrigerate leftovers.

VANILLA CREAM PUFFS *Omit cherry-chocolate filling. In a bowl, whisk 1½ cups milk, 1 package (5.1 ounces) instant vanilla pudding mix and ½ teaspoon almond extract for 2 minutes. Let stand 2 minutes or until soft-set. Fold in 4 cups whipped cream. Spoon into cream puffs.*

Coconut Cashew Crunch

My husband doesn't normally care for coconut, but this nutty crunch is one of his favorite treats. It makes an incredible topping for ice cream or frozen yogurt.

—**DANA NEMECEK** SKIATOOK, OK

COCONUT CASHEW CRUNCH

PREP: 20 MIN. • **BAKE:** 50 MIN.
MAKES: 3 QUARTS

- 9 **cups Rice Krispies**
- 2 **cups flaked coconut**
- 1 **can (8 ounces) salted cashew pieces**
- 1 **cup packed brown sugar**
- ½ **cup butter, cubed**
- ½ **cup light corn syrup**
- 1 **teaspoon vanilla extract**
- ½ **teaspoon baking soda**

1. In a large bowl, combine the cereal, coconut and cashews.

2. In a large saucepan, combine the brown sugar, butter and corn syrup; bring to a boil over medium heat, stirring constantly. Cook and stir for 5 minutes. Remove from the heat; stir in vanilla and baking soda. Pour over cereal mixture; toss to coat.

3. Transfer to two foil-lined 15-in. x 10-in. x 1-in. baking pans. Bake at 250° for 50-60 minutes or until golden brown, stirring every 15 minutes. Cool completely in the pan on a wire rack. Serve as is or use as a topping for ice cream, fruit or yogurt. Store in airtight containers.

Apple Kolaches

A fellow home economist gave me a recipe for kolaches, and I couldn't wait to bake a batch of the fruit-filled pastries. My son, who isn't normally a fan of sweets, was disappointed when he came home to find his dad had polished off the last one!

—**ANN JOHNSON** EVANSVILLE, IN

PREP: 30 MIN. + CHILLING • **BAKE:** 10 MIN.
MAKES: 2½ DOZEN

- 1 cup butter, softened
- 1 package (8 ounces) cream cheese, softened
- 2 cups all-purpose flour
- 1½ cups finely chopped peeled apples
- ¼ teaspoon ground cinnamon

ICING

- 1 cup confectioners' sugar
- 4½ teaspoons 2% milk
- ½ teaspoon vanilla extract

1. In a large bowl, beat the butter and cream cheese until light and fluffy. Gradually add the flour and mix well. Divide dough into two portions; cover and refrigerate for 2 hours or until easy to handle.

2. Preheat oven to 400°. In a small bowl, combine apples and cinnamon. On a lightly floured surface, roll one portion of the dough into a 15x9-in. rectangle; cut into 3-in. squares. Place a teaspoonful of apple mixture in the center of each square. Overlap two opposite corners of dough over filling; pinch tightly to seal.

3. Place 2 in. apart on ungreased baking sheets. Repeat with remaining dough and apple mixture. Bake 10-12 minutes or until the bottoms are lightly browned. Cool 1 minute before removing from pans to wire racks.

4. Combine icing ingredients; drizzle over warm kolaches.

LEMONY COCONUT FROZEN YOGURT

APPLE KOLACHES

EAT SMART Lemony Coconut Frozen Yogurt

Whenever I crave something cold to beat the summer heat, I whip up my lemony frozen yogurt. I like it served in a crunchy waffle bowl with coconut, blueberries and raspberries sprinkled on top.

—**CAITLYN HEINZ** OVID, NY

PREP: 15 MIN. + CHILLING
PROCESS: 15 MIN. • **MAKES:** 1¼ QUARTS

- 4 cups (32 ounces) plain yogurt
- ¾ cup sugar
- ½ cup lemon juice
- 3 tablespoons grated lemon peel
- 1 cup half-and-half cream
- ½ cup flaked coconut, toasted
  Ice cream waffle bowls, optional
  Fresh blueberries and raspberries, optional

1. Line a strainer or colander with four layers of cheesecloth or one coffee filter; place over a bowl. Place yogurt in the prepared strainer; refrigerate, covered, 3 hours. Remove yogurt from cheesecloth and place in a large bowl; discard drained liquid.

2. Whisk the sugar, lemon juice and lemon peel into yogurt until the sugar is dissolved. Stir in cream. Pour into cylinder of ice cream freezer; freeze according to the manufacturer's directions, adding coconut during the last 5 minutes of processing time. If desired, serve in waffle bowls and top with berries.

NOTE *To toast coconut, spread in a 15x10x1-in. baking pan. Bake at 350° for 5-10 minutes or until golden brown, stirring frequently.*

PER SERVING *177 cal., 7 g fat (5 g sat. fat), 25 mg chol., 69 mg sodium, 24 g carb., trace fiber, 4 g pro.* **Diabetic Exchanges:** *1½ starch, 1½ fat.*

Mocha Cream Cheese Mousse

Coffee and dessert come together in a whole new way in this smooth, velvety mousse. Java lovers just can't get enough, and neither can chocoholics!

—BETH ALLARD BELMONT, NH

PREP: 25 MIN. + CHILLING
MAKES: 2 SERVINGS

- ⅔ cup semisweet chocolate chips
- 3 tablespoons plus 1 teaspoon half-and-half cream
- 1 teaspoon instant coffee granules
- ⅔ cup heavy whipping cream
- 3 tablespoons confectioners' sugar
- 1 package (3 ounces) cream cheese, softened
- ½ teaspoon vanilla extract
  Whipped cream and chocolate curls

1. In a small bowl, microwave the chocolate chips, half-and-half cream and coffee granules at 80% power for 45-60 seconds or until the chips are melted; stir until smooth. Cool to room temperature.

2. In another bowl, beat the heavy whipping cream until it begins to thicken. Add the confectioners' sugar; beat until stiff peaks form. Add the cream cheese and vanilla to the cooled chocolate mixture; beat until smooth. Fold in whipped cream.

3. Spoon mousse into serving dishes. Garnish with whipped cream and chocolate curls.

NOTE *This recipe was tested in a 1,100-watt microwave.*

⑤INGREDIENTS FAST FIX
Raspberry Parfaits

Want an easy but elegant treat for lunch with a friend? You'll need only 10 minutes and four basic ingredients—berries, jam, whipped topping and cream cheese—to put together decadent parfaits.

—JOELYN HANHAM CHESTER, NY

START TO FINISH: 10 MIN.
MAKES: 2 SERVINGS

- 2 ounces cream cheese, softened
- 2 tablespoons seedless raspberry jam
- ½ cup whipped topping, divided
- ½ cup fresh or frozen raspberries

1. In a small bowl, beat cream cheese and jam until smooth. Fold in ¼ cup whipped topping.

2. Place 2 tablespoons raspberries in each of two small parfait glasses or dessert dishes; layer with cream cheese mixture and remaining berries. Top with remaining whipped topping. Refrigerate until serving.

Spiced Peach Puffs

We used to make cream puffs for special occasions when I was growing up in a family of seven. This spiced peach version has always been my favorite.

—AGNES WARD STRATFORD, ON

PREP: 70 MIN. • **BAKE:** 25 MIN. + COOLING
MAKES: 3 DOZEN

- 1 cup water
- ½ cup butter, cubed
- 1 teaspoon ground nutmeg
- ⅛ teaspoon salt
- 1 cup all-purpose flour
- 4 eggs
- 2 cups heavy whipping cream
- ½ cup confectioners' sugar
- 1 teaspoon vanilla extract
- 2 cups chopped peeled fresh or frozen peaches, thawed
  Additional confectioners' sugar

1. In a large saucepan, bring the water, butter, nutmeg and salt to a boil. Add flour all at once and stir until a smooth ball forms. Remove from the heat; let stand for 5 minutes. Add eggs, one at a time, beating well after each addition. Continue beating until mixture is smooth and shiny.

2. Drop dough by tablespoonfuls 2 in. apart onto greased baking sheets. Bake at 400° for 25-30 minutes or until golden brown. Remove to a wire rack. Immediately split puffs open; remove tops and set aside. Discard soft dough from inside. Cool puffs.

3. For the filling, in a large bowl, beat cream until it begins to thicken. Add confectioners' sugar and vanilla; beat until stiff peaks form.

4. Just before serving, fill puffs with whipped cream and peaches. Dust with confectioners' sugar.

SPICED PEACH PUFFS

Kidding Around

Children (and grown-ups, too) just can't resist recipes like S'Moreos and Banana Pudding. In an especially playful mood? Fool 'em with two yummy desserts that resemble breakfast!

BANANA PUDDING

(5) INGREDIENTS FAST FIX ▶ S'Moreos

While camping, our family enjoyed a cookie-filled variation of classic s'mores. If you have a jar of Nutella, go one step further and slather it on the inside of the graham cracker halves.

—**CHRISTINA SMITH** SANTA ROSA, CA

START TO FINISH: 15 MIN. • **MAKES:** 4 SERVINGS

- 4 **Oreo cookies**
- 3 **tablespoons creamy peanut butter**
- 4 **whole graham crackers, halved**
- 1 **milk chocolate candy bar (1.55 ounces), quartered**
- 4 **large marshmallows**

1. Spread both sides of each Oreo cookie with peanut butter; place over half of the halved graham crackers. Top with chocolate.

2. Using a long metal skewer or long-handled fork, toast marshmallows 6 in. from medium-hot heat until golden brown, turning occasionally. Place on chocolate; cover with remaining graham crackers. Serve immediately.

Banana Pudding

I didn't see my son, Lance Corporal Eric Harris, for more than two years after he enlisted in the Marines after high school. I'll always remember spotting him for the first time at the airport when he returned. When we got home, he ate two big bowls of my banana pudding, his favorite treat. He's a true Southern boy!

—**STEPHANIE HARRIS** MONTPELIER, VA

PREP: 15 MIN. + CHILLING • **COOK:** 20 MIN. + COOLING
MAKES: 9 SERVINGS

- ¾ **cup sugar**
- ¼ **cup all-purpose flour**
- ¼ **teaspoon salt**
- 3 **cups 2% milk**
- 3 **eggs**
- 1½ **teaspoons vanilla extract**
- 58 **vanilla wafers (about 8 ounces), divided**
- 4 **large ripe bananas, cut into ¼-inch slices**

1. In a large saucepan, mix sugar, flour and salt. Whisk in milk. Cook and stir over medium heat until thickened and bubbly. Reduce heat to low; cook and stir 2 minutes longer. Remove from heat.

2. In a small bowl, whisk the eggs. Whisk a small amount of the hot mixture into the eggs; return all to the pan, whisking constantly. Bring to a gentle boil; cook and stir 2 minutes. Remove from the heat. Stir in the vanilla. Cool 15 minutes, stirring occasionally.

3. In an ungreased 8-in.-square baking dish, layer 25 vanilla wafers, half of the banana slices and half of the pudding. Repeat layers.

4. Press plastic wrap onto surface of pudding. Refrigerate 4 hours or overnight. Just before serving, crush remaining wafers and sprinkle over top.

S'MOREOS

EDIBLE JUICE
SUNNY-SIDE-UP DESSERT

(5)INGREDIENTS Edible Juice

PREP: 5 MIN. • **COOK:** 5 MIN. + CHILLING • **MAKES:** 4 SERVINGS

- 2 envelope unflavored gelatin
- 4 cups orange juice, divided
- 4 teaspoons sugar
- 4 drinking straws

1. In a small bowl, sprinkle gelatin over 1 cup orange juice; let stand 1 minute.

2. In a large saucepan, bring sugar and remaining juice to a boil. Stir in gelatin mixture. Cook and stir over low heat until gelatin is completely dissolved. Pour into four glasses; insert straws. Refrigerate, covered, until firm.

(5)INGREDIENTS FAST FIX
Sunny-Side-Up Dessert

START TO FINISH: 10 MIN. • **MAKES:** 4 SERVINGS

- 1 tablespoon butter, softened
- 4 slices pound cake
- ½ cup vanilla yogurt
- 4 canned apricot halves

1. Spread butter over both sides of cake slices. In a skillet, toast pound cake over medium-high heat 15-30 seconds on each side or until golden brown. Transfer to dessert plates.

2. Spoon yogurt over cake to resemble fried egg whites. Top with apricots to resemble yolks.

Lemon Pudding Dessert

Here's a fluffy, tangy treat we always have during the holidays. I love the fact that I can prepare it in advance and keep it in the refrigerator until dinnertime.
—**JANICE HURD** CHURCH HILL, TN

PREP: 35 MIN. + CHILLING
MAKES: 20 SERVINGS

- 1 **cup all-purpose flour**
- ½ **cup chopped pecans**
- ½ **cup butter, melted**
- 1 **tablespoon sugar**

FILLING

- 1 **package (8 ounces) cream cheese, softened**
- 1 **cup confectioners' sugar**
- 1 **carton (12 ounces) frozen whipped topping, thawed, divided**
- 4 **cups cold 2% milk**
- 3 **packages (3.4 ounces each) instant lemon pudding mix**

1. In a small bowl, combine the flour, pecans, butter and sugar. Press onto the bottom of a greased 13-in. x 9-in. baking dish. Bake at 350° for 12-15 minutes or until the edges are lightly browned. Cool crust completely on a wire rack.

2. In a large bowl, beat cream cheese and confectioners' sugar until smooth. Fold in half of the whipped topping. Spread over crust.

3. In a large bowl, whisk the milk and instant lemon pudding mix for 2 minutes (the mixture will be thick). Spread over the cream cheese layer; top with the remaining whipped topping. Refrigerate until chilled.

CINNAMON-TOFFEE CROISSANT BREAD PUDDING

"I've been a bread pudding fan from the moment I first tasted this spiced toffee version. Served warm from the oven, it's the ultimate comfort food."
—**AMBER MASSEY** ARGYLE, TX

LEMON PUDDING DESSERT

Cinnamon-Toffee Croissant Bread Pudding

PREP: 30 MIN. + STANDING • **BAKE:** 30 MIN.
MAKES: 12 SERVINGS (1¼ CUPS SAUCE)

- 3 **eggs, beaten**
- 4 **cups 2% milk**
- 2 **cups sugar**
- 4½ **teaspoons vanilla extract**
- 3 **teaspoons ground cinnamon**
- ½ **teaspoon ground nutmeg**
- 10 **croissants, torn into pieces**
- 1 **cup toffee bits**
- 1 **cup chopped pecans, toasted**
- 1 **cup milk chocolate chips**

SAUCE

- 1 **cup sugar**
- ½ **cup half-and-half cream**
- ¼ **cup butter, cubed**
- ½ **teaspoon vanilla extract**

1. In a large bowl, combine the eggs, milk, sugar, vanilla, cinnamon and nutmeg. Gently stir in the croissants, toffee bits, pecans and chocolate chips; let stand for 15 minutes or until the croissants are softened.

2. Transfer to a greased 13-in. x 9-in. baking dish. Bake, uncovered, at 350° for 30-35 minutes or until a knife inserted near the center of pudding comes out clean.

3. For the sauce, bring the sugar, cream and butter to a boil in a small saucepan. Reduce heat; simmer, uncovered, for 5 minutes. Remove from the heat; stir in vanilla. Serve with warm bread pudding.

Lemon-Ginger Creme Brulee

Tongue-tingling lemon and ginger give classic creme brulee a delectable update.

—SCOTT HUNTER SHERMAN OAKS, CA

PREP: 20 MIN. • **BAKE:** 25 MIN. + CHILLING
MAKES: 6 SERVINGS

- 2 cups heavy whipping cream
- 1/3 cup plus 2 tablespoons sugar, divided
- 1/2 teaspoon ground ginger
- 8 egg yolks, beaten
- 1 teaspoon lemon extract
- 1/2 teaspoon vanilla extract
- 2 tablespoons brown sugar

1. In a large heavy saucepan, heat the heavy whipping cream, 1/3 cup sugar and ginger until bubbles form around the sides of the pan. Remove from the heat; stir a small amount of the hot mixture into the egg yolks. Return all to the pan, stirring constantly. Stir in the extracts.

2. Transfer to six 6-oz. ramekins or custard cups. Place in a baking pan; add 1 in. of boiling water to pan. Bake, uncovered, at 325° for 25-30 minutes or until centers are just set (mixture will jiggle). Remove ramekins from water bath; cool for 10 minutes. Cover and refrigerate for at least 4 hours.

3. Combine the brown sugar and remaining sugar. If using a creme brulee torch, sprinkle the custards with sugar mixture. Heat the sugar with the torch until caramelized. Serve immediately.

4. If broiling the custards, place ramekins on a baking sheet; let stand at room temperature for 15 minutes. Sprinkle with sugar mixture. Broil 8 in. from the heat for 4-7 minutes or until sugar is caramelized. Refrigerate for 1-2 hours or until firm.

top tip

Chocolate Chip Tip

I let leftover melted chocolate harden, then chop it into chunks and store it in the fridge to use later when I need chocolate chips.
—RENEE Z. TACOMA, WA

Chocolate Lover's Custards

A swirled white and bittersweet chocolate topping will tempt you to dip a spoon into these smooth, rich, individual-sized desserts. And when you get to the silky custard underneath, it seals the deal!

—LORRAINE CALAND SHUNIAH, ON

PREP: 25 MIN. • **BAKE:** 30 MIN. + CHILLING
MAKES: 8 SERVINGS

- 2½ cups heavy whipping cream
- ½ cup sugar
- 5 ounces white baking chocolate, chopped
- 6 egg yolks
- 1 teaspoon vanilla extract

TOPPING
- 3 ounces bittersweet chocolate, melted
- 1 ounce white baking chocolate, melted

1. In a small saucepan, heat cream and sugar until bubbles form around sides of pan. Add white chocolate; stir until smooth. Remove from the heat. In a small bowl, whisk egg yolks; stir a small amount of hot cream mixture into egg yolks. Return all to the pan, stirring constantly. Stir in vanilla.

2. Transfer to eight 6-oz. ramekins or custard cups. Place in a baking pan; add 1 in. of boiling water to pan. Bake, uncovered, at 325° for 30-35 minutes or until centers are just set (mixture will jiggle). Remove the ramekins from water bath; cool for 10 minutes. Cover and refrigerate for at least 4 hours.

3. Working one at a time, spread bittersweet chocolate over each custard. Immediately place drops of white chocolate over the top and swirl with a toothpick. Refrigerate for 15 minutes or until chocolate is firm.

CHOCOLATE LOVER'S CUSTARDS

Cranberry Celebration Cheesecake

PREP: 45 MIN. • **BAKE:** 1¾ HOURS + CHILLING • **MAKES:** 16 SERVINGS

- ½ cup dried cranberries
- 2 cups cake flour
- ½ cup ground almonds
- ¼ cup confectioners' sugar
- ½ cup cold butter, cubed

FILLING
- ¾ cup plus 1½ cups sugar, divided
- 2 tablespoons cornstarch
- ¼ cup cranberry juice
- 2 cups fresh or frozen cranberries
- 4 packages (8 ounces each) cream cheese, softened
- 1 teaspoon vanilla extract
- 4 eggs, lightly beaten

TOPPING
- 2 cups (16 ounces) sour cream
- ¼ cup sugar
- 2 teaspoons vanilla extract
- 1 cup heavy whipping cream
- ¼ cup ground almonds
- ¼ cup sliced almonds, toasted

1. In a food processor, finely chop the dried cranberries. Add the flour, almonds and confectioners' sugar; process until blended. Add butter; pulse just until crumbly.

2. Press onto the bottom and 1½ in. up the sides of a greased 10-in. springform pan. Place on a baking sheet. Bake at 350° for 10 minutes.

3. In a small saucepan, combine ¾ cup sugar and the cornstarch; stir in the cranberry juice until smooth. Add berries. Cook and stir until thickened and bubbly. Set aside.

4. In a large bowl, beat cream cheese, vanilla and remaining sugar until smooth. Add the eggs; beat just until combined. Pour half of batter into crust. Carefully spoon ¾ cup berry mixture over batter; top with remaining batter.

5. Bake for 45 minutes. Reduce heat to 250°. Bake 25-30 minutes longer or until the center is almost set. Combine the sour cream, sugar and vanilla; spread over the top. Bake 20-30 minutes or until set. Cool on a wire rack for 10 minutes. Run a knife around the edge of pan to loosen; cool 1 hour longer. Spread remaining berry mixture over the top. Refrigerate overnight.

6. Beat the cream until stiff peaks form; fold in the ground almonds. Pipe around top edge of cheesecake; sprinkle with sliced almonds.

"Cranberry Celebration Cheesecake is perfect for holiday parties, special events...any day at all."
—**TERI LEE RASEY** CADILLAC, MI

Cherry-Blackberry Crisp

I've used mulberries instead of blackberries in this old family recipe. Whichever you choose, it's a sure crowd-pleaser.
—**WANDA ALLENSWORTH** WEBSTER CITY, IA

PREP: 20 MIN. • **BAKE:** 55 MIN. • **MAKES:** 14 SERVINGS

- ⅔ cup packed brown sugar
- 2 tablespoons quick-cooking tapioca
- ½ teaspoon almond extract
- ¼ teaspoon ground cinnamon
- 4 cups frozen pitted tart cherries, thawed
- 2 cups frozen unsweetened blackberries, thawed

TOPPING
- 1½ cups all-purpose flour
- 1½ cups sugar
-    Dash salt
- ⅔ cup cold butter
- 1½ cups finely chopped walnuts
-    Whipped cream

1. In a large bowl, combine brown sugar, tapioca, extract and cinnamon. Gently stir in cherries and blackberries. Allow to stand for 10 minutes. Pour into a greased 13-in. x 9-in. baking dish.

2. In another bowl, combine the flour, sugar and salt. Cut in the butter until crumbly. Add the walnuts; sprinkle over the fruit. Bake, uncovered, at 350° for 55-60 minutes or until the topping is golden brown and the filling is bubbly. Serve warm with whipped cream.

CRANBERRY CELEBRATION CHEESECAKE

Orange Cheesecake Dessert

This is my "Dreamsicle Cheesecake" because the flavor makes me think of my favorite childhood treat. The luscious raspberry syrup gives each piece a touch of grown-up sophistication.
—**PATRICIA HARMON** BADEN, PA

PREP: 30 MIN. • **BAKE:** 35 MIN. + CHILLING
MAKES: 18 SERVINGS

- 1¾ cups shortbread cookie crumbs (about 22 cookies)
- ⅔ cup sliced almonds, finely chopped
- 2 tablespoons plus 1 cup sugar, divided
- ⅓ cup butter, melted
- 4 packages (8 ounces each) cream cheese, softened
- ½ cup thawed orange juice concentrate
- 1¼ teaspoons almond extract
- 4 eggs, lightly beaten
- 2 packages (10 ounces each) frozen sweetened raspberries, thawed
- 2 tablespoons cornstarch

1. In a small bowl, combine the cookie crumbs, almonds and 2 tablespoons sugar; stir in butter. Press into a greased 13-in. x 9-in. baking dish. Cover and refrigerate for at least 15 minutes.

2. In a large bowl, beat cream cheese and remaining sugar until smooth. Add orange juice concentrate and extract; beat until smooth. Add eggs; beat on low speed just until combined. Pour over crust.

3. Bake at 350° for 35-40 minutes or until center is almost set. Cool on a wire rack for 1 hour. Cover and refrigerate for 8 hours or overnight.

4. Drain raspberries, reserving juice; set berries aside. In a small saucepan, combine cornstarch and reserved juice until smooth. Bring to a boil; cook and stir for 1-2 minutes or until thickened. Remove from the heat; gently stir in raspberries. Cool. Serve with cheesecake dessert.

ORANGE CHEESECAKE DESSERT

PRETZEL FRUIT PIZZA

Pretzel Fruit Pizza

While working as an independent kitchen consultant, I created a dessert pizza. Top it with whatever fresh fruit you like.
—**BETHANY PERRY** BEVERLY, MA

PREP: 15 MIN. + CHILLING • **BAKE:** 10 MIN. + CHILLING
MAKES: 8 SERVINGS

- 3 cups finely crushed pretzels
- ⅔ cup sugar
- 1¼ cups cold butter, cubed
- 1 can (14 ounces) sweetened condensed milk
- ¼ cup lime juice
- 1 tablespoon grated lime peel
- 1½ cups whipped topping
- 7 to 8 cups assorted fresh fruit, such as plums, berries, kiwi and oranges

1. Preheat oven to 375°. In a large bowl, mix the crushed pretzels and sugar. Cut in the butter until the mixture resembles coarse crumbs. Press into a 14-in. pizza pan. Bake 8-10 minutes or until set. Cool on a wire rack; refrigerate 30 minutes.

2. In a large bowl, mix milk, lime juice and lime peel. Fold in whipped topping; spread over crust. Refrigerate until cold. Just before serving, top with fruit.

BERNICE SMITH'S ORANGE-CINNAMON FRENCH TOAST PAGE 142

Breakfast & Brunch

Thanks to these **rise-and-shine recipes**, a homemade breakfast is as easy as can be. Cheesy egg bakes, chocolaty pancakes, gooey bread pudding, spiced coffee...**what a way to start the day!**

**JUDY WILSON'S
CHILLY COFFEE PUNCH**
PAGE 147

**JENNIFER BECKMAN'S DUTCH BAKED
PANCAKE WITH STRAWBERRY-
ALMOND COMPOTE** PAGE 148

**HEATHER KING'S
FARM FRESH QUICHE**
PAGE 151

FAST FIX ▶ Orange-Cinnamon French Toast

Using the oven to make this tasty toast means everyone eats at the same time.
—**BERNICE SMITH** STURGEON LAKE, MN

START TO FINISH: 30 MIN.
MAKES: 6 SLICES

- 2 to 4 tablespoons butter, melted
- 2 tablespoons honey
- ½ teaspoon ground cinnamon
- 3 eggs
- ½ cup orange juice
- ⅛ teaspoon salt, optional
- 6 slices bread
  Additional honey, optional

1. In a small bowl, mix the butter, honey and cinnamon. Pour into a greased 13-in. x 9-in. baking pan; spread to coat bottom of pan.
2. In a shallow bowl, whisk the eggs, orange juice and, if desired, salt. Dip both sides of bread in egg mixture. Place in prepared pan.
3. Bake at 400° for 15-20 minutes or until golden brown. Invert onto a serving platter; serve with honey if desired.

MINI-CHIP COCOA PANCAKES

ORANGE-CINNAMON FRENCH TOAST

"Get your chocoholic fix early with a stack of cocoa pancakes dotted with chocolate chips. Add a sprinkling of powdered sugar or a dollop of whipped cream."
—**JOYCE MOYNIHAN** LAKEVILLE, MN

FAST FIX ▶ Mini-Chip Cocoa Pancakes

START TO FINISH: 30 MIN.
MAKES: 4 SERVINGS

- 1¼ cups all-purpose flour
- ¼ cup baking cocoa
- ¼ cup sugar
- 3 teaspoons baking powder
- ½ teaspoon salt
- 2 eggs
- 1 cup 2% milk
- 3 tablespoons butter, melted
- 1½ teaspoons vanilla extract
- ⅔ cup miniature semisweet chocolate chips
  Powdered sugar and whipped cream, optional

1. In a large bowl, whisk the first five ingredients. In another bowl, whisk the eggs, milk, butter and vanilla until blended. Add to the flour mixture; stir just until moistened. Fold in the chocolate chips.
2. Coat a griddle with cooking spray; heat over medium heat. Pour the batter by ¼ cupfuls onto the griddle. Cook until the bubbles on top begin to pop. Turn; cook until the second side is lightly browned. If desired, dust with powdered sugar and serve with whipped cream.

Oatmeal Brulee with Ginger Cream

Here's an extra-special dish for a chilly morning. I love the crispy, caramelized top and raspberry surprise at the bottom.

—YVONNE STARLIN HERMITAGE, TN

PREP: 30 MIN. • **BROIL:** 10 MIN.
MAKES: 4 SERVINGS

GINGER CREAM
- ½ cup heavy whipping cream
- 2 slices fresh gingerroot (about ¾-inch diameter)
- 1 cinnamon stick (3 inches)
- 1 tablespoon grated orange peel
- 3 tablespoons maple syrup
- ⅛ teaspoon ground nutmeg

OATMEAL
- 4 cups water
- 2 cups old-fashioned oats
- ¼ cup chopped dried apricots
- ¼ cup dried cherries, chopped
- ½ teaspoon salt
- 3 tablespoons brown sugar
- 2 tablespoons butter, softened
- 1 cup fresh or frozen unsweetened raspberries, thawed
- ¼ cup sugar

1. In a small saucepan, combine the cream, ginger, cinnamon stick and orange peel; bring to a boil. Reduce heat; simmer, covered, for 10 minutes. Remove from the heat; strain and discard solids. Stir in syrup and nutmeg.

2. In a large saucepan, bring water to a boil; stir in the oats, apricots, cherries and salt. Reduce heat to medium; cook for 5 minutes, stirring occasionally. Remove from the heat; stir in brown sugar and ¼ cup ginger cream. Let stand, covered, for 2 minutes.

3. Grease four 10-oz. broiler-safe ramekins with butter; place on a baking sheet. Divide raspberries among ramekins. Spoon oatmeal over raspberries; sprinkle evenly with sugar. Broil 4-6 in. from the heat for 7-9 minutes or until sugar is caramelized. Serve with remaining ginger cream.

OVERNIGHT ASPARAGUS STRATA

Overnight Asparagus Strata

This is no ordinary strata! The delicious egg bake filled with ham is wonderful not only for breakfast, but also for dinner.

—LYNN LICATA SYLVANIA, OH

PREP: 15 MIN. + CHILLING • **BAKE:** 40 MIN.
MAKES: 8 SERVINGS

- 1 pound fresh asparagus, trimmed and cut into 1-inch pieces
- 4 English muffins, split and toasted
- 2 cups (8 ounces) shredded Colby-Monterey Jack cheese, divided
- 1 cup cubed fully cooked ham
- ½ cup chopped sweet red pepper
- 8 eggs
- 2 cups 2% milk
- 1 teaspoon salt
- 1 teaspoon ground mustard
- ¼ teaspoon pepper

1. In a large saucepan, bring 8 cups water to a boil. Add asparagus; cook, uncovered, 2-3 minutes or just until crisp-tender. Drain and immediately drop into ice water. Drain and pat dry.

2. Arrange six English muffin halves in a greased 13-in. x 9-in. baking dish, cut side up. Trim remaining halves to fill spaces. Layer with 1 cup cheese, asparagus, ham and red pepper.

3. In a large bowl, whisk eggs, milk, salt, mustard and pepper. Pour over top. Refrigerate, covered, overnight.

4. Preheat oven to 375°. Remove strata from refrigerator while oven heats. Sprinkle with remaining cheese. Bake, uncovered, 40-45 minutes or until a knife inserted near the center comes out clean. Let stand 5 minutes before cutting.

OATMEAL BRULEE WITH GINGER CREAM

BRUNCH STRATA

"With ham, zucchini, mushrooms and cheese, this popular egg dish is hearty and satisfying. The recipe makes two stratas, so keep it in mind when you need to feed a crowd in the morning."
—**ARLENE BUTLER** OGDEN, UT

Brunch Strata

PREP: 45 MIN. • **BAKE:** 35 MIN. + STANDING
MAKES: 2 CASSEROLES (8 SERVINGS EACH)

- ⅓ cup canola oil
- ½ pound sliced fresh mushrooms
- 3 small zucchini, chopped
- 2 medium onions, chopped (about 1½ cups)
- 1 medium green pepper, chopped
- 2 cups cubed fully cooked ham
- 2 garlic cloves, minced
- 2 packages (8 ounces each) cream cheese, softened
- ½ cup half-and-half cream
- 12 eggs, lightly beaten
- 4 cups cubed day-old bread
- 3 cups (12 ounces) shredded cheddar cheese
- 1 teaspoon salt
- ½ teaspoon pepper

1. In a Dutch oven, heat oil over medium-high heat. Add the vegetables and ham; cook and stir until vegetables are tender. Add garlic; cook 1 minute longer. Drain and pat dry.
2. In a large bowl, beat the cream cheese and cream until smooth. Gradually beat in the eggs. Stir in the remaining ingredients and vegetable mixture.
3. Transfer to two greased 11-in. x 7-in. baking dishes. Bake, uncovered, at 350° for 35-40 minutes or until a knife inserted near the center comes out clean. Let stand for 10 minutes before serving.

Gruyere & Prosciutto Strata

Prosciutto, sweet onions and Gruyere combine for a wonderful make-ahead breakfast. I never have to worry about leftovers!
—**PATTI LAVELL** ISLAMORADA, FL

PREP: 15 MIN. + CHILLING • **BAKE:** 35 MIN. • **MAKES:** 9 SERVINGS

- 2 teaspoons canola oil
- 4 ounces thin slices prosciutto, chopped
- 2 large sweet onions, chopped (4 cups)
- 1 carton (8 ounces) egg substitute
- 2½ cups 2% milk
- ¼ teaspoon ground mustard
- ⅛ teaspoon pepper
- 8 cups cubed French bread
- 1½ cups (6 ounces) shredded Gruyere or Swiss cheese, divided

1. In a large skillet, heat oil over medium-high heat. Add prosciutto; cook and stir until crisp. Remove from pan with a slotted spoon. Add onions to the same pan; cook and stir until tender.
2. In a large bowl, whisk egg substitute, milk, mustard and pepper. Stir in the bread and onions. Reserve 2 tablespoons cooked prosciutto for the topping; stir remaining prosciutto into bread mixture.
3. Transfer half of the mixture to a greased 13-in. x 9-in. baking dish; sprinkle with half of the Gruyere cheese. Top with the remaining bread mixture. Separately cover and refrigerate strata and reserved prosciutto overnight.
4. Preheat oven to 350°. Remove strata from refrigerator while oven heats. Bake, uncovered, 20 minutes. Sprinkle with the remaining Guyere cheese; top with the reserved prosciutto. Bake 15-20 minutes longer or until a knife inserted near the center comes out clean. Let stand 5-10 minutes before serving.

GRUYERE & PROSCIUTTO STRATA

ASPARAGUS PHYLLO BAKE

3. Spread the ricotta mixture over the phyllo layers. Top with the remaining phyllo sheets, brushing each with butter. Cut into 12 rectangles. Bake 50-55 minutes or until golden brown.

NOTE *To toast nuts, spread in a 15-in. x 10-in. x1-in. baking pan. Bake at 350° for 5-10 minutes or until lightly browned, stirring occasionally. Or, spread in a dry nonstick skillet and heat over low heat until lightly browned, stirring occasionally.*

Breakfast Praline Bread Pudding

This warm, ooey-gooey treat is perfect for a large holiday brunch. The pecan-filled pudding also travels well.

—**ERIN FURBY** ANCHORAGE, AK

PREP: 20 MIN. + CHILLING • **BAKE:** 40 MIN. • **MAKES:** 12 SERVINGS

- 8 **eggs, lightly beaten**
- 2 **cups half-and-half cream**
- 1 **cup 2% milk**
- 2 **tablespoons brown sugar**
- 3 **teaspoons vanilla extract**
- 1 **teaspoon ground cinnamon**
- ¾ **teaspoon ground nutmeg**
- ½ **teaspoon salt**
- 1 **loaf (1 pound) French bread, cut into 1-inch cubes**
- 1 **cup chopped pecans**
- ½ **cup packed brown sugar**
- ½ **cup butter, melted**

1. In a large bowl, whisk the first eight ingredients until blended; stir in the bread cubes. Transfer to a greased 13-in. x 9-in. baking dish. Sprinkle with the pecans and brown sugar; drizzle with butter. Refrigerate, covered, several hours or overnight.

2. Preheat oven to 350°. Remove the bread pudding from refrigerator; uncover and let stand while oven heats. Bake 40-50 minutes or until puffed, golden and a knife inserted near the center comes out clean. Serve warm.

Asparagus Phyllo Bake

I'm Greek and grew up wrapping everything in phyllo. When asparagus is in season, I get some dough and start baking.
—**BONNIE GEAVARAS-BOOTZ** SCOTTSDALE, AZ

PREP: 25 MIN. • **BAKE:** 50 MIN. • **MAKES:** 12 SERVINGS

- 2 **pounds fresh asparagus, trimmed and cut into 1-inch pieces**
- 5 **eggs, lightly beaten**
- 1 **carton (15 ounces) ricotta cheese**
- 1 **cup (4 ounces) shredded Swiss cheese**
- 2 **tablespoons grated Parmesan cheese**
- 2 **garlic cloves, minced**
- ½ **teaspoon salt**
- ½ **teaspoon grated lemon peel**
- ½ **teaspoon pepper**
- ½ **cup slivered almonds, toasted**
- ¾ **cup butter, melted**
- 16 **sheets phyllo dough (14 x 9 inches)**

1. In a large saucepan, bring 8 cups water to a boil. Add the asparagus; cook, uncovered, 30 seconds or just until the asparagus turns bright green. Remove the asparagus and immediately drop into ice water. Drain and pat dry. In a large bowl, mix eggs, cheeses and seasonings; stir in almonds and asparagus.

2. Preheat oven to 375°. Brush a 13-in. x 9-in. baking dish with some of the butter. Unroll phyllo dough. Layer eight sheets of phyllo in prepared dish, brushing each with butter. Keep the remaining phyllo covered with plastic wrap and a damp towel to prevent it from drying out.

BREAKFAST PRALINE BREAD PUDDING

Bacon Breakfast Cups

My son once joked about adding bacon to cupcakes. I surprised him with these cheesy cups the next morning. The look on his face was priceless!

—**KAREN BURKETT** RESEDA, CA

PREP: 30 MIN. • **BROIL:** 5 MIN.
MAKES: 6 SERVINGS

- 18 **turkey bacon strips, cut in half**
- 1 **cup frozen shredded hash brown potatoes**
- 2 **eggs**
- 2 **teaspoons 2% milk**
  Dash each salt and pepper
- 2 **teaspoons butter**
- ¼ **cup shredded Mexican cheese blend**
  Chopped green onion and fresh parsley

1. Preheat oven to 375°. Line 12 alternating cups in a mini-muffin pan with bacon pieces, crisscrossing three strips in each so they resemble spokes of a wheel. Loosely crumple twelve 3-in. strips of aluminum foil into balls; place in cups to keep bacon from sliding. Bake 15-20 minutes or until bacon is crisp.
2. Meanwhile, cook the potatoes according to the package directions. In a small bowl, whisk the eggs, milk, salt and pepper. In a small skillet, heat the butter over medium heat. Pour in egg mixture; cook and stir until eggs are thickened and no liquid egg remains.
3. Transfer the bacon cups to a baking sheet; remove foil. Spoon hash browns and scrambled eggs into cups; sprinkle with cheese. Broil 3-4 in. from heat 3-5 minutes or until cheese is melted. Sprinkle with green onion and parsley.

CROISSANT BREAKFAST CASSEROLE

BACON BREAKFAST CUPS

Croissant Breakfast Casserole

Croissants and orange marmalade come together in a wonderful treat for family and guests. I serve strawberries alongside for a refreshing accompaniment.

—**JOAN HALLFORD** N. RICHLAND HILLS, TX

PREP: 15 MIN. + CHILLING • **BAKE:** 25 MIN.
MAKES: 12 SERVINGS

- 1 **jar (18 ounces) orange marmalade**
- ½ **cup apricot preserves**
- ⅓ **cup orange juice**
- 3 **teaspoons grated orange peel**
- 6 **croissants, split**
- 5 **eggs**
- 1 **cup half-and-half cream**
- 1 **teaspoon almond or vanilla extract**
  Quartered fresh strawberries

1. In a small bowl, mix the orange marmalade, apricot preserves, orange juice and orange peel. Arrange the croissant bottoms in a greased 13-in. x 9-in. baking dish. Spread with 1½ cups marmalade mixture. Add the croissant tops.
2. In another bowl, whisk the eggs, half-and-half cream and extract; pour over croissants. Spoon the remaining marmalade mixture over the tops. Refrigerate, covered, overnight.
3. Preheat oven to 350°. Remove the casserole from the refrigerator while the oven heats. Bake, uncovered, 25-30 minutes or until a knife inserted near the center comes out clean. Let stand 5 minutes before serving. Serve with strawberries.

Italian Brunch Torte

We enjoy this hearty layered torte with a salad of mixed greens and tomato wedges.
—**DANNY DIAMOND** FARMINGTON HILLS, MI

PREP: 50 MIN. • **BAKE:** 1 HOUR + STANDING
MAKES: 12 SERVINGS

- 2 tubes (8 ounces each) refrigerated crescent rolls, divided
- 1 teaspoon olive oil
- 1 package (6 ounces) fresh baby spinach
- 1 cup sliced fresh mushrooms
- 7 eggs
- 1 cup grated Parmesan cheese
- 2 teaspoons Italian seasoning
- ⅛ teaspoon pepper
- ½ pound thinly sliced deli ham
- ½ pound thinly sliced hard salami
- ½ pound sliced provolone cheese
- 2 jars (12 ounces each) roasted sweet red peppers, drained, sliced and patted dry

1. Preheat oven to 350°. Place a greased 9-in. springform pan on a double thickness of heavy-duty foil (about 18 in. square). Securely wrap foil around pan. Unroll one tube of dough and separate into triangles. Press onto bottom of pan for crust, sealing seams well. Bake 10-15 minutes or until set.

2. Meanwhile, in a large skillet, heat oil over medium-high heat. Add the spinach and mushrooms; cook and stir until mushrooms are tender. Drain on several layers of paper towels, blotting well. In a large bowl, whisk six eggs, Parmesan cheese, Italian seasoning and pepper.

3. Layer crust with half of the ham, salami, provolone cheese, red peppers and spinach mixture. Pour half of the egg mixture over the top. Repeat layers; top with remaining egg mixture.

4. On a work surface, unroll and separate the remaining dough into triangles. Press together to form a circle and seal the seams; place over the filling. Whisk the remaining egg; brush over dough.

5. Bake, uncovered, 1 to 1¼ hours or until a thermometer reads 160°, covering loosely with foil if needed to prevent overbrowning. Carefully loosen sides from pan with a knife; remove rim. Let stand 20 minutes.

Chilly Coffee Punch

Here's a sweet punch for coffee lovers. Whipped cream, chocolate syrup and shaved chocolate make yummy toppings.
—**JUDY WILSON** SUN CITY WEST, AZ

PREP: 10 MIN. + CHILLING
MAKES: 24 SERVINGS

- 6 cups hot strong brewed coffee
- ¼ cup sugar
- ½ cup coffee liqueur
- 1 carton (1½ quarts) vanilla ice cream, softened
- 1 carton (1½ quarts) chocolate ice cream, softened
  Optional toppings: whipped cream, chocolate syrup and chocolate shavings

1. In a pitcher, combine the coffee and sugar, stirring to dissolve the sugar. Refrigerate, covered, until cold, about 45 minutes.

2. Stir liqueur into coffee. Just before serving, spoon ice cream into a punch bowl. Stir in coffee mixture. If desired, serve with toppings.

Sausage Loaf

A dear family friend always brought this flavorful loaf of pork sausage to our Christmas brunch. The menu included Mom's homemade overnight cinnamon rolls, a big bowl of fruit salad and plenty of scrambled eggs. What a feast!
—**JEANNE AMBROSE** MILWAUKEE, WI

PREP: 10 MIN. • **BAKE:** 50 MIN. + STANDING
MAKES: 6 SERVINGS

- 1 cup seasoned stuffing cubes
- 1 can (5 ounces) evaporated milk
- 1 egg, lightly beaten
- 1 tablespoon prepared horseradish
- 1 tablespoon ketchup
- 2 teaspoons Dijon mustard
- 2 packages (12 ounces each) reduced-fat bulk pork sausage

1. In a large bowl, combine the first six ingredients. Add the sausage; mix lightly but thoroughly. Transfer to an ungreased 8-in. x 4-in. loaf pan.

2. Bake at 375° for 50-55 minutes or until a thermometer reads 160°. Let stand 10 minutes before slicing.

CHILLY COFFEE PUNCH

PECAN APPLE PANCAKES

Pecan Apple Pancakes

Weekend breakfasts are a big deal here in Texas. These from-scratch buttermilk flapjacks are loaded with shredded apples, chopped pecans and four spices.
—**SHARON RICHARDSON** DALLAS, TX

PREP: 15 MIN. • **COOK:** 10 MIN./BATCH
MAKES: 18 PANCAKES

- 2 **cups all-purpose flour**
- 1 **cup sugar**
- 2 **teaspoons baking powder**
- 1 **teaspoon baking soda**
- 1 **teaspoon ground cinnamon**
- ½ **teaspoon salt**
- ½ **teaspoon ground ginger**
- ½ **teaspoon ground mace**
- ½ **teaspoon ground cloves**
- 2 **eggs**
- 1¾ **cups buttermilk**
- 3 **tablespoons canola oil**
- 1¾ **cups shredded peeled apples**
- ½ **cup chopped pecans**

1. In a large bowl, mix the first nine ingredients. In another bowl, whisk the eggs, buttermilk and oil until blended. Add to the flour mixture; stir just until moistened. Stir in the apples and pecans.

2. Lightly grease a griddle; heat over medium-low heat. Pour the pancake batter by ¼ cupfuls onto the griddle. Cook until the bubbles on top begin to pop and the bottoms are golden brown. Turn; cook until the second side is golden brown.

Dutch Baked Pancake with Strawberry-Almond Compote

Pannekoeken, or Dutch baked pancakes, are a treat in my husband's family. Now they're a favorite of mine, too!
—**JENNIFER BECKMAN** FALLS CHURCH, VA

PREP: 15 MIN. • **BAKE:** 20 MIN.
MAKES: 6 SERVINGS (3 CUPS TOPPING)

- 2 **tablespoons butter**
- 4 **eggs**
- ⅔ **cup 2% milk**
- 2 **tablespoons grated orange peel**
- ½ **teaspoon almond extract**
- ⅔ **cup all-purpose flour**
- 2 **tablespoons sugar**
- ½ **teaspoon kosher salt**

TOPPING

- 1 **pound fresh strawberries, hulled and quartered**
- ½ **cup slivered almonds, toasted**
- 2 **tablespoons orange juice**
- 1 **tablespoon sugar**

1. Preheat oven to 400°. Place the butter in a 9-in. pie plate. Place in oven for 4-5 minutes or until the butter is melted; carefully swirl to coat evenly.

2. Meanwhile, in a large bowl, whisk eggs, milk, orange peel and extract until blended. Whisk in flour, sugar and salt. Pour into hot pie plate. Bake 20-25 minutes or until puffed and sides are golden brown and crisp.

3. In a small bowl, combine topping ingredients. Serve with pancake.

NOTE *To toast nuts, spread in a 15-in. x 10-in. x 1-in. baking pan. Bake at 350° for 5-10 minutes or until lightly browned, stirring occasionally. Or, spread in a dry nonstick skillet and heat over low heat until lightly browned, stirring occasionally.*

DUTCH BAKED PANCAKE WITH STRAWBERRY-ALMOND COMPOTE

MAPLE-BACON GRITS PUFF

Turkey Sage Sausage Patties

I love the flavor of these nicely seasoned patties that use a lighter meat option— lean ground turkey. Prefer garlic? Add that in place of the sage.

—**JANICE WUERTZER** DUBUQUE, IA

PREP: 10 MIN. + CHILLING • **COOK:** 15 MIN.
MAKES: 6 PATTIES

- 1 **small onion, finely chopped**
- ¼ **cup dry bread crumbs**
- 1 **teaspoon rubbed sage**
- ½ **teaspoon salt**
- ½ **teaspoon paprika**
- ¼ **teaspoon pepper**
- 1 **pound lean ground turkey**
- 2 **teaspoons canola oil**

1. In a large bowl, combine the first six ingredients. Crumble the turkey over mixture; mix lightly but thoroughly. Shape into six patties. Refrigerate, covered, for 2 hours.

2. In a large nonstick skillet, heat oil over medium heat. Add patties; cook for 6-7 minutes on each side or until a thermometer reads 165°.

⑤INGREDIENTS
Maple-Bacon Grits Puff

Make ordinary grits extraordinary with chopped bacon and maple syrup. They lend salty sweetness to the yummy puff. For a special finishing touch, sprinkle on minced fresh chives after baking.

—**LOTTE WASHBURN** SEBRING, FL

PREP: 20 MIN. • **BAKE:** 1 HOUR
MAKES: 8 SERVINGS

- 8 **bacon strips, chopped**
- 2 **cups 2% milk**
- 1¼ **cups water**
- ½ **teaspoon salt**
- 1 **cup quick-cooking grits**
- ½ **cup maple syrup**
- 4 **eggs, lightly beaten**
  Minced fresh chives, optional

1. Preheat the oven to 350°. In a large skillet, cook bacon over medium heat until crisp, stirring occasionally. Remove with a slotted spoon; drain on paper towels. Reserve 2 tablespoons bacon drippings.

2. In a large saucepan, bring milk, water and salt to a boil. Slowly stir in grits. Reduce heat to medium-low; cook, covered, 5-7 minutes or until thickened, stirring occasionally. Remove from heat; stir in the maple syrup, half of the cooked bacon and reserved drippings.

3. In a small bowl, whisk a small amount of hot grits into eggs until blended; return all to pan, mixing well. Transfer to a greased 8-in.-square baking dish.

4. Bake, uncovered, 1 hour or until a knife inserted near the center comes out clean. Sprinkle with the remaining bacon and, if desired, chives; let stand 5 minutes before serving.

FAST FIX ▶ Crunchy Baked French Toast

What do you do when one child wants cereal and the other wants French toast? You combine them for a crunchy new breakfast treat, of course!

—ANNDREA BAILEY HUNTINGTON BEACH, CA

START TO FINISH: 30 MIN.
MAKES: 6 SERVINGS

- 5 eggs
- ¾ cup 2% milk
- ¾ teaspoon ground cinnamon
- ¾ teaspoon vanilla extract
- ⅛ teaspoon salt
- 4 cups Cap'n Crunch cereal, crushed
- 12 slices French bread (1 inch thick)

1. Preheat oven to 450°. In a shallow bowl, whisk the first five ingredients until blended. Place crushed cereal in another shallow bowl. Dip both sides of bread in egg mixture, then in cereal, patting to help cereal adhere.

2. Place on greased baking sheets. Bake 12-15 minutes or until golden brown, turning once.

CRUNCHY BAKED FRENCH TOAST

top tip — Sticky Situation

I like to wipe a bit of vegetable oil inside my measuring cup when I'm measuring peanut butter or molasses. This keeps the sticky ingredients from clinging to the cup, so I don't have to scrape—and cleanup's a snap.

—LYNN HAYES ST. JOHN, NB

Chocolate Chip Elvis Pancakes

I'm one of 13 children, so in our family, finding menus that everyone liked was challenging. These chocolaty peanut butter-and-banana pancakes were a Saturday favorite we all loved.

—KEENAN MCDERMOTT SPRINGFIELD, MO

PREP: 15 MIN. • **COOK:** 5 MIN./BATCH
MAKES: 16 PANCAKES

- 1¼ cups all-purpose flour
- 2 tablespoons brown sugar
- 3 teaspoons baking powder
- ½ teaspoon salt
- 1 egg
- ¼ cup peanut butter
- 1½ cups 2% milk
- 3 tablespoons butter, melted
- 1 teaspoon vanilla extract
- ½ cup chopped ripe banana
- ½ cup semisweet chocolate chips

1. In a large bowl, whisk the flour, brown sugar, baking powder and salt. In another bowl, whisk egg, peanut butter, milk, melted butter and vanilla until blended. Add to flour mixture; stir just until moistened. Fold in the banana and chocolate chips.

2. Lightly grease a griddle; heat over medium heat. Pour pancake batter by ¼ cupfuls onto griddle. Cook until the bubbles on top begin to pop and the bottoms are golden brown. Turn; cook until second side is golden brown.

Spiced Coffee

Chocolate syrup, cinnamon, anise and cloves make ordinary coffee special. It all comes together in my slow cooker.

—**JOANNE HOLT** BOWLING GREEN, OH

PREP: 10 MIN. • **COOK:** 2 HOURS
MAKES: 8 SERVINGS

- 8 **cups brewed coffee**
- ⅓ **cup sugar**
- ¼ **cup chocolate syrup**
- ½ **teaspoon anise extract**
- 4 **cinnamon sticks (3 inches)**
- 1½ **teaspoons whole cloves**
  Additional cinnamon sticks, optional

1. In a 3-qt. slow cooker, combine the coffee, sugar, chocolate syrup and anise extract. Place cinnamon sticks and cloves on a double thickness of cheesecloth. Gather corners of cloth to enclose spices; tie securely with string. Add to slow cooker. Cook, covered, on low 2-3 hours.

2. Discard the spice bag. Ladle the coffee into mugs. If desired, serve with cinnamon sticks.

SPICED COFFEE

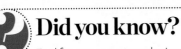

? Did you know?

Feel free to use your choice of brown or white eggs in recipes. Though different colors, brown and white eggs have the same nutritional value, and they cook the same. The color of the egg is based on the breed of the chicken. Generally speaking, hens with white feathers lay white eggs, and hens with reddish-brown feathers lay brown eggs.

FARM FRESH QUICHE

Farm Fresh Quiche

Going to the farmers market inspires me to create recipes like this one, a cheesy vegetable quiche loaded with broccoli, onion, mustard greens and rosemary.

—**HEATHER KING** FROSTBURG, MD

PREP: 35 MIN. • **BAKE:** 30 MIN. + STANDING
MAKES: 6 SERVINGS

- ¼ **cup olive oil**
- 1 **bunch broccoli, cut into florets**
- 1 **small onion, finely chopped**
- 3 **cups chopped fresh mustard greens or spinach**
- 3 **garlic cloves, minced**
- 1 **sheet refrigerated pie pastry**
- 4 **eggs**
- 1 **cup 2% milk**
- 1 **tablespoon minced fresh rosemary or 1 teaspoon dried rosemary, crushed**
- ½ **teaspoon salt**
- ½ **teaspoon pepper**
- ½ **cup shredded smoked cheddar cheese, divided**
- ½ **cup shredded Swiss cheese, divided**

1. Preheat oven to 375°. In a large skillet, heat oil over medium-high heat. Add the broccoli and onion; cook and stir until broccoli is crisp-tender. Stir in the greens and garlic; cook and stir 4-5 minutes longer or until greens are wilted.

2. Unroll the pastry sheet into a 9-in. pie plate; flute edge. Fill with broccoli mixture. In a small bowl, whisk eggs, milk, rosemary, salt and pepper. Stir in ¼ cup cheddar cheese and ¼ cup Swiss cheese; pour over vegetables. Sprinkle with remaining cheeses.

3. Bake 30-35 minutes or until a knife inserted near the center comes out clean. Let quiche stand 15 minutes before cutting.

MARLA CLARK'S GRILLED SAUSAGE & PEPPER HEROES *PAGE 158*

Potluck Pleasers

Friends and family will line up for the **crowd-size recipes** in this chapter. With favorites such as Game Time Stromboli, Beer Brat Chili and Chunky Veggie Slaw, you'll always **bring home an empty dish!**

**KRISTINE CHAYES'
GERMAN BUTTER POUND CAKE**
PAGE 165

**CONNIE EATON'S
TORTELLINI SALAD**
PAGE 160

**MELISSA MILLWOOD'S
BUFFALO CHICKEN LASAGNA**
PAGE 161

Tomato, Sausage & Cheddar Bread Pudding

Love bread pudding? Here's the perfect excuse to have it as the main dish of your meal, not merely as dessert afterward.

—**HOLLY JONES** KENNESAW, GA

PREP: 30 MIN. • **BAKE:** 45 MIN.
MAKES: 12 SERVINGS

- 3 cups (12 ounces) shredded sharp cheddar cheese
- 1 can (28 ounces) diced tomatoes, drained
- 1 pound bulk Italian sausage, cooked and crumbled
- 4 green onions, thinly sliced
- ¼ cup minced fresh basil or 1 tablespoon dried basil
- ¼ cup packed brown sugar
- 1 teaspoon dried oregano
- 1 teaspoon garlic powder
- 3 cups cubed French bread
- 6 eggs
- 1½ cups heavy whipping cream
- ½ teaspoon salt
- ½ teaspoon pepper
- ½ cup grated Parmesan cheese

1. Preheat oven to 350°. In a large bowl, combine first eight ingredients. Stir in the bread. Transfer to a greased 13-in. x 9-in. baking dish.

2. In the same bowl, whisk the eggs, cream, salt and pepper; pour over the bread mixture. Sprinkle with the Parmesan cheese. Bake 45-50 minutes or until a knife inserted near center comes out clean.

TOMATO, SAUSAGE & CHEDDAR BREAD PUDDING

"This chunky chili smells so good in the slow cooker. I can't think of a better way to use up leftover brats, and my husband can't think of a better way to eat them!"

—**KATRINA KRUMM** APPLE VALLEY, MN

BEER BRAT CHILI

SLOW COOKER
Beer Brat Chili

PREP: 10 MIN. • **COOK:** 5 HOURS
MAKES: 8 SERVINGS (2½ QUARTS)

- 1 can (15 ounces) white kidney or cannellini beans, rinsed and drained
- 1 can (15 ounces) pinto beans, rinsed and drained
- 1 can (15 ounces) Southwestern black beans, undrained
- 1 can (14½ ounces) Italian diced tomatoes, undrained
- 1 can (10 ounces) diced tomatoes and green chilies, undrained
- 1 package (14 ounces) fully cooked beer bratwurst links, sliced
- 1½ cups frozen corn
- 1 medium sweet red pepper, chopped
- 1 medium onion, finely chopped
- ¼ cup chili seasoning
- 1 garlic clove, minced

In a 5-qt. slow cooker, combine all ingredients. Cook, covered, on low 5-6 hours.

Mushroom & Wild Rice Soup

You can tell how much I like mushrooms by looking at this soup recipe. I added four different kinds! I also used a packaged rice mix to speed up the preparation.
—**MARY MCVEY** COLFAX, NC

PREP: 25 MIN. + STANDING • **COOK:** 45 MIN.
MAKES: 12 SERVINGS (2¼ QUARTS)

- 2½ cups water
- 1 ounce dried porcini mushrooms
- 1 ounce dried shiitake mushrooms
- 3 tablespoons butter
- 1 small onion, diced
- ½ pound sliced fresh mushrooms
- ½ pound sliced baby portobello mushrooms
- 3 garlic cloves, minced
- 4 cups chicken broth
- 1 package (6 ounces) long grain and wild rice mix
- ½ teaspoon salt
- ¼ teaspoon white pepper
- ½ cup cold water
- 4 teaspoons cornstarch
- 1 cup heavy whipping cream

1. In a small saucepan, bring the water to a boil; add the dried mushrooms. Remove from the heat; let stand for 25-30 minutes or until softened.

2. Using a slotted spoon, remove the softened mushrooms; rinse. Trim and discard the stems from the shiitake mushrooms. Chop mushrooms. Strain soaking liquid through a fine-mesh strainer. Reserve mushrooms and soaking liquid.

3. In a Dutch oven, heat the butter over medium-high heat. Add onion; cook and stir until tender. Add fresh and baby portobello mushrooms; cook and stir until tender. Add garlic; cook 1 minute longer.

4. Stir in the chicken broth, rice mix with the contents of the seasoning packet, reserved dried mushrooms and soaking liquid, salt and pepper. Bring to a boil. Reduce heat; cover and simmer for 20-25 minutes or until the rice is tender.

5. In a small bowl, mix the cold water and cornstarch until smooth; stir into soup. Bring to a boil; cook and stir for 2 minutes or until thickened. Stir in cream; heat through.

SWEET POTATO PANCAKES WITH CINNAMON CREAM

Sweet Potato Pancakes with Cinnamon Cream

Topped with a smooth cinnamon cream and loaded with apples, my sweet potato pancakes have flavors and aromas that just seem to say "autumn."
—**TAMMY REX** NEW TRIPOLI, PA

PREP: 25 MIN. • **COOK:** 5 MIN./BATCH
MAKES: 12 SERVINGS (1½ CUPS TOPPING)

- 1 package (8 ounces) cream cheese, softened
- ¼ cup packed brown sugar
- ½ teaspoon ground cinnamon
- ½ cup sour cream

PANCAKES
- 6 eggs
- ¾ cup all-purpose flour
- ½ teaspoon ground nutmeg
- ½ teaspoon salt
- ¼ teaspoon pepper
- 6 cups shredded sweet potatoes (about 3 large)
- 3 cups shredded peeled apples (about 3 large)
- ⅓ cup grated onion
- ½ cup canola oil

1. In a small bowl, beat the cream cheese, brown sugar and cinnamon until blended; beat in the sour cream. Set aside.

2. In a large bowl, whisk the eggs, flour, nutmeg, salt and pepper. Add the sweet potatoes, apples and onion; toss to coat.

3. In a large nonstick skillet, heat 2 tablespoons oil over medium heat. Working in batches, drop the sweet potato mixture by ⅓ cupfuls into the oil; press slightly to flatten. Fry for 2-3 minutes on each side until golden brown, using remaining oil as needed. Drain on paper towels. Serve with cinnamon topping.

? Did you know?

Sweet potatoes and yams are often confused with one another, and canned sweet potatoes are often labeled yams. True yams, though, are not readily available in the United States and are seldom grown here.

"Make this stromboli as a snack when the big game is on TV...or serve it for dinner with your favorite tossed salad."

—JANE MCMILLAN DANIA BEACH, FL

GAME TIME STROMBOLI

Game Time Stromboli

PREP: 30 MIN. • **BAKE:** 20 MIN.
MAKES: 2 STROMBOLI (6 SERVINGS EACH)

- 2 tubes (13.8 ounces each) refrigerated pizza crust
- 8 ounces thinly sliced part-skim mozzarella cheese
- 8 ounces thinly sliced mortadella
- 8 ounces thinly sliced capocollo or prosciutto
- 8 ounces thinly sliced hard salami
- 1 large green pepper, thinly sliced
- 2 tablespoons shredded Asiago cheese
- 1 teaspoon garlic powder
- 1 teaspoon dried parsley flakes
  Marinara sauce, warmed

1. On a greased baking sheet, unroll one pizza crust and pat into a 16-in. x 13-in. rectangle. Layer half of the mozzarella cheese, deli meats and pepper lengthwise down the center third of the crust, leaving a ½-in. border at each end. Fold up the long sides of the crust over the filling, pinching the seam and ends to seal. Fold up ends. Cut slits in top. Repeat with remaining ingredients.

2. Sprinkle each stromboli with half of the Asiago cheese, garlic powder and parsley. Bake at 425° for 16-20 minutes or until golden brown. Serve with marinara sauce.

FAST FIX ▶ **Brussels Sprouts & Kale Saute**

In an effort to add more greens to our meals, I combined Brussels sprouts and kale with crispy salami. My kids eat it up.
—**JENNIFER MCNABB** BRENTWOOD, TN

START TO FINISH: 30 MIN. • **MAKES:** 12 SERVINGS (½ CUP EACH)

- ¼ pound thinly sliced hard salami, cut into ¼-inch strips
- 1½ teaspoons olive oil
- 2 tablespoons butter
- 2 pounds fresh Brussels sprouts, thinly sliced
- 2 cups shredded fresh kale
- 1 large onion, finely chopped
- ½ teaspoon kosher salt
- ⅛ teaspoon cayenne pepper
- ¼ teaspoon coarsely ground pepper
- 1 garlic clove, minced
- ½ cup chicken broth
- ½ cup chopped walnuts
- 1 tablespoon balsamic vinegar

1. In a Dutch oven, cook and stir the salami in oil over medium-high heat for 3-5 minutes or until crisp. Remove to paper towels with a slotted spoon; reserve drippings in pan.

2. Add butter to the drippings; heat over medium-high heat. Add Brussels sprouts, kale, onion, salt, cayenne and black pepper; cook and stir until vegetables are crisp-tender. Add garlic; cook 1 minute longer.

3. Stir in the broth; bring to a boil. Reduce heat; cover and cook for 4-5 minutes or until Brussels sprouts are tender. Stir in walnuts and vinegar. Serve with salami strips.

BRUSSELS SPROUTS & KALE SAUTE

SPICY COWBOY CHILI

3. In the same skillet, heat 1 tablespoon oil over medium-high heat. Brown the beef in batches, adding more oil if needed; transfer to a 6-qt. slow cooker. In the skillet, heat 2 teaspoons oil over medium heat. Add onions; cook and stir until tender. Add to beef.

4. Stir in the remaining ingredients, mashed garlic and dried chilies mixture. Cover and cook on low for 7-9 hours or until meat is tender. If desired, serve with cheese.

NOTE *One-half teaspoon ground chipotle pepper may be substituted for the dried chipotle chilies; add ground chipotle with mashed garlic and beer mixture to slow cooker.*

PER SERVING *301 cal., 9 g fat (3 g sat. fat), 60 mg chol., 588 mg sodium, 27 g carb., 8 g fiber, 27 g pro.* **Diabetic Exchanges:** *4 lean meat, 1½ starch, 1 vegetable.*

SLOW COOKER

Sweet & Hot Baked Beans

At a barbecue, baked beans are a must. They get a little sweetness and heat when I mix in bits of pineapple and jalapenos.
—**ROBIN HAAS** CRANSTON, RI

PREP: 20 MIN. • **COOK:** 5 HOURS
MAKES: 12 SERVINGS (½ CUP EACH)

- 4 **cans (15 ounces each) white kidney or cannellini beans, rinsed and drained**
- 2 **cans (8 ounces each) crushed pineapple, undrained**
- 2 **large onions, finely chopped**
- 1 **cup packed brown sugar**
- 1 **cup ketchup**
- 10 **bacon strips, cooked and crumbled**
- ½ **cup molasses**
- ¼ **cup canned diced jalapeno peppers**
- 2 **tablespoons white vinegar**
- 4 **garlic cloves, minced**
- 4 **teaspoons ground mustard**
- ¼ **teaspoon ground cloves**

In a 3- or 4-qt. slow cooker, combine all ingredients. Cook, covered, on low 5-6 hours.

SLOW COOKER **EAT SMART**

Spicy Cowboy Chili

Toasting the ancho and chipotle peppers for this slow-cooked chili releases their earthy flavors and gives each bowl plenty of zip. We think a sprinkling of cheddar cheese is the perfect finishing touch.
—**RACHEL SPRINKEL** HILO, HI

PREP: 45 MIN. • **COOK:** 7 HOURS • **MAKES:** 14 SERVINGS (3½ QUARTS)

- 1 **whole garlic bulb**
- 2 **to 3 tablespoons olive oil, divided**
- 2 **dried ancho chilies**
- 2 **dried chipotle chilies**
- 1 **bottle (12 ounces) dark beer**
- 3 **pounds beef stew meat, cut into ¾-inch pieces**
- 2 **large onions, chopped**
- 3 **cans (16 ounces each) kidney beans, rinsed and drained**
- 3 **cans (14½ ounces each) diced tomatoes, undrained**
- 2 **cans (8 ounces each) tomato sauce**
- 2 **tablespoons Worcestershire sauce**
- 1 **tablespoon chili powder**
- 1 **teaspoon pepper**
- ½ **teaspoon salt**
  Shredded cheddar cheese, optional

1. Remove the papery outer skin from garlic bulb, but do not peel or separate the cloves. Cut off top of garlic bulb, exposing individual cloves. Brush cut cloves with 1 teaspoon oil. Wrap in foil. Bake at 425° for 30-35 minutes or until cloves are soft. Unwrap and cool slightly. Squeeze garlic from skins; mash with a fork.

2. Meanwhile, in a large dry skillet over medium-high heat, toast chilies on both sides until puffy, about 3-6 minutes. (Do not blacken.) Cool. Remove stems and seeds; coarsely chop chilies. Place in a small bowl; cover with beer. Let stand to soften, about 30 minutes.

SWEET & HOT BAKED BEANS

Grilled Sausage & Pepper Heroes

Chicken sausage lightens up these grilled sandwiches a bit without sacrificing flavor.

—**MARLA CLARK** MORIARTY, NM

PREP: 20 MIN. • **GRILL:** 30 MIN.
MAKES: 12 SERVINGS

- 2 jars (24 ounces each) roasted garlic Parmesan spaghetti sauce
- ⅛ teaspoon crushed red pepper flakes
- 2 medium green peppers
- 2 medium sweet red peppers
- 2 medium sweet yellow peppers
- 1 large sweet onion, cut crosswise into ¼-inch slices
- 3 packages (12 ounces each) fully cooked Italian chicken sausage links
- 12 brat or hoagie buns, split
- 12 slices provolone cheese, halved

1. In a Dutch oven, combine spaghetti sauce and red pepper flakes. Heat through over medium heat, stirring occasionally; keep warm.

2. Cut the peppers in half. Remove and discard the stems and seeds. Grill the peppers and onion, covered, over medium heat 8-10 minutes on each side or until tender. Slice the peppers. Stir onion and peppers into the sauce; heat through.

3. Grill sausages, covered, over medium heat for 10-12 minutes or until heated through, turning occasionally. Place buns on baking sheets, cut side up. Top with cheese. Broil 3-4 in. from the heat 2-3 minutes or until cheese is melted. Top with sausages and pepper mixture.

GRILLED SAUSAGE & PEPPER HEROES

"Garden-fresh vegetables always go over well at our community potlucks. I bring my homemade vinaigrette in a mason jar to pour on just before serving."

—**JEANETTE HILDEBRAND** STAFFORD, KS

ITALIAN FRESH VEGETABLE SALAD

EAT SMART **FAST FIX** ▸ ## Italian Fresh Vegetable Salad

START TO FINISH: 25 MIN.
MAKES: 20 SERVINGS (1 CUP EACH)

SALAD

- 1 bunch romaine, torn
- 4 cups fresh baby spinach
- 2 cups grape tomatoes
- 1 can (14 ounces) water-packed artichoke hearts, rinsed, drained and quartered
- 1 medium zucchini, thinly sliced
- 1 small green pepper, sliced
- 1 small sweet red pepper, sliced
- 1 cup thinly sliced fresh mushrooms
- 1 cup thinly sliced red onion
- 1 cup (4 ounces) shredded part-skim mozzarella cheese
- ½ cup sliced pepperoncini
- 1 can (2¼ ounces) sliced ripe olives, drained

VINAIGRETTE

- ⅔ cup canola oil
- ½ cup red wine vinegar
- ¼ cup minced fresh basil
- 1½ teaspoons garlic powder
- 1½ teaspoons ground mustard
- 1 teaspoon honey
- ½ teaspoon salt

1. In a large bowl, combine the salad ingredients. In a small bowl, whisk the vinaigrette ingredients.

2. Just before serving, pour ¾ cup vinaigrette over salad; toss to coat. Refrigerate remaining vinaigrette for another use.

PER SERVING *84 cal., 6 g fat (1 g sat. fat), 3 mg chol., 149 mg sodium, 5 g carb., 1 g fiber, 3 g pro.* **Diabetic Exchanges:** *1 vegetable, 1 fat.*

Mashed Cauliflower Au Gratin

Unless you tell them, your guests might not even realize they're eating cauliflower when they sample this crumbed-topped side dish. It's buttery, cheesy and creamy.
—**SANDIE PARKER** ELK RAPIDS, MI

PREP: 40 MIN. • **BAKE:** 40 MIN.
MAKES: 12 SERVINGS (¾ CUP)

- 2 large heads cauliflower, broken into florets
- 1½ cups shredded Parmesan cheese
- 1 cup shredded Colby-Monterey Jack cheese
- 6 tablespoons butter, cubed
- ¾ teaspoon garlic salt
- ½ teaspoon Montreal steak seasoning

TOPPING
- 1 cup (4 ounces) Italian-style panko (Japanese) bread crumbs
- ¼ cup butter, melted

1. Preheat oven to 350°. Place the cauliflower in a stockpot; add water to cover. Bring to a boil. Reduce heat; simmer, uncovered, 10-12 minutes or until very tender. Drain; transfer to a large bowl. Mash the cauliflower; stir in the cheeses, cubed butter and seasonings. Transfer to a greased 13-in. x 9-in. baking dish.

2. In a small bowl, mix bread crumbs and melted butter until evenly coated; sprinkle over the cauliflower mixture. Bake, uncovered, 40-50 minutes or until heated through and topping is golden brown.

MASHED CAULIFLOWER AU GRATIN

BLUEBERRY-APPLE COBBLER WITH ALMOND TOPPING

Blueberry-Apple Cobbler with Almond Topping

For a comforting dessert or brunch treat, combine the richness of a cobbler with the satisfying crunch of a crumble.
—**CATHY RAU** NEWPORT, OR

PREP: 25 MIN. • **BAKE:** 30 MIN. + COOLING
MAKES: 12 SERVINGS

- ⅔ cup sugar
- 3 tablespoons cornstarch
- ½ teaspoon ground cinnamon
- ⅛ teaspoon ground nutmeg
- 5 cups fresh or frozen unsweetened blueberries
- 1¼ cups shredded peeled apples (about 2 medium)
- 2 tablespoons lemon juice

BISCUIT TOPPING
- 1¾ cups all-purpose flour
- ¼ cup sugar
- 3 teaspoons baking powder
- ½ teaspoon salt
- ½ cup cold butter, cubed
- ½ cup half-and-half cream
- ½ cup plain yogurt
- 1 teaspoon vanilla extract

ALMOND CRUMBLE
- ½ cup sliced almonds, coarsely chopped
- ⅓ cup all-purpose flour
- ⅓ cup packed brown sugar
- 2 tablespoons cold butter

1. In a large bowl, combine the sugar, cornstarch, cinnamon and nutmeg. Add the blueberries, apples and lemon juice; toss to coat. Transfer to a greased 13-in. x 9-in. baking dish.

2. For the biscuit topping, in a small bowl, mix the flour, sugar, baking powder and salt. Cut in the cold butter until crumbly. In a separate bowl, whisk cream, plain yogurt and vanilla; stir into the flour mixture just until moistened. Drop by spoonfuls over the fruit mixture.

3. For the almond crumble, in another bowl, combine the almonds, flour and brown sugar. Cut in butter until crumbly. Sprinkle over top.

4. Bake at 375° for 30-40 minutes or until filling is bubbly and topping is golden brown. Cool on a wire rack for 30 minutes before serving.

Oodles of Noodles

Lots of pasta makes these potluck-sized dishes especially popular. Choose from a signature tortellini medley, two macaroni-and-cheese favorites and a delicious spin on lasagna.

"My mac combines Swiss, Gouda, Parmesan, white cheddar and goat cheese for an ooey-gooey treat."
—MYA ZERONIS PITTSBURGH, PA

FIVE-CHEESE MACARONI WITH PROSCIUTTO BITS

FAST FIX ▶ Connie's Tortellini Salad

I like to make this colorful salad when we're spending a long weekend at the lake. I keep a big bowlful in the refrigerator, and family members just grab some whenever they're hungry. It's quick and convenient.
—CONNIE EATON PITTSBURGH, PA

START TO FINISH: 30 MIN. • **MAKES:** 16 SERVINGS (¾ CUP EACH)

- 1 package (13 ounces) dried cheese tortellini
- 1 medium zucchini, halved and sliced
- 1 cup Italian salad dressing
- 1 pint grape tomatoes
- 1 can (14 ounces) water-packed artichoke hearts, rinsed, drained and quartered
- 1 jar (11.1 ounces) pitted Greek olives, drained
- 1 carton (8 ounces) miniature fresh mozzarella cheese balls, drained

In a large saucepan, cook tortellini according to package directions. Drain; transfer to a large bowl. Immediately add zucchini and dressing; toss to coat. Stir in the remaining ingredients. Serve warm or refrigerate and serve cold.

CONNIE'S TORTELLINI SALAD

Five-Cheese Macaroni with Prosciutto Bits

PREP: 25 MIN. • **BAKE:** 20 MIN.
MAKES: 12 SERVINGS (1¼ CUPS EACH)

- 1 package (16 ounces) elbow macaroni
- ⅓ cup unsalted butter, cubed
- 1 medium onion, halved and thinly sliced
- 1 garlic clove, minced
- ⅓ cup all-purpose flour
- ½ cup white wine or reduced-sodium chicken broth
- 4 cups heavy whipping cream
- 1 teaspoon white pepper
- ¼ teaspoon salt
- 5 ounces fresh goat cheese, crumbled
- 5 ounces white cheddar cheese, shredded
- 5 ounces Swiss cheese, shredded
- 3 ounces smoked Gouda cheese, shredded
- ¾ cup grated Parmesan cheese
- ½ cup panko (Japanese) bread crumbs
- 4 ounces thinly sliced prosciutto, chopped

1. Cook the macaroni according to the package directions until al dente.
2. Meanwhile, in a Dutch oven, heat the butter over medium-high heat. Add onion; cook and stir for 4-6 minutes or until golden brown. Add garlic; cook 1 minute longer. Stir in the flour until blended; gradually stir in the wine. Add the cream, pepper and salt; bring to a boil, stirring constantly. Cook and stir for 2 minutes or until thickened.
3. Reduce heat to medium-low. Add goat cheese; stir gently until melted. Gradually stir in the remaining cheeses; cook until melted. Remove from the heat.
4. Drain the macaroni; stir into sauce. Transfer to a greased 13-in. x 9-in. baking dish. Sprinkle with bread crumbs. Bake, uncovered, at 375° for 15-20 minutes or until lightly browned.
5. Meanwhile, in a small nonstick skillet, cook prosciutto over medium heat for 5-7 minutes or until crisp, stirring frequently. Sprinkle over macaroni just before serving.

Beer Macaroni & Cheese

PREP: 20 MIN. • **BAKE:** 15 MIN. • **MAKES:** 12 SERVINGS

- 1 package (16 ounces) elbow macaroni
- ¼ cup butter
- 2 garlic cloves, minced
- ¼ cup all-purpose flour
- 1 tablespoon ground mustard
- 1 teaspoon salt
- ¾ teaspoon pepper
- 2½ cups 2% milk
- ¾ cup amber beer
- ¼ cup heavy whipping cream
- 3 cups (12 ounces) shredded cheddar cheese, divided
- 2 cups (8 ounces) shredded fontina cheese
- 2 tablespoons grated Parmesan cheese, divided
- 2 tablespoons minced chives
- 5 bacon strips, cooked and crumbled

1. Cook the macaroni according to the package directions for al dente.
2. Meanwhile, in a Dutch oven, heat the butter over medium-high heat. Add garlic; cook and stir for 1 minute. Stir in the flour, mustard, salt and pepper until smooth; gradually whisk in the milk, beer and cream. Bring to a boil; cook and stir for 2 minutes or until thickened.
3. Reduce heat. Stir in 2 cups cheddar cheese, fontina cheese and 1 tablespoon Parmesan cheese until melted. Add the chives.
4. Drain macaroni; stir into sauce. Transfer to a greased 3-qt. baking dish. Sprinkle with remaining cheddar and Parmesan cheeses.
5. Bake, uncovered, at 400° for 15-20 minutes or until golden brown and heated through. Top with crumbled bacon. Let stand for 5 minutes before serving.

> "Take classic comfort food to a whole new level with bacon bits, minced chives and a hint of beer."
> —**LAUREN PETERSEN** EVERETT, WA

BEER MACARONI & CHEESE

BUFFALO CHICKEN LASAGNA

Buffalo Chicken Lasagna

The inspiration for this zippy lasagna came from my daughter, whose favorite food is buffalo wings. She was thrilled!
—**MELISSA MILLWOOD** LYMAN, SC

PREP: 1 HOUR 40 MIN. • **BAKE:** 40 MIN. + STANDING
MAKES: 12 SERVINGS

- 1 tablespoon canola oil
- 1½ pounds ground chicken
- 1 small onion, chopped
- 1 celery rib, finely chopped
- 1 large carrot, grated
- 2 garlic cloves, minced
- 1 can (14½ ounces) diced tomatoes, drained
- 1 bottle (12 ounces) buffalo wing sauce
- ½ cup water
- 1½ teaspoons Italian seasoning
- ½ teaspoon salt
- ¼ teaspoon pepper
- 9 lasagna noodles
- 1 carton (15 ounces) ricotta cheese
- 1¾ cups (7 ounces) crumbled blue cheese, divided
- ½ cup minced Italian flat leaf parsley
- 1 egg, lightly beaten
- 3 cups (12 ounces) shredded part-skim mozzarella cheese
- 2 cups (8 ounces) shredded white cheddar cheese

1. In a Dutch oven, heat the oil over medium heat. Add the chicken, onion, celery and carrot; cook and stir until meat is no longer pink and vegetables are tender. Add garlic; cook 2 minutes longer. Stir in the tomatoes, wing sauce, water, Italian seasoning, salt and pepper; bring to a boil. Reduce heat; cover and simmer for 1 hour.
2. Meanwhile, cook the noodles according to the package directions; drain. In a small bowl, mix ricotta cheese, ¾ cup blue cheese, parsley and egg.
3. Spread 1½ cups sauce into a greased 13-in. x 9-in. baking dish. Layer with three noodles, 1½ cups sauce, ⅔ cup ricotta mixture, 1 cup mozzarella cheese, ⅔ cup cheddar cheese and ⅓ cup blue cheese. Repeat layers twice.
4. Bake, covered, at 350° for 20 minutes. Uncover; bake 20-25 minutes longer or until bubbly and cheese is melted. Let stand for 10 minutes before serving.

CREAMY HERB DEVILED EGGS

"Deviled eggs come in so many different varieties." This version incorporates plain Greek-style yogurt and bottled ranch salad dressing. I never have to bring home leftovers."
—**JENNI DISE** PHOENIX, AZ

(5) INGREDIENTS FAST FIX ▶ Creamy Herb Deviled Eggs

START TO FINISH: 20 MIN.
MAKES: 2 DOZEN

- 12 hard-cooked eggs
- ¼ cup prepared ranch salad dressing
- 3 tablespoons plain Greek yogurt
- 2 teaspoons Dijon mustard
- ¼ teaspoon pepper
- ⅛ teaspoon paprika

Cut eggs lengthwise in half. Remove the yolks, reserving the whites. In a small bowl, mash yolks. Stir in ranch salad dressing, yogurt, mustard and pepper. Spoon or pipe into egg whites. Refrigerate, covered, until serving. Sprinkle with paprika.

Autumn Vegetable Mash

I stop mashing before these vegetables get too smooth because I prefer a chunky texture. But go ahead and keep mashing if your family likes them smoother.
—**DANA BALTER** NAPLES, FL

PREP: 20 MIN. • **COOK:** 20 MIN.
MAKES: 12 SERVINGS (¾ CUP EACH)

- 8 medium Yukon Gold potatoes, cut into 1-inch pieces
- 6 medium parsnips, peeled and cut into 1-inch pieces
- 2 large celery roots, peeled and cut into 1-inch pieces
- 3 cups chicken broth
- 2½ teaspoons salt, divided
- ⅔ cup 2% milk
- 2 teaspoons garlic powder
- ½ teaspoon pepper

1. In a Dutch oven, combine potatoes, parsnips, celery roots, broth and 2 teaspoons salt. Add water to cover vegetables. Bring to a boil. Reduce heat; cook, covered, for 15-20 minutes or until vegetables are tender.
2. Using a slotted spoon, transfer the vegetables to a large bowl; reserve the cooking liquid. Mash the vegetables, gradually adding the milk, garlic powder, pepper, remaining salt and enough reserved cooking liquid to reach desired consistency.

Winter Squash, Sausage & Feta Bake

During fall, I love to add seasonal flavor and color to my cooking with butternut squash. Combining it with Italian sausage and cheese creates a tasty potluck dish.
—**CRAIG SIMPSON** SAVANNAH, GA

PREP: 30 MIN. • **BAKE:** 45 MIN.
MAKES: 20 SERVINGS (¾ CUP EACH)

- 1 pound bulk Italian sausage
- 2 large onions, chopped
- ½ teaspoon crushed red pepper flakes, divided
- ¼ cup olive oil
- 2 teaspoons minced fresh rosemary
- 1½ teaspoons salt
- 1 teaspoon Worcestershire sauce
- 1 teaspoon pepper
- 1 medium butternut squash (about 4 pounds), peeled and cut into 1-inch cubes
- 1 medium acorn squash, peeled and cut into 1-inch cubes
- 2 cups (8 ounces) crumbled feta cheese
- 2 small sweet red peppers, chopped

1. In a large skillet, cook the sausage, onions and ¼ teaspoon pepper flakes over medium heat for 8-10 minutes or until the sausage is no longer pink and the onions are tender, breaking up the sausage into crumbles; drain.
2. In a large bowl, combine the oil, rosemary, salt, Worcestershire sauce, pepper and remaining pepper flakes. Add the butternut and acorn squash, feta cheese, red peppers and sausage mixture; toss to coat.
3. Transfer mixture to an ungreased shallow roasting pan. Cover and bake at 375° for 35 minutes. Uncover; bake 10-15 minutes longer or until the squash is tender.

WINTER SQUASH, SAUSAGE & FETA BAKE

Hearty Quinoa & Corn Chowder

My grandmother lived in the Appalachian Mountains and always served beans and corn straight from the garden. To give her yummy chowder recipe a bit of an update, I mixed in quinoa and herbs.

—**KARI NAPIER** LOUISVILLE, KY

PREP: 25 MIN. + STANDING • **COOK:** 15 MIN.
MAKES: 14 SERVINGS (¾ CUP EACH)

- 3 **medium sweet red peppers**
- 1 **cup quinoa, rinsed**
- 1 **tablespoon butter**
- 1 **tablespoon olive oil**
- 1 **medium onion, chopped**
- 2 **garlic cloves, minced**
- ⅓ **cup all-purpose flour**
- 4 **cups vegetable stock**
- 2 **cups heavy whipping cream**
- 6 **medium ears sweet corn, kernels removed (about 4 cups) or 2 packages (10 ounces) frozen corn, thawed**
- 1 **can (15 ounces) pinto beans, rinsed and drained**
- 2 **tablespoons minced fresh parsley**
- ½ **teaspoon minced fresh thyme**
- 1½ **teaspoons salt**
- ½ **teaspoon pepper**

1. Broil peppers 4 in. from the heat until skins blister, about 5 minutes. With tongs, rotate peppers a quarter turn. Broil and rotate until all sides are blistered and blackened. Immediately place peppers in a large bowl; cover and let stand for 20 minutes.

2. Peel off and discard the charred skin. Remove stems and seeds. Finely chop peppers.

3. Meanwhile, in a Dutch oven, cook and stir quinoa over medium-high heat for 3-5 minutes or until lightly toasted; remove from the pan.

4. In the same pan, heat the butter and oil over medium-high heat. Add onion; cook and stir until tender. Add garlic; cook 1 minute longer. Stir in flour until blended. Gradually whisk in stock and cream.

5. Add corn, beans, roasted peppers and quinoa; bring to a boil, stirring frequently. Reduce the heat; simmer, uncovered, for 15-20 minutes or until quinoa is tender, stirring occasionally. Stir in the remaining ingredients.

"When I needed to feed my son and a dozen of his buddies at his 21st birthday bonfire, I fired up the grill. These brats topped with sauerkraut were a big hit."
—**KEELEY WEBER** STERLING HEIGHTS, MI

Grilled Beer Brats with Kraut

PREP: 45 MIN. • **GRILL:** 35 MIN.
MAKES: 12 SERVINGS

- 6 **bacon strips, chopped**
- 1 **large onion, chopped**
- 1 **medium apple, peeled and thinly sliced**
- 2 **garlic cloves, minced**
- 1 **can (14 ounces) sauerkraut, rinsed and well drained**
- 3 **tablespoons spicy brown mustard**
- 1 **tablespoon brown sugar**
- 12 **uncooked bratwurst links**
- 1 **bottle (12 ounces) dark beer**
- 12 **hoagie buns, split**

1. In a large skillet, cook bacon over medium heat until crisp, stirring occasionally. Remove with a slotted spoon; drain on paper towels.

2. Cook and stir the onion in bacon drippings until softened. Reduce heat to medium-low; cook 15-20 minutes or until deep golden brown, stirring occasionally. Add the apple and garlic; cook 2 minutes longer. Stir in the sauerkraut, mustard, brown sugar and cooked bacon.

3. Transfer to a 13-in. x 9-in. disposable foil pan. Arrange bratwurst over top. Pour beer over bratwurst. Place pan on grill rack over medium heat; cook, covered, 30-35 minutes or until the sausages are no longer pink. Remove pan from heat.

4. Remove bratwurst and return to grill. Grill, covered, 2-3 minutes on each side or until browned. Serve on buns with sauerkraut mixture.

Ruby Red Beet & Apple Salad

Because I grow beets, I eat them a lot. In this salad, they often turn the apples—and sometimes my fingers—pinkish-red. But with such a great dish, I don't mind!
—**KATHY RAIRIGH** MILFORD, IN

PREP: 10 MIN. + COOLING
COOK: 35 MIN. + CHILLING
MAKES: 12 SERVINGS

- 2½ pounds fresh beets (about 8 medium)
- 2 medium apples, peeled and chopped
- 1 cup chopped fresh kale
- 1 cup chopped red cabbage
- 1 cup shredded carrots
- ½ cup chopped onion
- ½ cup cider vinegar
- ⅓ cup olive oil
- 2 tablespoons honey
- 1 teaspoon salt
- ¾ teaspoon curry powder
- ⅛ teaspoon each ground ginger, garlic powder and pepper

1. Scrub beets and trim tops to 1 in. Place in a Dutch oven; add water to cover. Bring to a boil. Reduce heat; simmer, covered, 30-60 minutes or until tender. Remove from water; cool.
2. Peel beets and cut into ½-in. cubes. In a large bowl, combine the apples, kale, cabbage, carrots, onion and beets.
3. In a small bowl, whisk remaining ingredients. Pour over the salad; toss to coat. Refrigerate, covered, for at least 4 hours or until chilled, stirring occasionally.

CHUNKY VEGGIE SLAW

RUBY RED BEET & APPLE SALAD

EAT SMART FAST FIX
Chunky Veggie Slaw

Traditional coleslaw gets a fresh approach when you add broccoli, cucumbers, snap peas and crunchy walnuts. Reduced-fat mayonnaise lightens it up.
—**NICHOLAS KING** DULUTH, MN

START TO FINISH: 25 MIN.
MAKES: 14 SERVINGS (1 CUP EACH)

- 1 small head cabbage, chopped
- 6 cups (1½ pounds) fresh broccoli florets
- 1 medium cucumber, chopped
- 2 celery ribs, sliced
- 12 fresh sugar snap peas, halved
- 1 small green pepper, chopped
- ¾ cup buttermilk
- ½ cup reduced-fat mayonnaise
- 3 tablespoons cider vinegar
- 2 tablespoons sugar
- ½ teaspoon salt
- 1 cup chopped walnuts, toasted
- 2 green onions, thinly sliced

In a large bowl, combine the first six ingredients. In a small bowl, whisk the buttermilk, mayonnaise, cider vinegar, sugar and salt. Pour over the salad; toss to coat. Top with the walnuts and green onions. Refrigerate leftovers.
NOTE *To toast nuts, spread in a 15-in. x 10-in. x 1-in. baking pan. Bake at 350° for 5-10 minutes or until lightly browned, stirring occasionally. Or, spread in a dry nonstick skillet and heat over low heat until lightly browned, stirring occasionally.*
PER SERVING *125 cal., 9 g fat (1 g sat. fat), 4 mg chol., 189 mg sodium, 10 g carb., 3 g fiber, 4 g pro.* **Diabetic Exchanges:** *2 vegetable, 1½ fat.*

Roasted Brussels Sprouts & Cauliflower

My grandchildren were never huge fans of cauliflower, but crispy chopped bacon makes a big difference in this vegetable bake. They like it even more when I use golden cauliflower instead of white.

—**PATRICIA HUDSON** RIVERVIEW, FL

PREP: 25 MIN. • **COOK:** 20 MIN.
MAKES: 12 SERVINGS (½ CUP EACH)

- 8 bacon strips, chopped
- 6 garlic cloves, minced
- 1 tablespoon olive oil
- 1 tablespoon butter, melted
- ¼ teaspoon kosher salt
- ¼ teaspoon coarsely ground pepper
- 4 cups Brussels sprouts, halved
- 4 cups fresh cauliflowerets
- ¼ cup grated Parmesan cheese
  Additional grated Parmesan cheese, optional

1. In a large skillet, cook bacon over medium heat until crisp, stirring occasionally. Remove with a slotted spoon; drain on paper towels. Discard drippings, reserving 1 tablespoon.
2. In a large bowl, mix the garlic, oil, butter, salt, pepper and reserved drippings. Add Brussels sprouts and cauliflowerets; toss to coat. Transfer to two greased 15-in. x 10-in. x 1-in. baking pans.
3. Bake at 350° for 15 minutes. Sprinkle each pan with 2 tablespoons cheese. Bake 3-5 minutes longer or until vegetables are tender. Sprinkle with bacon and, if desired, additional cheese.

ROASTED BRUSSELS SPROUTS & CAULIFLOWER

"Cardamom, lemon, almond and vanilla flavors all come together beautifully in German Butter Pound Cake. A little confectioners' sugar is the perfect finish."
—**KRISTINE CHAYES** SMITHTOWN, NY

GERMAN BUTTER POUND CAKE

German Butter Pound Cake

PREP: 30 MIN. • **BAKE:** 1 HOUR
MAKES: 16 SERVINGS

- 6 eggs, separated
- 1 cup butter, softened
- 2 cups sugar
- 1 tablespoon grated lemon peel
- 1 teaspoon vanilla extract
- ½ teaspoon almond extract
- 1½ cups all-purpose flour
- 2 teaspoons baking powder
- ½ teaspoon salt
- ½ teaspoon ground cardamom
- 6 tablespoons 2% milk
- 2 tablespoons confectioners' sugar

1. Place the egg whites in a large bowl; let stand at room temperature for 30 minutes. Generously grease and flour a 10-in. tube pan.
2. In a large bowl, cream the butter and sugar until light and fluffy. Add the egg yolks, one at a time, beating well after each addition. Beat in the lemon peel and extracts. In another bowl, mix the flour, baking powder, salt and cardamom; add to creamed mixture alternately with milk, beating well after each addition.
3. With clean beaters, beat egg whites on medium speed until soft peaks form. Fold into cake batter.
4. Transfer the cake batter to the prepared pan. Bake at 350° for 60-70 minutes or until a toothpick inserted into the center comes out clean. Cool in pan for 10 minutes before removing to a wire rack to cool. Sprinkle with confectioners' sugar.
NOTE *For easier removal of cake, use solid shortening when greasing a fluted or plain tube pan.*

ATHENA RUSSELL'S
SANTA FE CHICKEN
PITA PIZZAS PAGE 173

Weeknight Solutions

Even the busiest days are no match for these **convenient recipes**. Each main course and side dish requires just 30 minutes or less of prep time—so you can fix a **family-pleasing dinner** in a snap.

**KELLY WESTPHAL'S
BBQ HOT DOG & POTATO PACKS**
PAGE 168

**ADELE ZUERNER'S
SLOW-SIMMERING BEEF
BOURGUIGNON** *PAGE 170*

**ARTLAND CAMPBELL'S
SHRIMP FRIED RICE QUESADILLAS**
PAGE 180

(5) INGREDIENTS FAST FIX
BBQ Hot Dog & Potato Packs

Kids like to help with these fun foil packs. Small hands can easily top the potatoes with the hot dogs, onions and cheese.

—KELLY WESTPHAL WIND LAKE, WI

START TO FINISH: 20 MIN.
MAKES: 4 SERVINGS

- 1 package (20 ounces) refrigerated red potato wedges
- 4 hot dogs
- 1 small onion, cut into wedges
- ¼ cup shredded cheddar cheese
- ½ cup barbecue sauce

1. Divide the potato wedges among four pieces of heavy-duty foil (about 18 in. square). Top each with a hot dog, onion wedges and cheese. Drizzle with barbecue sauce. Fold the foil around mixture, sealing tightly.
2. Grill, covered, over medium heat 10-15 minutes or until heated through. Open the foil carefully to allow steam to escape.

BBQ HOT DOG & POTATO PACKS

"Hot soup is always a welcome sight on a chilly day. Get Slow & Easy Minestrone cooking in the morning, then just stir in the barley and beans before dinner."
—SALLY GOEB NEW EGYPT, NJ

SLOW COOKER
Slow & Easy Minestrone

PREP: 25 MIN. • **COOK:** 7 HOURS
MAKES: 6 SERVINGS (2¼ QUARTS)

- 1 can (28 ounces) diced tomatoes, undrained
- 3 celery ribs, cut into ½-inch slices
- 2 medium carrots, cut into ½-inch slices
- 2 small zucchini, halved and cut into ¾-inch slices
- 2 cups vegetable broth
- 1 cup shredded cabbage
- ¼ pound sliced fresh mushrooms
- 1 small onion, chopped
- 2 garlic cloves, minced
- 1 teaspoon dried basil
- 1 teaspoon salt
- ⅓ cup quick-cooking barley
- 1 can (15 ounces) white kidney or cannellini beans, rinsed and drained

1. In a 4- or 5-qt. slow cooker, combine the first 11 ingredients. Cover and cook on low for 7-9 hours.
2. Cook barley according to package directions; stir into soup. Add beans; heat through.

top tip
Ladle up Leftovers

I keep a heavy-duty resealable plastic bag in the freezer for soup ingredients. When we have extra cooked veggies, chicken or beef from dinner, I put the leftovers in the bag. In no time at all, I have enough to simmer up a pot of soup. All I have to do is cook some rice or noodles to stir in.

—LEE D. LANSING, MI

Simple Sparerib & Sauerkraut Supper

Thanks to this home-style meal from the slow cooker, I can spend less time in the kitchen and more time with my family.

—DONNA HARP CINCINNATI, OH

PREP: 30 MIN. • **COOK:** 6 HOURS
MAKES: 4 SERVINGS

- 1 **pound fingerling potatoes**
- 1 **medium onion, chopped**
- 1 **medium Granny Smith apple, peeled and chopped**
- 3 **thick-sliced bacon strips, cooked and crumbled**
- 1 **jar (16 ounces) sauerkraut, undrained**
- 2 **pounds pork spareribs**
- ½ **teaspoon salt**
- ¼ **teaspoon pepper**
- 1 **tablespoon vegetable oil**
- 3 **tablespoons brown sugar**
- ¼ **teaspoon caraway seeds**
- ½ **pound smoked Polish sausage, cut into 1-inch slices**
- 1 **cup beer**

1. In a 6-qt. slow cooker, place the potatoes, onion, apple and bacon. Drain sauerkraut, reserving ⅓ cup of the liquid; add sauerkraut and reserved liquid to slow cooker.
2. Cut spareribs into serving-size portions; sprinkle with salt and pepper. In a large skillet, heat the oil over medium-high heat; brown ribs in batches. Transfer to slow cooker; sprinkle with brown sugar and seeds.
3. Add sausage; pour in beer. Cover and cook on low for 6-7 hours or until ribs are tender.

SIMPLE SPARERIB & SAUERKRAUT SUPPER

"Here's a surefire winner—whole wheat fettuccine tossed with fresh sweet corn, tomatoes, red peppers, green onions and a little feta cheese. Try it and see!"
—ANGELA SPENGLER CLOVIS, NM

FRESH CORN & TOMATO FETTUCCINE

Fresh Corn & Tomato Fettuccine

START TO FINISH: 30 MIN.
MAKES: 4 SERVINGS

- 8 **ounces uncooked whole wheat fettuccine**
- 2 **medium ears sweet corn, husks removed**
- 2 **teaspoons plus 2 tablespoons olive oil, divided**
- ½ **cup chopped sweet red pepper**
- 4 **green onions, chopped**
- 2 **medium tomatoes, chopped**
- ½ **teaspoon salt**
- ½ **teaspoon pepper**
- 1 **cup crumbled feta cheese**
- 2 **tablespoons minced fresh parsley**

1. In a Dutch oven, cook fettuccine according to the package directions, adding corn during the last 8 minutes of cooking.
2. Meanwhile, in a small skillet, heat 2 teaspoons oil over medium-high heat. Add the red pepper and green onions; cook and stir until tender.
3. Drain the pasta and corn; transfer the pasta to a large bowl. Cool the corn slightly; cut corn from the cob and add to pasta. Add tomatoes, salt, pepper, remaining oil and pepper mixture; toss to combine. Sprinkle with cheese and parsley.
PER SERVING *422 cal., 15 g fat (4 g sat. fat), 15 mg chol., 580 mg sodium, 56 g carb., 10 g fiber, 17 g pro.*

Rainbow Vegetable Skillet

My kids happily eat their veggies when this spiced side is on the table. To create a main course instead, I stir in cooked chicken.
—**JENNIFER SCHMIDT** DICKENS, TX

START TO FINISH: 30 MIN. • **MAKES:** 9 SERVINGS

- 1 medium butternut squash (about 2 pounds)
- ¼ cup reduced-fat butter, melted
- 2 tablespoons brown sugar
- 1 tablespoon chili powder
- 1 tablespoon minced fresh cilantro
- 1 teaspoon salt
- ½ teaspoon pepper
- ¼ teaspoon ground cinnamon
- 1 medium green pepper, cut into 1-inch pieces
- 1 medium sweet yellow pepper, cut into 1-inch pieces
- 1 medium red onion, cut into wedges
- 1 tablespoon olive oil
- 2 cups grape tomatoes

1. Cut the squash in half; discard the seeds. Place cut side down in a microwave-safe dish; add ½ in. water. Microwave, uncovered, on high for 10-12 minutes or until almost tender.
2. Meanwhile, in a small bowl, combine the butter, brown sugar, chili powder, cilantro, salt, pepper and cinnamon; set aside. When the squash is cool enough to handle, peel and discard rind. Cut pulp into ½-in. pieces.
3. In a large skillet, saute the peppers and onion in oil until tender. Add tomatoes and squash; heat through. Transfer to a large bowl; add butter mixture and toss to coat.
NOTE *This recipe was tested with Land O'Lakes light stick butter in a 1,100-watt microwave.*
PER SERVING *106 cal., 5 g fat (2 g sat. fat), 7 mg chol., 322 mg sodium, 18 g carb., 4 g fiber, 2 g pro.* **Diabetic Exchanges:** *1 starch, 1 vegetable, ½ fat.*

RAINBOW VEGETABLE SKILLET

"Warm up cool fall days with tender chunks of beef simmered in a rich sauce and ladled over steaming noodles."
—**ADELE ZUERNER** ARDEN, NC

SLOW-SIMMERING BEEF BOURGUIGNON

Slow-Simmering Beef Bourguignon

PREP: 30 MIN. • **COOK:** 8 HOURS • **MAKES:** 6 SERVINGS

- 3 pounds beef stew meat
- ¾ teaspoon salt
- ¾ teaspoon pepper
- 3 tablespoons all-purpose flour
- 1½ cups beef broth
- 1½ cups dry red wine or additional beef broth, divided
- ¾ pound medium fresh mushrooms, quartered
- 1 large sweet onion, chopped
- 2 medium carrots, sliced
- 1 thick-sliced bacon strip, chopped
- 2 garlic cloves, minced
- 2 tablespoons Italian tomato paste
  Hot cooked egg noodles

1. Sprinkle beef with salt and pepper. In a large nonstick skillet coated with cooking spray, brown beef in batches. Remove with a slotted spoon to a 4- or 5-qt. slow cooker. Add flour; toss to coat. Add broth and 1 cup wine.
2. In the same skillet, add the mushrooms, onion, carrots and bacon; cook and stir over medium heat until carrots are tender. Add garlic; cook 1 minute longer. Add the remaining wine, stirring to loosen browned bits from the pan; stir in tomato paste. Transfer to slow cooker.
3. Cover and cook on low for 8-10 hours or until the beef is tender. Serve with noodles.

(5) INGREDIENTS FAST FIX

Blue Cheese-Crusted Sirloin Steaks

START TO FINISH: 30 MIN. • **MAKES:** 4 SERVINGS

- 2 tablespoons butter, divided
- 1 medium onion, chopped
- 1 beef top sirloin steak (1 inch thick and 1½ pounds)
- ¾ teaspoon salt
- ½ teaspoon pepper
- ⅓ cup crumbled blue cheese
- 2 tablespoons soft bread crumbs

1. In a large ovenproof skillet, heat 1 tablespoon butter over medium heat. Add the onion; cook and stir until tender. Transfer to a small bowl.

2. Cut steak into four equal portions; season with salt and pepper. In the same skillet, heat the remaining butter over medium heat. Brown steaks, about 5 minutes on each side. Meanwhile, add blue cheese and bread crumbs to onion; mix well. Spread over steaks.

3. Broil the steaks 4-6 in. from the heat for 3-5 minutes or until the steaks reach the desired doneness (for medium-rare, a thermometer should read 145°; medium, 160°; well-done, 170°).

FAST FIX # Steakhouse Mushrooms

A friend shared her recipe for buttery seasoned mushrooms with me when we were in nursing school. Now I prepare them whenever my husband cooks meat on the grill.

—**KENDA BURGETT** RATTAN, OK

START TO FINISH: 20 MIN. • **MAKES:** 4 SERVINGS

- ¼ cup butter, cubed
- 1 pound medium fresh mushrooms
- 2 teaspoons dried basil
- ½ teaspoon dried oregano
- ½ teaspoon seasoned salt
- ¼ teaspoon garlic powder
- 1 teaspoon browning sauce, optional

In a large skillet, heat butter over medium-high heat. Add mushrooms; cook and stir until tender. Stir in seasonings and, if desired, browning sauce. Reduce heat to medium; cook, covered, for 3-5 minutes to allow flavors to blend.

STEAKHOUSE MUSHROOMS
BLUE CHEESE-CRUSTED SIRLOIN STEAKS

FAST FIX ▸ Tilapia with Citrus Sauce

Tilapia is a mild, delicate fish, but the tangy sauce in this recipe adds a burst of flavor.
—FRANCIS GARLAND ANNISTON, AL

START TO FINISH: 30 MIN.
MAKES: 4 SERVINGS

- ½ cup 2% milk
- ½ cup all-purpose flour
- ½ teaspoon salt
- ½ teaspoon pepper
- 4 tilapia fillets (4 ounces each)
  Olive oil-flavored cooking spray
- 3 garlic cloves, minced
- 1 tablespoon butter
- 2 teaspoons olive oil
- ½ small lemon, sliced
- ½ medium lime, sliced
- ½ small navel orange, sliced
- 3 tablespoons lemon juice
- 3 tablespoons lime juice
- 2 tablespoons orange juice
- 2 green onions, finely chopped

1. Place milk in a shallow bowl. In another shallow bowl, combine the flour, salt and pepper. Dip fish in milk, then coat with flour mixture.

2. Spray fillets with cooking spray. In a large nonstick skillet coated with cooking spray, cook fish over medium-high heat for 3-4 minutes on each side or until fish flakes easily with a fork. Remove and keep warm.

3. In the same pan, saute garlic in butter and oil for 1 minute. Add the lemon, lime and orange slices, juices and onions; cook 1 minute longer. Serve with fish.

TILAPIA WITH CITRUS SAUCE

"I'm always looking for new ways to use the slow cooker. Tempting Teriyaki Chicken Stew balances salty and sweet ingredients for a combination I love."
—AMY SIEGEL CLIFTON, NJ

TEMPTING TERIYAKI CHICKEN STEW

SLOW COOKER Tempting Teriyaki Chicken Stew

PREP: 20 MIN. • **COOK:** 7 HOURS
MAKES: 6 SERVINGS

- 1 tablespoon olive oil
- 6 bone-in chicken thighs (about 2 pounds)
- 2 medium sweet potatoes, cut into 1-inch pieces
- 3 medium carrots, cut into 1-inch pieces
- 1 medium parsnip, peeled and cut into 1-inch pieces
- 1 medium onion, sliced
- 1 cup apricot preserves
- ½ cup maple syrup
- ½ cup teriyaki sauce
- ½ teaspoon ground ginger
- ⅛ teaspoon cayenne pepper
- 2 tablespoons cornstarch
- 2 tablespoons cold water

1. In a large skillet, heat the oil over medium-high heat; brown chicken on both sides. Place vegetables in a 4-qt. slow cooker; add chicken. In a small bowl, mix the preserves, maple syrup, teriyaki sauce, ginger and cayenne; pour over chicken.

2. Cover and cook on low for 6-8 hours or until chicken is tender. Remove chicken and vegetables to a platter; keep warm.

3. Transfer the cooking liquid to a small saucepan. Skim the fat. Bring the cooking liquid to a boil. In a small bowl, combine the cornstarch and cold water until smooth; gradually stir into the pan. Return to a boil, stirring constantly; cook and stir for 2 minutes or until thickened. Serve with chicken and vegetables.

Santa Fe Chicken Pita Pizzas

START TO FINISH: 30 MIN.
MAKES: 4 SERVINGS

- 4 whole pita breads
- ½ cup refried black beans
- ½ cup salsa
- 1 cup cubed cooked chicken breast
- 2 tablespoons chopped green chilies
- 2 tablespoons sliced ripe olives
- ¾ cup shredded Colby-Monterey Jack cheese
- 1 green onion, chopped
- ½ cup reduced-fat sour cream

1. Preheat oven to 350°. Place pita breads on an ungreased baking sheet; spread with beans. Top with salsa, chicken, chilies and olives; sprinkle with cheese.

2. Bake 8-10 minutes or until cheese is melted. Top with green onion; serve with sour cream.

PER SERVING *380 cal., 11 g fat (6 g sat. fat), 56 mg chol., 776 mg sodium, 44 g carb., 3 g fiber, 24 g pro.* **Diabetic Exchanges:** *3 starch, 2 lean meat, 1 fat.*

"Without any fuss, personal pizzas can be altered to please anyone. I give mine a Southwestern spin with salsa, green chilies and refried black beans."

—ATHENA RUSSELL FLORENCE, SC

SANTA FE CHICKEN PITA PIZZA

SLOW-COOKED HAM WITH PINEAPPLE SAUCE
DILL POTATO WEDGES

SLOW COOKER

Slow-Cooked Ham with Pineapple Sauce

Our holiday ham has a yummy pineapple sauce and is slow-cooked to perfection. It's so good, I'll make it any time of year.

—TERRY ROBERTS YORKTOWN, VA

PREP: 10 MIN. • **COOK:** 6 HOURS
MAKES: 12 SERVINGS

- 1 fully cooked boneless ham (4 to 5 pounds)
- 1 can (20 ounces) unsweetened crushed pineapple, undrained
- 1 cup packed brown sugar
- 1 tablespoon cornstarch
- ¼ teaspoon salt
- 2 tablespoons lemon juice
- 1 tablespoon yellow mustard

Place the ham in a 5-qt. slow cooker. In a small saucepan, mix the remaining ingredients, stirring to dissolve the cornstarch. Bring to a boil, stirring occasionally. Pour over ham, covering completely. Cover and cook on low for 6-8 hours.

---

⑤ INGREDIENTS | FAST FIX ▶

Dill Potato Wedges

These seasoned potato wedges are my absolute favorites. They're not only great with just about any main dish, but they're also quick and easy to prepare.

—JEANNIE KLUGH LANCASTER, PA

START TO FINISH: 15 MIN.
MAKES: 4 SERVINGS

- 1 tablespoon olive oil
- 1 package (20 ounces) refrigerated red potato wedges
- ½ teaspoon salt
- ½ teaspoon pepper
- 2 tablespoons grated Parmesan cheese
- 1 teaspoon snipped fresh dill or ¼ teaspoon dill weed

In a large skillet, heat oil over medium heat. Add the red potato wedges; sprinkle with salt and pepper. Cook for 10-12 minutes or until tender and golden brown, stirring occasionally. Remove from the heat; sprinkle with cheese and dill.

ASPARAGUS, BACON & HERBED CHEESE PIZZA

FAST FIX ▶ Asparagus, Bacon & Herbed Cheese Pizza

This zesty pizza is especially nice with spring asparagus but is good year-round. Red pepper flakes add a bit of a kick.
—**DAHLIA ABRAMS** DETROIT, MI

START TO FINISH: 30 MIN. • **MAKES:** 6 SERVINGS

- 1 prebaked 12-inch pizza crust
- 6 teaspoons olive oil, divided
- 1 cup (4 ounces) shredded part-skim mozzarella cheese
- 2¼ cups cut fresh asparagus (1-inch pieces)
- 8 bacon strips, cooked and crumbled
- ½ cup garlic-herb spreadable cheese (about 3 ounces)
- ¼ teaspoon crushed red pepper flakes

1. Preheat oven to 450°. Place crust on an ungreased 12-in. pizza pan or baking sheet; brush top with 4 teaspoons oil. Top with mozzarella cheese, asparagus and bacon. Drop spreadable cheese by teaspoonfuls over pizza. Sprinkle with pepper flakes; drizzle with remaining oil.
2. Bake 12-15 minutes or until cheese is lightly browned.

FAST FIX ▶ Chicken Lo Mein Stir-Fry

In the mood for Asian? Skip expensive takeout food and enjoy an easy, delicious stir-fry from your own kitchen.
—**DONNA NOECKER** PLANO, TX

START TO FINISH: 20 MIN. • **MAKES:** 4 SERVINGS

- 6 ounces uncooked lo mein noodles or vermicelli
- 1 pound boneless skinless chicken breasts, cut into thin strips
- 4 tablespoons reduced-sodium soy sauce, divided
- 3 garlic cloves, minced
- ¼ cup hoisin sauce
- 3 tablespoons water
- 1 teaspoon sugar
- 4 teaspoons sesame oil
- 1 package (9 ounces) fresh spinach

1. Cook the noodles according to the package directions. In a large bowl, combine the chicken, 1 tablespoon soy sauce and garlic; toss to coat. Marinate at room temperature for 10 minutes.
2. Meanwhile, in a small bowl, mix the hoisin sauce, water, sugar and remaining soy sauce until smooth. In a large skillet, heat oil over medium-high heat. Add the chicken mixture; stir-fry until no longer pink. Stir in the sauce mixture and spinach.
3. Drain noodles; add to skillet and toss to combine. Cook and stir just until spinach is wilted.

FAST FIX ▶ Sweet and Sour Carrots

I've rounded out many dinners with these carrots. I like them best with a main dish of roast turkey, brisket or braised short ribs.
—**HELEN ORESTAD** POWDERVILLE, MT

START TO FINISH: 30 MIN. • **MAKES:** 8 SERVINGS

- ¼ cup sugar
- ¼ cup orange juice
- ⅔ cup dried cranberries
- 2 tablespoons grated orange peel
- 3 tablespoons butter
- 2 pounds fresh carrots, sliced
- ⅓ cup water
- ¼ cup pine nuts, toasted
- 4 teaspoons sherry vinegar
- ½ teaspoon salt

1. In a small saucepan, combine the sugar and orange juice. Cook and stir over low heat for 2 minutes or until sugar is dissolved. Remove from the heat. Stir in cranberries and orange peel; set aside.
2. In a large saucepan, melt butter. Add carrots and water; stir until well coated. Bring to a boil. Reduce heat; cover and simmer for 5-7 minutes or until carrots are crisp-tender.
3. Stir in the pine nuts, sherry vinegar, salt and cranberry mixture. Simmer, uncovered, for 5-7 minutes or until the carrots are tender.

SWEET AND SOUR CARROTS

CORNMEAL-CHIVE DROP BISCUITS
GREENS WITH BACON & CRANBERRIES

Cornmeal-Chive Drop Biscuits

Cornmeal gives these biscuits a satisfying crunch. You can use this recipe to make drop dumplings for soups or stews, too. Just drop the dough on top, cover and simmer for 10 minutes.
—**ANGELA BUCHANAN** LONGMONT, CO

START TO FINISH: 30 MIN. • **MAKES:** 6 BISCUITS

- 1 cup all-purpose flour
- ¼ cup cornmeal
- 1 teaspoon baking soda
- ¼ teaspoon salt
- ¼ cup cold butter
- ⅔ cup buttermilk
- 1 tablespoon minced chives

1. In a small bowl, mix the flour, cornmeal, baking soda and salt. Cut in butter until mixture resembles coarse crumbs. Add buttermilk and chives; stir just until moistened.
2. Drop the dough by ¼ cupfuls 2 in. apart onto a greased baking sheet. Bake at 375° for 12-16 minutes or until golden brown. Serve warm.

Greens with Bacon & Cranberries

START TO FINISH: 15 MIN.
MAKES: 4 SERVINGS (ABOUT ⅔ CUP VINAIGRETTE)

- ¼ cup olive oil
- ¼ cup maple syrup
- 2 tablespoons cider vinegar
- ¼ teaspoon ground mustard
- ½ teaspoon salt
- ⅛ teaspoon coarsely ground pepper

SALAD

- 12 cups torn mixed salad greens
- 2 medium pears, sliced
- 8 bacon strips, cooked and crumbled
- ½ cup coarsely chopped walnuts, toasted
- ¼ cup dried cranberries
- ¼ cup crumbled Gorgonzola cheese

In a small bowl, whisk the first six ingredients; set aside. Just before serving, place the salad greens in a large bowl. Drizzle with the vinaigrette and toss to coat. Top with the remaining ingredients.
NOTE *To toast nuts, spread in a 15-in. x 10-in. x 1-in. baking pan. Bake at 350° for 5-10 minutes or until lightly browned, stirring occasionally. Or, spread in a dry nonstick skillet and heat over low heat until lightly browned, stirring occasionally.*

? **Did you know?**

Cider vinegar, made from apples, has a slightly fruity flavor and is frequently used as a substitute for wine vinegars. Flavored vinegars and wine vinegars are generally more subtle in flavor than white vinegar.

"After discovering an amazing dinner salad at a restaurant while we were on vacation, I couldn't wait to try to re-create it at home. I think I came pretty close, and it's been a big success in our family."
—**BRENDA NAKHLA** LAC DU FLAMBEAU, WI

FAST FIX ▶ Spaghetti with Four Cheeses

Creamy and cheesy, this spaghetti is a mainstay whenever I'm expecting guests. The recipe was handed down from my aunt and takes less than half an hour to prepare, so I don't feel rushed.
—NELLA PARKER HERSEY, MI

START TO FINISH: 25 MIN.
MAKES: 6 SERVINGS

- 8 ounces uncooked spaghetti
- ¼ cup butter, cubed
- 1 tablespoon all-purpose flour
- ¼ teaspoon salt
- ¼ teaspoon pepper
- 1½ cups half-and-half cream
- 1 cup (4 ounces) shredded part-skim mozzarella cheese
- 4 ounces fontina cheese, shredded
- ½ cup shredded provolone cheese
- ¼ cup shredded Parmesan cheese
- 2 tablespoons minced fresh parsley

1. Cook the spaghetti according to package directions. Meanwhile, in a large saucepan, melt butter. Stir in the flour, salt and pepper until smooth. Gradually stir in cream. Bring to a boil; cook and stir for 2 minutes or until thickened. Remove from the heat; stir in cheeses until melted.
2. Drain spaghetti; toss with cheese sauce and parsley.

SPAGHETTI WITH FOUR CHEESES

BAKED CHEDDAR EGGS & POTATOES
CRUNCHY VEGETABLE SALAD

"I love having breakfast at dinnertime— especially when it's this combo of eggs, potatoes and cheese started in a skillet and popped into the oven to bake."
—NADINE MERHEB TUCSON, AZ

Baked Cheddar Eggs & Potatoes

PREP: 20 MIN. • **BAKE:** 15 MIN.
MAKES: 4 SERVINGS

- 3 tablespoons butter
- 1½ pounds red potatoes, chopped
- ¼ cup minced fresh parsley
- 2 garlic cloves, minced
- ¾ teaspoon kosher salt
- ⅛ teaspoon pepper
- 8 eggs
- ½ cup shredded extra-sharp cheddar cheese

1. Preheat oven to 400°. In a 10-in. ovenproof skillet, heat butter over medium-high heat. Add potatoes; cook and stir until golden brown and tender. Stir in parsley, garlic, salt and pepper. With back of a spoon, make four wells in the potato mixture; break two eggs into each well.
2. Bake 9-11 minutes or until egg whites are completely set and yolks begin to thicken but are not hard. Sprinkle with cheese; bake 1 minute or until cheese is melted.

FAST FIX ▶ Crunchy Vegetable Salad

Here's a quick vegetable salad even kids will eat. They'll like the colorful variety, crunchy texture and Italian dressing.
—LINDA RUSSELL EXETER, ON

START TO FINISH: 10 MIN.
MAKES: 6 SERVINGS

- 2 cups cauliflowerets
- 2 cups broccoli florets
- 2 carrots, thinly sliced
- 1 small zucchini, sliced
- 1 small red onion, sliced
- 1 to 1½ cups Italian salad dressing

In a large bowl, combine all ingredients; toss to coat. Refrigerate until serving.

Roast Chicken Breasts with Peppers

This zippy entree is a real winner in our household. The seasonings and peppery topping deliver loads of flavor.
—**MELISSA GALINAT** LAKELAND, FL

START TO FINISH: 30 MIN.
MAKES: 4 SERVINGS

- ¾ teaspoon fennel seed, crushed
- ¾ teaspoon salt, divided
- ½ teaspoon pepper, divided
- ¼ teaspoon garlic powder
- ¼ teaspoon dried oregano
- 4 boneless skinless chicken breast halves (5 ounces each)
- 2 teaspoons plus 1 tablespoon olive oil, divided
- 1 large sweet red pepper, thinly sliced
- 1 medium sweet yellow pepper, thinly sliced
- 4 shallots, thinly sliced
- 1 cup chicken broth
- 1½ teaspoons minced fresh rosemary
- 1 tablespoon balsamic vinegar

1. In a large dry skillet, toast the fennel, ½ teaspoon salt, ¼ teaspoon pepper, garlic powder and oregano over medium heat for 1-2 minutes or until aromatic, stirring frequently. Cool slightly. Sprinkle over chicken.
2. In same skillet, heat 2 teaspoons oil over medium-high heat. Brown the chicken, about 2 minutes on each side. Transfer to an ungreased 15-in. x 10-in. x 1-in. baking pan. Bake at 450° for 10-15 minutes or until a thermometer reads 170°.
3. Meanwhile, heat remaining oil in the same skillet. Add the peppers and shallots; cook and stir over medium heat until crisp-tender.
4. Add broth and rosemary, stirring to loosen browned bits from pan. Bring to a boil; cook for 4-6 minutes or until the broth is almost evaporated. Stir in vinegar and remaining salt and pepper. Serve with chicken.

⑤ INGREDIENTS
Noodle Rice Pilaf

Can't decide between the usual rice or pasta side dish? Combine the two into one deliciously different medley. You'll need only three more ingredients—chicken broth, butter and fresh parsley—and just 5 minutes of prep time.
—**KATHY SCHRECENGOST** OSWEGO, NY

PREP: 5 MIN. • **COOK:** 30 MIN.
MAKES: 4 SERVINGS

- ¼ cup butter, cubed
- 1 cup uncooked long grain rice
- ½ cup uncooked fine egg noodles or broken vermicelli (1-inch)
- 2¾ cups chicken broth
- 2 tablespoons minced fresh parsley

1. In a large saucepan, heat the butter over medium-high heat. Add rice and noodles; cook and stir for 3-4 minutes or until noodles are lightly browned.
2. Stir in the chicken broth; bring to a boil. Reduce the heat; simmer, covered, for 20-25 minutes or until the broth is absorbed and the rice is tender. Stir in the parsley.

ROAST CHICKEN BREASTS WITH PEPPERS
NOODLE RICE PILAF

WORTH EVERY PENNE

FAST FIX Worth Every Penne

My husband is usually a meat-and-potatoes kind of guy. But when I fixed him a main-dish salad of sauteed chicken, vegetables and penne pasta, he asked me to make it again.

—JANET REIMER ARMSTRONG, BC

START TO FINISH: 30 MIN. • **MAKES:** 5 SERVINGS

- ¼ cup balsamic vinegar
- ¼ cup prepared pesto
- 2 tablespoons olive oil, divided
- 1 teaspoon honey
- ½ teaspoon salt
- ½ teaspoon pepper
- 2 cups uncooked penne pasta
- 3 cups sliced fresh mushrooms
- 1 large red onion, chopped
- 1 small sweet red pepper, julienned
- 1 small green pepper, julienned
- 3 cups fresh baby spinach
- 3 cups cubed cooked chicken breast
- 12 cherry tomatoes, halved
- ½ cup crumbled feta cheese or ¼ cup grated Parmesan cheese

1. In a small bowl, combine the vinegar, pesto, 1 tablespoon oil, honey, salt and pepper; set aside. Cook pasta according to package directions.

2. Meanwhile, in a Dutch oven, saute mushrooms, onion and peppers in the remaining oil until tender. Stir in the spinach, chicken and tomatoes; cook until spinach is wilted.

3. Drain the pasta; place in a large serving bowl. Add the chicken mixture, tomatoes and pesto mixture; toss to coat. Sprinkle with cheese.

FAST FIX
Alfredo Bacon Mushroom Pizza

This hearty pie is so convenient to prepare but looks and tastes like a specialty pizza from a restaurant. Creamy Alfredo sauce complements the distinctive mix of toppings.

—KAMI HORCH FRANKFORT, ME

START TO FINISH: 30 MIN. • **MAKES:** 8 SLICES

- 1 loaf (1 pound) frozen pizza dough, thawed
- ½ pound bacon strips
- 1 cup roasted garlic Alfredo sauce
- 1½ cups (6 ounces) shredded part-skim mozzarella cheese
- ¼ cup grated Parmesan cheese
- 2 large portobello mushrooms, stems removed
- ¼ teaspoon pepper

1. Roll pizza dough into a 15-in. circle; transfer to a greased 14-in. pizza pan and build up edges slightly. Bake at 425° for 6-8 minutes or until lightly browned. Meanwhile, in a large skillet, cook bacon just until done. Drain on paper towels; cut into 1-in. pieces.

2. Spread Alfredo sauce over crust; sprinkle with cheeses. Cut mushrooms into ½-in. strips; place over cheese so they resemble the spokes of a wheel. Sprinkle with bacon and pepper. Bake for 10-15 minutes or until heated through and cheese is melted.

ALFREDO BACON MUSHROOM PIZZA

WASABI BEEF FAJITAS

Momma's Turkey Stew with Dumplings

Each year, my mother transformed our Thanksgiving leftovers into a comforting turkey stew. It's still one of my favorite meals.
—**STEPHANIE RABBITT-SCHAPP** CINCINNATI, OH

PREP: 20 MIN. • **COOK:** 6½ HOURS • **MAKES:** 6 SERVINGS

- 3 **cups shredded cooked turkey**
- 1 **large sweet onion, chopped**
- 1 **large potato, peeled and cubed**
- 2 **large carrots, chopped**
- 2 **celery ribs, chopped**
- 2 **bay leaves**
- 1 **teaspoon salt**
- ½ **teaspoon poultry seasoning**
- ½ **teaspoon dried thyme**
- ¼ **teaspoon pepper**
- 1 **carton (32 ounces) chicken broth**
- ⅓ **cup cold water**
- 3 **tablespoons cornstarch**
- ½ **cup frozen corn, thawed**
- ½ **cup frozen peas, thawed**
- 1 **cup biscuit/baking mix**
- ⅓ **cup 2% milk**

1. In a 6-qt. slow cooker, combine the first 10 ingredients; stir in chicken broth. Cover and cook on low for 6-7 hours.
2. Remove bay leaves. In a small bowl, mix the cold water and cornstarch until smooth; stir into the turkey mixture. Add corn and peas. Cover and cook on high until mixture reaches a simmer.
3. Meanwhile, in a small bowl, mix the baking mix and milk just until moistened. Drop by rounded tablespoonfuls on top of the simmering liquid. Reduce heat to low; cover and cook for 20-25 minutes or until a toothpick inserted in a dumpling comes out clean.

MOMMA'S TURKEY STEW WITH DUMPLINGS

FAST FIX **Wasabi Beef Fajitas**

Beef fajitas take on the flavors of the Far East when you add soy sauce, ginger and Japanese horseradish, also known as wasabi. Look for it in the Asian food section of your supermarket.
—**TASTE OF HOME TEST KITCHEN**

START TO FINISH: 20 MIN. • **MAKES:** 8 SERVINGS

- 1 **large sweet red pepper, julienned**
- 12 **green onions with tops, cut in half lengthwise**
- 2 **tablespoons sesame oil, divided**
- 1 **pound uncooked beef stir-fry strips**
- 2 **teaspoons cornstarch**
- 3 **tablespoons reduced-sodium soy sauce**
- 2 **teaspoons prepared wasabi**
- 2 **teaspoons minced fresh gingerroot**
- 1 **teaspoon minced garlic**
- 8 **flour tortillas (8 inches), warmed**
- 1 **cup coleslaw mix**

1. In a large skillet, stir-fry the red pepper and green onions in 1 tablespoon oil for 3 minutes or until tender; remove and set aside. In the same skillet, stir-fry beef in remaining oil for 5 minutes or until no longer pink.
2. In a small bowl, combine cornstarch, soy sauce, wasabi, ginger and garlic until blended; pour over beef. Bring to a boil; cook and stir for 2 minutes or until thickened. Return red pepper mixture to the pan; heat through.
3. Spoon ½ cup beef mixture down the center of each tortilla; top with 2 tablespoons coleslaw mix. Fold one side of tortilla over filling and roll up.

Lemon-Olive Chicken with Orzo

Trying to lighten up your meals? Here's a better-for-you choice that still satisfies. Because it's quick to fix, I have time to toss together a green salad as a side dish.

—NANCY BROWN DAHINDA, IL

START TO FINISH: 30 MIN.
MAKES: 4 SERVINGS

- 1 tablespoon olive oil
- 4 boneless skinless chicken thighs (about 1 pound)
- 1 can (14½ ounces) reduced-sodium chicken broth
- ⅔ cup uncooked whole wheat orzo pasta
- ½ medium lemon, cut into 4 wedges
- ½ cup pitted Greek olives, sliced
- 1 tablespoon lemon juice
- 1 teaspoon dried oregano
- ¼ teaspoon salt
- ¼ teaspoon pepper

1. In a large nonstick skillet, heat oil over medium heat. Brown chicken on both sides; remove from pan.
2. Add broth to the skillet; increase heat to medium-high. Cook, stirring to loosen browned bits from pan. Stir in the remaining ingredients. Return to a boil. Reduce heat; simmer, uncovered, 5 minutes, stirring occasionally.
3. Return chicken to the pan. Cook, covered, 5-8 minutes or until pasta is tender and a thermometer inserted into chicken reads 170°.
PER SERVING 346 cal., 17 g fat (3 g sat. fat), 76 mg chol., 784 mg sodium, 22 g carb., 5 g fiber, 26 g pro. **Diabetic Exchanges:** 3 lean meat, 2 fat, 1 starch.

LEMON-OLIVE CHICKEN WITH ORZO

SHRIMP FRIED RICE QUESADILLAS

Shrimp Fried Rice Quesadillas

Cheesy quesadillas get a surprising but delicious twist when you add shrimp, soy sauce and rice. Feel free to use leftover fried rice from last night's takeout.

—ARTLAND CAMPBELL HYANNIS, MA

START TO FINISH: 25 MIN.
MAKES: 2 SERVINGS

- ¼ pound uncooked small shrimp, peeled and deveined
- 2 tablespoons chopped onion
- 2 tablespoons chopped sweet red pepper
- 2 tablespoons chopped green pepper
- 3 tablespoons butter, divided
- 1 egg, beaten
- ⅓ cup cooked long grain rice
- 1 tablespoon reduced-sodium soy sauce
- 2 flour tortillas (8 inches)
- 2 slices pepper jack cheese (¾ ounce each)

1. In a small skillet, saute the shrimp, onion and peppers in 1 tablespoon butter until shrimp turn pink; remove and keep warm.
2. In a small bowl, whisk the egg. In the same skillet, heat 1 tablespoon butter until hot. Add egg; cook and stir over medium heat until egg is completely set. Stir in the rice, soy sauce and shrimp mixture.
3. Spread the remaining butter over one side of each flour tortilla. Place tortillas butter side down, on a griddle. Place a slice of cheese on each tortilla. Sprinkle the shrimp mixture over half of each tortilla. Fold over and cook over low heat for 1-2 minutes on each side or until the cheese is melted. Cut into wedges.

Beefy French Onion Potpie

My husband is a fan of French onion soup, so I used the canned variety as a quick base for my beef potpie. He loved it!

—SARA HUTCHENS DU QUOIN, IL

START TO FINISH: 30 MIN.
MAKES: 4 SERVINGS

- 1 **pound ground beef**
- 1 **small onion, chopped**
- 1 **can (10½ ounces) condensed French onion soup**
- 1½ **cups (6 ounces) shredded part-skim mozzarella cheese**
- 1 **tube (12 ounces) refrigerated buttermilk biscuits**

1. Preheat oven to 350°. In a large skillet, cook the beef and onion over medium heat 6-8 minutes or until beef is no longer pink, breaking beef into crumbles; drain. Stir in soup; bring to a boil.

2. Transfer to an ungreased 9-in. deep dish pie plate; sprinkle with cheese. Bake 5 minutes or until the cheese is melted. Top with the biscuits. Bake 15-20 minutes longer or until biscuits are golden brown.

BBQ Meat Loaf Minis

Both children and adults enjoy these tasty meat loaves baked in muffin cups. If you'd like a bit of a kick, mix in 2 teaspoons chili powder and 1 cup of salsa.

—LINDA CALL FALUN, KS

START TO FINISH: 30 MIN.
MAKES: 6 SERVINGS

- 1 **package (6 ounces) stuffing mix**
- 1 **cup water**
- 2 **tablespoons hickory smoke-flavored barbecue sauce**
- 1 **pound ground beef**
- 1 **cup (4 ounces) shredded cheddar cheese**
  Additional hickory smoke-flavored barbecue sauce, optional

1. Preheat oven to 375°. In a large bowl, combine stuffing mix, water and 2 tablespoons sauce. Add beef; mix lightly but thoroughly. Place ⅓ cup mixture into each of 12 ungreased muffin cups, pressing lightly.

2. Bake, uncovered, 18-22 minutes or until a thermometer reads 160°. Sprinkle the tops with cheese; bake 2-4 minutes longer or until the cheese is melted. If desired, serve with additional barbecue sauce.

Coconut Curry Shrimp

Jasmine rice makes a fragrant bed for this flavorful seafood stir-fry. The sweetness of the coconut milk is complemented by the spiciness of the curry. I serve each plate with tangy lime wedges.

—CINDY ROMBERG MISSISSAUGA, ON

START TO FINISH: 25 MIN.
MAKES: 3 SERVINGS

- ⅔ **cup coconut milk**
- 1 **tablespoon fish sauce**
- 1½ **teaspoons curry powder**
- 1 **teaspoon brown sugar**
- ¼ **teaspoon salt**
- ¼ **teaspoon pepper**
- 1 **pound uncooked large shrimp, peeled and deveined**
- 1 **medium sweet red pepper, finely chopped**
- 2 **green onions, chopped**
- ¼ **cup minced fresh cilantro**
  Hot cooked jasmine rice
  Lime wedges

1. In a small bowl, combine the first six ingredients. In a large skillet or wok, stir-fry shrimp in 2 tablespoons coconut milk mixture until shrimp turn pink. Remove and keep warm.

2. Add the red pepper, green onions and remaining coconut milk mixture to pan. Bring to a boil; cook and stir for 3-4 minutes or until vegetables are crisp-tender.

3. Add the shrimp and cilantro; heat through. Serve with jasmine rice and lime wedges.

COCONUT CURRY SHRIMP

ADRI BARR CROCETTI'S
CRANBERRY-APPLE
LATTICE PIE *PAGE 202*

Holiday & Seasonal Celebrations

Gather your friends and family for scrumptious food, festivities and fun. When it's time to celebrate a **special occasion**, you'll find everything you need in this extra-big chapter.

LARA PENNELL'S MINI CHOCOLATE WAFER CAKES *PAGE 185*

JUDITH FOREMAN'S TOMATOES WITH BUTTERMILK VINAIGRETTE *PAGE 192*

ANGELA HANKS' FLYING BAT PIZZAS *PAGE 195*

Chocolate Valentines

Surprise that special someone on February 14 with dark and dreamy chocolate. These rich, decadent cupcakes, cookies and more are perfect to share with the one you love.

JUMBO BROWNIE COOKIES

Judy's Chocolate Chip Banana Bread

My co-worker and dear friend, Judy, gave me her scrumptious banana bread recipe more than 30 years ago. I still use it and added just one simple ingredient—semisweet chocolate chips to please all the sweet tooths I know.

—DEBRA KEISER ST. CLOUD, MN

PREP: 20 MIN. • **BAKE:** 1 HOUR + COOLING
MAKES: 1 LOAF (16 SLICES)

- ½ cup butter, softened
- 1¼ cups sugar
- 2 eggs
- 1 cup mashed ripe bananas (about 2 medium)
- ¼ cup buttermilk
- 1 teaspoon vanilla extract
- 2 cups all-purpose flour
- 1 teaspoon baking powder
- ¾ teaspoon baking soda
- ½ teaspoon salt
- ¾ cup semisweet chocolate chips
- ¼ cup chopped walnuts, optional

1. Line the bottom of a greased 9-in. x 5-in. loaf pan with parchment paper; grease paper.
2. In a large bowl, beat the butter and sugar until crumbly. Add eggs, one at a time, beating well after each addition. Beat in the bananas, buttermilk and vanilla. In another bowl, mix the flour, baking powder, baking soda and salt; stir into creamed mixture. Fold in chocolate chips and, if desired, walnuts.
3. Transfer to the prepared pan. Bake at 350° for 60-65 minutes or until a toothpick inserted in center comes out clean. Cool for 10 minutes before removing from pan to a wire rack; remove paper.

 ## Did you know?

Chocolate should be stored tightly wrapped in a cool, dry place. When stored in a spot that's too warm, it develops grayish-white streaks or blotches, called a fat bloom. In damp storage, it develops a rough feel, called a sugar bloom. You can still melt chocolate with blooms and incorporate it into batter or dough for baked goods.

Jumbo Brownie Cookies

Treat family and friends on Valentine's Day or any day at all with a fresh-baked batch of rich, fudgy cookies. Mixing a little instant espresso powder into the dough puts them over the top.

—REBECCA CABABA LAS VEGAS, NV

PREP: 20 MIN. • **BAKE:** 15 MIN./BATCH • **MAKES:** ABOUT 1½ DOZEN

- 2⅔ cups (16 ounces) 60% cacao bittersweet chocolate baking chips
- ½ cup unsalted butter, cubed
- 4 eggs
- 1½ cups sugar
- 4 teaspoons vanilla extract
- 2 teaspoons instant espresso powder, optional
- ⅔ cup all-purpose flour
- ½ teaspoon baking powder
- ¼ teaspoon salt
- 1 package (11½ ounces) semisweet chocolate chunks

1. Preheat oven to 350°. In a large saucepan, melt the chocolate chips and butter over low heat, stirring until smooth. Remove from the heat; cool slightly.
2. In a small bowl, whisk eggs, sugar, vanilla and, if desired, espresso powder until blended. Whisk into the chocolate mixture. In another bowl, mix the flour, baking powder and salt; add to the chocolate mixture, mixing well. Fold in the chocolate chunks.
3. Drop dough by ¼ cupfuls 3 in. apart onto parchment paper-lined baking sheets. Bake 12-14 minutes or until set. Cool on pans 1-2 minutes. Remove to wire racks to cool.
NOTE *This recipe was tested with Ghirardelli 60% Cacao Bittersweet Chocolate Baking Chips; results may vary when using a different product.*

Chocolate & Peanut Butter Mousse Cheesecake

PREP: 50 MIN. + CHILLING • **MAKES:** 16 SERVINGS

- 1½ cups chocolate wafer crumbs (about 24 wafers)
- ¼ cup butter, melted

MOUSSE LAYERS
- 1¼ cups heavy whipping cream
- ¾ cup creamy peanut butter
- 5 ounces cream cheese, softened
- 2 tablespoons butter, softened
- 1¼ cups confectioners' sugar
- 5 ounces bittersweet chocolate, chopped
- 1 milk chocolate candy bar (3½ ounces), chopped
- ⅓ cup sugar
- ¼ cup 2% milk
- 1 teaspoon vanilla extract

GANACHE
- 6 ounces bittersweet chocolate, chopped
- ⅔ cup heavy whipping cream
- 1 teaspoon vanilla extract

1. In a small bowl, mix wafer crumbs and butter. Press onto bottom of a greased 9-in. springform pan.

2. In another bowl, beat cream until stiff peaks form. In a large bowl, beat peanut butter, cream cheese and butter until smooth. Beat in confectioners' sugar. Fold in half of the whipped cream. Spread evenly over crust. Refrigerate while preparing the next layer.

"Chocolate and Peanut Butter Mousse Cheesecake takes a little time to make, but it's definitely worth it."
—**JANON FURRER** PRESCOTT, AZ

CHOCOLATE & PEANUT BUTTER MOUSSE CHEESECAKE

MINI CHOCOLATE WAFER CAKES

3. Place the bittersweet and milk chocolates in a small bowl. In a small saucepan, combine the sugar and milk; bring just to a boil, stirring constantly. Pour over the chocolate; stir with a whisk until smooth. Stir in vanilla. Cool to room temperature, stirring occasionally. Fold in the remaining whipped cream. Spread evenly over peanut butter layer. Freeze 2 hours or until firm.

4. For the ganache, place chocolate in a small bowl. In a small saucepan, bring cream just to a boil. Pour over the chocolate; whisk until smooth. Stir in vanilla. Cool to room temperature or until the ganache thickens to a spreading consistency, stirring occasionally. Spread over cheesecake. Refrigerate 1 hour or until set. Remove rim from pan.

Mini Chocolate Wafer Cakes

I first prepared these for a friend when I lived in the dorms at college and had no access to appliances. Little did I know I'd be fixing the same cakes for my children 20 years later!
—**LARA PENNELL** MAULDIN, SC

PREP: 15 MIN. + CHILLING • **MAKES:** 8 SERVINGS

- 1½ cups heavy whipping cream
- 3 tablespoons baking cocoa
- 2 tablespoons sugar
- 1½ teaspoons vanilla extract
- 24 chocolate wafers
  - Chocolate syrup
  - Heart-shaped sprinkles

1. In a large bowl, beat the cream, cocoa, sugar and vanilla until soft peaks form. Arrange eight wafers on the bottom of a foil-lined 9-in.-square baking pan. Spoon or pipe about 2 tablespoons cream mixture onto each. Repeat the layers twice, making eight stacks. Refrigerate, covered, overnight.

2. To serve, transfer to dessert plates. Drizzle with chocolate syrup; top with sprinkles.

Silky Chocolate Pie

Our family loves this smooth-as-silk, Cognac-splashed dessert. It's fancy enough to serve guests on special occasions but too good not to enjoy other times, too!

—KATHY HEWITT CRANSTON, RI

PREP: 25 MIN. • **COOK:** 15 MIN.+ CHILLING
MAKES: 8 SERVINGS

> **Pastry for single-crust pie (9 inches), see below**
> ⅓ **cup sugar**
> ¼ **cup cornstarch**
> 2½ **cups half-and-half cream**
> 4 **egg yolks**
> 6 **ounces semisweet chocolate, finely chopped**
> 3 **tablespoons Cognac or brandy**
> 1 **teaspoon vanilla extract**
> **TOPPING**
> 1 **cup heavy whipping cream**
> 1 **tablespoon Cognac or brandy**
> 1 **teaspoon confectioners' sugar**
> **Baking cocoa**

1. On a lightly floured surface, roll the pastry dough to a ⅛-in.-thick circle; transfer to a 9-in. pie plate. Trim the pastry to ½ in. beyond the rim of the plate; flute the edge. Line unpricked pastry with a double thickness of foil. Fill with pie weights, dried beans or uncooked rice.

2. Bake crust at 400° for 20 minutes. Remove foil and weights; bake 10-12 minutes longer or until golden brown. Cool on a wire rack.

3. In a heavy saucepan, mix sugar and cornstarch. Whisk in cream. Cook and stir over medium heat until thickened and bubbly. Remove from the heat. In a small bowl, whisk a small amount of hot mixture into egg yolks; return all to the pan, whisking constantly. Cook and stir over low heat 1 minute longer. Remove from heat; stir in chocolate, Cognac and vanilla until the chocolate is melted.

4. Transfer to a clean bowl; press plastic wrap onto the surface of filling. Cool the filling to room temperature. Spoon into crust. Refrigerate, covered, until cold, about 4 hours.

5. For topping, in a small bowl, beat cream until it begins to thicken. Add Cognac and confectioners' sugar; beat until soft peaks form. Spread over pie. Sprinkle with cocoa.

PASTRY FOR SINGLE-CRUST PIE (9 INCHES) *Combine 1¼ cups of all-purpose flour and ⅛ tsp. salt; cut in ½ cup cold butter until crumbly. Gradually add 3-4 Tbsp. ice water, tossing with a fork until dough holds together when pressed. Wrap in plastic wrap and refrigerate 1 hour.*

NOTE *Let pie weights cool before storing. Beans and rice may be reused for pie weights, but not for cooking.*

CHOCOLATE CREAM CUPCAKES

---

⑤INGREDIENTS Chocolate Cream Cupcakes

My favorite hockey team, the Boston Bruins, inspired me to create cupcakes based on Boston cream pie.

—ALISA CHRISTENSEN
RANCHO SANTA MARGARITA, CA

PREP: 30 MIN. + CHILLING
BAKE: 20 MIN. + COOLING
MAKES: 20 CUPCAKES

> 1 **package yellow cake mix (regular size)**
> 1 **package (3.4 ounces) cook-and-serve chocolate pudding mix**
> **GLAZE**
> ⅔ **cup semisweet chocolate chips**
> 2½ **tablespoons butter**
> 1¼ **cups confectioners' sugar**
> 3 **tablespoons hot water**

1. Prepare and bake the cake mix according to the package directions for cupcakes, using 20 paper-lined muffin cups. Cool completely.

2. Meanwhile, in a small bowl, prepare pudding mix according to package directions. Press plastic wrap onto surface of pudding; refrigerate until cold.

3. Cut a small hole in the tip of a pastry bag or in a corner of a food-safe plastic bag; insert a small pastry tip. Transfer the pudding to the bag. Using a wooden or metal skewer, poke a hole through the bottom of the cupcake liners. Push tip through hole and pipe filling into cupcakes.

4. In a microwave, melt chocolate chips and butter; stir until smooth. Whisk in confectioners' sugar and hot water. Dip the tops of the cupcakes into the glaze.

Deep & Dark Ganache Cake

PREP: 40 MIN. + COOLING
BAKE: 30 MIN. + COOLING
MAKES: 24 SERVINGS

- 6 ounces bittersweet chocolate, chopped
- 1½ cups hot brewed coffee
- 4 eggs
- 3 cups sugar
- ¾ cup canola oil
- 2 teaspoons vanilla extract
- 2½ cups all-purpose flour
- 1 cup baking cocoa
- 2 teaspoons baking soda
- ¾ teaspoon baking powder
- 1¼ teaspoons salt
- 1½ cups buttermilk

GANACHE FROSTING

- 16 ounces bittersweet chocolate, chopped
- 2 cups heavy whipping cream
- 5 teaspoons light corn syrup

1. Line bottoms of three greased 8-in.-square baking pans with parchment paper; grease paper.

2. Place the chocolate in a small bowl. Pour hot coffee over the chocolate; stir with a whisk until smooth. Cool mixture slightly.

3. In a large bowl, beat eggs on high speed until lemon-colored. Gradually add sugar, oil, vanilla and chocolate mixture, beating until well blended. In another bowl, mix the flour, cocoa, baking soda, baking powder and salt; add to chocolate mixture alternately with buttermilk, beating well after each addition.

4. Transfer to the prepared pans. Bake at 325° for 30-35 minutes or until a toothpick inserted in center comes out clean. Cool for 10 minutes before removing from pans to wire racks; remove paper. Cool completely.

5. For ganache, place chocolate in a large bowl. In a small saucepan, bring cream and corn syrup just to a boil. Pour over chocolate; stir with a whisk until smooth.

6. Let stand at room temperature to cool and thicken slightly, about 45 minutes, stirring occasionally. (Mixture will be very soft, but will thicken when spread onto cake.)

7. Place one cake layer on a serving plate; spread with ⅓ cup ganache. Repeat layers. Top with remaining cake layer. Spread remaining ganache over top and sides of cake.

TWO-LAYERED DEEP & DARK GANACHE CAKE & CUPCAKES
Prepare cake as directed, using twelve paper-lined muffin cups and two greased and parchment-lined 8-in.-square baking pans. Fill muffin cups three-fourths full; bake at 375° for 15-17 minutes or until a toothpick comes out clean. Divide remaining batter between prepared cake pans. Reduce oven setting to 325°; bake cake layers as directed. Yield: One 2-layered cake and 1 dozen cupcakes (24 servings).

Did you know?

Ganache is a French term referring to a smooth mixture of chocolate and cream used as a cake filling, as a glaze and in candy-making. Traditionally, ganache is made by pouring hot cream over chopped chocolate and stirring until the mixture is velvety smooth. The proportions of cream to chocolate vary depending on the use. As in the Deep & Dark Ganache Cake recipe at left, corn syrup may be added to give a shiny finish to the poured ganache. Flavorings may also be added.

"Chocoholics, here's the cure for your craving! Deep & Dark Ganache Cake is incredibly rich, decadent and satisfying. No one has been able to resist a slice."
—**TARRA KNIGHT** BENBROOK, TX

DEEP & DARK GANACHE CAKE

Fresh for Easter

Set a joyful table for your Sunday dinner with these revamped springtime favorites. From a showstopping main course to a delectable dessert, they're sure to delight guests.

GLAZED PINEAPPLE HAM

Roasted Potatoes with Garlic Butter

A platter of these golden and orange potatoes is so colorful and aromatic, it could replace flowers as a centerpiece!

—**ELIZABETH KELLEY** CHICAGO, IL

PREP: 30 MIN. • **BAKE:** 20 MIN. • **MAKES:** 10 SERVINGS

- 8 medium Yukon Gold potatoes, peeled
- 3 medium sweet potatoes, peeled
- 2 tablespoons canola oil
- ½ teaspoon salt
- ¼ teaspoon pepper
- ¼ cup butter
- 3 garlic cloves, minced
- 1 tablespoon minced fresh thyme or 1 teaspoon dried thyme
- ½ cup shredded cheddar cheese
- ⅓ cup grated Parmesan cheese
  Additional minced fresh thyme, optional

1. Cut Yukon Gold and sweet potatoes into ⅛-in. slices; toss with oil and sprinkle with salt and pepper. Divide between two greased 15-in. x 10-in. x 1-in. baking pans. Roast at 425° for 17-20 minutes or until tender.
2. Meanwhile, in a small skillet, heat butter over medium heat. Add the garlic and thyme; cook and stir for 1 minute. Transfer the roasted potatoes to a large bowl. Drizzle with the butter mixture; toss to coat. Sprinkle with cheeses and, if desired, additional thyme; toss to combine.

ROASTED POTATOES WITH GARLIC BUTTER

Glazed Pineapple Ham

Here's the recipe I used the first time I prepared a holiday ham. I was so happy with the results, it became a new tradition.

—**CHRISSY CLARK** BOISE, ID

PREP: 15 MIN. • **BAKE:** 2¼ HOURS + STANDING
MAKES: 20 SERVINGS

- 1 fully cooked bone-in ham (7 to 9 pounds)
  Whole cloves

GLAZE/SAUCE
- 2 tablespoons cornstarch
- ¼ cup cold water
- 2½ cups packed dark brown sugar, divided
- 1 can (20 ounces) unsweetened crushed pineapple, undrained
- ¼ cup lemon juice
- 2 tablespoons Dijon mustard
- ¼ teaspoon salt
- 1 cup packed light brown sugar

1. Place ham on a rack in a shallow roasting pan. Using a sharp knife, score the surface of ham with ¼-in.-deep cuts in a diamond pattern; insert a clove in each diamond. Cover and bake at 325° for 2 to 2½ hours or until a thermometer reaches 130°.
2. Meanwhile, in a large saucepan, dissolve the cornstarch in water; stir in 2 cups dark brown sugar, pineapple, lemon juice, Dijon mustard and salt. Bring to a boil; cook and stir for 1-2 minutes or until slightly thickened. Reserve 2 cups for sauce; keep warm.
3. Remove ham from oven. Increase the oven setting to 425°. Pour the remaining pineapple mixture over ham. In a small bowl, mix the light brown sugar and remaining dark brown sugar; spread over ham.
4. Bake ham, uncovered, 10-15 minutes longer or until a thermometer reads 140°. Serve with reserved sauce.

Tuscan-Style Roasted Asparagus

PREP: 20 MIN. • **BAKE:** 15 MIN. • **MAKES:** 8 SERVINGS

- 1½ pounds fresh asparagus, trimmed
- 1½ cups grape tomatoes, halved
- 3 tablespoons pine nuts
- 3 tablespoons olive oil, divided
- 2 garlic cloves, minced
- 1 teaspoon kosher salt
- ½ teaspoon pepper
- 1 tablespoon lemon juice
- ⅓ cup grated Parmesan cheese
- 1 teaspoon grated lemon peel

1. Preheat oven to 400°. Place the asparagus, tomatoes and pine nuts on a foil-lined 15x10x1-in. baking pan. Mix 2 tablespoons oil, garlic, salt and pepper; add to asparagus and toss to coat.

2. Bake 15-20 minutes or just until asparagus is tender. Drizzle with remaining oil and lemon juice; sprinkle with cheese and lemon peel. Toss to combine.

PER SERVING *95 cal., 8 g fat (2 g sat. fat), 3 mg chol., 294 mg sodium, 4 g carb., 1 g fiber, 3 g pro.* **Diabetic Exchanges:** *1½ fat, 1 vegetable.*

"I like using locally grown produce for Tuscan-Style Roasted Asparagus. It can be served hot or cold."
—**JANNINE FISK** MALDEN, MA

TUSCAN-STYLE ROASTED ASPARAGUS

Strawberry Walnut Torte

Everyone looks forward to a slice of this Easter-worthy dessert. The frosted torte has lots of fresh strawberries on top.
—**BONNIE MALLOY** NORWOOD, PA

PREP: 30 MIN. • **BAKE:** 25 MIN. + COOLING • **MAKES:** 16 SERVINGS

- ¾ cup chopped walnuts, toasted and cooled
- ¼ cup plus 1¼ cups sugar, divided
- 1½ cups heavy whipping cream
- 3 eggs
- 3 teaspoons vanilla extract
- 1¾ cups all-purpose flour
- 2 teaspoons baking powder
- ½ teaspoon salt

FROSTING

- 1½ cups heavy whipping cream
- 1 package (8 ounces) cream cheese, softened
- 1 cup sugar
- 1 teaspoon vanilla extract
- ⅛ teaspoon salt
- 1 jar (12 ounces) strawberry preserves, divided
- 4 cups halved fresh strawberries

1. Preheat oven to 350°. Line bottoms of two greased 9-in. round baking pans with parchment paper; grease paper.

2. Place the walnuts and ¼ cup sugar in a food processor; pulse until walnuts are ground. In a small bowl, beat the heavy whipping cream until stiff peaks form. Set aside the walnut mixture and cream.

3. In a large bowl, beat the eggs and remaining sugar until thick and lemon-colored; beat in vanilla. In another bowl, mix flour, baking powder, salt and walnut mixture; fold into egg mixture alternately with whipped cream.

4. Transfer to prepared pans. Bake 25-30 minutes or until a toothpick inserted in center comes out clean. Cool in pans 10 minutes before removing to wire racks; remove paper. Cool completely.

5. For frosting, in a small bowl, beat cream until stiff peaks form. In a large bowl, beat cream cheese, sugar, vanilla and salt until blended. Fold in whipped cream.

6. Using a long serrated knife, cut each cake horizontally in half. Place one cake layer on a serving plate; spread with ½ cup frosting. Top with a second cake layer. Reserve 2 tablespoons preserves for strawberries; spread half of the remaining preserves over top of cake to within ½ inch of edge. Repeat layers.

7. Frost the sides of the cake with the remaining frosting. For a basket weave design, run a small offset spatula around cake to form ridges, stopping and starting at short intervals. Arrange strawberries over top. In a microwave, melt the reserved preserves; brush over strawberries. Refrigerate until serving.

NOTE *To toast nuts, spread in a 15x10x1-in. baking pan. Bake at 350° for 5-10 minutes or until lightly browned, stirring occasionally. Or, spread in a dry nonstick skillet and heat over low heat until lightly browned, stirring occasionally.*

Best for the Bride

Any blushing bride-to-be will love a blissful shower featuring delicious, easy-to-eat foods. Toast the guest of honor and quench everyone's thirst with festive sangria, too.

Mixed Berry Sangria

Refreshing and colorful, this sparkling beverage always goes over well at ladies' luncheons and other special events. Serve each glass with a spoon so guests can easily eat the berries once the sangria is gone.
—**LINDA CIFUENTES** MAHOMET, IL

PREP: 10 MIN. + CHILLING • **MAKES:** 10 SERVINGS (¾ CUP EACH)

- 1 bottle (750 milliliters) sparkling white wine
- 2½ cups white cranberry juice
- ⅔ cup light or coconut rum
- ⅓ cup each fresh blackberries, blueberries and raspberries
- ⅓ cup chopped fresh strawberries
  Ice cubes

In a large pitcher, mix the wine, juice and rum; add fruit. Refrigerate at least 2 hours; serve over ice.

MIXED BERRY SANGRIA

FLUFFY HERB DROP BISCUITS

FAST FIX ▶ Fluffy Herb Drop Biscuits

With a large herb garden, I can go out and pick whatever I need for cooking. I put fresh rosemary and dill in my biscuits.
—**MELISSA MCCABE** LONG BEACH, CA

START TO FINISH: 20 MIN. • **MAKES:** 1 DOZEN

- 2 cups all-purpose flour
- 2 teaspoons baking powder
- ½ teaspoon salt
- ¼ teaspoon baking soda
- ¾ cup buttermilk
- ⅓ cup canola oil
- 2 tablespoons minced fresh basil
- 2 teaspoons minced fresh rosemary

1. Preheat oven to 450°. In a large bowl, whisk flour, baking powder, salt and baking soda. In another bowl, whisk the buttermilk, oil, basil and rosemary; stir into dry ingredients just until moistened.
2. Drop the dough by rounded tablespoonfuls 2 in. apart onto an ungreased baking sheet. Bake 10-12 minutes or until light brown. Serve warm.

Fresh Berry & Almond Tarts

PREP: 15 MIN. • **BAKE:** 10 MIN. + COOLING
MAKES: 16 INDIVIDUAL TARTS

- 1 package (14.1 ounces) refrigerated pie pastry
- 1 package (8 ounces) cream cheese, softened
- ¼ cup confectioners' sugar
- ¼ teaspoon almond extract
- 2 cups fresh blueberries
- 2 cups fresh raspberries
- ¼ cup sliced almonds, toasted
  Additional confectioners' sugar, optional

1. Preheat oven to 400°. On a lightly floured surface, unroll the pastry sheets. Roll each to ⅛-inch thickness. Cut with a floured 3-in. cookie cutter to make eight circles or other shapes. Transfer to ungreased baking sheets; prick holes in pastries with a fork.

2. Bake 8-10 minutes or until golden brown. Remove from pans to wire racks to cool completely.

3. Meanwhile, in a small bowl, mix the cream cheese, confectioners' sugar and almond extract until blended. Spread over cooled pastries. Top with berries, pressing lightly to adhere. Sprinkle with almonds and, if desired, confectioners' sugar. Refrigerate leftovers.

NOTE *To toast nuts, spread in a 15x10x1-in. baking pan. Bake at 350° for 5-10 minutes or until lightly browned, stirring occasionally. Or, spread in a dry nonstick skillet and heat over low heat until lightly browned, stirring occasionally.*

"At a party with friends who like to sample new recipes, these fruity appetizers were a hit."
—**SHEILA WYUM** RUTLAND, ND

FRESH BERRY & ALMOND TARTS

TARRAGON CHICKEN & ROMAINE SALAD

Tarragon Chicken & Romaine Salad

I combine the best of romaine, chicken and potato salads for this three-in-one medley. A sprinkling of bacon is the finishing touch.
—**KATHY YAROSH** APOPKA, FL

PREP: 30 MIN. • **COOK:** 15 MIN. + COOLING • **MAKES:** 12 SERVINGS

- 1½ cups cubed red potatoes

DRESSING
- ¼ cup finely chopped onion
- ¼ cup Dijon mustard
- ¼ cup white wine vinegar
- ¼ cup lemon juice
- 2 teaspoons dried tarragon
- 1 garlic clove, minced
- ½ teaspoon salt
- ½ teaspoon pepper
- 1 cup canola oil

SALAD
- 2 packages (10 ounces each) hearts of romaine salad mix
- 4 cups cubed cooked chicken
- 1 cup chopped celery
  Small romaine heart leaves, optional
- 16 bacon strips, cooked and crumbled

1. Place potatoes in a small saucepan; add water to cover. Bring to a boil. Reduce heat; cook, uncovered, 10-15 minutes or until tender. Drain; cool completely.

2. In a small bowl, whisk the onion, Dijon mustard, white wine vinegar, lemon juice and seasonings. Gradually whisk in the oil until blended.

3. In a large bowl, combine the salad mix, chicken, celery and potatoes. Just before serving, add dressing; toss to coat. If desired, serve on small romaine leaves. Top with bacon.

July Fourth Reunion

When you need to satisfy everyone at a family reunion, try the summery menu of favorites here. From the delicious main dish to dessert, they're sure to please everyone.

Cream Cheese Cutouts

Decorating cookies always puts me in a happy mood. These yummy cutouts are especially nice because they don't rise a lot or lose their shape. For a July Fourth party, cut them into stars.
—**JULIE DAWSON** GALENA, OH

PREP: 15 MIN. + CHILLING • **BAKE:** 10 MIN./BATCH + COOLING
MAKES: ABOUT 7 DOZEN

- 1 cup butter, softened
- 1 package (3 ounces) cream cheese, softened
- 1 cup sugar
- ¼ teaspoon salt
- 1 egg
- 1 teaspoon vanilla extract
- 2½ cups all-purpose flour

FROSTING

- 3 cups confectioners' sugar
- ⅓ cup butter, softened
- 1½ teaspoons vanilla extract
- 2 to 3 tablespoons 2% milk
  Food coloring, optional
  Assorted sprinkles or candies

1. In a large bowl, cream the butter, cream cheese, sugar and salt until light and fluffy. Beat in the egg and vanilla. Gradually beat in flour. Refrigerate, covered, 1-2 hours or until firm enough to roll.
2. Preheat oven to 375°. On a lightly floured surface, roll dough to ⅛-in. thickness. Cut with floured cookie cutters. Place 1 in. apart on ungreased baking sheets.
3. Bake 7-8 minutes or until the edges are lightly browned. Cool on the pans 1 minute. Remove to wire racks to cool completely.
4. In a small bowl, beat the confectioners' sugar, butter, vanilla and enough milk to reach the desired consistency. If desired, add food coloring. Decorate the cookies with frosting and sprinkles.

"To make the most of my garden tomatoes, I drizzle on a homemade buttermilk dressing."
—**JUDITH FOREMAN** ALEXANDRIA, VA

TOMATOES WITH BUTTERMILK VINAIGRETTE

EAT SMART **FAST FIX**

Tomatoes with Buttermilk Vinaigrette

START TO FINISH: 20 MIN. • **MAKES:** 12 SERVINGS (¾ CUP EACH)

- ¾ cup buttermilk
- ¼ cup minced fresh tarragon
- ¼ cup white wine vinegar
- 3 tablespoons canola oil
- 1½ teaspoons sugar
- ½ teaspoon ground mustard
- ¼ teaspoon celery salt
- ¼ teaspoon pepper
- 4 pounds cherry tomatoes, halved
- ⅓ cup minced fresh chives

1. In a small bowl, whisk the first eight ingredients until blended. Refrigerate, covered, until serving.
2. Just before serving, arrange tomatoes on a platter; drizzle with vinaigrette. Sprinkle with chives.
PER SERVING *79 cal., 4 g fat (trace sat. fat), 1 mg chol., 63 mg sodium, 10 g carb., 2 g fiber, 2 g pro.* **Diabetic Exchanges:** *1 vegetable, ½ starch, ½ fat.*

Red, White & Blue Berry Trifle

This patriotic dessert is best prepared the day before serving. Keep additional fresh berries on hand for garnishing.

—**KAIA MCSHANE** MUNSTER, IN

PREP: 20 MIN. + CHILLING • **MAKES:** 12 SERVINGS

- 1 can (14 ounces) sweetened condensed milk
- 1½ cups 2% milk
- 2 packages (3.4 ounces each) instant lemon pudding mix
- ½ cup sour cream
- 2 cups fresh blueberries
- 2 cups fresh raspberries
- 1 tablespoon lemon juice
- 1 package (16 ounces) frozen pound cake, thawed and cubed
- 1 container (8 ounces) frozen whipped topping, thawed
  Additional blueberries and raspberries, optional

1. In a large bowl, whisk the sweetened condensed milk, 2% milk and lemon pudding mix 2 minutes. Fold in sour cream. In another bowl, toss blueberries and raspberries with lemon juice.

2. In a greased 9-in. springform pan, layer half of the cake cubes, half of the berry mixture and half of the pudding mixture; repeat. Refrigerate, covered, at least 2 hours before serving.

3. To serve, remove rim from springform pan. Serve with whipped topping and, if desired, additional berries.

Chicken Riggies

PREP: 30 MIN. + MARINATING • **COOK:** 15 MIN.
MAKES: 12 SERVINGS (1¾ CUPS EACH)

- ½ cup dry sherry
- 2 tablespoons olive oil
- 3 garlic cloves, minced

RED, WHITE & BLUE BERRY TRIFLE

CHICKEN RIGGIES

"Creamy, cheesy rigatoni pasta mixed with tender marinated chicken just says comfort food."
—**JACKIE SCANLAN** DAYTON, OH

- 1 teaspoon dried oregano
- 2 pounds boneless skinless chicken breasts, cubed

SAUCE

- 2 tablespoons butter
- 1 each medium sweet red and green pepper, chopped
- 4 pickled hot cherry peppers, chopped
- 1 medium onion, chopped
- 2 garlic cloves, minced
- 1 cup dry sherry
- 2 cans (one 29 ounces, one 15 ounces) tomato puree
- ¼ teaspoon salt
- ⅛ teaspoon pepper
- 2 packages (16 ounces each) uncooked rigatoni
- 1½ cups heavy whipping cream
- 6 ounces cream cheese, cut up
- 1½ cups grated Romano cheese

1. In a large resealable plastic bag, combine sherry, oil, garlic and oregano. Add chicken; seal bag and turn to coat. Refrigerate 1 hour.

2. Drain chicken, discarding marinade. Heat a Dutch oven over medium-high heat. Add chicken in batches; cook and stir until no longer pink. Remove from pan.

3. In same pan, heat butter over medium-high heat. Add peppers, onion and garlic; cook and stir until tender. Add sherry; bring to a boil. Stir in tomato puree, salt and pepper; return to a boil. Reduce heat; simmer 8-10 minutes or until slightly thickened, stirring occasionally. Add chicken; heat through.

4. Meanwhile, in a stockpot, cook rigatoni according to package directions. In a small saucepan, combine cream and cream cheese over medium heat; cook and stir until blended. Add to chicken mixture; stir in Romano cheese.

5. Drain rigatoni; return to stockpot. Add sauce to pasta; toss to combine.

Happy Halloween

These frightfully yummy foods are guaranteed to scare up smiles on October 31. Surprise your costumed party guests with an assortment of not-so-tricky treats—or even a complete meal.

"I always bake extra sweet potatoes so I can quickly mash the pulp for hummus. The recipe calls for pita chips as dippers, but it's fun to arrange fresh veggies around the bowl in the shape of a skeleton. It gets everyone gobbling up a wholesome, healthy snack."
—**MARY MARLOWE LEVERETTE** COLUMBIA, SC

Halloween Candy Bark

Let children customize this chunky fall bark using their favorite candies, cookies and munchies. They'll love it!
—**PEGGIE BROTT** CARTHAGE, NY

PREP: 20 MIN. + STANDING • **MAKES:** 2¾ POUNDS

- 2 teaspoons butter
- 1½ pounds white candy coating, coarsely chopped
- 2 cups pretzels, coarsely chopped
- 10 Oreo cookies, chopped
- ¾ cup candy corn
- ¾ cup dry roasted peanuts
- ½ cup milk chocolate M&M's
- ½ cup Reese's Pieces

1. Line a 15x10x1-in. baking pan with foil; grease the foil with butter. In a microwave, melt the white candy coating; stir until smooth. Spread into the prepared pan. Sprinkle with the remaining ingredients; press into the candy coating. Let stand about 1 hour.

2. Break or cut the bark into pieces. Store in an airtight container.

SWEET POTATO HUMMUS

HALLOWEEN CANDY BARK

FAST FIX ▶ Sweet Potato Hummus

START TO FINISH: 10 MIN. • **MAKES:** 16 SERVINGS (¼ CUP EACH)

- 4 cups mashed sweet potatoes
- ¼ cup tahini
- ¼ cup lime juice
- 2 garlic cloves, minced
- 2 teaspoons ground cumin
- 1½ teaspoons salt
- ¼ teaspoon cayenne pepper
- Baked pita chips

Place the first seven ingredients in a food processor; process until blended. Transfer to a bowl. Serve with baked pita chips.

Flying Bat Pizzas

PREP: 30 MIN. • **BAKE:** 10 MIN. • **MAKES:** 2 PIZZAS (8 SLICES EACH)

- 1 package (16 ounces) frozen corn, thawed
- 1 can (16 ounces) kidney beans, rinsed and drained
- 1 can (15 ounces) black beans, rinsed and drained
- 1 medium sweet red pepper, finely chopped
- 1 tablespoon chili powder
- 1 tablespoon cider vinegar
- 2 teaspoons olive oil
- 1 teaspoon ground cumin
- 2 prebaked 12-inch pizza crusts
- 2 cups (8 ounces) shredded cheddar cheese
- 2 spinach tortillas (10 inches)
- 1 can (4¼ ounces) chopped ripe olives
  Sour cream, optional

1. Preheat oven to 450°. In a large bowl, combine the first eight ingredients. Transfer half of the mixture to a food processor. Process until blended; spread over crusts. Top with remaining bean mixture; sprinkle with cheese.

2. For bats, cut three 7-in. strips from edges of each tortilla. Using kitchen shears, cut scallops along the straight edge of each strip. From each center portion, cut three bat faces. Assemble three bats on each pizza. Arrange olive pieces on bats to make eyes and mouths. Sprinkle remaining olives over pizzas.

3. Bake 10-15 minutes or until cheese is melted. If desired, serve with sour cream.

"Pizza is a great way to lure kids to the kitchen. They can help add the toppings before baking."
—**ANGELA HANKS** ST. ALBANS, WV

FLYING BAT PIZZAS

Haunted Antipasto Salad

Even grown-up foods like antipasto salad can get dressed up for Halloween night. Finish each plate with a ghost-shaped slice of provolone cheese cut with a cookie cutter.
—**CYNTHIA BENT** NEWARK, DE

PREP: 35 MIN. • **MAKES:** 12 SERVINGS

- 12 slices provolone cheese
- 10 cups torn romaine
- 2 jars (7½ ounces each) marinated quartered artichoke hearts, drained
- 1 jar (7 ounces) roasted sweet red peppers, drained and julienned
- 4 plum tomatoes, cut into ¼-inch slices
- 1 small red onion, halved and thinly sliced
- 10 slices thinly sliced hard salami, julienned
- 1 can (6 ounces) pitted ripe olives, drained
- ½ cup Italian salad dressing

1. Using a 4-in. ghost-shaped cutter, cut one ghost from each slice of provolone cheese. (Reserve remaining cheese for another use.)

2. In a large bowl, combine vegetables, salami and olives; toss to combine. Just before serving, drizzle with Italian salad dressing and toss to coat. Transfer to serving plates; top with ghosts.

⑤ INGREDIENTS

Trick-or-Treat Pizza

Hosting a party for kids? Instead of tossing out leftover Halloween candy, pile it onto a sugar cookie crust for a dessert pizza everyone will go crazy for. With a variety of goodies on top, it always looks colorful, festive and fun.

—**KENDRA BOWEN** LOUISVILLE, IL

PREP: 10 MIN. • **BAKE:** 20 MIN. + CHILLING
MAKES: 16 SLICES

- 1 tube (16½ ounces) refrigerated sugar cookie dough
  Assorted Halloween candies, unwrapped
- 2 cups semisweet chocolate chips
- 3 tablespoons creamy peanut butter

1. Let the sugar cookie dough stand at room temperature for 5-10 minutes to soften. Press onto an ungreased 14-in. pizza pan. Bake at 350° for 18-22 minutes or until deep golden brown. Cool on pan on a wire rack.
2. Coarsely chop the large candies; set aside. In a microwave, melt semisweet chocolate chips and peanut butter; stir until smooth. Spread over the cookie crust; top with candies. Refrigerate, covered, until the chocolate mixture is set. Cut into wedges.

HALLOWEEN WITCH HATS

TRICK-OR-TREAT PIZZA

Halloween Witch Hats

Children and adults alike love finding the cake inside these cute cones.

—**BETSY KING** DULUTH, MN

PREP: 20 MIN.
BAKE: 15 MIN./BATCH + COOLING
MAKES: 24 WITCH HATS AND 11 CUPCAKES

- 24 ice cream sugar cones
- 1 package yellow cake mix (regular size)
- ½ cup chocolate frosting
- 24 chocolate wafers
- 1 can (16 ounces) vanilla frosting
- ¼ teaspoon orange paste food coloring
- 12 green apple Jolly Rancher Chews, halved
  Purple nonpareils

1. Cover the top of a 10-in. fluted tube pan with a double layer of heavy-duty aluminum foil. Using a skewer or paring knife, poke 12 holes in the foil, making one hole in the center and eleven holes around it, about 2½ in. apart. Gently insert a cone in each hole, leaving the top 1 in. of the cone above the foil.
2. Prepare the cake batter according to the package directions. Spoon 1 tablespoon plus 1 teaspoon batter into each cone. Bake at 350° for 14-16 minutes or until a toothpick inserted in center comes out clean. Cool in pan on a wire rack.
3. Repeat with the remaining cones and additional batter. Use remaining batter to bake cupcakes.
4. Spread 1 teaspoon of the chocolate frosting onto center of each chocolate wafer. Top with cone, cake side down.
5. In a large bowl, beat the vanilla frosting and orange food coloring. Cut a small hole in the tip of a pastry bag or in a corner of a food-safe plastic bag; insert a #45 round tip. Fill the bag with orange frosting. Pipe around the cone rims; attach halved green candies for buckles. Frost the cupcakes with the remaining frosting; sprinkle with purple nonpareils.

Owl Tree

PREP: 1 HOUR • **BAKE:** 20 MIN. + COOLING
MAKES: 21 CUPCAKES AND 6 MINI CUPCAKES

- 1 package chocolate fudge cake mix (regular size)
- 1 cup water
- ½ cup canola oil
- ¼ cup brewed coffee, room temperature
- 3 eggs
- 1 cup (6 ounces) miniature semisweet chocolate chips

FROSTING AND DECORATIONS
- 1 can (16 ounces) chocolate frosting, divided
- 1 teaspoon black paste food coloring
- 12 mini Oreo cookies
  Brown and yellow milk chocolate M&M's
- 3¾ cups confectioners' sugar
- ½ cup butter, softened
- ½ cup shortening
- ¼ to ⅓ cup water

OWL TREE

1. Preheat the oven to 350°. Line 21 muffin cups and 6 mini-muffin cups with paper liners.
2. In a bowl, combine the cake mix, water, oil, coffee and eggs; beat on low speed 30 seconds. Beat on medium 2 minutes. Stir in the chips. Fill the prepared cups two-thirds full. Bake for 18-22 minutes for regular-sized cupcakes and 10-12 minutes for mini cupcakes or until a toothpick inserted in center comes out clean. Cool in the pans 10 minutes before removing to wire racks to cool completely.
3. Place 1⅓ cups chocolate frosting in a small bowl. Tint black with food coloring. Cut a small hole in the tip of a pastry bag or in a corner of a food-safe plastic bag; insert #125 or other large petal or flat pastry tip. Fill bag with black frosting and set aside.
4. Frost mini cupcakes with some of the remaining chocolate frosting. Separate cookies, leaving cream filling on one side of cookies. Place filling sides of cookies on frosted cupcakes for eyes, cream side up; attach brown M&M's with chocolate frosting.
5. Trim plain cookies into triangles for ears; place above eyes. Insert #16 or other star pastry tip into another pastry bag. Fill bag with remaining

"I've been 'cooking' since I was 3 years old. Now I cook for my two teenage sons and bake decorated cakes. I came up with my Owl Tree for an online contest."
—**TAMMY BAKER** BOWLING GREEN, KY

chocolate frosting. Pipe feathers on ears and around eyes. Place yellow M&M's between eyes for beaks.
6. In a large bowl, beat confectioners' sugar, butter, shortening and enough water to reach spreading consistency; frost the large cupcakes. Arrange the cupcakes side by side on a covered cake board.
7. Pipe black frosting across tops of cupcakes for tree trunk and branches. Place owl cupcakes on branches.

❓ Did you know?

Tinted black frosting will come together quickly and easily if you add black paste food coloring to canned chocolate frosting rather than a light-colored frosting. Use this simple technique for decorative cakes such as the Owl Tree (recipe at left), cutout cookies and other desserts that call for tinting frosting black.

Candy Corn Quesadillas

This autumn main dish is so tasty and easy to make, you'll want to enjoy it year-round. Let children join in the fun—fill a bag with the nacho tortilla chips for them to crush with a rolling pin while you do the rest.

—MARIE PARKER MILWAUKEE, WI

PREP: 25 MIN. • **COOK:** 10 MIN. • **MAKES:** 2 DOZEN

- 1 rotisserie chicken, cut up
- 1 jar (16 ounces) salsa
- 1 cup frozen corn, thawed
- ¼ cup barbecue sauce
- ½ teaspoon ground cumin
- ½ cup butter, melted
- 8 flour tortillas (10 inches)
- 1 jar (15½ ounces) salsa con queso dip, warmed
- 4 cups (16 ounces) shredded Mexican cheese blend
- 2⅔ cups crushed nacho-flavored tortilla chips
- ½ cup sour cream

1. In a Dutch oven, combine the first five ingredients; heat through, stirring occasionally. Brush butter over one side of each tortilla.
2. Place one tortilla in a large skillet, buttered side down. Spread with 1 cup chicken mixture; top with another tortilla, buttered side up. Cook over medium heat 1-2 minutes or until bottom is lightly browned. Turn quesadilla.
3. Spread ½ cup salsa con queso dip over the quesadilla; carefully sprinkle cheese along outer edge. Cook, covered, 1-2 minutes or until cheese begins to melt.
4. Remove the quesadilla to a cutting board. Sprinkle the crushed tortilla chips over the salsa con queso dip. Cut the quesadilla into six wedges. Place a small dollop of the sour cream at the narrow point of each quesadilla wedge. Repeat with the remaining ingredients.

BAT CUPCAKES

(5) INGREDIENTS Bat Cupcakes

With chocolate kisses, cookies and icing, I turn plain cupcakes into batty ones. We serve them at our pumpkin-carving party.

—JOYCE MOYNIHAN LAKEVILLE, MN

PREP: 25 MIN. • **BAKE:** 20 MIN. + COOLING • **MAKES:** 2 DOZEN

- 1 package chocolate cake mix (regular size)
- 1 can (16 ounces) chocolate frosting
- 24 fudge-striped cookies
- 24 milk chocolate kisses
  White decorating icing

1. Prepare and bake the cake mix according to the package directions for cupcakes. Cool completely.
2. Spread frosting over cupcakes. For bat wings, cut cookies in half; insert two cookie halves into each cupcake.
3. Gently press chocolate kisses into frosting for heads. Add eyes with decorating icing.

CANDY CORN QUESADILLAS

(5) INGREDIENTS Gruesome Green Toes

At a Halloween bash, these creepy toes are a real kick! To create them, simply dip Nutter Butters into tinted candy coating, then attach halved black candies for the toenails.

—JAMEY JACKSON GILE, WI

PREP: 25 MIN. + STANDING • **MAKES:** 22 COOKIES

- 12 **ounces white candy coating, coarsely chopped**
  Green paste food coloring
- 22 **Nutter Butter cookies**
- 11 **Crows candies, halved lengthwise**

1. In a microwave, melt candy coating; stir until smooth. Tint green.

2. Dip one cookie into the tinted candy coating. Let excess drip off and place on waxed paper. Immediately place a candy half, cut side down, on the cookie. Repeat. Let stand for 15 minutes or until set.

LI'L LIPS

GRUESOME GREEN TOES

(5) INGREDIENTS FAST FIX ▶ Li'l Lips

My kids loved putting mini marshmallow "teeth" between apple slices to resemble little mouths. We usually used red apples, but green ones would be a playful alternative.

—AGNES WARD STRATFORD, ON

START TO FINISH: 20 MIN. • **MAKES:** 8 SERVINGS

- 1 **medium red apple**
- 1 **teaspoon lemon juice**
- ¼ **cup chunky peanut butter**
- 2 **tablespoons reduced-fat cream cheese**
- ⅛ **teaspoon ground cinnamon**
  Miniature marshmallows, optional

1. Cut the apple into 16 wedges; toss with lemon juice.

2. In a small bowl, mix peanut butter, cream cheese and cinnamon until blended. Spread about 2 teaspoons onto one side of half of the apple slices; top each with a second slice, pressing to form lips. If desired, press marshmallows onto peanut butter for teeth. Refrigerate until serving.

Turkey Day Feast

Start with one big bird, then take your pick of mix-and-match side dishes and dazzling desserts. Your family will never guess how easy this Thanksgiving dinner was to prepare!

FOOLPROOF GRAVY

FAST FIX ▶ Foolproof Gravy

Homemade gravy doesn't get much simpler than this. Turkey drippings make it flavorful, yet it's basic enough for a beginner to fix. And you'll never have to worry about lumps!
—**EDIE DESPAIN** LOGAN, UTAH

START TO FINISH: 20 MIN. • **MAKES:** 2⅓ CUPS

Drippings from 1 roasted turkey
½ to 1 cup turkey or chicken broth
¼ cup plus 1 tablespoon all-purpose flour
½ cup fat-free milk
1 teaspoon chicken bouillon granules
¼ teaspoon poultry seasoning
⅛ teaspoon white pepper

1. Pour drippings into a 2-cup measuring cup. Skim and discard fat. Add enough broth to the drippings to measure 2 cups; transfer to a small saucepan and bring to a boil.

2. In a small bowl, whisk the flour and milk until smooth; gradually stir into drippings mixture. Stir in the bouillon granules, poultry seasoning and white pepper. Return to a boil, stirring constantly; cook and stir for 2 minutes or until thickened.

Parmesan-Rosemary Mashed Potatoes

To dress up ordinary mashed potatoes, I include plenty of add-ins. The combination of fresh rosemary, garlic, Parmesan cheese and mayonnaise always draws compliments.
—**DAWN MILLER** EAST STROUDSBURG, PA

PREP: 20 MIN. • **COOK:** 20 MIN.
MAKES: 12 SERVINGS (¾ CUP EACH)

5 large russet potatoes, peeled and cubed (about 4 pounds)
3 medium red potatoes, cubed (about ¾ pound)
½ cup butter, softened
2 tablespoons mayonnaise
3 garlic cloves, minced
2 teaspoons minced fresh rosemary
1 teaspoon salt
½ teaspoon pepper
1 to 1¼ cups whole milk
3 tablespoons shredded Parmesan cheese

1. Place potatoes in a Dutch oven; add water to cover. Bring to a boil. Reduce heat; cook, uncovered, for 15-20 minutes or until tender.

2. Drain; return to pan. Mash potatoes, gradually adding the butter, mayonnaise, garlic, rosemary, salt, pepper and enough milk to reach the desired consistency. Stir in the Parmesan cheese.

PARMESAN-ROSEMARY MASHED POTATOES

POTATO-PUMPKIN MASH

Potato-Pumpkin Mash

PREP: 20 MIN. • **COOK:** 25 MIN. • **MAKES:** 8 SERVINGS

- 8 cups cubed peeled pie pumpkin (about 2 pounds)
- 8 medium Yukon Gold potatoes, peeled and cubed (about 2 pounds)
- ½ to ¾ cup 2% milk, divided
- 8 tablespoons butter, softened, divided
- 1 teaspoon salt, divided
- 1 tablespoon olive oil
- ¼ teaspoon coarsely ground pepper

1. Place the pumpkin in a large saucepan; add water to cover. Bring to a boil. Reduce heat; cook, uncovered, for 20-25 minutes or until tender.

2. Meanwhile, place potatoes in another saucepan; add water to cover. Bring to a boil. Reduce heat; cook, uncovered, for 10-15 minutes or until tender.

3. Drain potatoes; return to the pan. Mash potatoes, adding ¼ cup milk, 4 tablespoons butter and ½ teaspoon salt. Add additional milk if needed to reach the desired consistency. Transfer to a serving bowl; keep warm.

4. Drain pumpkin; return to pan. Mash pumpkin, gradually adding the remaining butter and salt and enough remaining milk to reach the desired consistency; spoon evenly over potatoes. Cut through mashed vegetables with a spoon or knife to swirl. Drizzle with olive oil; sprinkle with pepper. Serve immediately.

Peach-Blueberry Crumble Tart

PREP: 30 MIN. + COOLING • **BAKE:** 35 MIN. • **MAKES:** 12 SERVINGS

- 1⅓ cups all-purpose flour
- ¼ cup sugar
- ¼ teaspoon ground cinnamon
- ½ cup butter, melted
- 2 cups frozen unsweetened blueberries, thawed
- 2 cups frozen unsweetened sliced peaches, thawed
- 1 tablespoon honey

CRUMB TOPPING
- ¼ cup all-purpose flour
- ¼ cup packed brown sugar
- ¼ cup old-fashioned oats
- ¼ cup chopped pecans
- ⅛ teaspoon ground cloves
- 2 tablespoons butter, melted

1. Preheat oven to 350°. In a small bowl, mix flour, sugar and cinnamon; stir in butter just until blended. Press onto the bottom and up the side of a 9-in. fluted tart pan with removable bottom. Bake 15-20 minutes or until lightly browned. Cool on a wire rack.

2. In a large bowl, combine blueberries, peaches and honey; toss to coat. In a small bowl, combine the first five topping ingredients; stir in butter.

3. Spoon fruit mixture into crust; sprinkle with topping. Bake at 350° 35-40 minutes or until the topping is golden brown and the filling is bubbly. Cool on a wire rack at least 15 minutes before serving.

PEACH-BLUEBERRY CRUMBLE TART

Cranberry-Apple Lattice Pie

PREP: 40 MIN. + CHILLING
BAKE: 1 HOUR 5 MIN. + COOLING
MAKES: 8 SERVINGS

- 2½ cups all-purpose flour
- 1 tablespoon sugar
- ¾ teaspoon salt
- ½ cup cold unsalted butter, cubed
- ⅓ cup cold shortening
- 5 to 7 tablespoons ice water

FILLING

- ½ cup dried currants or raisins
- 2 tablespoons dark rum or water
- 1 cup fresh or frozen cranberries, divided
- ¾ cup sugar, divided
- 6 medium baking apples, such as Fuji or Braeburn (about 2 pounds), peeled and cut into ¼-inch slices
- 2 tablespoons quick-cooking tapioca
- 1 tablespoon lemon juice
- 2 teaspoons grated lemon peel
- ½ teaspoon ground cinnamon

GLAZE

- 2 teaspoons sugar
  Dash ground cinnamon
- 1 egg
- 1 tablespoon 2% milk or heavy whipping cream

1. In a small bowl, mix the flour, sugar and salt; cut in butter and shortening until crumbly. Gradually add ice water, tossing with a fork until dough holds together when pressed. Divide the dough in half. Shape each half into a disk; wrap in plastic wrap. Refrigerate for 30 minutes or overnight.

2. In a small bowl, combine the dried currants and dark rum; let stand for 20 minutes.

3. Place ¾ cup cranberries and ¼ cup sugar in a food processor; pulse until the cranberries are coarsely chopped. Transfer to a large bowl. Add the apple slices, tapioca, lemon juice, lemon peel, cinnamon, remaining sugar and currant mixture; toss to combine. Let stand for 15 minutes.

4. On a lightly floured surface, roll one half of the dough to a ⅛-in.-thick circle; transfer to a 9-in. deep-dish pie plate. Trim the pastry to ½ in. beyond the rim of the plate. Add the filling.

5. Roll the remaining dough into a ⅛-in.-thick circle; cut into ½-in.-wide strips. Arrange over the filling in a lattice pattern. Trim and seal the strips to the edge of the bottom pastry; flute the edge. Place the remaining cranberries in the spaces between the lattice strips.

6. For the glaze, in a small bowl, mix the sugar and cinnamon; set aside. In another bowl, whisk egg and milk; brush over lattice top. Sprinkle with sugar mixture.

7. Bake on a lower oven rack at 400° for 25 minutes. Reduce the oven temperature to 325°; bake 40-45 minutes longer or until the crust is golden brown and the filling is bubbly.

8. Cool on a wire rack for 30 minutes; serve warm.

CRANBERRY-APPLE LATTICE PIE

"Two perennially popular fruits come together—and get a splash of rum—in this beautiful holiday dessert. I've found that very few people can pass up a piece."
—**ADRI BARR CROCETTI** SHERMAN OAKS, CA

Roast Turkey with Sausage-Cabbage Stuffing

PREP: 30 MIN.
BAKE: 3 HOURS + STANDING
MAKES: 12 SERVINGS (ABOUT 8 CUPS STUFFING)

⅓ cup unsalted butter, softened
3 tablespoons minced fresh thyme
1 teaspoon salt
¼ teaspoon pepper
1 turkey (12 to 14 pounds)

STUFFING

1 pound bulk Italian sausage
3 cups chopped cabbage
1 large carrot, shredded
1 celery rib, chopped
1 small onion, chopped
2 tablespoons half-and-half cream
¾ teaspoon poultry seasoning
¼ teaspoon salt
⅛ teaspoon pepper
3 cups seasoned stuffing cubes
1 egg, lightly beaten
⅔ to ¾ cup chicken broth

1. In a small bowl, mix the butter, thyme, salt and pepper. Place the turkey on a rack in a shallow roasting pan, breast side up. With your fingers, carefully loosen skin from the turkey breast; rub half of the butter mixture under the skin. Rub the remaining butter mixture over the turkey. Tuck the wings under the turkey; tie the drumsticks together.

2. Bake at 325° for 3 to 3¾ hours or until a thermometer inserted in thigh reads 180°. Baste occasionally with pan drippings.

3. For the stuffing, in a Dutch oven, cook the sausage over medium heat for 6-8 minutes or until no longer pink, breaking into crumbles. Remove with a slotted spoon; drain on paper towels. Discard the drippings, reserving 1 tablespoon.

4. Add the cabbage, carrot, celery and onion to reserved drippings; cook and stir over medium heat until tender. Stir in cream, poultry seasoning, salt and pepper.

5. Add the stuffing cubes, egg and sausage; toss to combine. Stir in enough chicken broth to reach the desired moistness; transfer to a greased 11-in. x 7-in. baking dish. Bake, covered, for 30 minutes. Uncover and bake 10-15 minutes longer or until lightly browned.

6. Remove the turkey from the oven; cover loosely with foil and let stand for 20 minutes before carving. Serve with the stuffing.

"Here's a Thanksgiving staple in our family. The golden bird is moist, flavorful and impressive. Guests always rave about the sausage-and-cabbage stuffing, too."
—ALMA WINBERRY GREAT FALLS, MT

ROAST TURKEY WITH SAUSAGE-CABBAGE STUFFING

FAST FIX ▶ Mashed Potatoes with Garlic-Olive Oil

We're big fans of garlic mashed potatoes. To intensify the flavor, I combine the fresh cloves and olive oil in my food processor, then drizzle it over the spuds.
—**EMORY DOTY** JASPER, GA

START TO FINISH: 30 MIN.
MAKES: 12 SERVINGS (¾ CUP EACH)

4 pounds red potatoes, quartered
½ cup olive oil
2 garlic cloves
⅔ cup heavy whipping cream
¼ cup butter, softened
2 teaspoons salt
½ teaspoon pepper
⅔ to ¾ cup whole milk
3 green onions, chopped
¾ cup grated Parmesan cheese, optional

1. Place potatoes in a Dutch oven; add water to cover. Bring to a boil. Reduce the heat; cook, uncovered, for 15-20 minutes or until tender. Meanwhile, place the oil and garlic in a small food processor; process until blended.

2. Drain the potatoes; return to the pan. Mash potatoes, gradually adding the heavy whipping cream, butter, salt, pepper and enough milk to reach the desired consistency. Stir in the green onions. Serve with garlic olive oil and, if desired, cheese.

NOTE *For food safety purposes, prepare garlic olive oil just before serving; do not store leftover oil mixture.*

Cheery Cookies

Spread Christmas spirit this yuletide season with platters, jars and tins of sweet treats. You'll see smiles by the dozen when you share batches of the fresh-baked goodies here.

"I use candy canes of different flavors in the dough to give my blossom cookies fun variety."
—JOAN COSSETTE COLBERT, WA

CANDY CANE
BLOSSOM COOKIES

FAST FIX ▶ Holiday Rum Balls

This recipe is a must for special occasions with my family and friends. The little no-bake bites come together in just 30 minutes and pack a festive rum punch for the holidays.
—DIANE DUSCHANEK COUNCIL BLUFFS, IA

START TO FINISH: 30 MIN. • **MAKES:** ABOUT 2½ DOZEN

- 1 package (12 ounces) vanilla wafers, finely crushed
- 2 cups confectioners' sugar
- 1 cup finely chopped walnuts
- ¼ cup baking cocoa
- ½ cup light corn syrup
- ¼ cup rum
   Additional confectioners' sugar

1. In a large bowl, combine the crushed vanilla wafers, confectioners' sugar, walnuts and cocoa; mix until blended. In another bowl, mix the light corn syrup and rum; stir into crumb mixture.

2. Shape into 1-in. balls. Roll in additional confectioners' sugar. Store in an airtight container.

HOLIDAY RUM BALLS

Candy Cane Blossom Cookies

PREP: 45 MIN. • **BAKE:** 10 MIN./BATCH • **MAKES:** 4 DOZEN

- 1 cup butter, softened
- 1 cup sugar
- 1 egg
- 1 teaspoon vanilla extract
- 3 cups all-purpose flour
- 2 teaspoons baking powder
- ¼ teaspoon salt
- 4 candy canes, finely crushed
- 48 milk chocolate kisses, candy cane kisses or miniature chocolate-covered peppermint patties, unwrapped

1. In a large bowl, cream the butter and sugar until light and fluffy. Beat in the egg and vanilla. In another bowl, mix the flour, baking powder and salt; gradually beat into the creamed mixture.

2. Shape into 1-in. balls; roll in crushed candy canes. Place 2 in. apart on ungreased baking sheets.

3. Bake at 350° for 10-12 minutes or until the bottoms are golden brown. Immediately press a chocolate candy into the center of each cookie. Remove from the pans to wire racks to cool.

Ginger-Macadamia Nut Snowballs

Loaded with chopped crystallized ginger and macadamia nuts, these wintry balls have a hint of lemon and always go over well. Don't be surprised if you see guests lick the confectioners' sugar from their fingers—and then grab another!

—**JENNY HUMPHRIES** OCEAN VIEW, HI

PREP: 25 MIN. • **BAKE:** 15 MIN./BATCH • **MAKES:** ABOUT 5 DOZEN

- 1 **cup butter, softened**
- ¾ **cup plus 1½ cups confectioners' sugar, divided**
- 2 **teaspoons grated lemon peel**
- 2 **teaspoons lemon extract**
- 2¼ **cups cake flour**
- 1 **cup chopped macadamia nuts**
- 1 **cup chopped crystallized ginger**

1. In a large bowl, cream butter and ¾ cup confectioners' sugar until blended. Beat in lemon peel and lemon extract. Gradually beat the flour into the creamed mixture. Stir in macadamia nuts and ginger. Refrigerate for 1 hour or until easy to handle.

2. Shape the dough into 1-in. balls; place 2 in. apart on parchment paper-lined baking sheets. Bake at 350° for 14-16 minutes or until lightly browned.

3. Roll warm cookies in remaining confectioners' sugar. Cool on wire racks. When cooled, roll the cookies again in confectioners' sugar.

GINGER-MACADAMIA NUT SNOWBALLS

"Hazelnut Yule Logs are tasty and travel well, too. They're ideal take-along treats at Christmastime."

—**BARBARA BURGE** LOS GATOS, CA

HAZELNUT YULE LOGS

Hazelnut Yule Logs

PREP: 30 MIN. • **BAKE:** 10 MIN./BATCH • **MAKES:** 4½ DOZEN

- 1 **cup butter, softened**
- ¾ **cup packed brown sugar**
- 1 **tablespoon lemon juice**
- 1 **teaspoon grated lemon peel**
- 2½ **cups all-purpose flour**
- ¼ **teaspoon salt**
- 1½ **cups finely chopped hazelnuts**
- 2 **tablespoons water**

1. In a large bowl, cream butter and brown sugar until light and fluffy. Beat in lemon juice and peel. In another bowl, mix flour and salt; gradually beat into creamed mixture.

2. Place the hazelnuts in a small bowl. On a lightly floured surface, roll ½ cupfuls of dough into ½-in.-thick ropes about 22 inches long. Cut the ropes into 2-in. logs. Lightly brush each log with water; roll in hazelnuts to coat. Place 1 in. apart on ungreased baking sheets.

3. Bake at 375° for 8-10 minutes or until light brown. Remove to wire racks to cool.

Coconut Slice & Bake Cookies

This recipe's tinted coconut reminds me of snowflakes falling under holiday lights.
—**LEE ROBERTS**
RACINE, WI

PREP: 25 MIN. + CHILLING
BAKE: 15 MIN./BATCH
MAKES: ABOUT 4½ DOZEN

- 1 **cup butter, softened**
- ¾ **cup sugar**
- 2 **cups all-purpose flour**
- 3 **cups flaked coconut, divided**
- 15 **drops red food coloring**
- 10 **drops green food coloring**

1. In a large bowl, cream butter and sugar until light and fluffy; gradually beat in the flour. Stir in 1 cup coconut. Divide dough in half; shape each into a 7-in.-long roll.

2. Place 1 cup coconut into each of two large resealable plastic bags. Add red food coloring to one bag; seal the bag and shake to tint the coconut. Repeat with remaining coconut and green coloring. Roll one log in red coconut; roll remaining log in green coconut. Wrap logs separately in plastic wrap; refrigerate for 1-2 hours or until firm.

3. Cut dough crosswise into ¼-in. slices. Place 1 in. apart on ungreased baking sheets. Bake cookies at 325° for 12-14 minutes or until the bottoms are light brown. Remove cookies from pans to wire racks to cool.

COCONUT SLICE & BAKE COOKIES

"Double Whammy Eggnog Cookies are a great way to use up the last little bit in your carton of holiday nog. It goes into both the dough and the frosting."
—**TERESA MORRIS** LAUREL, DE

DOUBLE WHAMMY EGGNOG COOKIES

Double Whammy Eggnog Cookies

PREP: 30 MIN. + CHILLING
BAKE: 15 MIN./BATCH + COOLING
MAKES: 4 DOZEN

- 1⅓ **cups butter, softened**
- 1 **cup packed brown sugar**
- 4 **egg yolks**
- 2 **tablespoons eggnog**
- ½ **teaspoon rum extract**
- 3 **cups all-purpose flour**

EGGNOG FROSTING

- 4½ **cups confectioners' sugar**
- ¾ **cup butter, softened**
- 1½ **teaspoons rum extract**
- ½ **teaspoon ground nutmeg**
- ¼ **teaspoon ground cinnamon**
- 2 **to 3 tablespoons eggnog**
  Additional ground nutmeg

1. In a large bowl, cream butter and brown sugar until light and fluffy. Beat in the egg yolks, eggnog and extract. Gradually beat in flour. Refrigerate, covered, for at least 2 hours.

2. Shape the cookie dough into 1-in. balls; place 2 in. apart on ungreased baking sheets. Bake cookies at 325° for 13-16 minutes or until the bottoms are brown. Remove to wire racks to cool completely.

3. In a large bowl, beat the first five frosting ingredients until blended; beat in enough eggnog to reach the desired consistency. Spread over cookies; sprinkle with additional nutmeg. Let stand until set. Store in airtight containers.

NOTE *This recipe was tested with commercially prepared eggnog.*

Mom's Old-Fashioned Cutouts

Old family memories come rushing back as soon as I start mixing up a batch of these traditional cutouts.

—**LOIS SMIT** MONEE, IL

PREP: 50 MIN.
BAKE: 10 MIN./BATCH + COOLING
MAKES: 5 DOZEN

- 1   **cup butter, softened**
- 1½ **cups sugar**
- 1   **egg**
- ½   **cup sour cream**
- 1   **teaspoon vanilla extract**
- 4   **cups all-purpose flour, sifted**
- 1   **teaspoon baking powder**
- ½   **teaspoon baking soda**
- ½   **teaspoon salt**
- ½   **teaspoon ground cinnamon or ground nutmeg**
- 2   **cups confectioners' sugar**
- 1   **teaspoon vanilla extract**
- ¼   **teaspoon salt**
- 3   **to 4 tablespoons heavy whipping cream**
      Food coloring, optional

1. In a large bowl, cream the butter and sugar until light and fluffy. Beat in the egg, then the sour cream and vanilla. In another bowl, mix the flour, baking powder, baking soda, salt and cinnamon; gradually beat into the creamed mixture.

2. Divide dough into three portions. Shape each into a disk; wrap in plastic wrap. Refrigerate for 30 minutes or until easy to handle.

3. On a lightly floured surface, roll each portion of dough to ¼-in. thickness. Cut with a floured 3-in. cookie cutter. Place 2 in. apart on greased baking sheets.

4. Bake at 350° for 10-12 minutes or until light browned. Remove to wire racks to cool completely.

5. In a small bowl, mix confectioners' sugar, vanilla, salt and enough cream to reach the desired consistency. If desired, tint frosting with food coloring. Decorate cookies as desired.

MOM'S OLD-FASHIONED CUTOUTS

Christmas Party Fun

Invite your family and friends for some holiday merrymaking and the sweet goodies here, from chocolate-coated stirrers in mugs of cocoa to a snow globe cake that's almost too cute to eat.

"These sticks are popular at bake sales. To change things up, I use all sorts of different decorations."
—**TERI LEE RASEY** CADILLAC, MI

CHOCOLATE-TOPPED MARSHMALLOW STICKS

⑤INGREDIENTS Melting Snowman

After a day of sledding, skating or other wintry activities, kids will love warming up with hot chocolate featuring a sweet surprise. As they sip, the creamy snowman will slowly disappear—and so will the chill in their fingers and toes!

—TASTE OF HOME TEST KITCHEN

PREP: 10 MIN. + FREEZING • **MAKES:** 1 DOZEN

¾ cup whipped topping
  Miniature semisweet chocolate chips
  Orange jimmies
  Hot cocoa

Using a small cookie scoop, shape snowmen by dropping 1-tablespoon portions of whipped topping onto a waxed paper-lined baking sheet. Decorate with chocolate chips and jimmies to create faces. Freeze until firm. Place over servings of hot cocoa just before serving.

MELTING SNOWMAN

⑤INGREDIENTS Chocolate-Topped Marshmallow Sticks

PREP: 20 MIN. + STANDING • **COOK:** 10 MIN. • **MAKES:** 3 DOZEN

2 cups (12 ounces) semisweet chocolate chips
3 teaspoons shortening, divided
36 lollipop sticks
1 package (10 ounces) large marshmallows (about 36)
½ cup white baking chips
  Optional toppings: assorted nonpareils, colored sugars, small or crushed candies and flaked coconut

1. In a microwave, melt chocolate chips and 2 teaspoons shortening; stir until smooth.
2. Insert one lollipop stick into each marshmallow. Dip marshmallows in melted chocolate, turning to coat; allow excess to drip off. Place on waxed paper.
3. In a microwave, melt white baking chips with remaining shortening; drizzle over chocolate. Decorate with toppings if desired. Let stand until set.
4. Use to stir servings of hot cocoa. Store in an airtight container.

(5) INGREDIENTS Chocolate-Dipped Candy Canes

PREP: 20 MIN. + STANDING • **COOK:** 5 MIN. • **MAKES:** 1 DOZEN

- 1 cup semisweet chocolate chips
- 12 candy canes (6 inches each)
- 3 ounces white baking chocolate, chopped
  Optional toppings: assorted colored sugars or sprinkles and crushed candies

1. In a microwave, melt chocolate chips; stir until smooth. Dip curved ends of candy canes in chocolate; allow excess to drip off. Place on waxed paper.

2. In a microwave, melt white baking chocolate; stir until smooth. Drizzle over chocolate. Decorate with toppings if desired. Let stand until set.

3. Use to stir servings of hot cocoa.

DIY HOT COCOA MIX

"I couldn't resist pairing my two loves—chocolate and peppermint."
—SANDRA BAUMGARTEN
VANCOUVER, WA

CHOCOLATE-DIPPED CANDY CANES

FAST FIX ▶ DIY Hot Cocoa Mix

During our long, cold winters here in Idaho, a steaming beverage is a welcome sight. Thanks to this make-ahead mix, I can have one ready in the time it takes to pull off mittens and boots.
—**TRACY DALIN** GOODING, ID

START TO FINISH: 10 MIN.
MAKES: 21 SERVINGS (7 CUPS HOT COCOA MIX)

- 2¾ cups nonfat dry milk powder
- 2 cups powdered nondairy creamer
- 1 cup confectioners' sugar
- ¾ cup baking cocoa
- 1 package (3.9 ounces) instant chocolate pudding mix
- 1 cup miniature marshmallows, optional
- ½ cup miniature semisweet chocolate chips, optional

EACH SERVING
- ¾ cup hot 2% milk

In a large airtight container, mix the first five ingredients. If desired, stir in marshmallows and chocolate chips. Store in a cool, dry place for up to 6 months.
TO PREPARE HOT COCOA *Place ⅓ cup mix in a mug. Stir in hot milk until blended.*

? Did you know?

There are endless ways to dress up mugs of hot chocolate. Add a bit of cherry, strawberry, orange, mint or coconut flavoring. Like a bit of spice? Sprinkle on a little cinnamon or use a cinnamon stick as a stirrer. You could even dissolve a dab of peanut butter in the hot beverage.

(5) INGREDIENTS Chocolate-Hazelnut Spoons

My daughter has fun using bright candies and sprinkles to decorate coated spoons. She likes to stir them into her mug of hot cocoa—or eat them all by themselves!

—JANUARY BRYLOW MILWAUKEE, WI

PREP: 15 MIN. + STANDING • **COOK:** 5 MIN.
MAKES: 1 DOZEN

½ cup Nutella
12 metal or plastic spoons
¾ pound white candy coating, melted
    Optional toppings: assorted colored sugars, small or crushed candies and colored sprinkles

1. Place 2 teaspoons Nutella onto each spoon. Dip the spoons quickly in the melted candy coating; allow excess to drip off. Decorate with toppings if desired. Place spoons on waxed paper; let stand until set.
2. Use to stir servings of hot cocoa.

WINTER WONDERLAND CEREAL TREATS

CHOCOLATE-HAZELNUT SPOONS

FAST FIX

Winter Wonderland Cereal Treats

Here's a great recipe to make with kids. They can dress up the crispy snowmen and trees with all sorts of goodies. Try Airheads Sour Belts for the scarves and snipped marshmallows for the hats.

—BRENDA AUSTIN MANLIUS, NY

START TO FINISH: 30 MIN.
MAKES: ABOUT 10 TREES OR 6 SNOWMEN

¼ cup butter, cubed
2 teaspoons ground cinnamon or pumpkin pie spice
1 package (10 ounces) large marshmallows
6 cups Rice Krispies
    Pretzel sticks, assorted candies and/or Fruit Roll-ups, cut into thin strips
    Vanilla frosting
    Flaked coconut

1. In a large saucepan, melt the butter over medium heat. Add the cinnamon and marshmallows; stir until blended and the marshmallows are melted. Remove from the heat. Stir in the cereal until coated. Use mixture to shape trees or snowmen.
2. For trees, press the mixture into a greased 13-in. x 9-in. baking pan; cool completely. Cut into triangles.
3. For snowmen, cool cereal mixture slightly; shape into different-sized balls using buttered hands. Stack balls to make snowmen.
4. To decorate, attach pretzel sticks, candies and/or Fruit Roll-ups with frosting. Arrange cereal treats on a platter; surround with coconut. Serve the same day for best texture.

Holiday Snow Globe Cake

PREP: 65 MIN. • **BAKE:** 25 MIN. + COOLING
MAKES: 12 SERVINGS

- 4 **eggs, separated**
- ⅔ **cup butter, softened**
- 1 **cup sugar, divided**
- 2 **tablespoons dark rum**
- 2 **cups cake flour**
- 3 **teaspoons baking powder**
- ½ **teaspoon salt**
- ⅔ **cup coconut milk**

FROSTING/FILLING

- 1¼ **cups heavy whipping cream**
- 2 **tablespoons confectioners' sugar**
- ¾ **teaspoon vanilla extract**
- ¾ **cup seedless raspberry jam**
- 2 **cups flaked coconut**

DECORATIONS

- **Frosted Christmas Tree
  (see directions above right)**
- **Porcelain snowman ornament**
- **8-inch glass bubble bowl
  (about 6-inch opening)**

1. Line bottoms of two greased 8-in. round baking pans with parchment paper; grease paper. Place egg whites in a large bowl; let stand at room temperature for 30 minutes.

2. In another bowl, cream butter and ½ cup sugar until light and fluffy. Add egg yolks, beating well. Beat in rum. In another bowl, mix the flour, baking powder and salt; add to the creamed mixture alternately with coconut milk, beating well after each addition.

3. With clean beaters, beat the egg whites on medium speed until soft peaks form. Gradually add remaining sugar, 1 tablespoon at a time, beating on high after each addition until sugar is dissolved. Continue beating until stiff glossy peaks form. Fold into batter. Transfer to prepared pans.

4. Bake at 350° for 20-25 minutes or until a toothpick inserted in the center comes out clean. Cool in the pans for 10 minutes before removing to wire racks; remove paper. Cool completely.

5. If cake layers have rounded tops, trim with a long serrated knife to make level; set aside. In a large bowl, beat cream until it begins to thicken. Add confectioners' sugar and vanilla; beat until stiff peaks form.

6. Place one cake layer on a serving plate, bottom side down. Spread jam over top to within ¾ in. of edge; top with ½ cup whipped cream. Place the second cake layer over whipped cream, bottom side up.

7. Spread remaining whipped cream over top and sides of cake; sprinkle with coconut. Refrigerate for at least 15 minutes.

8. Just before serving, place frosted tree and snowman on center of cake. Carefully invert bowl over top.

FROSTED CHRISTMAS TREE

Lightly brush a small star-shaped sugar cookie with corn syrup; sprinkle with silver edible glitter. For the Christmas tree, tint canned vanilla frosting with green paste food coloring. Stack two ice cream sugar cones. Using a #32 open star tip, pipe tree branches onto the top cone to resemble a pine tree. Decorate with candy-coated sunflower kernels or colored sprinkles; sprinkle with coarse sugar. Place star sugar cookie at top of tree.

HOLIDAY SNOW GLOBE CAKE

"Yes, this snow globe is meant to be eaten! Remove the bowl and snowman ornament, then slice into a cake covered with coconut-topped whipped cream."
—MARIE LOUISE LUDWIG PHOENIXVILLE, PA

Noel Cakes & Breads

Special cakes and irresistible loaves are always favorites on Christmastime menus. Bake your own showstoppers for the holiday season with the best-loved recipes featured here.

Russian Krendl Bread

During dinner with a Russian immigrant family, they served this traditional, pretzel-shaped bread. I couldn't wait to get the recipe. Now, when I need hugs from the grandchildren, I surprise them with this fruit-filled favorite—it works every time!

—ANN SODMAN EVANS, CO

PREP: 45 MIN. + RISING • **BAKE:** 45 MIN. + COOLING
MAKES: 24 SERVINGS

- 1 **package (¼ ounce) active dry yeast**
- 3 **tablespoons sugar**
- ¾ **cup warm half-and-half cream or milk (110° to 115°)**
- ¼ **cup butter, softened**
- 2 **egg yolks**
- 1½ **teaspoons vanilla extract**
- ½ **teaspoon salt**
- 2¾ to 3¼ **cups all-purpose flour**

FILLING

- 1 **cup apple juice**
- 1 **large apple, peeled and chopped**
- ⅔ **cup finely chopped dried apples**
- ⅓ **cup finely chopped dried apricots**
- ⅓ **cup chopped pitted dried plums**
- 2 **tablespoons plus ¼ cup butter, divided**
- 4 **tablespoons sugar, divided**
- ½ **teaspoon ground cinnamon**
  Confectioners' sugar

1. In a small bowl, dissolve the yeast and sugar in warm cream. In a large bowl, combine the softened butter, egg yolks, vanilla, salt, yeast mixture and 1½ cups flour; beat on medium speed until smooth. Stir in enough remaining flour to form a soft dough (dough will be sticky).

2. Turn onto a floured surface; knead until smooth and elastic, about 6-8 minutes. Place in a greased bowl, turning once to grease the top. Cover with plastic wrap and let rise in a warm place until doubled, about 1 hour.

3. In a large saucepan, combine first five filling ingredients; add 2 tablespoons butter and 2 tablespoons sugar. Bring to a boil. Reduce the heat; simmer for 30 minutes or until the mixture reaches a jam-like consistency, stirring occasionally. Cool completely.

4. Punch down dough. Turn onto a lightly floured surface;

RUSSIAN KRENDL BREAD

roll into a 32-in. x 10-in. rectangle. Melt remaining butter; brush over dough. Sprinkle with the remaining sugar and cinnamon. Spread fruit mixture to within 1 in. of edges. Roll up jelly-roll style, starting with a long side; pinch seam and ends to seal.

5. Place on a greased baking sheet, seam side down; form into a pretzel shape. Cover with a kitchen towel; let rise in a warm place until almost doubled, about 30 minutes.

6. Bake at 350° for 40-45 minutes or until golden brown. Remove from pan to a wire rack to cool. Just before serving, sprinkle with confectioners' sugar.

Candy Cane Rolls

PREP: 30 MIN. + RISING • **BAKE:** 15 MIN. • **MAKES:** 2 DOZEN

- 1 package (¼ ounce) active dry yeast
- ¼ cup warm water (110° to 115°)
- ¾ cup warm milk (110° to 115°)
- ¼ cup sugar
- ¼ cup shortening
- 1 egg
- 1 teaspoon salt
- 3¼ to 3¾ cups all-purpose flour
- 1 cup red candied cherries, quartered
- 1 cup confectioners' sugar
- 1 to 2 tablespoons milk

1. In a small bowl, dissolve yeast in warm water. In a large bowl, combine the warm milk, sugar, shortening, egg, salt, yeast mixture and 2 cups flour; beat until smooth. Add cherries. Stir in enough remaining flour to form a soft dough (dough will be sticky).

2. Turn onto a floured surface; knead until smooth and elastic, about 6-8 minutes. Place in a greased bowl, turning once to grease the top. Cover with plastic wrap and let rise in a warm place until doubled, about 1 hour.

3. Punch down dough; let rest for 10 minutes. Turn onto a lightly floured surface; divide. Roll each half into a 12-in. x 7-in. rectangle. Cut each into twelve 1-in.-wide strips. Twist each and place 2 in. apart on greased baking sheets, curving one end like a cane. Cover with a kitchen towel; let rise in a warm place until doubled, about 45 minutes.

4. Bake at 375° for 12-15 minutes or until golden brown. Remove from pans to wire racks to cool. In a small bowl, mix confectioners' sugar and enough milk to reach desired consistency. Drizzle over rolls.

CINNAMON-ROLL CHRISTMAS TREE

Cinnamon-Roll Christmas Tree

It's so easy to prepare these spiced goodies using frozen dough. What a sweet way to celebrate on Christmas morning!
—**ALYSSA HELM** CALEDONIA, MI

PREP: 20 MIN. + RISING • **BAKE:** 20 MIN. • **MAKES:** 1 DOZEN

- 1 loaf (1 pound) frozen bread dough, thawed
- 2 tablespoons butter, softened
- ⅓ cup packed brown sugar
- ¼ cup sugar
- 1 tablespoon ground cinnamon
- 1 cup vanilla frosting of your choice

1. On a lightly floured surface, roll dough into a 12-in. x 8-in. rectangle. Spread butter to within ½ in. of edges. In a small bowl, mix the brown sugar, sugar and cinnamon; sprinkle over butter. Roll up jelly-roll style, starting with a long side; pinch seam to seal. Cut into 12 slices.

2. Line a baking sheet with parchment paper. Center one slice near the top of the pan, cut side down. Closely arrange nine more slices to form three additional rows, adding one slice per row, to form a tree. Center remaining two slices at base of tree for trunk. Cover with a kitchen towel; let rise in a warm place until doubled, about 30 minutes.

3. Bake at 350° for 18-20 minutes or until golden brown. Spread with frosting; serve warm.

"Candy Cane Rolls are fun for a special brunch, teatime treat or even a cheery homemade gift."
—**JANICE PETERSON** HURON, SD

CANDY CANE ROLLS

Peppermint Cake Rolls

This recipe makes two decadent cake rolls—enough to serve a crowd or to have an extra you can freeze for another time. I sprinkle each dessert with crushed peppermints.

—SUELLEN CALHOUN DES MOINES, IA

PREP: 25 MIN. • **BAKE:** 15 MIN. + COOLING
MAKES: 2 CAKES (10 SLICES EACH)

- 1 package (16 ounces) angel food cake mix
  Confectioners' sugar
- 1 carton (16 ounces) frozen whipped topping, thawed
- 1½ teaspoons peppermint extract
- 1 cup hot fudge ice cream topping
- ½ cup crushed peppermint candies, divided
  Fresh mint leaves, optional

1. Line two greased 15x10x1-in. baking pans with waxed paper. Prepare cake mix according to package directions. Divide batter evenly into prepared pans, spreading evenly.

2. Bake at 350° for 12-15 minutes or until tops spring back when lightly touched. Cool for 5 minutes.

3. Invert each cake onto a kitchen towel dusted with confectioners' sugar. Gently peel off the paper. Roll up cake in the towel jelly-roll style, starting with a short side. Cool completely on a wire rack.

4. In a small bowl, mix the whipped topping and extract until blended. Unroll the cakes; spread each with 1½ cups peppermint mixture to within ½ in. of edges.

5. Cut a small hole in the corner of a food-safe plastic bag; fill with fudge topping. Drizzle each cake with half of the fudge topping; sprinkle with 2 tablespoons crushed peppermint candies. Roll up again, without towel.

6. Transfer to platters. Frost with the remaining peppermint mixture. Cakes can be served immediately or frozen, covered, for later use. Remove from the freezer 10 minutes before serving. Top with the remaining peppermint candies and, if desired, mint leaves just before serving.

CANDIED CITRUS
SUGARED CRANBERRIES
CRANBERRY CAKE WITH TANGERINE FROSTING

Cranberry Cake with Tangerine Frosting

Use special garnish recipes (on the next page) to decorate this showstopper.

—SANDY GAULITZ
SPRING, TX

PREP: 30 MIN. • **BAKE:** 35 MIN. + COOLING
MAKES: 16 SERVINGS

- ¼ cup butter, softened
- 2 cups sugar
- 2 teaspoons vanilla extract
- 4 cups plus 2 tablespoons cake flour, divided
- 2 tablespoons baking powder
- 1 teaspoon salt
- 2 cups 2% milk
- 4 cups fresh or frozen cranberries

FROSTING
- 2 packages (8 ounces each) cream cheese, softened
- ¾ cup butter, softened
- 4 cups confectioners' sugar
- 2 tablespoons tangerine or orange juice
- ½ teaspoon grated tangerine or orange peel
  Optional toppings: Sugared Cranberries, Candied Citrus (see next page), red sprinkles

1. Line the bottoms of two greased 8-in. square or 9-in. round baking pans with parchment paper; grease paper. In a large bowl, beat butter and sugar until crumbly, about 2 minutes. Beat in vanilla.

2. In another bowl, mix 4 cups flour, baking powder and salt; add to butter mixture alternately with milk, beating well after each addition. In a large bowl, toss cranberries with remaining flour; fold into batter.

3. Transfer to the prepared pans. Bake at 400° for 35-40 minutes or until a toothpick inserted in center comes out clean. Cool for 10 minutes before removing from pans to wire racks; remove parchment paper. Cool completely.

4. For frosting, in a large bowl, beat cream cheese and butter until smooth. Gradually beat in the confectioners' sugar, tangerine juice and peel. Spread between cake layers and over top and sides of cake. Refrigerate, covered, until serving.

5. If desired, top cake with Sugared Cranberries, Candied Citrus (recipes on next page) and red sprinkles.
NOTE *This recipe does not use eggs.*

Candied Citrus and Sugared Cranberries make perfect decorations for Cranberry Cake with Tangerine Frosting shown at left. Use the helpful how-to photos below as a guide.

❶ For Candied Citrus:
Add thin tangerine or orange slices to boiling water and sugar. Cook at medium heat until the slices are translucent, about 20 minutes, turning occasionally. Reduce heat and simmer until tender, about 10 minutes, turning occasionally.

❷ With a slotted spoon or tongs, place slices on a wire rack or parchment-lined baking pan. Let dry at room temperature overnight.

❸ For Sugared Cranberries:
Lightly coat cranberries in a mixture of water and egg substitute. Place cranberries on a baking pan and sprinkle with coarse and superfine sugars until coated. Let dry on a wire rack at room temperature for 2 hours or until dry.

❹ To add flair to frosting:
Press the back side of a small offset spatula against the frosting and gently drag the spatula in an upward motion. Repeat around the sides of the cake.

(5) INGREDIENTS
Candied Citrus
This technique for dressing up oranges or tangerines is as easy as can be.
—**TASTE OF HOME TEST KITCHEN**

PREP: 5 MIN. • **COOK:** 30 MIN. + STANDING
MAKES: 10-12 TANGERINE SLICES

- 2¼ cups sugar
- 2 cups water
- 10 to 12 large tangerine or medium orange slices

1. In a Dutch oven, combine sugar and water; bring to a boil. Add tangerine slices; reduce heat to medium. Cook until the slices are translucent, about 20 minutes, turning occasionally. Reduce the heat; simmer until slices are tender but still intact, about 10 minutes, turning occasionally.
2. Using a slotted spoon or tongs, remove the slices to a wire rack or parchment paper-lined baking pan. Let stand at room temperature overnight to dry. (Save the syrup for another use.) If desired, cut slices in half; use to decorate a cake, pie or other dessert.

(5) INGREDIENTS
Sugared Cranberries
With their frosty look, sugared berries always add a festive seasonal touch to autumn and winter events.
—**TASTE OF HOME TEST KITCHEN**

PREP: 10 MIN. + STANDING • **MAKES:** 3 CUPS

- 1 package (12 ounces) fresh or frozen cranberries
- 2 tablespoons water
- 1 tablespoon egg substitute
- ½ cup coarse sugar
- ½ cup superfine sugar

1. In a small bowl, stir together the water and egg substitute. Lightly coat the cranberries in the mixture. Place cranberries on a baking pan; sprinkle with sugars until coated.
2. Transfer the cranberries to a wire rack; let stand at room temperature for 2 hours or until dry. Use to decorate a cake, pie or other dessert.

DAVID FEDER'S LEMON-ROASTED CHICKEN WITH OLIVE COUSCOUS *PAGE 220*

Mom's Best

Share the love with the heartwarming stories and made-by-mom dishes in this chapter. These **treasured specialties** will surely inspire you to make them for your own family.

JUDY CLARK'S
ICEBOX BUTTERHORNS
PAGE 218

CATHY BRANCIAROLI'S
STRAWBERRIES & CREAM TORTE
PAGE 229

JAYE BEELER'S
HEARTY BUTTERNUT SQUASH SOUP
PAGE 227

From Scratch, With Love

Our mother was an expert at **bringing family to the table**. Her memorable meal featuring spareribs debuted on the pages of *Taste of Home* magazine 18 years ago.

STORY BY JUDY CLARK | ELKHART, IN

ICEBOX BUTTERHORNS

M y mother, Thelma Arnold, has always been a Suzy Homemaker. I first shared her story with *Taste of Home* magazine because I knew readers would appreciate her devotion to cooking from scratch, the flavors of her food and its "old-time U.S.A." character.

We grew up on a busy farm in Elkhart, Indiana. Everything we ate—her wonderful Tangy Spareribs and Icebox Butterhorns included—was homemade.

I still remember coming home from church to the smell of ribs baking in the oven alongside potatoes. Mom's golden-brown butterhorns were the perfect accompaniment.

During planting and harvesting season, the number of mouths to feed grew from our family of six to include everyone helping in the field. Mom would prepare a big midday meal to sustain the men for an afternoon of work, often taking entire pies, baskets of sandwiches and kettles of soup out to where they were working.

It wasn't just her cooking that let us know we were Mom's first priority. She never missed a single sporting event or concert that we kids participated in, and that was true for all the grandchildren, too.

My mother is truly an amazing woman. I forget it sometimes, but whenever I tell others about her, I'm reminded of just how wonderful she is. She has a fighting spirit and is incredibly independent, still insisting on hosting the entire family for holiday get-togethers. There are 40 of us now, 16 of whom are her great-grandchildren.

Thanksgiving belongs to my mom. Many of her specialties, such as her oyster dressing, don't have recipes. She adds this and that until it looks and feels right. That's true for her old-fashioned sugar cookies, too. One of my nieces is already working hard to perfect the recipe.

We'll be gathering together in Mom's home again soon, and I know we'll all feel grateful for the time she gave us, whether it was cooking a special meal or cheering us on from the bleachers.

Icebox Butterhorns

PREP: 15 MIN. + CHILLING • **BAKE:** 15 MIN. • **MAKES:** 2 DOZEN

- 2 packages (¼ ounce each) active dry yeast
- ¼ cup warm water (110° to 115°)
- 2 cups warm milk (110° to 115°)
- ¾ cup butter, melted
- ½ cup sugar
- 1 egg
- 1 teaspoon salt
- 6½ cups all-purpose flour
  Additional melted butter

1. In a small bowl, dissolve the yeast in the warm water. In a large bowl, combine the warm milk, butter, sugar, egg, salt, yeast mixture and 3 cups flour; beat on medium speed until smooth. Stir in enough remaining flour to form a soft dough (dough will be sticky).

2. Do not knead dough. Place in a greased bowl, turning once to grease the top. Cover with plastic wrap and refrigerate overnight.

3. Punch down dough. Turn onto a lightly floured surface; divide in half. Roll each half into a 12-in. circle; cut each into 12 wedges. Roll up the wedges from the wide ends. Place 2 in. apart on greased baking sheets, point side down. Cover with kitchen towels; let rise in a warm place until doubled, about 1 hour.

4. Bake at 350° for 15-20 minutes or until golden brown. Immediately brush with additional melted butter. Remove from pans to wire racks to cool.

Tangy Spareribs

PREP: 30 MIN. • **BAKE:** 1½ HOURS • **MAKES:** 6 SERVINGS

- 4 to 5 pounds pork spareribs
- 2 tablespoons butter
- 1 medium onion, finely chopped
- ½ cup finely chopped celery
- 1 cup water
- 1 cup ketchup
- ⅓ cup lemon juice
- 2 tablespoons brown sugar
- 2 tablespoons white vinegar
- 1 tablespoon Worcestershire sauce
- ½ teaspoon ground mustard
- ⅛ teaspoon pepper
- ⅛ teaspoon chili powder

1. Cut ribs into serving-size pieces; place in a shallow roasting pan, bone side down. Bake, uncovered, at 350° for 45 minutes.

2. Meanwhile, in a large saucepan, heat the butter over medium-high heat. Add the onion and celery; cook and stir for 4-5 minutes or until tender. Stir in the remaining ingredients. Bring to a boil; reduce heat. Simmer for about 10 minutes or until slightly thickened, stirring occasionally; remove from the heat.

3. Drain fat from roasting pan. Pour sauce over ribs. Bake 45-60 minutes longer or until ribs are tender.

TANGY SPARERIBS

Hanukkah at Mom's House

For some families, Hanukkah means latkes. For ours, thanks to Mom, **it's all about the sufganiyot.** STORY BY DAVID FEDER | BUFFALO GROVE, IL

Puffy fried doughnuts—called sufganiyot—are a Hanukkah tradition in our family. Of course, we certainly eat our share of great latkes (potato pancakes). But sufganiyot became a "must" after we moved to Israel when I was a boy. During our time there, each neighborhood held a block party, complete with sufganiyot kiosks.

My mom, Golda Edwards, always keeps her house—now in Beaverton, Oregon—filled with wonderful smells of baking. She knocks out loaf after loaf of fresh-baked bread, including sourdough rounds, whole-wheat challahs for Sabbath and black currant and cinnamon bread for my daughter, Yael (shown in the photo with Mom, at top right).

For Hanukkah, Mom's best cooking advice is "Let the men do it." So I'm in charge of the kitchen, with help from Yael, while Mom keeps an eye on us.

Our Festival of Lights feast sings of my mom, whose Sephardic Jewish heritage means she's drawn to the flavors of the Iberian peninsula, where her ancestors probably settled 1,000 years ago, and to the ingredients of nearby North Africa.

We love Mom's Lemon-Roasted Chicken with Olive Couscous and Spiced Garlic Carrots—and, of course, the sweet sufganiyot of my childhood. Try them filled with jelly or preserves and dusted with powdered sugar. You can even add a modern twist and replace the jelly with Nutella. It's got Mom's seal of approval.

LEMON-ROASTED CHICKEN WITH OLIVE COUSCOUS

Lemon-Roasted Chicken with Olive Couscous

PREP: 20 MIN. • **BAKE:** 1½ HOURS + STANDING
MAKES: 8 SERVINGS (4 CUPS COUSCOUS)

- 1 **roasting chicken (5 to 6 pounds)**
- 1 **medium lemon, thinly sliced**
- 1 **teaspoon fennel seeds, crushed**
- 1 **tablespoon olive oil**
- ¾ **teaspoon coarsely ground pepper**
- ¼ **teaspoon salt**

OLIVE COUSCOUS

- 1 **cup uncooked whole wheat couscous**
- ½ **teaspoon dried thyme**
- ¼ **teaspoon salt**
- ½ **cup coarsely chopped pitted green olives**
- 1 **tablespoon pine nuts**

1. Place the chicken on a rack in a shallow roasting pan, breast side up. Tuck the wings under the chicken; tie the drumsticks together.

2. With your fingers, carefully loosen skin from the chicken breast; place lemon slices and fennel under the skin. Secure skin to underside of breast with toothpicks. Rub skin with oil; sprinkle with pepper and salt.

3. Roast at 350° for 1½ to 2 hours or until a thermometer inserted into thigh reads 180°, basting occasionally with pan drippings. Remove chicken from the oven; cover loosely with foil and let stand for 15 minutes before carving.

4. Meanwhile, prepare the couscous according to package directions, adding thyme and salt to water before heating. Stir in the olives and pine nuts during the last minute of cooking. Serve with chicken.

Sufganiyot

PREP: 35 MIN. + RISING • **COOK:** 10 MIN. • **MAKES:** 1½ DOZEN

- ½ cup whole wheat flour
- 1 package (¼ ounce) active dry yeast
- ¼ teaspoon ground cloves
- 1½ to 2 cups all-purpose flour
- ½ cup water
- ¼ cup honey
- 2 teaspoons canola or peanut oil
- 1 egg
- ½ teaspoon vanilla extract
  Oil for deep-fat frying
- ¾ cup seedless raspberry preserves
  Confectioners' sugar

1. In a large bowl, mix the whole wheat flour, yeast, cloves and 1¼ cups all-purpose flour. In a small saucepan, heat the water, honey and oil to 120°-130°. Add to dry ingredients; beat on medium speed for 2 minutes. Add egg and vanilla; beat 2 minutes longer. Stir in enough remaining flour to form a soft dough (dough will be sticky).

2. Turn onto a floured surface; knead until smooth and elastic, about 6-8 minutes. Place in a greased bowl, turning once to grease the top. Cover with plastic wrap and let rise in a warm place until doubled, about 1 hour.

3. Punch down dough. Turn onto a lightly floured surface; roll dough to ¼-in. thickness. Cut with a floured 2-in. biscuit cutter.

SPICED GARLIC CARROTS

SUFGANIYOT

4. In an electric skillet or deep fryer, heat oil to 375°. Fry doughnuts, a few at a time, for 45 seconds on each side or until golden brown. Drain on paper towels.

5. Cut a small hole in the tip of a pastry bag or in a corner of a food-safe plastic bag; insert a small tip. Fill bag with raspberry preserves.

6. With a small knife, pierce a hole into the side of each doughnut; fill with preserves. Dust with confectioners' sugar. Serve warm.

FAST FIX ▶ Spiced Garlic Carrots

START TO FINISH: 30 MIN. • **MAKES:** 6 SERVINGS

- 2 pounds medium carrots, cut diagonally into ¼-inch slices
- 2 cinnamon sticks (3 inches)
- 1 teaspoon cumin seeds
- ¼ cup olive oil
- 12 garlic cloves, peeled and slightly crushed
- ½ teaspoon crushed red pepper flakes
- ¼ teaspoon salt

1. Place carrots in a large saucepan and cover with water. Bring to a boil. Cover and cook for 5-8 minutes or until tender; drain.

2. In a large dry skillet, toast the cinnamon sticks and cumin seeds over medium heat until aromatic, stirring occasionally. Add the oil; heat over medium-high heat. Add the carrots, crushed garlic, pepper flakes and salt; cook and stir for 3-5 minutes or until the carrots and garlic are lightly browned. Remove cinnamon sticks.

Irish Charm in Every Bite

The aromas of pie and cookies greet us as we walk in the door. **Mom knows the way to our hearts.**

STORY BY REBECCA LITTLE | PARK RIDGE, IL

T he Irish don't just drink beer and sing dirges. Sometimes we eat. A lot. My mom, Mary Little, is one of eight children in an Irish Catholic family that gathers to laugh, gossip, celebrate and eat. Many memories have sound tracks; mine have food tracks.

My parents' harvest table is the center of their home in Flossmoor, Illinois. It's where everyone gathers—sometimes just our immediate family of five, sometimes 45 McInerney relatives for holidays, sometimes an assortment of family and friends.

There's always plenty of food. My mom's entire family suffers from an inability to gauge when enough is enough. They make an absurd variety for every holiday, then panic the day before because there's not enough! So everyone makes an additional treat or three, then stands before the bounty and says, "Why do we always have so much food?" It might be our oldest family tradition.

My mom is an amazing cook, famous for her pork tenderloin, brunches and baked goods. I've shared some favorites here—Mom's Maple-Apple Pie, Jam Thumbprint Cookies, Creamy Irish Coffee and Lemon-Blueberry Pound Cake.

Much to her chagrin and mine, her talent has skipped me entirely. Most of this is sheer lack of skill, but it's also because Mom can't help but take over. She doesn't even realize she's doing it. I'll be making cookies, and suddenly Mom is next to me. Next thing you know, she's got the mixing bowl and I'm sitting at the kitchen island, licking the spoon. It's not such a bad gig, so no complaints.

MOM'S MAPLE-APPLE PIE

Mom's Maple-Apple Pie

PREP: 30 MIN. • **BAKE:** 40 MIN. + COOLING • **MAKES:** 8 SERVINGS

- 1 cup sugar
- 2 tablespoons all-purpose flour
- 1½ teaspoons ground cinnamon
- ½ teaspoon ground nutmeg
- ¼ teaspoon salt
- 6 medium tart apples, peeled and thinly sliced (about 2¼ pounds)
- 1 tablespoon lemon juice
- 1 (14.1 ounces) refrigerated pie pastry
- 2 tablespoons butter
- 3 tablespoons maple syrup, divided
  Warm maple syrup, optional

1. In a small bowl, combine the first five ingredients. In a large bowl, toss apples with lemon juice. Add sugar mixture; toss to coat.

2. Unroll one pastry sheet into a 9-in. pie plate; trim even with the rim. Add the filling. Dot with butter; drizzle with 2 tablespoons maple syrup. Unroll remaining pastry; place over filling. Trim, seal and flute edge. Cut slits in top. Brush pastry with 1 tablespoon maple syrup.

⑤INGREDIENTS FAST FIX ▶ Creamy Irish Coffee

START TO FINISH: 10 MIN. • **MAKES:** 4 SERVINGS

- 3 cups hot strong brewed coffee
- 4 ounces Irish cream liqueur
  Sweetened whipped cream, optional
  Chocolate shavings, optional

Divide coffee and liqueur among four mugs; stir. If desired, top with whipped cream and chocolate shavings.

3. Bake at 425° for 40-45 minutes or until the crust is golden brown and the filling is bubbly. Cover pie loosely with foil during the last 20 minutes if needed to prevent overbrowning. Remove foil. Cool on a wire rack. If desired, serve with warm maple syrup.

Jam Thumbprint Cookies

PREP: 20 MIN. + CHILLING • **BAKE:** 20 MIN./BATCH
MAKES: ABOUT 5 DOZEN

- 1½ cups butter, softened
- 1 cup sugar
- 1 teaspoon vanilla extract
- ¼ teaspoon salt
- 3½ cups all-purpose flour
- ⅓ cup flaked coconut
- 1 egg
- 1 tablespoon water
- ⅓ cup apricot or red raspberry preserves
  Confectioners' sugar, optional

1. In a large bowl, cream the butter, sugar, vanilla and salt until light and fluffy. Gradually beat in flour. Wrap in plastic wrap and refrigerate 30 minutes or until easy to handle.
2. Preheat oven to 350°. Place coconut in a small bowl. In a separate bowl, whisk egg and water. Shape cookie dough into 1-in. balls; dip the tops in egg mixture, then in coconut, pressing slightly to adhere. Place 2 in. apart on parchment paper-lined baking sheets, coconut side up.
3. Press a deep indentation into center of each with the end of a wooden spoon handle. Fill with preserves.
4. Bake 18-20 minutes or until the bottoms are browned. Remove to wire racks to cool. If desired, dust the tops with confectioner's sugar.

JAM THUMBPRINT COOKIES

LEMON-BLUEBERRY POUND CAKE

Lemon-Blueberry Pound Cake

PREP: 25 MIN. • **BAKE:** 55 MIN. + COOLING • **MAKES:** 12 SERVINGS

- ⅓ cup butter, softened
- 4 ounces cream cheese, softened
- 2 cups sugar
- 3 eggs
- 1 egg white
- 1 tablespoon grated lemon peel
- 2 teaspoons vanilla extract
- 2 cups fresh or frozen unsweetened blueberries
- 3 cups all-purpose flour, divided
- 1 teaspoon baking powder
- ½ teaspoon baking soda
- ½ teaspoon salt
- 1 cup (8 ounces) lemon yogurt

GLAZE
- 1½ cups confectioners' sugar
- ¼ cup lemon juice

1. Grease and flour a 10-in. fluted tube pan. In a large bowl, cream butter, cream cheese and sugar until blended. Add the eggs and egg white, one at a time, beating well after each addition. Beat in lemon peel and vanilla.
2. Toss the blueberries with 2 tablespoons flour. In another bowl, mix the remaining flour with baking powder, baking soda and salt; add to the creamed mixture alternately with yogurt, beating after each addition just until combined. Fold in blueberry mixture.
3. Transfer the batter to the prepared pan. Bake at 350° for 55-60 minutes or until a toothpick inserted into center comes out clean. Cool in pan 10 minutes before removing to wire rack; cool for 15 minutes.
4. In a small bowl, mix the confectioners' sugar and lemon juice until smooth. Gradually brush onto warm cake, about one-third at a time, allowing glaze to soak into cake before adding more. Cool completely.
NOTE *For easier removal of cake, use solid shortening when greasing a fluted or plain tube pan.*

Keeping It *Classic*

Mom's dinner table was a magnet that attracted our huge family—and a random mix of neighborhood kids. It was where we shared so much more than a meal.

STORY BY PATTY LANOUE STEARNS | TRAVERSE CITY, MI

A s a child of the Great Depression, my late mother, Irene LaNoue, never took a meal for granted. Her formative years were achingly poor. By the 1970s, Mom was a newspaper columnist married to Charles LaNoue, an automotive engineer, with seven children (that's me in the photo above right) and an open-door policy for a bunch of rowdy neighborhood kids. Plus there was our collie, Lassie.

Our suburban Detroit home was a hangout for our friends, and at dinnertime, Mom invited them to stay. Our table was jammed, but Mom found a way to squeeze everyone in. Her big heart and sense of humor made her a human magnet. Her classic meals—with recipes such as Pastry Chicken a la King, Creamy Dilled Cucumber Salad and Pistachio Cake with Walnuts—were priceless.

Mom's favorite hangout was a stool at the counter next to the stove in her aqua kitchen, where she read the paper and planned meals. Her cooking style was '60s modern, with a nod to her Norwegian mother and Moravian father.

Meals were always big, quick and tasty. After we said grace, the cacophony of clanging silverware was followed by appreciative *mmms*, then more dish passing and chatter as Mom's dinner disappeared. Before long, everyone had left—except the unlucky person whose turn it was to do the dishes.

PISTACHIO CAKE WITH WALNUTS

Pistachio Cake with Walnuts

PREP: 20 MIN. • **BAKE:** 40 MIN. + COOLING • **MAKES:** 12 SERVINGS

- 1 **package white cake mix (regular size)**
- 1 **package (3.4 ounces) instant pistachio pudding mix**
- 3 **eggs**
- 1 **cup club soda**
- ¾ **cup canola oil**
- 1 **cup chopped walnuts**

FROSTING

- 1 **package (3.4 ounces) instant pistachio pudding mix**
- 1 **cup 2% milk**
- 1 **carton (8 ounces) frozen whipped topping, thawed**

1. Preheat oven to 350°. Grease and flour a 10-in. fluted tube pan.

2. In a large bowl, combine the first five ingredients; beat on low speed 30 seconds. Beat on medium 2 minutes. Fold in walnuts. Transfer to prepared pan. Bake 40-45 minutes or until a toothpick inserted into center comes out clean. Cool in pan 10 minutes before removing to a wire rack to cool completely.

3. For frosting, in a large bowl, combine pudding mix and milk; beat on low speed 1 minute. Fold in whipped topping. Spread over cake. Refrigerate leftovers.

NOTE *For easier removal of cakes, use solid shortening to grease plain and fluted tube pans.*

Creamy Dilled Cucumber Salad

PREP: 20 MIN. + CHILLING • **MAKES:** 6 SERVINGS

- 2 English cucumbers, thinly sliced
- 1 teaspoon salt
- 1½ cups (12 ounces) sour cream
- ¼ cup thinly sliced red onion
- ¼ cup snipped fresh dill
- 2 tablespoons white wine vinegar
- 2 garlic cloves, minced
- 1 teaspoon sugar
- 1 teaspoon coarsely ground pepper

1. Place the cucumbers in a colander; sprinkle with salt and toss. Let stand 15 minutes. Squeeze and blot dry with paper towels.
2. In a large bowl, combine the remaining ingredients; stir in cucumbers. Refrigerate, covered, at least 1 hour.

PASTRY CHICKEN A LA KING

CREAMY DILLED CUCUMBER SALAD

Pastry Chicken a la King

PREP: 25 MIN. • **COOK:** 20 MIN. • **MAKES:** 6 SERVINGS

- 1 package (10 ounces) frozen puff pastry shells
- 3 tablespoons butter
- 1 cup sliced fresh mushrooms
- 1 medium sweet red pepper, finely chopped
- 1 celery rib, finely chopped
- 1 small onion, finely chopped
- 3 tablespoons all-purpose flour
- 2 cups 2% milk
- 2 egg yolks
- 2 tablespoons heavy whipping cream
- ¼ teaspoon lemon juice
- ½ teaspoon salt
- ¼ teaspoon paprika
- ¼ teaspoon pepper
- 2 cups cubed cooked chicken
- 1 cup frozen petite peas

1. Bake the pastry shells according to package directions.
2. Meanwhile, in a large skillet, heat butter over medium-high heat. Add mushrooms, red pepper, celery and onion; cook and stir until tender. Stir in the flour until blended; gradually add milk. Bring to a boil; cook and stir 2 minutes or until thickened.
3. In a small bowl, mix egg yolks and cream. Stir a small amount of hot mixture into egg yolk mixture; return all to pan, stirring constantly. Add lemon juice, salt, paprika and pepper; cook and stir over low heat for 2 minutes or until thickened. Add chicken and peas; heat through. Serve over pastry shells.

A Growing Family

Special memories inspire our searches for the freshest produce, which is found close to home.

STORY BY JAYE BEELER | GRAND RAPIDS, MI

Every Sunday and holiday, the food of my Kentucky childhood overflowed from the kitchen to the sideboard, the coffee table, even the tops of the washer and dryer. It was the work of my maternal grandmother, Odessa Moore, a retired cook. She learned from her Tennessee mother, Myrtle Sain, called Big Mama even though she was under 5 feet.

In Logan County, Kentucky, Grandaddy and Granny's garden was full of practical produce. They'd bring us sacks of vegetables, warm from the sun. Our peach trees and blackberry bushes yielded pies, cobblers, jams and ice cream. My mom, Gloria Beeler, and her sisters inherited Granny's connection to the earth and everyday food.

Now my own family of five hunts for fun, locally grown foods here in Michigan. We've found green eggs, purple potatoes, orange cauliflower and yellow watermelon in markets and fields. Our small garden also inspires our cooking. It sprouts produce with names my children find magical—Cinderella squash, Purple Ruffles basil and Green Zebra tomatoes.

We all enjoy the fruits of our labor in recipes such as Hearty Butternut Squash Soup, Harvest Salad with Cherry Vinaigrette, Spinach-Basil Pesto, Pesto Twists and Cherry-Chocolate Oatmeal Cookies. I'm raising the sixth generation whose childhood meals will be as flavor-packed and fresh-from-the-garden as I remember mine back in Kentucky.

CHERRY-CHOCOLATE OATMEAL COOKIES

Cherry-Chocolate Oatmeal Cookies

PREP: 25 MIN. • **BAKE:** 10 MIN./BATCH • **MAKES:** 6 DOZEN

- 1 cup butter, softened
- 1½ cups packed brown sugar
- 2 eggs
- 1 teaspoon vanilla extract
- 1½ cups all-purpose flour
- 1 teaspoon ground cinnamon
- ½ teaspoon baking powder
- ½ teaspoon baking soda
- ½ teaspoon salt
- 2 cups old-fashioned oats
- 1 cup dried tart cherries
- 1 cup dark chocolate chips

1. Preheat oven to 350°. In a large bowl, cream butter and brown sugar until light and fluffy. Beat in eggs and vanilla. In another bowl, whisk the flour, cinnamon, baking powder, baking soda and salt; gradually beat into creamed mixture. Stir in oats, cherries and chocolate chips.

2. Drop dough by tablespoonfuls 2 in. apart onto ungreased baking sheets. Bake 9-11 minutes or until edges are golden brown. Cool on pans 1 minute. Remove to wire racks to cool.

Harvest Salad with Cherry Vinaigrette

PREP: 10 MIN. • **BAKE:** 50 MIN. + COOLING
MAKES: 10 SERVINGS (1 CUP EACH)

- 3 **medium fresh beets (about 1 pound)**
- 1 **package (5 ounces) spring mix salad greens**
- 2 **medium apples, thinly sliced**
- 1 **medium carrot, shredded**
- ½ **cup grape tomatoes, halved**
- ½ **cup yellow grape tomatoes or pear tomatoes, halved**
- ½ **cup garbanzo beans or chickpeas, rinsed and drained**
- ½ **cup coarsely chopped walnuts, toasted**
- 4 **thick-sliced bacon strips, cooked and crumbled**

CHERRY VINAIGRETTE

- ½ **cup tart cherry preserves**
- 3 **tablespoons olive oil**
- 2 **tablespoons red wine vinegar**
- 2 **teaspoons Dijon mustard**
- 1 **garlic clove, minced**
- ¼ **teaspoon salt**
- ⅛ **teaspoon pepper**

1. Preheat oven to 400°. Scrub beets and trim tops to 1 in. Wrap in foil; place on a baking sheet. Bake 50-60 minutes or until tender. Remove foil; cool completely. Peel beets and cut into ½-in. pieces.

2. In a large bowl, combine the salad greens, apples, carrot, tomatoes, beans, walnuts, bacon and cooled beets. In a small bowl, whisk vinaigrette ingredients until blended. Serve with salad.

HEARTY BUTTERNUT SQUASH SOUP

HARVEST SALAD WITH CHERRY VINAIGRETTE

Hearty Butternut Squash Soup

PREP: 20 MIN. • **COOK:** 40 MIN. • **MAKES:** 12 SERVINGS (4½ QUARTS)

- 1 **pound bulk Italian sausage**
- 1 **medium onion, chopped**
- 1 **medium sweet red pepper, chopped**
- 4 **garlic cloves, minced**
- 1 **large butternut squash (about 5 pounds), peeled, seeded and cut into 1-inch pieces**
- 1 **package (16 ounces) frozen corn, divided**
- 4 **cups water**
- 1 **tablespoon chicken base**
- 2 **cans (15½ ounces each) great northern beans, rinsed and drained**
- 2 **cans (14½ ounces each) fire-roasted diced tomatoes, undrained**
- 1 **teaspoon salt**
- ¼ **teaspoon pepper**
  Heavy whipping cream and minced fresh parsley, optional

1. In a stockpot, cook sausage, onion and red pepper over medium heat 9-11 minutes or until sausage is no longer pink and onion is tender, breaking up sausage into crumbles. Add garlic; cook 1 minute longer. Remove with a slotted spoon; discard drippings.

2. Add the squash, 1½ cups corn, water and chicken base to the same pan; bring to a boil. Reduce heat; simmer, covered, 15-20 minutes or until squash is tender.

3. Remove the soup from the heat; cool slightly. Process in batches in a blender until smooth. Return to pot. Add beans, tomatoes, salt, pepper, sausage mixture and remaining corn; heat through. If desired, drizzle servings with cream and sprinkle with parsley.

FAST FIX ▶ Spinach-Basil Pesto

START TO FINISH: 10 MIN. • **MAKES:** 1¾ CUPS

- 6 garlic cloves, halved
- 3 cups fresh baby spinach
- 1½ cups loosely packed basil leaves
- ¾ cup chopped walnuts or pine nuts, toasted
- 1 cup grated Parmesan cheese
- ½ teaspoon salt
  Dash pepper
- ¾ cup olive oil

Place garlic in a food processor; pulse until finely chopped. Add spinach, basil and walnuts. Pulse until chopped. Add the cheese, salt and pepper. Continue processing while gradually adding oil in a steady stream.

⑤ INGREDIENTS FAST FIX ▶ Pesto Twists

START TO FINISH: 25 MIN. • **MAKES:** 12 SERVINGS

- 1 package (17.3 ounces) frozen puff pastry, thawed
- ½ cup prepared pesto
- ½ cup shredded Parmesan cheese

1. Preheat oven to 400°. Unfold the puff pastry sheets on a lightly floured surface. Roll each sheet into a 12-in. square. Spread the pesto onto one pastry sheet to within ¼ in. of the edges. Sprinkle with the Parmesan cheese. Top with the remaining puff pastry, pressing lightly. Cut into twelve 1-in.-wide strips. Twist each strip four times. Place 2 in. apart on parchment paper-lined baking sheets, pressing down the ends.

2. Bake 12-15 minutes or until golden brown. Serve warm.

SPINACH-BASIL PESTO
PESTO TWISTS

Strawberries of Summer

When the mercury rises, **take a cue from my mom** and keep your family cool with a refreshing berry dessert.

STORY BY CATHY BRANCIAROLI | WILMINGTON, DE

I grew up in northeast Ohio at a time when summer stretched endlessly, school days ended in the early afternoon and playdates had yet to be invented. My sister and I had the most fun baking with our mom, Virginia. Spring and summer yielded fruit that made its way into many of our desserts. My mother's strawberry torte was a high-rise construction, alternating layers of whipped cream and strawberries with a cake baked under a meringue crown.

Mom nearly lost her family's recipes because they were never written down, and she waited too long to master them. It took years of experimenting before she felt she had re-created her favorites.

We made sure that her Strawberries & Cream Torte lives on. Mom always provided pointers while guiding me through each step of the recipe. For instance, to get the fluffiest whipped cream, we put the beaters and bowl in the refrigerator to chill before using. And meringue, Mom explained, is really nothing but a big collection of bubbles whipped into egg whites. It puffs up while baking, then flattens as it cools on the cake.

Once assembled, her torte offers amazing flavors and textures. And it whisks me back to carefree days in the kitchen with my mom and sister.

1. Place egg whites in a large bowl; let stand at room temperature 30 minutes. Preheat oven to 350°. Line the bottoms of two greased 8-in. round baking pans with parchment paper; grease paper.
2. In a large bowl, cream butter and ½ cup sugar until light and fluffy. Add egg yolks, beating well. Beat in vanilla.
3. In another bowl, whisk the flour, baking powder and salt; add to creamed mixture alternately with milk, beating well after each addition. Transfer to prepared pans.
4. With clean beaters, beat egg whites on medium speed until foamy. Add remaining sugar, beating on high until sugar is dissolved. Continue beating until soft peaks form. Spread over batter in pans.
5. Bake 12-15 minutes or until a toothpick inserted into the center comes out clean. Cool completely in pans on wire racks. (Cake layers will be thin.)
6. In a large bowl, beat cream until stiff peaks form. Loosen edges of cakes from pans with a knife. Carefully remove one cake to a serving plate, meringue side up.
7. Arrange sliced strawberries over top; sprinkle with sugar. Gently spread with half of the whipped cream. Top with remaining cake layer, meringue side up; spread with remaining whipped cream. Top with whole strawberries. Refrigerate until serving.

STRAWBERRIES & CREAM TORTE

Strawberries & Cream Torte

PREP: 25 MIN. • **BAKE:** 15 MIN. + COOLING • **MAKES:** 12 SERVINGS

- 2 **eggs, separated**
- ¼ **cup butter, softened**
- ½ **cup plus ½ teaspoon sugar, divided**
- ½ **teaspoon vanilla extract**
- 1 **cup all-purpose flour**
- 1½ **teaspoons baking powder**
- ¼ **teaspoon salt**
- ½ **cup 2% milk**

ASSEMBLY

- 2 **cups heavy whipping cream**
- 1 **pint fresh strawberries, hulled and sliced**
- ½ **teaspoon sugar**
- **Additional fresh strawberries**

**JUDY BATSON'S
MUFFULETTA OLIVE SALAD**
PAGE 237

Field Editor Favorites

Taste of Home's Field Editors **love to share** their most popular, sought-after recipes. Page through this special chapter to find a **scrumptious array** of main dishes, sides, desserts and more.

**PRECI D'SILVA'S
WARM GREEN BEAN & POTATO
SALAD** PAGE 233

**MARIETTA SLATER'S
CHRISTMAS TORTELLINI & SPINACH
SOUP** PAGE 235

**SARAH HAENGEL'S
CARAMEL APPLE STRUDEL**
PAGE 238

Molded Cranberry-Orange Salad

When I take this gelatin mold to potlucks during the holidays, people always ooh and aah. If you prefer, garnish it with whipped cream instead of celery.

—**CAROL MEAD** LOS ALAMOS, NM

PREP: 20 MIN. + CHILLING
MAKES: 12 SERVINGS

- 1 teaspoon unflavored gelatin
- 1 tablespoon plus 1 cup cold water, divided
- 1 cup boiling water
- 1 package (3 ounces) raspberry gelatin
- 1 package (12 ounces) fresh or frozen cranberries, divided
- 2 medium apples, cut into wedges
- 1 medium navel orange, peeled
- 1 cup sugar
- ½ cup chopped walnuts
- ½ cup finely chopped celery

1. In a bowl, sprinkle the unflavored gelatin over 1 tablespoon cold water; let stand for 1 minute. Add boiling water and raspberry gelatin; stir for 2 minutes to completely dissolve gelatin. Stir in remaining cold water. Refrigerate for 45 minutes or until thickened.

2. Place 2⅓ cups cranberries, apples and orange in a food processor; pulse until chopped. Transfer to a bowl; stir in sugar. Stir into thickened gelatin. Fold in walnuts, celery and remaining whole cranberries.

3. Pour into a 10-in. fluted tube pan or 8-cup ring mold coated with cooking spray. Cover and refrigerate overnight or until firm. Unmold onto a platter.

MOLDED CRANBERRY-ORANGE SALAD

"I became a fan of seafood appetizers as soon as I tasted these simple skewers of pineapple, onion and marinated shrimp cooked to perfection on the grill."
—**MICHELE TUNGETT** ROCHESTER, IL

GRILLED SHRIMP APPETIZER KABOBS

EAT SMART Grilled Shrimp Appetizer Kabobs

PREP: 15 MIN. + MARINATING • **GRILL:** 5 MIN.
MAKES: 10 SERVINGS

- ⅓ cup tomato sauce
- ⅓ cup olive oil
- 3 tablespoons minced fresh basil
- 3 tablespoons red wine vinegar
- 5 garlic cloves, minced
- ¾ teaspoon salt
- ½ teaspoon cayenne pepper
- 10 uncooked jumbo shrimp, peeled and deveined (8-10 ounces)
- 10 fresh pineapple chunks
- 1 small onion, cut into 1-inch chunks

1. In a large bowl, whisk the first seven ingredients until blended. Reserve ¼ cup marinade for basting. Add shrimp to remaining marinade; toss to coat. Refrigerate, covered, for 30 minutes.

2. On each of 10 metal or soaked wooden appetizer skewers, alternately thread one shrimp, one pineapple chunk and onion. Grill, covered, over medium heat or broil 4 in. from heat for 4-6 minutes or until shrimp turn pink, turning occasionally and basting with reserved marinade during the last 2 minutes.

PER SERVING *68 cal., 4 g fat (1 g sat. fat), 31 mg chol., 138 mg sodium, 4 g carb., trace fiber, 4 g pro.* **Diabetic Exchanges:** *1 lean meat, ½ fat.*

Festive King's Cake

For our Mardi Gras parties, I make the traditional king's cake and bake it with a tiny toy baby inside. Whoever gets the piece with the baby is supposed to have a year of good luck. The catch is that they must also throw a party next year!

—STACEY FEATHER JAY, OK

PREP: 40 MIN. + RISING
BAKE: 30 MIN. + COOLING
MAKES: 1 CAKE (16 SLICES)

- ½ cup sugar
- 2 tablespoons active dry yeast
- 2 teaspoons salt
- 4 to 4½ cups all-purpose flour
- 1 cup 2% milk
- ¾ cup butter, cubed
- 5 egg yolks
- **FILLING**
- 1 cup sugar
- 1 tablespoon ground cinnamon
- **TOPPING**
- 1⅓ cups confectioners' sugar
- ½ teaspoon vanilla extract
- 2 to 3 tablespoons 2% milk
  Purple, yellow and green colored sugars

1. In a bowl, mix the sugar, yeast, salt and 2 cups flour. In a small saucepan, heat milk and butter to 120°-130°. Add to dry ingredients; beat on medium speed for 2 minutes. Add the egg yolks; beat 2 minutes longer. Stir in enough remaining flour to form a soft dough.

2. Turn dough onto a floured surface; knead until smooth and elastic, about 6-8 minutes. Place in a greased bowl, turning once to grease the top. Cover with plastic wrap and let rise in a warm place until doubled, about 1½ hours.

3. For filling, mix sugar and cinnamon in a small bowl. Punch down dough. Turn onto a lightly floured surface; roll into a 24-in. x 6-in. rectangle. Sprinkle cinnamon-sugar lengthwise down one half of dough. Fold dough lengthwise over filling; pinch the seam to seal. Transfer to a greased baking sheet, seam side down. Shape into a ring, pinching ends together to seal. Cover with a kitchen towel; let rise in a warm place until doubled, about 1 hour.

4. Bake at 350° for 30-35 minutes or until golden brown. Remove from pan to a wire rack to cool completely. For topping, mix the confectioners' sugar, vanilla and enough milk to reach the desired consistency. Spread over cake; sprinkle with colored sugars.

FAST FIX ▶ Warm Green Bean & Potato Salad

The pairing of green beans and red potatoes, also known as Green Beans Pierre, is one of my go-to side dishes. It's especially good with chicken.

—PRECI D'SILVA DUBAI, UAE

START TO FINISH: 30 MIN.
MAKES: 10 SERVINGS

- 1 pound small red potatoes, quartered
- ¼ cup olive oil
- 2 tablespoons white wine vinegar
- ½ teaspoon salt
- ⅛ teaspoon each garlic powder, ground mustard and pepper
- ⅛ teaspoon each dried basil, parsley flakes and tarragon
- 1 pound fresh green beans, cut into 2-inch pieces
- 2 medium tomatoes, coarsely chopped
- 2 tablespoons chopped onion

1. Place potatoes in a large saucepan; add water to cover. Bring to a boil. Cook, uncovered, for 10 minutes. Meanwhile, in a large bowl, whisk the oil, vinegar and seasonings.

2. Add green beans to potatoes; return to a boil. Cook 3-5 minutes longer or until vegetables are tender. Drain; add to dressing and toss to coat. Stir in tomatoes and onion. Serve warm.

WARM GREEN BEAN & POTATO SALAD

EAT SMART Veg Jambalaya

PREP: 10 MIN. • **COOK:** 30 MIN. • **MAKES:** 6 SERVINGS

- 1 tablespoon canola oil
- 1 medium green pepper, chopped
- 1 medium onion, chopped
- 1 celery rib, chopped
- 3 garlic cloves, minced
- 2 cups water
- 1 can (14½ ounces) diced tomatoes, undrained
- 1 can (8 ounces) tomato sauce
- ½ teaspoon Italian seasoning
- ¼ teaspoon salt
- ¼ teaspoon crushed red pepper flakes
- ⅛ teaspoon fennel seed, crushed
- 1 cup uncooked long grain rice
- 1 can (16 ounces) butter beans, rinsed and drained
- 1 can (16 ounces) red beans, rinsed and drained

1. In a Dutch oven, heat the oil over medium-high heat. Add the green pepper, onion and celery; cook and stir until tender. Add garlic, cook 1 minute longer.

2. Add the water, tomatoes, tomato sauce and seasonings. Bring to a boil; stir in rice. Reduce heat; cover and simmer for 15-18 minutes or until the liquid is absorbed and the rice is tender. Stir in beans; heat through.

PER SERVING *281 cal., 3 g fat (trace sat. fat), 0 chol., 796 mg sodium, 56 g carb., 9 g fiber, 11 g pro.*

"Here's a mild jambalaya my sons like. My husband prefers more of a kick, so I add hot sauce to his."
—**CRYSTAL BRUNS** ILIFF, CO

VEG JAMBALAYA

CHOCOLATE-DRIZZLED GINGERBREAD

Chocolate-Drizzled Gingerbread

This decadent gingerbread looks extra special when I top it off with whipped cream, crystallized ginger and shaved chocolate.
—**PRECI D'SILVA** DUBAI, UAE

PREP: 25 MIN. • **BAKE:** 40 MIN. • **MAKES:** 9 SERVINGS

- ½ cup butter, softened
- ½ cup packed brown sugar
- 1 egg
- ½ cup molasses
- 1¾ cups all-purpose flour
- 1 teaspoon baking powder
- ½ teaspoon ground ginger
- ¼ teaspoon salt
- ⅛ teaspoon ground cloves
- ½ cup water
- 4 ounces bittersweet chocolate, melted and slightly cooled

TOPPING
- ¾ cup heavy whipping cream
- 2 tablespoons confectioners' sugar
- ¼ teaspoon ground ginger
  Chopped crystallized ginger and chocolate shavings, optional

1. Preheat oven to 325°. In a large bowl, cream butter and brown sugar until light and fluffy. Add egg, then molasses, beating well after each addition.

2. In another bowl, mix the flour, baking powder, ground ginger, salt and cloves; gradually add to creamed mixture alternately with water, beating well after each addition.

3. Pour half of the batter into a greased 8-in. square baking dish. Drizzle with half of the melted chocolate. Top with remaining batter and chocolate. Bake 40-45 minutes or until a toothpick inserted into center comes out clean. Cool completely on a wire rack.

4. For topping, in a small bowl, beat cream until it begins to thicken. Add confectioners' sugar and ginger; beat until soft peaks form. Serve with cake. If desired, sprinkle with crystallized ginger and chocolate shavings.

Christmas Tortellini & Spinach Soup

I came up with my tortellini and spinach soup during the summer. But seeing the bright red and green colors mixed together made me think of a first course for Christmas dinner.

—**MARIETTA SLATER** JUSTIN, TX

START TO FINISH: 25 MIN. • **MAKES:** 6 SERVINGS

- 2 cans (14½ ounces each) vegetable broth
- 1 package (9 ounces) refrigerated cheese tortellini or tortellini of your choice
- 1 can (15 ounces) white kidney or cannellini beans, rinsed and drained
- 1 can (14½ ounces) Italian diced tomatoes, undrained
- ¼ teaspoon salt
- ⅛ teaspoon pepper
- 3 cups fresh baby spinach
- 3 tablespoons minced fresh basil
- ¼ cup shredded Asiago cheese

1. In a large saucepan, bring broth to a boil. Add tortellini; reduce heat. Simmer, uncovered, for 5 minutes. Stir in the beans, tomatoes, salt and pepper; return to a simmer. Cook 4-5 minutes longer or until tortellini are tender.

2. Stir in spinach and basil; cook until spinach is wilted. Top servings with cheese.

CHRISTMAS TORTELLINI & SPINACH SOUP

"Put those orchard-fresh fall apples to perfect use in this upside-down cake. I like to finish off each warm piece with a scoop of vanilla bean ice cream."

—**RAYMONDE BOURGEOIS** SWASTIKA, ON

GINGERED APPLE UPSIDE-DOWN CAKE

Gingered Apple Upside-Down Cake

PREP: 30 MIN. • **BAKE:** 30 MIN.+ COOLING • **MAKES:** 8 SERVINGS

- ¼ cup butter, cubed
- ¼ cup packed brown sugar
- 1 tablespoon finely chopped crystallized ginger
- 2 large apples, peeled and cut into ⅛-in. slices

BATTER
- ¼ cup butter, softened
- ⅔ cup packed brown sugar
- 2 eggs
- 1 teaspoon vanilla extract
- 1½ cups all-purpose flour
- 2 teaspoons baking powder
- 1 teaspoon ground ginger
- ¼ teaspoon salt
- ½ cup 2% milk

1. Preheat oven to 375°. Place butter in a 9-in. round baking pan; heat in oven until melted. Tilt pan to coat bottom and sides. Sprinkle brown sugar and ginger onto bottom of pan. Arrange apple slices in circles over brown sugar mixture.

2. For batter, in a large bowl, beat butter and brown sugar until blended. Add the eggs, one at a time, beating well after each addition. Beat in vanilla. In another bowl, whisk flour, baking powder, ginger and salt; add to the creamed mixture alternately with milk. Spoon over apples.

3. Bake 30-35 minutes or until a toothpick inserted into the center comes out clean. Cool 10 minutes before inverting onto a serving plate. Serve warm.

Brown Sugar Salmon with Strawberries

The relish for this grilled salmon features strawberries and cucumber, a flavor pairing I discovered in the U.K.

—**JUDITH FOREMAN** ALEXANDRIA, VA

PREP: 20 MIN. + CHILLING • **GRILL:** 10 MIN.
MAKES: 4 SERVINGS (2 CUPS RELISH)

- ⅓ **cup packed brown sugar**
- 1 **tablespoon canola oil**
- 1 **teaspoon ground mustard**
- 1 **teaspoon ground allspice**
- ½ **teaspoon salt**
- 4 **salmon fillets (5 ounces each)**

RELISH

- 1 **tablespoon minced fresh mint**
- 1 **tablespoon canola oil**
- 1 **tablespoon lemon juice**
- 2 **teaspoons grated lemon peel**
- ⅛ **teaspoon sugar**
- 1 **cup finely chopped fresh strawberries**
- 1 **small cucumber, finely chopped**

1. In a small bowl, mix the first five ingredients; rub over the flesh side of salmon. Refrigerate, covered, 1 hour.
2. For relish, in another bowl, mix mint, oil, lemon juice, lemon peel and sugar. Add the strawberries and cucumber; toss to coat.
3. Moisten a paper towel with cooking oil; using long-handled tongs, rub on the grill rack to coat lightly. Place the salmon on the grill rack, skin side down. Grill, covered, over medium heat 8-10 minutes or until fish flakes easily with a fork. Serve with relish.

BROWN SUGAR SALMON WITH STRAWBERRIES

"I like to toss together a bowlful of crunchy apples, juicy pears and veggies, then pour on a spicy homemade dressing. It's a combination that works beautifully."

—**JEAN ECOS** HARTLAND, WI

FRESH APPLE & PEAR SALAD

Pork Chops with Corn Bread Stuffing

In our family, we often choose stuffing instead of potatoes as a side dish. Here's one of our favorite dinners.

—**JO GROTH** PLAINFIELD, IA

PREP: 20 MIN. • **BAKE:** 20 MIN.
MAKES: 6 SERVINGS

- 1 **can (14½ ounces) chicken broth**
- 1 **can (7 ounces) Mexicorn, drained**
- 1 **celery rib, chopped**
- ¼ **cup chopped onion**
- 1 **egg, lightly beaten**
- ¼ **teaspoon dried sage leaves, crushed**
- 4 **cups corn bread stuffing mix**
- 6 **bone-in pork loin chops (6 ounces each)**
- 1½ **teaspoons Montreal steak seasoning**
- 1 **tablespoon canola oil**

1. In a large bowl, combine the first six ingredients; stir in stuffing mix. Transfer to a greased 13-in. x 9-in. baking dish.
2. Sprinkle the pork chops with steak seasoning. In a large skillet, heat the oil over medium heat; brown the chops on both sides. Place over the stuffing. Bake, uncovered, at 400° for 18-22 minutes or until a thermometer inserted into pork reads 145°. Let stand for 5 minutes before serving.

EAT SMART **FAST FIX** ▶ ## Fresh Apple & Pear Salad

START TO FINISH: 20 MIN.
MAKES: 8 SERVINGS

- 4 **medium apples, thinly sliced**
- 2 **medium pears, thinly sliced**
- 1 **medium cucumber, seeded and chopped**
- 1 **medium red onion, halved and thinly sliced**
- ¼ **cup apple cider or juice**
- 1 **tablespoon snipped fresh dill**
- 1 **tablespoon olive oil**
- 1 **tablespoon spicy brown mustard**
- 2 **teaspoons brown sugar**
- ½ **teaspoon salt**
- ¼ **teaspoon pepper**

In a large bowl, combine apples, pears, cucumber and onion. In a small bowl, whisk remaining ingredients until blended. Pour over apple mixture; toss to coat. Refrigerate until serving.
PER SERVING 96 cal., 2 g fat (trace sat. fat), 0 mg chol., 175 mg sodium, 20 g carb., 4 g fiber, 1 g pro. **Diabetic Exchanges:** 1 fruit, ½ fat.

Muffuletta Olive Salad

This is my version of a famous New Orleans salad. Enjoy it as a sandwich topping, or on toasted baguette slices as an appetizer. You could also make the recipe with diced ham and salami.

—**JUDY BATSON** TAMPA, FL

PREP: 25 MIN. + CHILLING
MAKES: 16 SERVINGS (¼ CUP EACH)

- ½ cup olive oil
- ¼ cup red wine vinegar
- 6 garlic cloves, minced
- 1 tablespoon dried oregano
- 1 tablespoon thinly sliced green onion
- 1 tablespoon minced fresh parsley
- 1 teaspoon crushed red pepper flakes
- 1½ cups green olives with pimientos, halved
- 1 cup coarsely chopped giardiniera
- ½ cup coarsely chopped pickled beets
- ½ cup pitted Greek olives, halved
- ⅓ cup roasted sweet red peppers, chopped
- ¼ cup finely chopped celery
- 1 tablespoon drained capers

In a large bowl, whisk the first seven ingredients. Add the remaining ingredients; toss to coat. Cover and refrigerate for at least eight hours, stirring occasionally. If desired, serve with toasted baguette slices.

MUFFULETTA OLIVE SALAD

PRALINE-TOPPED APPLE BREAD

Praline-Topped Apple Bread

Wondering what to serve your overnight guests for breakfast or brunch? Treat them to a delightful iced bread loaded with tangy apples and pecans.

—**SONJA BLOW** NIXA, MO

PREP: 30 MIN. • **BAKE:** 50 MIN. + COOLING
MAKES: 1 LOAF (16 SLICES)

- 2 cups all-purpose flour
- 2 teaspoons baking powder
- ½ teaspoon baking soda
- ½ teaspoon salt
- 1 cup sugar
- 1 cup (8 ounces) sour cream
- 2 eggs
- 3 teaspoons vanilla extract
- 1½ cups chopped peeled Granny Smith apples
- 1¼ cups chopped pecans, toasted, divided
- ½ cup butter, cubed
- ½ cup packed brown sugar

1. In a large bowl, mix flour, baking powder, baking soda and salt. In another bowl, beat sugar, sour cream, eggs and vanilla until well blended. Stir into flour mixture just until moistened. Fold in apples and 1 cup pecans.

2. Pour into a greased 9-in. x 5-in. loaf pan. Bake at 350° for 50-55 minutes or until a toothpick inserted into center comes out clean. Cool in pan 10 minutes. Remove to a wire rack; cool completely.

3. In a saucepan, mix butter and brown sugar. Bring to a boil; stir constantly to dissolve sugar. Boil 1 minute. Spoon over bread. Sprinkle with remaining pecans; let stand until set.

NOTE *To toast nuts, spread in a 15-in. x 10-in. x 1-in. baking pan. Bake at 350° for 5-10 minutes or until lightly browned, stirring occasionally. Or, spread in a dry nonstick skillet and heat over low heat until lightly browned, stirring occasionally.*

GREENS WITH HOMEMADE CROUTONS

Greens with Homemade Croutons

Fresh mixed greens get a flavorful boost from homemade croutons baked with tarragon, thyme and basil. It's one of my favorite salads because it's so simple to prepare and goes with everything.

—**ANN BUSH** COLORADO CITY, CO

PREP: 25 MIN. • **BAKE:** 15 MIN. • **MAKES:** 4 SERVINGS

- 5 slices day-old French bread (½ inch thick), cubed
- ¼ cup unsalted butter, melted
- 2 teaspoons minced fresh tarragon
- 2 teaspoons minced fresh thyme
- 1 teaspoon minced fresh basil
- ¼ teaspoon onion powder
- ¼ teaspoon garlic salt

DRESSING
- 3 tablespoons canola oil
- 2 tablespoons lime juice
- 2 teaspoons sugar
- ¼ teaspoon salt
  Dash celery salt

SALAD
- 2 cups spring mix salad greens
- 2 cups torn romaine or fresh baby spinach
- ½ small cucumber, thinly sliced
- 1 cup cherry tomatoes, halved
- 1 green onion, thinly sliced

1. Preheat oven to 325°. Place the bread cubes in a bowl. Drizzle with butter; toss lightly. Sprinkle with seasonings; toss to combine. Arrange in a single layer on an ungreased baking sheet. Bake 14-18 minutes or until golden brown, turning occasionally.

2. Meanwhile, in a small bowl, whisk dressing ingredients. In a large bowl, combine the salad ingredients. Just before serving, drizzle dressing over the salad; toss to coat. Top with croutons.

Caramel Apple Strudel

PREP: 35 MIN. + COOLING • **BAKE:** 25 MIN. • **MAKES:** 8 SERVINGS

- 5 medium apples, peeled and chopped (5 cups)
- ¾ cup apple cider or juice
- ¼ cup sugar
- ½ teaspoon ground cinnamon
- ¼ teaspoon ground allspice
- ¼ teaspoon ground cloves
- 1 frozen puff pastry sheet, thawed
- ¼ cup fat-free caramel ice cream topping
- 1 egg
- 1 tablespoon water
- 1 tablespoon coarse sugar
  Sweetened whipped cream and additional caramel ice cream topping, optional

1. Preheat oven to 375°. In a large saucepan, combine the first six ingredients. Bring to a boil. Reduce heat; simmer, uncovered, 15-20 minutes or until the apples are tender, stirring occasionally. Cool completely.

2. Unfold the puff pastry on a large sheet of parchment paper; roll into a 16-in. x 12-in. rectangle. Place a short side of the rectangle facing you. Using a slotted spoon, arrange apples on bottom half of pastry to within 1 in. of the edges. Drizzle apples with the caramel topping. Roll up jelly-roll style, starting with the bottom side. Pinch the seams to seal and tuck ends under.

3. In a small bowl, whisk the egg with water; brush over the pastry. Sprinkle with coarse sugar. Cut slits in the top. Bake 25-30 minutes or until golden brown. If desired, serve with whipped cream and additional caramel topping.

"Born in Vienna, my father told us how his mother used to cover all the kitchen counters with dough when making strudel. Caramel Apple Strudel is an easier, modern version of that dessert." —**SARAH HAENGEL** BOWIE, MD

CARAMEL APPLE STRUDEL

"Even guys who have big, hearty appetites snatch up these little bites filled with spinach dip."
—**KELLY WILLIAMS** FORKED RIVER, NJ

SPINACH DIP PULL-APARTS

Spinach Dip Pull-Aparts

PREP: 35 MIN. • **BAKE:** 45 MIN. + COOLING • **MAKES:** 15 SERVINGS

- 1 package (8 ounces) cream cheese, softened
- 2 garlic cloves, minced
- ¼ teaspoon pepper
- 1 package (10 ounces) frozen chopped spinach, thawed and squeezed dry
- ½ cup shredded part-skim mozzarella cheese
- ¼ cup grated Parmesan cheese
- ¼ cup mayonnaise
- 2 tubes (one 6 ounces, one 12 ounces) refrigerated buttermilk biscuits
  Marinara sauce, warmed, optional

1. Preheat oven to 350°. In a small bowl, beat the cream cheese, garlic and pepper until blended. Stir in spinach, cheeses and mayonnaise.

2. Separate the biscuit dough. Using a serrated knife, cut each biscuit horizontally in half. Wrap each half around 1 tablespoon of the spinach mixture, pinching to seal and forming a ball.

3. Layer in a greased 10-in. fluted tube pan. Bake 45 to 50 minutes or until golden brown. Cool in pan 10 minutes before inverting onto a serving plate. Serve warm with marinara sauce if desired.

Portobello Pasta Bake

Here's a recipe I always pull out after our Thanksgiving dinner. Leftover turkey never tasted so good!
—**PRECI D'SILVA** DUBAI, UAE

PREP: 20 MIN. • **BAKE:** 20 MIN. • **MAKES:** 4 SERVINGS

- 2½ cups uncooked multigrain spiral pasta
- 3 large portobello mushrooms
- 1 tablespoon olive oil
- 1 tablespoon butter
- 3 garlic cloves, minced
- 3 tablespoons all-purpose flour
- 1½ cups 2% milk
- ⅓ cup heavy whipping cream
- 2 cups cubed cooked turkey
- ¾ teaspoon salt
- ¼ teaspoon pepper
- 1 cup (4 ounces) shredded part-skim mozzarella cheese, divided
- 2 tablespoons grated Parmesan cheese

1. Cook pasta according to package directions. With a spoon, scrape and remove gills of mushrooms; slice caps.

2. In a large skillet, heat oil and butter over medium-high heat. Add sliced mushrooms; cook and stir until tender. Add garlic; cook 1 minute longer. Stir in flour until blended; gradually add milk and cream. Bring to a boil; cook and stir for 2 minutes or until thickened. Stir in the turkey, salt and pepper; heat through.

3. Drain pasta; add to turkey mixture and toss to coat. Stir in ¾ cup mozzarella cheese.

4. Transfer to a greased 8-in. square baking dish. Sprinkle with Parmesan cheese and remaining mozzarella cheese. Bake, uncovered, at 350° for 20-25 minutes or until cheese is melted.

PORTOBELLO PASTA BAKE

NICOLE CLAYTON'S PORK
CHOPS WITH HONEY-BALSAMIC
GLAZE *PAGE 250*

Quick Fixes

When there's **little time to cook**, skip pricey takeout and turn to this chapter for favorites that are ready to serve in **30 minutes or less**. Your family is sure to love the flavor-packed fare.

**SHARON REHM'S
QUICK & EASY HONEY MUSTARD**
PAGE 244

**BETH ROYALS' GRILLED SIRLOIN
KABOBS WITH PEACH SALSA**
PAGE 243

**STEPHANIE BARRON'S
TURKEY VERDE LETUCE WRAPS**
PAGE 245

(5) INGREDIENTS **EAT SMART**
Sesame Noodles with Shrimp & Snap Peas

Sometimes I stir chopped fresh cilantro into this tasty stir-fry just before serving.
—**NEDRA SCHELL** FORT WORTH, TX

START TO FINISH: 25 MIN.
MAKES: 4 SERVINGS

- 8 **ounces uncooked multigrain linguine**
- 1 **tablespoon canola oil**
- 1 **pound uncooked medium shrimp, peeled and deveined**
- 2 **cups fresh sugar snap peas, trimmed**
- ⅛ **teaspoon salt**
- ⅛ **teaspoon crushed red pepper flakes**
- ¾ **cup reduced-fat Asian toasted sesame salad dressing**

1. Cook linguine according to package directions for al dente.
2. Meanwhile, in a large skillet, heat oil over medium-high heat. Add the shrimp, peas, salt and pepper flakes; stir-fry 2-3 minutes or until shrimp turn pink and peas are crisp-tender. Drain linguine, reserving ¼ cup pasta water. Add the linguine, pasta water and salad dressing to shrimp mixture; toss to combine.

PER SERVING *418 cal., 10 g fat (1 g sat. fat), 138 mg chol., 646 mg sodium, 60 g carb., 8 g fiber, 29 g pro.*

HAM & BROCCOLI PASTA

SESAME NOODLES WITH SHRIMP & SNAP PEAS

(5) INGREDIENTS
Ham & Broccoli Pasta

My kids actually thank me when I make my all-in-one dinner of leftover cooked ham, broccoli and bow tie noodles. The simple but yummy sauce starts with spreadable chive and onion cream cheese.
—**JANA CATHEY** ADA, MI

START TO FINISH: 15 MIN.
MAKES: 6 SERVINGS

- 4½ **cups uncooked bow tie pasta (12 ounces)**
- 1 **package (16 ounces) frozen broccoli florets**
- 3 **cups cubed fully cooked ham**
- 1 **carton (8 ounces) spreadable chive and onion cream cheese**
- ⅓ **cup milk**
- ¼ **teaspoon salt**
- ½ **teaspoon pepper**

1. In a Dutch oven, cook the pasta according to package directions, adding the broccoli during the last 5 minutes of cooking; drain.
2. In the same pan, combine the remaining ingredients; cook and stir over medium heat until heated through and cream cheese is melted. Return the pasta mixture to the pan and toss to combine.

❓ Did you know?

Known as farfalle in Italian, bow tie pasta is believed to have been created in northern Italy as early as the 1500s. The sturdy pasta holds its shape well and is a great choice for heavy tomato and cream sauces as well as hearty casseroles.

Pork Tenderloin with Zesty Italian Sauce

We think my Italian pork entree goes best with garlic mashed potatoes and fresh green beans or corn on the cob.

—JOE VINCE PORT HURON, MI

START TO FINISH: 25 MIN.
MAKES: 4 SERVINGS

- 1 **pork tenderloin (1 pound), cut into 8 slices**
- ½ **teaspoon salt**
- ¼ **teaspoon pepper**
- 1 **tablespoon canola oil**
- ½ **cup white wine or chicken broth**
- ½ **cup zesty Italian salad dressing**
- 1 **tablespoon butter**

1. Sprinkle the pork with salt and pepper. In a large skillet, heat oil over medium-high heat. Brown pork, about 2 minutes on each side; remove from the pan.

2. Add wine to pan, stirring to loosen browned bits from the bottom. Bring to a boil; cook until liquid is reduced by about half. Stir in the dressing. Reduce heat; simmer, uncovered, 1-2 minutes or until slightly thickened.

3. Return the pork to pan; simmer, covered, for 3-5 minutes or until a thermometer inserted in pork reads 145°. Stir in butter. Let pork rest for 5 minutes before serving.

Grilled Sirloin Kabobs with Peach Salsa

Fresh peaches, peach preserves and peach salsa combine for a fruity addition to these kabobs. It's a wonderful balance of sweet and zippy flavors.

—BETH ROYALS RICHMOND, VA

START TO FINISH: 25 MIN.
MAKES: 6 SERVINGS

- 3 **tablespoons peach preserves**
- 1 **tablespoon finely chopped seeded jalapeno pepper**
- 1 **beef top sirloin steak (1½ pounds), cut into 1-inch cubes**
- ½ **teaspoon salt**
- ¼ **teaspoon pepper**
- 3 **medium peaches, cut into sixths**
- 1½ **cups peach salsa**

1. In a small bowl, mix the peach preserves and jalapeno pepper. Season the beef with salt and pepper. Alternately thread the beef and the peaches onto six metal or soaked wooden skewers.

2. Moisten a paper towel with cooking oil; using long-handled tongs, rub on grill rack to coat lightly. Grill kabobs, covered, over medium heat or broil 4 in. from heat 6-8 minutes or until beef reaches the desired doneness, turning occasionally. Remove from grill; brush with preserves mixture. Serve with salsa.

PER SERVING *219 cal., 5 g fat (2 g sat. fat), 46 mg chol., 427 mg sodium, 17 g carb., 3 g fiber, 25 g pro.* **Diabetic Exchanges:** *3 lean meat, ½ starch, ½ fruit.*

GRILLED SIRLOIN KABOBS WITH PEACH SALSA

BBQ CHICKEN POLENTA WITH FRIED EGG

QUICK FIXES

"In college, I used to fix myself a fried egg breakfast with chicken and polenta before class. Now I cook it for friends and family."

—**EVAN JANNEY** LOS ANGELES, CA

BBQ Chicken Polenta with Fried Egg

START TO FINISH: 25 MIN.
MAKES: 4 SERVINGS

- 2 **cups shredded cooked chicken breasts**
- ¾ **cup barbecue sauce**
- 1 **tablespoon minced fresh cilantro**
- 2 **tablespoons olive oil, divided**
- 1 **tube (1 pound) polenta, cut into 8 slices**
- 1 **small garlic clove, minced**
- 4 **eggs**

1. In a small saucepan, combine the chicken, barbecue sauce and cilantro; heat through over medium heat, stirring occasionally.
2. In a large skillet, heat 1 tablespoon oil over medium-high heat. Add the polenta; cook 2-3 minutes on each side or until lightly browned. Transfer to a serving plate; keep warm.
3. In the same pan, heat the remaining oil over medium-high heat. Add the garlic; cook and stir 1 minute. Break the eggs, one at a time, into the pan. Reduce heat to low. Cook until desired doneness, turning after the whites are set, if desired. Serve over polenta with chicken mixture.

⑤ INGREDIENTS

Quick & Easy Honey Mustard

This simple homemade mustard has more flavor than any store-bought version or restaurant specialty I've ever tried. And the recipe requires just three ingredients!
—**SHARON REHM** NEW BLAINE, AR

START TO FINISH: 5 MIN. • **MAKES:** 1 CUP

- ½ **cup stone-ground mustard**
- ¼ **cup honey**
- ¼ **cup rice vinegar**

In a small bowl, whisk all ingredients. Refrigerate until serving.

QUICK & EASY HONEY MUSTARD

TURKEY VERDE LETTUCE WRAPS

Blueberry-Rhubarb Crisp

For a special treat, top this microwaved dessert with a scoop of vanilla ice cream.

—**LORRI CAMPBELL** MANKATO, MN

PREP/TOTAL TIME: 25 MIN.
MAKES: 6 SERVINGS

- 2-½ cups diced fresh or frozen rhubarb, thawed
- ⅓ cup sugar
- 2 tablespoons all-purpose flour
- 1 can (21 ounces) blueberry pie filling

TOPPING
- ¾ cup all-purpose flour
- ¾ cup old-fashioned oats
- ⅓ cup packed brown sugar
- ¾ teaspoon ground cinnamon
- ½ cup cold butter, cubed

1. In a 2-qt. microwave-safe dish, combine the rhubarb, sugar and flour. Cover and microwave on high for 3 minutes; stir. Add pie filling.
2. In a small bowl, combine the flour, oats, brown sugar and cinnamon. Cut in butter until the mixture is crumbly; sprinkle over fruit. Cover and cook 4-5 minutes longer or until bubbly and rhubarb is tender. Serve warm.
NOTES *If using frozen rhubarb, measure rhubarb while still frozen, then thaw completely. Drain in a colander, but do not press liquid out. This recipe was tested in a 1,100-watt microwave.*

BLUEBERRY-RHUBARB CRISP

---

⑤INGREDIENTS EAT SMART
Turkey Verde Lettuce Wraps

Some lettuce wraps may seem like bland "health food," but this turkey filling with salsa will tingle your taste buds.

—**STEPHANIE BARRON** LAKE ORION, MI

START TO FINISH: 25 MIN.
MAKES: 6 SERVINGS

- 2 packages (17.6 ounces each) turkey breast cutlets, cut into 1-inch strips
- 4 teaspoons olive oil
- 1 teaspoon garlic salt
- ¼ teaspoon pepper
- 1 cup salsa verde
- 12 romaine leaves

1. In a large bowl, combine the turkey strips, oil, garlic salt and pepper. Heat a large skillet over medium-high heat. Add the turkey mixture in batches; cook and stir 2-4 minutes or until no longer pink.
2. Return all turkey to the pan. Stir in the salsa verde; heat through. Serve in romaine leaves.
PER SERVING *229 cal., 4 g fat (1 g sat. fat), 103 mg chol., 617 mg sodium, 3 g carb., 1 g fiber, 42 g pro.* **Diabetic Exchanges:** *5 lean meat, ½ fat.*

---

⑤INGREDIENTS Roasted
Salmon & White Bean Spinach Salad

Like salmon? Here's your catch of the day—baked fillets on a bed of greens and veggies dressed with a vinaigrette.

—**FRANCES PIETSCH** FLOWER MOUND, TX

START TO FINISH: 25 MIN.
MAKES: 4 SERVINGS

- 4 salmon fillets (6 ounces each)
- ¼ teaspoon salt
- ¼ teaspoon pepper
- 1 can (15½ ounces) great northern beans, rinsed and drained
- ½ cup prepared vinaigrette
- 1 package (11 ounces) fresh baby spinach
- 1 small red onion, cut into thin wedges

1. Place salmon on a greased 15-in. x 10-in. x 1-in. baking pan; sprinkle with salt and pepper. Bake at 400° for 11-13 minutes or until fish flakes easily with a fork. Cool slightly.
2. Meanwhile, in a large bowl, toss beans with the vinaigrette; set aside.
3. Just before serving, add spinach and onion to bean mixture; toss to combine. Divide among four plates. Top with salmon.

QUICK SHEPHERD'S PIE

Sliced apples and doughnut holes
or vanilla ice cream
Optional toppings: chopped salted
nuts, jimmies or miniature
chocolate chips

1. Place apple juice and cinnamon stick in a small saucepan. Bring to a boil; cook until liquid is reduced to ½ cup, about 10 minutes. Discard cinnamon stick.

2. Reduce the heat to medium; add the caramel bits, half at a time, whisking after each addition until the caramels are melted. Stir in the heavy whipping cream; keep warm until ready to serve.

3. Transfer to a serving dish; serve warm with apples slices and doughnut holes for dipping. Glaze can also be spooned over ice cream. If desired, sprinkle with toppings. (Warm the glaze in microwave if mixture becomes too thick.)

(5)INGREDIENTS
Quick Shepherd's Pie

Have homemade mashed potatoes left over from dinner? Use them instead of the refrigerated kind for this fuss-free, satisfying pie.

—JENNIFER EARLY EAST LANSING, MI

START TO FINISH: 20 MIN.
MAKES: 4 SERVINGS

- 1 tub (24 ounces) refrigerated cheddar mashed potatoes
- 1 pound lean ground beef (90% lean)
- 1 envelope mushroom gravy mix
- 1½ cups frozen mixed vegetables
- 1 cup water
- ⅛ teaspoon pepper

1. Heat the potatoes according to the package directions.

2. Meanwhile, in a large skillet, cook the beef over medium heat for 6-8 minutes or until no longer pink, breaking into crumbles; drain. Stir in the gravy mix. Add the vegetables and water; bring to a boil. Reduce the heat; simmer until heated through, stirring occasionally.

3. Transfer to a 9-in. square baking pan. Spread the potatoes over top; sprinkle with pepper. Broil 4-6 in. from the heat for 10-15 minutes or until golden brown.

(5)INGREDIENTS Creamy Caramel-Apple Glaze

This easy caramel was a happy discovery. The glaze is perfect not only for dipping, but also for drizzling over vanilla ice cream.
—SHANNON ROUM WAUKESHA, WI

START TO FINISH: 25 MIN. • **MAKES:** ¾ CUP

- 1½ cups unsweetened apple juice
- 1 cinnamon stick (3 inches)
- 1 cup Kraft caramel bits
- 1 tablespoon heavy whipping cream

? Did you know?

Granny Smith apples are ideal for caramel coatings and glazes when you want the tongue-tingling appeal of a sweet-tart flavor combination.

CREAMY CARAMEL-APPLE GLAZE

Cara's Crunchy Chicken Strips

Crushed croutons are the crunchy secret to my baked chicken tenders. Pair them with your family's favorite sauce.

—**CARA WINTERHOFF** TEMPE, AZ

START TO FINISH: 30 MIN.
MAKES: 6 SERVINGS

- ½ **cup biscuit/baking mix**
- ½ **teaspoon salt**
- ¼ **teaspoon pepper**
- 1 **cup crushed Caesar salad croutons**
- 2 **eggs, lightly beaten**
- 1½ **pounds boneless skinless chicken breasts, cut into 1-inch strips**
- 2 **tablespoons butter, melted**
  Dipping sauce of your choice

1. In a shallow bowl, mix the baking mix, salt and pepper. Place the crushed croutons and eggs in separate shallow bowls. Dip the chicken strips in the baking mix to coat both sides; shake off excess. Dip in the eggs, then in the croutons, patting to help the crouton coating adhere.

2. Arrange in a single layer on a greased 15-in. x 10-in. x 1-in. baking pan. Drizzle with butter. Bake chicken at 450° for 10-12 minutes or until it is no longer pink, turning once. Serve with dipping sauce.

CARA'S CRUNCHY CHICKEN STRIPS

GRILLED PROVOLONE & PEPPERONI

(5)INGREDIENTS
Grilled Provolone & Pepperoni

One day I wanted to try jazzing up this lunchtime favorite, so I exchanged the butter for some garlic spread and added slices of pepperoni. I couldn't resist having seconds!

—JENNIFER ZUNIGA DENVER, CO

START TO FINISH: 20 MIN. • **MAKES:** 4 SANDWICHES

- 4 slices provolone cheese
- 16 slices pepperoni
- 12 red onion rings
- 8 slices Italian bread (½ inch thick)
- 4 teaspoons garlic spread

1. Layer the cheese, pepperoni and onion on four bread slices; top with the remaining bread. Spread the outsides of sandwiches with garlic spread.

2. In a large skillet, toast the sandwiches over medium heat for 2-4 minutes on each side or until golden brown and the cheese is melted.

(5)INGREDIENTS
Ham & Swiss Melts

Who knew that the humble pickle could add so much pep to a ham melt? Splitting the big French baguette four ways gives each person a manageable size for devouring.

—LOUISE GILBERT QUESNEL, BC

START TO FINISH: 25 MIN. • **MAKES:** 4 SERVINGS

- 1 French bread baguette (10½ ounces)
- 16 slices Swiss cheese
- 8 thin sandwich pickle slices
- 4 slices deli ham
- ½ teaspoon paprika

1. Cut baguette in half without slicing through completely. Arrange half of the cheese on bottom half. Top with pickles, ham and remaining cheese; sprinkle with paprika. Close sandwich; cut crosswise into four pieces.

2. Transfer to an ungreased baking sheet. Bake at 350° for 12-15 minutes or until cheese is melted.

HAM & SWISS MELTS

(5) INGREDIENTS
Grilled Havarti & Mushrooms

This sandwich is in a league all its own. A crisp buttery exterior surrounds creamy Havarti and fresh mushrooms. A friend of mine said she didn't think she'd like it, but one bite won her over!
—**JUDITH POLITZER** BURTON, OH

START TO FINISH: 20 MIN. • **MAKES:** 4 SERVINGS

- 12 **ounces Havarti cheese with dill, thinly sliced**
- 8 **slices onion rye or other bakery bread (round loaf)**
- 2 **medium tomatoes, sliced**
- 1 **cup sliced fresh mushrooms**
- ¼ **cup butter, softened**

1. Place half of the cheese on four bread slices; top with tomatoes, mushrooms and remaining cheese. Spread outsides of sandwiches with butter.

2. In a large skillet, toast the sandwiches over medium heat for 3-4 minutes on each side or golden brown and the cheese is melted.

(5) INGREDIENTS
Tomato-Basil Grilled Cheese

When my teenage daughter and I were in a coffee shop, she tried a tomato-filled grilled cheese featuring fresh basil. She enjoyed it so much, I had to duplicate it at home.
—**KATHRYN HUDSON** BETHEL PARK, PA

START TO FINISH: 20 MIN. • **MAKES:** 4 SERVINGS

- 8 **ounces fresh mozzarella cheese, sliced**
- ¼ **cup minced fresh basil**
- 2 **medium tomatoes, sliced**
- 8 **slices sourdough bread**
  Salt and pepper to taste
- 2 **tablespoons butter, softened**

1. Layer the mozzarella cheese, basil and tomatoes on four bread slices. Sprinkle the tomatoes with salt and pepper. Top with the remaining bread. Spread the outsides of the sandwiches with butter.

2. Cook in a preheated panini maker or indoor electric grill until bread is browned and cheese is melted.

(5) INGREDIENTS
Grilled Cheese & Prosciutto

I found a kalamata olive loaf at my local market in central Missouri. Using that instead of the typical white bread is the key to these crowd-pleasers. They're good with herbed Italian bread, too.
—**AMY DODSON** COLUMBIA, MO

START TO FINISH: 15 MIN. • **MAKES:** 6 SANDWICHES

- 12 **slices provolone cheese**
- 12 **thin slices prosciutto**
- 12 **thin slices hard salami**
- 12 **slices Italian or kalamata olive bread**
- ¼ **cup butter, softened**

1. Layer the provolone, prosciutto and salami on six bread slices; top with remaining bread. Spread the outsides of sandwiches with butter.

2. In a large skillet, toast the sandwiches over medium heat for 2-3 minutes on each side or until golden brown and the cheese is melted.

TOMATO-BASIL GRILLED CHEESE

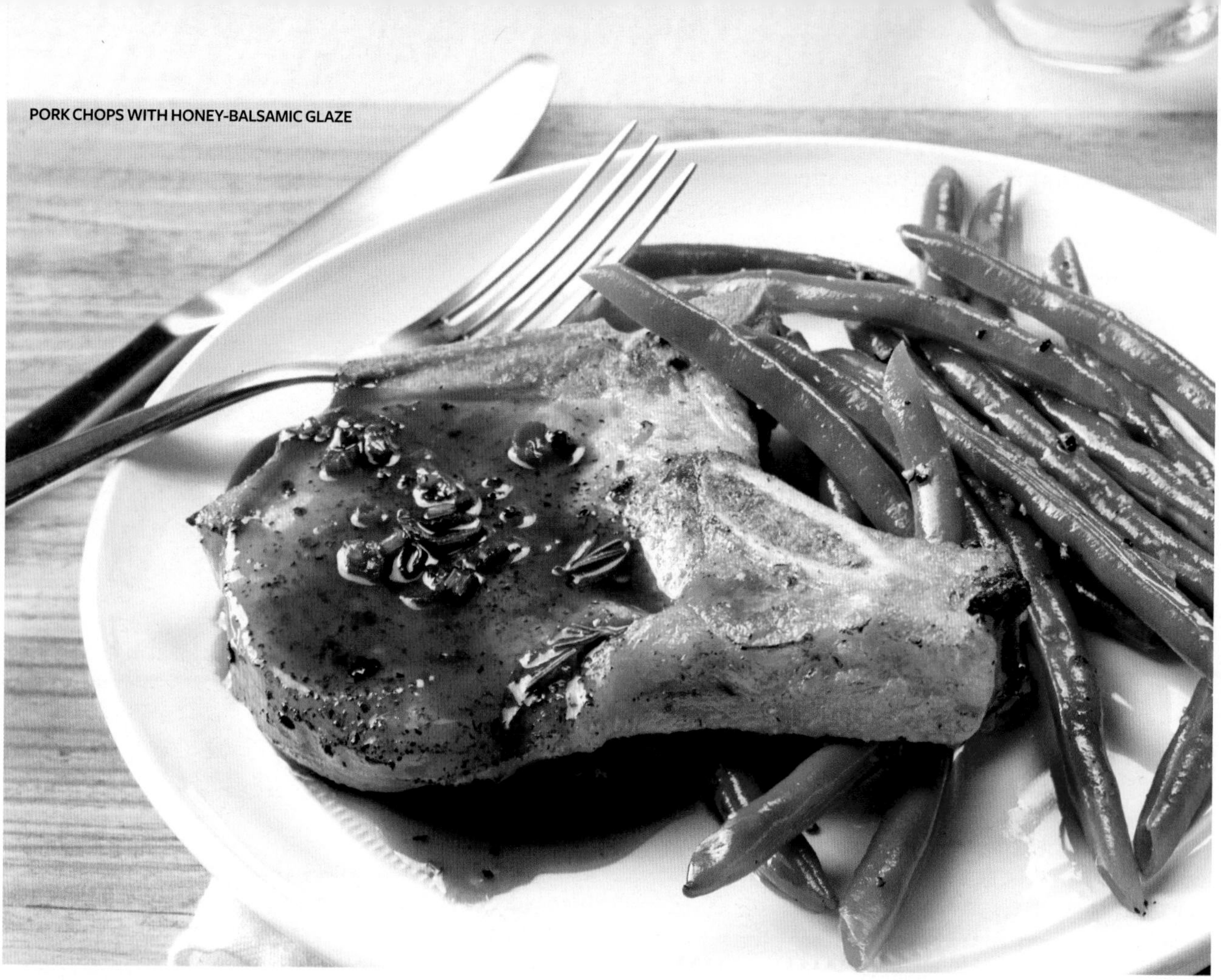

QUICK FIXES

PORK CHOPS WITH HONEY-BALSAMIC GLAZE

Pork Chops with Honey-Balsamic Glaze

My husband loves pork chops, so I try to find new ways to fix them. He says my glazed version belongs in a restaurant!

—**NICOLE CLAYTON** PRESCOTT, AZ

START TO FINISH: 30 MIN.
MAKES: 4 SERVINGS

- **4 bone-in pork loin chops (1 inch thick and 10 ounces each)**
- **½ teaspoon crushed red pepper flakes**
- **½ teaspoon salt**
- **½ teaspoon pepper**
- **2 tablespoons olive oil**

GLAZE

- **½ cup balsamic vinegar**
- **½ cup honey**
- **3 green onions, chopped**
- **2 garlic cloves, minced**
- **1 teaspoon minced fresh rosemary or ¼ teaspoon dried rosemary, crushed**
- **⅛ teaspoon salt**
- **⅛ teaspoon pepper**
- **¼ cup butter, cubed**

1. Sprinkle the pork chops with pepper flakes, salt and pepper. In a large skillet, heat oil over medium heat. Add pork; cook for 5-7 minutes on each side or until a thermometer reads 145°. Remove and keep warm.

2. In the same skillet, whisk vinegar, honey, green onions, garlic, rosemary, salt and pepper; bring to a boil. Reduce the heat; simmer glaze, uncovered, 6-8 minutes or until thickened slightly, stirring occasionally. Remove from the heat; whisk in the butter until melted. Serve with pork chops.

(5) INGREDIENTS

Apple & Cheddar Salad

Refreshing and easy to make, this medley is bound to become your go-to salad. Shredded cheddar cheese is the perfect complement to the crisp apples.

—**TASTE OF HOME TEST KITCHEN**

START TO FINISH: 10 MIN.
MAKES: 10 SERVINGS

- **12 cups fresh baby spinach**
- **⅔ cup honey Dijon vinaigrette**
- **1 large apple, thinly sliced**
- **⅔ cup salad croutons**
- **⅔ cup shredded cheddar cheese**

Place spinach in a large bowl. Drizzle with the vinaigrette; toss to coat. Top with apple slices, croutons and cheese. Serve immediately.

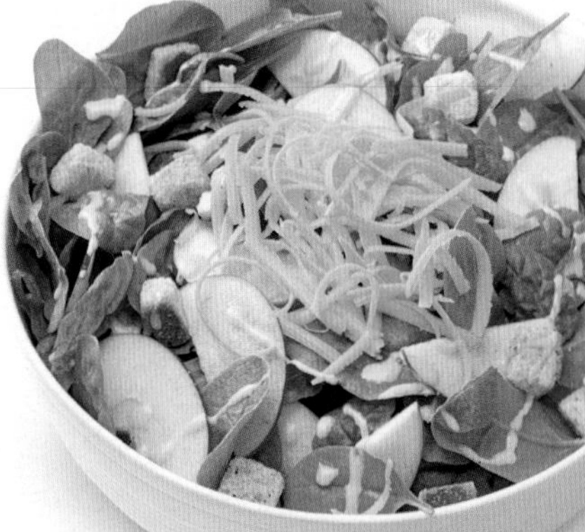

APPLE & CHEDDAR SALAD

BBQ & RANCH CHICKEN PIZZA

⑤ INGREDIENTS

BBQ & Ranch Chicken Pizza

I was looking for different dinner ideas for my kids and came up with a barbecue chicken pizza. They couldn't get enough!
—**SUE SITLER** BLOOMSBURG, PA

START TO FINISH: 30 MIN.
MAKES: 8 SERVINGS

- 2 **tubes (8 ounces each) refrigerated crescent rolls**
- ½ **cup hickory smoke-flavored barbecue sauce, divided**
- ¼ **cup prepared ranch salad dressing**
- 3 **cups cubed cooked chicken breasts**
- 2 **cups (8 ounces) shredded pizza cheese blend**

1. Unroll both tubes of crescent dough and press onto the bottom and up the sides of an ungreased 15-in. x 10-in. x 1-in. baking pan, pressing perforations to seal. Bake at 375° for 8-10 minutes or until lightly browned.
2. In a small bowl, mix ¼ cup of the barbecue sauce and salad dressing; spread over the crust. In another bowl, toss chicken with remaining barbecue sauce. Arrange over the top. Sprinkle with cheese. Bake for 15-20 minutes or until the crust is golden brown and the cheese is melted.

Garlic Guidelines

When buying fresh garlic, choose bulbs that feel firm and have a lot of dry, papery covering. Avoid bulbs with sprouts from the top of the cloves. Those garlic bulbs are older and may be bitter. The freshest sources of garlic are local farmers markets. Store garlic away from sunlight but in a well-ventilated container, such as a garlic keeper.

⑤ INGREDIENTS

Crispy Garlic-Broiled Chicken Thighs

These chicken thighs don't skimp on the garlic—and the resulting flavor is fantastic! During the summer months, I'll cook them on the grill instead of in the oven.
—**KELLEY FRENCH** COLCHESTER, VT

START TO FINISH: 25 MIN.
MAKES: 4 SERVINGS

- ⅓ **cup butter, melted**
- ¼ **cup reduced-sodium soy sauce**
- 7 **garlic cloves, minced**
- ½ **teaspoon pepper**
- 8 **bone-in chicken thighs (about 3 pounds)**

1. In a large bowl, mix the butter, soy sauce, garlic and pepper. Reserve ¼ cup soy mixture for basting. Add the chicken to remaining soy mixture; turn to coat.
2. Place the chicken on a broiler pan, skin side down. Broil 4-6 in. from the heat for 10-15 minutes on each side or until a thermometer reads 180°. Brush occasionally with the reserved soy mixture during the last 10 minutes of cooking.

CRISPY GARLIC-BROILED CHICKEN THIGHS

Speedy Soups

Why wait to enjoy a heartwarming bowlful of homemade soup? The comforting bean, tomato, turkey and ravioli specialties here all come together in just 30 minutes or less.

FIESTA TURKEY TORTILLA SOUP

Fire-Roasted Tomato Soup

Here's my take on a classic. The fire-roasted tomatoes add a bit of heat, which I like to balance with the coolness of sour cream.
—**CATHY HALL** LYNDHURST, VA

START TO FINISH: 25 MIN. • **MAKES:** 6 SERVINGS

- 2 **cans (10¾ ounces each) condensed tomato soup, undiluted**
- 2 **cans (one 12 ounces, one 5 ounces) evaporated milk**
- 1 **can (14½ ounces) fire-roasted diced tomatoes, undrained**
- ¼ **cup sour cream**
- ¼ **cup shredded cheddar cheese**
- 2 **tablespoons bacon bits**

In a large saucepan, combine the soup, evaporated milk and tomatoes; cook over medium heat until heated through, stirring occasionally. Top servings with sour cream, cheese and bacon bits.

"For this Southwestern recipe, I use leftover turkey or even rotisserie chicken for a great shortcut."
—**AMY MCFADDEN** CHELSEA, AL

Fiesta Turkey Tortilla Soup

START TO FINISH: 25 MIN. • **MAKES:** 8 SERVINGS

- 4 **cans (14½ ounces each) chicken broth**
- 3 **cups shredded cooked turkey or rotisserie chicken**
- 1 **can (15 ounces) black beans, rinsed and drained**
- 1 **can (15¼ ounces) whole kernel corn, drained**
- ½ **cup medium salsa**
- 5 **corn tortillas (6 inches), cut into ¼-inch strips**
- ¼ **cup chopped fresh cilantro**
  Additional salsa, optional

1. In a Dutch oven, combine the first five ingredients; bring to a boil. Reduce the heat; simmer for 10 minutes, stirring occasionally.
2. Meanwhile, spread tortilla strips in a single layer on a baking sheet. Bake at 400° for 4-6 minutes or until golden brown and crisp.
3. Stir cilantro into soup. Top servings with tortilla strips. If desired, serve with additional salsa.

FIRE-ROASTED TOMATO SOUP

QUICK RAVIOLI & SPINACH SOUP

(5) INGREDIENTS

Quick Ravioli & Spinach Soup

I love Italian food but wanted a quicker version of traditional wedding soup. Refrigerated ravioli speeds up the preparation.
—CYNTHIA BENT NEWARK, DE

START TO FINISH: 25 MIN. • **MAKES:** 6 SERVINGS

- 2 cartons (32 ounces each) chicken broth
- ¼ teaspoon onion powder
  Dash pepper
- 1 package (9 ounces) refrigerated small cheese ravioli
- 4 cups coarsely chopped fresh spinach (about 4 ounces)
- 3 cups shredded cooked chicken
  Grated Parmesan cheese, optional

In a large saucepan, combine the chicken broth, onion powder and pepper; bring to a boil. Add the cheese ravioli; cook, uncovered, for 7-10 minutes or until tender. Add the spinach and chicken during the last 3 minutes of cooking. If desired, serve with Parmesan cheese.

(5) INGREDIENTS

Hearty Cannellini & Sausage Soup

On a chilly fall or winter day, is there anything better than a bowl of flavorful broth filled with smoked sausage, creamy cannellini beans and chunks of hearty cabbage? I don't think so!
—PAULINE WHITE EL CAJON, CA

START TO FINISH: 30 MIN. • **MAKES:** 6 SERVINGS

- 12 ounces beef summer or smoked sausage, cut into ½-inch pieces
- 4½ cups vegetable broth
- 2 cans (15 ounces each) cannellini or white kidney beans, rinsed and drained
- 4 cups coarsely chopped napa or Chinese cabbage
- 3 green onions, chopped
- ¼ teaspoon salt
- ¼ teaspoon pepper

In a large saucepan, cook and stir sausage over medium heat until lightly browned; drain. Add the remaining ingredients; bring to a boil. Reduce heat; simmer for 5-10 minutes or until cabbage is tender and flavors are blended.

Napa Cabbage Clues

Napa cabbage—also known as Chinese, Peking or celery cabbage—has a mild flavor and is sweeter than regular cabbage. The long, thin leaves are crinkly pale green around the edge, and the centers and stem ends are white. Purchase heads that feel heavy and are compact, with crisp, fresh-looking leaves. Store them unwashed in an open plastic bag in the refrigerator crisper drawer for about 5 days. Napa cabbage can be used in many recipes that call for regular cabbage, such as stir-fries, salads and soups.

HEARTY CANNELLINI & SAUSAGE SOUP

⑤ INGREDIENTS EAT SMART
Chicken & Vegetable Curry Couscous

With just a few convenience items—frozen vegetables and a flavored couscous mix—you'll have dinner on the table in a flash.

—ELIZABETH HOKANSON ARBORG, MB

START TO FINISH: 25 MIN. • **MAKES:** 6 SERVINGS

- 1 **tablespoon butter**
- 1 **pound boneless skinless chicken breasts, cut into strips**
- 1 **package (16 ounces) frozen vegetable blend of your choice**
- 1¼ **cups water**
- 1 **package (5.7 ounces) curry-flavored couscous mix**
- ½ **cup raisins**

1. In a large nonstick skillet, heat butter over medium-high heat. Add chicken; cook and stir until no longer pink.

2. Add the vegetable blend, water and contents of couscous seasoning packet. Bring to a boil; stir in the couscous and raisins. Remove from heat; let stand, covered, 5 minutes or until water is absorbed. Fluff with a fork.

PER SERVING *273 cal., 4 g fat (2 g sat. fat), 47 mg chol., 311 mg sodium, 39 g carb., 4 g fiber, 21 g pro.* **Diabetic Exchanges:** *2 starch, 2 lean meat, 1 vegetable, ½ fat.*

SPICY CAJUN SALSA BURGERS

Spicy Cajun Salsa Burgers

Creole seasoning, red pepper flakes, garlic powder and salsa will really jazz up the burgers at your next cookout.

—DAVID DALTON ORLEANS, IN

START TO FINISH: 20 MIN. • **MAKES:** 4 SERVINGS

- ½ **cup salsa**
- 1 **teaspoon Creole seasoning**
- ½ **teaspoon garlic powder**
- ½ **teaspoon crushed red pepper flakes**
- ½ **teaspoon pepper**
- 1 **pound ground beef**
- 4 **kaiser rolls, split and toasted**

1. In a large bowl, combine the first five ingredients. Add the beef; mix lightly but thoroughly. Shape into four ½-in.-thick patties.

2. Grill burgers, covered, over medium heat or broil 4 in. from heat 4-5 minutes on each side or until a thermometer reads 160°. Serve on rolls.

NOTE *The following spices may be substituted for 1 teaspoon Creole seasoning: ¼ teaspoon each salt, garlic powder and paprika; and a pinch each of dried thyme, ground cumin and cayenne pepper.*

CHICKEN & VEGETABLE CURRY COUSCOUS

Creamy Tomato Tortellini with Sausage

It's hard to believe that only three simple ingredients go into this tomato sauce. It tastes like it bubbled away all day on top of the stove but takes less than half an hour to prepare.

—**JENNIFER EGGERT** SCOTTSDALE, AZ

START TO FINISH: 25 MIN. • **MAKES:** 6 SERVINGS

- 1 package (19 ounces) frozen cheese tortellini
- 2 fully cooked Italian chicken sausage links (3 ounces each), sliced
- 1 can (14½ ounces) diced tomatoes with garlic and onion, undrained
- 1 package (6 ounces) fresh baby spinach
- 4 ounces reduced-fat cream cheese

1. Cook the tortellini according to the package directions. Meanwhile, in a large nonstick skillet coated with cooking spray, cook and stir the sausage over medium-high heat 4-5 minutes or until browned. Add tomatoes and spinach; cook and stir just until spinach is wilted. Stir in the cream cheese until melted.

2. Drain the tortellini; add to the sausage mixture. Toss to combine.

PER SERVING *298 cal., 13 g fat (6 g sat. fat), 49 mg chol., 824 mg sodium, 31 g carb., 2 g fiber, 17 g pro.*

CREAMY TOMATO TORTELLINI WITH SAUSAGE

SAGE & BROWNED BUTTER RAVIOLI

Sage & Browned Butter Ravioli

After sampling a delicious ravioli specialty in Italy, we planted sage in our garden to be sure we could re-create that dish at home. Now we can enjoy an easy weeknight supper that uses the fruits of our labor and brings back memories of our trip.

—**RHONDA HAMILTON** PORTSMOUTH, OH

START TO FINISH: 30 MIN. • **MAKES:** 4 SERVINGS

- 1 package (20 ounces) refrigerated cheese ravioli or 2 packages (9 ounces each) mushroom agnolotti
- ½ cup butter, cubed
- ½ cup coarsely chopped fresh sage
- ½ teaspoon salt
- 2 tablespoons lemon juice
- ¼ cup shredded Parmesan cheese

1. Cook the cheese ravioli according to the package directions. In a large heavy saucepan, melt the butter over medium heat. Heat 5-7 minutes or until golden brown, stirring constantly. Immediately stir in the sage and salt; remove from the heat.

2. Drain the ravioli, reserving 2 tablespoons pasta water. Add ravioli, pasta water and lemon juice to butter mixture; gently toss to coat. Serve with cheese.

> "There's nothing better than turning out a really quick dinner that's also wholesome, hearty and popular with everyone. This Salsa Skillet Pork Chops recipe is a keeper."
>
> —**DEANNA ELLETT** BOYNTON BEACH, FL

⑤INGREDIENTS **EAT SMART**
Salsa Skillet Pork Chops

START TO FINISH: 30 MIN.
MAKES: 6 SERVINGS

- **6 boneless pork loin chops (6 ounces each)**
- **½ teaspoon salt**
- **¼ teaspoon pepper**
- **2 cups fresh whole kernel corn**
- **1 can (15 ounces) pinto beans, rinsed and drained**
- **1¼ cups chunky salsa**
- **2 tablespoons water**
- **1 teaspoon ground cumin**

1. Sprinkle chops with salt and pepper. Heat a large nonstick skillet coated with cooking spray over medium heat. Brown chops on both sides in batches.
2. Return all the chops to pan. Add the remaining ingredients; bring to a boil. Reduce heat; simmer, covered, 6-8 minutes or until thermometer inserted in pork reads 145°. Let stand 5 minutes before serving.
PER SERVING *366 cal., 11 g fat (4 g sat. fat), 82 mg chol., 548 mg sodium, 29 g carb., 4 g fiber, 38 g pro.* **Diabetic Exchanges:** *2 starch, 5 lean meat.*

APPLE-GOUDA MELTS

⑤INGREDIENTS
Apple-Gouda Melts
Here's a grown-up version of a classic sandwich our whole family loves.
—**CHERYLIN BIRKHOLZ** MARYSVILLE, CA

START TO FINISH: 15 MIN.
MAKES: 6 SERVINGS

- **6 slices seeded whole grain bread**
- **4 tablespoons butter, softened, divided**
- **6 ounces fresh mozzarella cheese, sliced**
- **1 large apple, thinly sliced**
- **6 ounces smoked Gouda cheese, sliced**

1. Arrange bread on a baking sheet; spread tops with half of the butter. Broil bread 4-6 in. from the heat for 1-2 minutes or until lightly toasted.
2. Turn bread over; spread tops with remaining butter. Layer with the mozzarella cheese, apple slices and Gouda cheese. Broil 3-4 minutes longer or until cheese is melted.

SALSA SKILLET PORK CHOPS

TANGY CHICKEN & PEPPERS

"We can't get enough of this tasty chicken. It's terrific!"
—**DONNA MCLEOD** BENTONVILLE, AR

(5) INGREDIENTS **EAT SMART**
Tangy Chicken & Peppers

START TO FINISH: 30 MIN.
MAKES: 6 SERVINGS

- 6 **boneless skinless chicken breast halves (6 ounces each)**
- ½ **teaspoon salt**
- ¼ **teaspoon pepper**
- 1 **package (16 ounces) frozen pepper and onion stir-fry blend**
- 1 **jar (16 ounces) pineapple salsa**
- 1 **can (11 ounces) mandarin oranges, drained**
- 4½ **cups hot cooked brown rice or hot cooked rice**

1. Sprinkle chicken with salt and pepper. Heat a large nonstick skillet coated with cooking spray over medium heat. Brown the chicken in batches; remove from pan.
2. In same pan, add stir-fry blend and pineapple salsa; bring to a boil, stirring occasionally. Return the chicken to pan; reduce heat. Simmer, covered, 12-15 minutes or until a thermometer inserted in chicken reads 165°. Stir in oranges; heat through. Serve with rice.
PER SERVING *422 cal., 5 g fat (1 g sat. fat), 94 mg chol., 519 mg sodium, 50 g carb., 6 g fiber, 39 g pro.*

(5) INGREDIENTS
Garlicky Beef & Tomatoes with Pasta

Feeling like pasta? Make it a complete meal with ground beef, chopped spinach, diced tomatoes and beans.
—**LISA DIFFELL** CORINTH, ME

START TO FINISH: 20 MIN.
MAKES: 6 SERVINGS

- 1 **package (16 ounces) uncooked bow tie pasta**
- 1 **pound ground beef**
- ¼ **teaspoon salt**
- 2 **cans (14½ ounces each) diced tomatoes with roasted garlic, undrained**
- 1 **can (15 ounces) white kidney or cannellini beans, rinsed and drained**
- 1 **package (10 ounces) frozen chopped spinach, thawed and squeezed dry**

Cook the bow tie pasta according to the package directions. Meanwhile, in a large skillet, cook the beef over medium heat 6-8 minutes or until no longer pink, breaking into crumbles; drain. Sprinkle the beef with salt. Stir in the remaining ingredients; heat through. Drain the pasta; serve with the beef mixture.

(5) INGREDIENTS
Super-Simple Garlic Broccoli

My kids like broccoli, especially when I add lots of garlic and a little Italian seasoning. I usually fix this side dish once a week.
—**CARAMIA SOMMERS** OSWEGO, NY

START TO FINISH: 20 MIN.
MAKES: 12 SERVINGS (¾ CUP EACH)

- 13 **cups fresh broccoli florets (about 2½ pounds)**
- 3 **tablespoons olive oil**
- 5 **garlic cloves, minced**
- ¾ **teaspoon Italian seasoning**
- ¼ **teaspoon salt**

In a Dutch oven, bring ½ in. of water to a boil. Add the broccoli; cover and cook for 3-5 minutes or until crisp-tender; drain. Combine the remaining ingredients. Add to the broccoli; toss to combine.

GARLICKY BEEF & TOMATOES WITH PASTA

JESS APFE'S SESAME CHICKEN NOODLE SALAD PAGE 275

Cooking Lighter

Every scrumptious dish in this chapter will fit into a healthier eating plan. With complete nutrition facts listed at the end of each recipe, you can **choose the best options** for you and your family.

ELIZABETH KELLEY'S SAUSAGE & VEGETABLE SKILLET DINNER *PAGE 270*

JENNIFER BECKMAN'S INDIAN-SPICED CHICKPEA WRAPS *PAGE 261*

AMBER NEEDHAM'S LEMON BLACKBERRY PARFAITS *PAGE 277*

Crunchy Salmon Cakes with Greek Yogurt Sauce

Whether you start with fresh salmon or a leftover cooked fillet from the fridge, these cakes make a great main course or appetizer. I've even put them in a salad.

—CINDY FAN ALHAMBRA, CA

PREP: 30 MIN. + CHILLING • **BAKE:** 15 MIN.
MAKES: 4 SERVINGS

- 1¼ **pounds salmon fillet**
- ⅛ **teaspoon pepper plus ¼ teaspoon pepper, divided**
- 1 **teaspoon olive oil**
- 1 **small onion, finely chopped**
- 2 **tablespoons minced fresh parsley**
- 1½ **cups panko (Japanese) bread crumbs, divided**
- ½ **cup reduced-fat mayonnaise**
- 1 **tablespoon lemon juice**
- ¼ **teaspoon salt**
- 1 **teaspoon hot pepper sauce, optional**
- 2 **egg whites, lightly beaten**
  Cooking spray

SAUCE
- ¼ **cup reduced-fat plain Greek yogurt**
- 1 **teaspoon snipped fresh dill**
- ¾ **teaspoon lemon juice**
- ¼ **teaspoon capers, drained and chopped**

1. Place salmon on a baking sheet coated with cooking spray; sprinkle with ⅛ teaspoon pepper. Bake, uncovered, at 350° for 14-17 minutes or until the fish flakes easily with a fork. Cool slightly; remove skin, if necessary. Transfer the salmon to a shallow dish; refrigerate, covered, for 2 hours or until chilled.

2. In a large skillet, heat the oil over medium-high heat. Add onion; cook and stir until tender. Stir in parsley.

3. In a large bowl, combine ½ cup bread crumbs, mayonnaise, lemon juice, salt, remaining pepper and onion mixture; if desired, add pepper sauce. Flake the salmon; add to bread crumb mixture, mixing lightly. Shape into eight 2½-in. patties.

4. Place egg whites and remaining crumbs in separate shallow bowls. Dip the patties in egg whites, then roll in crumbs to coat. Place on a baking sheet coated with cooking spray. Spritz tops with cooking spray. Bake, uncovered, at 425° for 14-17 minutes or until golden brown.

5. In a small bowl, mix the sauce ingredients; serve with salmon cakes.

PER SERVING *422 cal., 25 g fat (4 g sat. fat), 82 mg chol., 541 mg sodium, 17 g carb., 1 g fiber, 29 g pro.*

FAST FIX ▶ Baked Cod Piccata with Asparagus

It takes longer for the oven to preheat than it does to get my cod and asparagus in the oven. I love the speedy prep!

—BARBARA LENTO HOUSTON, PA

START TO FINISH: 30 MIN.
MAKES: 4 SERVINGS

- 1 **pound fresh asparagus, trimmed**
- ¼ **cup water**
- 1 **pound cod fillet, cut into four pieces**
- 2 **tablespoons lemon juice**
- 1 **teaspoon salt-free lemon-pepper seasoning**
- ½ **teaspoon garlic powder**
- 2 **tablespoons butter, cubed**
- 2 **teaspoons capers**
  Minced fresh parsley, optional

1. Place asparagus in an ungreased 11-in. x 7-in. baking dish; add water. Arrange cod over asparagus. Sprinkle with lemon juice, lemon-pepper and garlic powder. Dot with the butter; sprinkle with capers.

2. Bake, uncovered, at 400° for 12-15 minutes or until the fish flakes easily with a fork and asparagus is tender. If desired, sprinkle with parsley.

PER SERVING *150 cal., 7 g fat (4 g sat. fat), 58 mg chol., 265 mg sodium, 3 g carb., 1 g fiber, 20 g pro.* **Diabetic Exchanges:** *3 lean meat, 1 fat.*

BAKED COD PICCATA WITH ASPARAGUS

CRUNCHY SALMON CAKES
WITH GREEK YOGURT SAUCE

FAST FIX ▸ Hearty Turkey & Feta Sandwich

Here's a yummy sandwich I've served at get-togethers since my college days. The key ingredients are the roasted garlic hummus and pickles—everyone seems to notice if the pickles are missing!

—JACKIE TERMONT RUTHER GLEN, VA

START TO FINISH: 15 MIN.
MAKES: 8 SERVINGS

- 1 loaf (1 pound) unsliced French bread
- ½ cup roasted garlic hummus
- ¼ cup crumbled feta cheese
- 1 teaspoon dried oregano
- 1 pound sliced deli turkey
- 1 large sweet red pepper, sliced
- 4 thin sandwich pickle slices

1. Cut French bread lengthwise in half; hollow out each half, leaving a ¼-in. shell (save removed bread for another use).

2. Spread hummus over cut side of bread top. In a small bowl, combine cheese and oregano; sprinkle over bread bottom. Top with turkey, red pepper and pickles. Replace top; cut into slices.

PER SERVING 199 cal., 4 g fat (1 g sat. fat), 22 mg chol., 933 mg sodium, 24 g carb., 2 g fiber, 16 g pro.

HEARTY TURKEY & FETA SANDWICH

"Raita, an Indian condiment made with yogurt, elevates this vegetarian dish into a satisfying gourmet wrap. I sometimes substitute diced mango or cucumber for the pineapple and add fresh herbs like cilantro or mint." —JENNIFER BECKMAN FALLS CHURCH, VA

INDIAN-SPICED CHICKPEA WRAPS

FAST FIX ▸ Indian-Spiced Chickpea Wraps

START TO FINISH: 30 MIN.
MAKES: 4 SERVINGS (1⅓ CUPS SAUCE)

RAITA
- 1 cup (8 ounces) reduced-fat plain yogurt
- ½ cup drained unsweetened pineapple tidbits
- ¼ teaspoon salt
- ¼ teaspoon ground cumin

WRAPS
- 2 teaspoons canola oil
- 1 small onion, chopped
- 1 tablespoon minced fresh gingerroot
- 2 garlic cloves, minced
- ½ teaspoon curry powder
- ¼ teaspoon each salt, ground cumin and ground coriander
- ¼ teaspoon cayenne pepper, optional
- 1 can (15 ounces) chickpeas or garbanzo beans, rinsed and drained
- 1 cup canned crushed tomatoes
- 4 whole wheat tortillas (8 inches), warmed
- 3 cups fresh baby spinach

1. In a small bowl, mix the raita ingredients; set aside.

2. For wraps, in a nonstick skillet coated with cooking spray, heat oil over medium-high heat. Add onion; cook and stir until tender. Add ginger, garlic and seasonings; cook and stir 1 minute longer.

3. Stir in the chickpeas and tomatoes. Bring to a boil. Reduce heat; simmer, uncovered, for 5-8 minutes or until the mixture is slightly thickened, stirring occasionally.

4. Near the center of each tortilla, arrange spinach and chickpea mixture; top with the raita. Roll up tightly; serve immediately.

PER SERVING 355 cal., 9 g fat (1 g sat. fat), 3 mg chol., 745 mg sodium, 56 g carb., 9 g fiber, 13 g pro.

Rosemary Butternut Squash Lasagna

When our garden was overflowing with veggies, I came up with a lasagna recipe. It's our favorite way to use butternut squash.
—CHRISTINE WOOD TIPTON, IA

PREP: 30 MIN. • **BAKE:** 50 MIN. + STANDING • **MAKES:** 8 SERVINGS

- 9 uncooked whole grain lasagna noodles
- 1 medium butternut squash (about 3 pounds), peeled and cut crosswise into ¼-inch slices
- 2 tablespoons olive oil
- 1 teaspoon salt, divided
- 6 tablespoons all-purpose flour
- 4 cups fat-free milk
- 6 garlic cloves, minced
- 1 tablespoon minced fresh rosemary
- 1⅓ cups shredded Parmesan cheese

1. Preheat oven to 425°. Cook noodles according to the package directions; drain.

2. In a large bowl, combine the squash, oil and ½ teaspoon salt; toss to coat. Transfer to a 15-in. x 10-in. x 1-in. baking pan coated with cooking spray. Bake 10-15 minutes or until tender; remove from oven. Reduce heat to 375°.

3. Place the flour and remaining salt in a large saucepan; gradually whisk in milk. Bring to a boil, stirring constantly. Cook and stir 1-2 minutes or until thickened. Stir in garlic and rosemary.

4. Spread 1 cup sauce into a 13-in. x 9-in. baking dish coated with cooking spray. Layer with three noodles, ⅓ cup cheese, a third of the squash and 1 cup sauce. Repeat layers twice. Sprinkle with remaining cheese.

5. Cover and bake 40 minutes. Uncover; bake 10 minutes or until bubbly and the top is lightly browned. Let stand 10 minutes before serving.

PER SERVING *275 cal., 8 g fat (3 g sat. fat), 12 mg chol., 577 mg sodium, 40 g carb., 6 g fiber, 14 g pro.* **Diabetic Exchanges:** *2½ starch, ½ fat-free milk, ½ fat.*

ROSEMARY BUTTERNUT SQUASH LASAGNA

TURKEY SAUSAGE PIZZA

Turkey Sausage Pizza

If pizza night is a must in your house, double this recipe and freeze one pie for later. You'll have a quick treat for a hectic day.
—MELISSA JELINEK MENOMONEE FALLS, WI

PREP: 20 MIN. • **BAKE:** 15 MIN. • **MAKES:** 8 SLICES

- 1 loaf (1 pound) frozen bread dough, thawed
- ¾ pound Italian turkey sausage links, casings removed
- ½ cup sliced onion
- ½ cup sliced fresh mushrooms
- ½ cup chopped green pepper
- ½ cup pizza sauce
- 2 cups (8 ounces) shredded part-skim mozzarella cheese

1. With greased fingers, press the dough onto a 12-in. pizza pan coated with cooking spray. Prick the dough thoroughly with a fork. Bake at 400° for 10-12 minutes or until crust is lightly browned.

2. Meanwhile, in a large skillet, cook the turkey sausage, onion, mushrooms and green pepper over medium heat for 6-8 minutes or until sausage is no longer pink, breaking up sausage into crumbles; drain.

3. Spread crust with pizza sauce. Top with sausage mixture; sprinkle with cheese. Bake 12-15 minutes longer or until the crust is golden brown and the cheese is melted.

FREEZE OPTION *Wrap and freeze cooled pizza. To use, thaw overnight in the refrigerator. Unwrap; bake on a pizza pan at 400° for 18-22 minutes or until heated through.*

PER SERVING *283 cal., 9 g fat (4 g sat. fat), 32 mg chol., 668 mg sodium, 30 g carb., 3 g fiber, 18 g pro.* **Diabetic Exchanges:** *2 starch, 2 lean meat, ½ fat.*

Cajun Shrimp & Cucumber Wraps

START TO FINISH: 20 MIN. • **MAKES:** 4 SERVINGS

- ¼ cup lemon juice
- 4 tablespoons olive oil, divided
- 1½ teaspoons Cajun seasoning, divided
- ⅛ teaspoon pepper
- 1 pound uncooked large shrimp, peeled and deveined (tails removed)
- 8 Bibb or Boston lettuce leaves
- 4 flatbread wraps
- 2 small cucumbers, cut lengthwise into quarters
- 4 thin slices red onion
- ¼ cup fresh parsley leaves

1. In a small bowl, whisk lemon juice, 3 tablespoons oil, 1 teaspoon Cajun seasoning and pepper. Toss shrimp with the remaining Cajun seasoning. In a large skillet, heat the remaining oil over medium-high heat. Add shrimp mixture; cook and stir until shrimp turn pink.

2. Place lettuce on flatbread wraps; top with cucumbers, onion, parsley and shrimp. Drizzle with dressing; roll up and, if desired, secure with toothpicks.

PER SERVING *365 cal., 17 g fat (2 g sat. fat), 138 mg chol., 670 mg sodium, 29 g carb., 4 g fiber, 26 g pro.* **Diabetic Exchanges:** *3 lean meat, 2 starch, 2 fat.*

> "I like to balance spicy shrimp with cucumbers in a cool flatbread wrap."
> —**CHANTEL BEAUREGARD**
> LAKE ARROWHEAD, CA

CAJUN SHRIMP & CUCUMBER WRAPS

SPRING-THYME CHICKEN STEW

Spring-Thyme Chicken Stew

During a long, cold winter and spring, my husband and I craved comfort food. This slow-cooked stew was perfect! It fills the house with an aroma that reminds me of my mom's chicken soup.
—**AMY CHASE** VANDERHOOF, BC

PREP: 15 MIN. • **COOK:** 7 HOURS • **MAKES:** 4 SERVINGS

- 1 pound small red potatoes, halved
- 1 large onion, finely chopped
- ¾ cup shredded carrots
- 3 tablespoons all-purpose flour
- 6 garlic cloves, minced
- 2 teaspoons grated lemon peel
- 2 teaspoons dried thyme
- ½ teaspoon salt
- ¼ teaspoon pepper
- 1½ pounds boneless skinless chicken thighs, halved
- 2 cups reduced-sodium chicken broth
- 2 bay leaves
- 2 tablespoons minced fresh parsley

1. Place potatoes, onion and carrots in a 3-qt. slow cooker. Sprinkle with the flour, garlic, lemon peel, thyme, salt and pepper; toss to coat. Place chicken over top. Add the broth and bay leaves.

2. Cook, covered, on low 7-9 hours or until the chicken and vegetables are tender. Remove the bay leaves. Sprinkle with parsley.

PER SERVING *395 cal., 13 g fat (3 g sat. fat), 113 mg chol., 707 mg sodium, 32 g carb., 4 g fiber, 37 g pro.* **Diabetic Exchanges:** *5 lean meat, 2 vegetable, 1½ starch.*

HERBED-ROASTED MUSHROOMS

FAST FIX **Herbed-Roasted Mushrooms**

My husband grows herbs, and we use whatever's in season. I like to flavor three kinds of mushrooms with fresh-picked basil, rosemary and oregano.
—**JENNIFER NIEMI** TUCSON, AZ

START TO FINISH: 30 MIN.
MAKES: 4 SERVINGS

- ½ **pound medium fresh mushrooms**
- ½ **pound baby portobello mushrooms**
- 5 **ounces fresh shiitake mushrooms, stems removed**
- 2 **tablespoons olive oil**
- 2 **tablespoons minced fresh basil**
- 1 **tablespoon minced fresh oregano**
- 1 **tablespoon minced fresh rosemary**
- ¼ **teaspoon salt**
- ¼ **teaspoon pepper**
- 2 **tablespoons balsamic vinegar**

1. Cut the mushrooms into quarters; place in a large bowl. Add oil, herbs, salt and pepper; toss to combine. Place on two 15-in. x 10-in. x 1-in. baking pans coated with cooking spray.
2. Bake, uncovered, at 425° for 9-11 minutes or until tender. Transfer to a bowl. Drizzle with vinegar; toss to coat.
PER SERVING *104 cal., 7 g fat (1 g sat. fat), 0 chol., 154 mg sodium, 8 g carb., 2 g fiber, 4 g pro.* **Diabetic Exchanges:** *1½ fat, 1 vegetable.*

(5)INGREDIENTS SLOW COOKER **Overnight Cherry-Almond Oatmeal**

Put oatmeal in the slow cooker overnight, and you'll have a yummy breakfast that's ready when you get up in the morning.
—**GERALDINE SAUCIER** ALBUQUERQUE, NM

PREP: 10 MIN. • **COOK:** 7 HOURS
MAKES: 6 SERVINGS

- 4 **cups vanilla almond milk**
- 1 **cup steel-cut oats**
- 1 **cup dried cherries**
- ⅓ **cup packed brown sugar**
- ½ **teaspoon salt**
- ½ **teaspoon ground cinnamon**

In a 3-qt. slow cooker coated with cooking spray, combine all ingredients. Cover and cook on low 7-8 hours or until milk is absorbed.
PER SERVING *276 cal., 4 g fat (trace sat. fat), 0 chol., 306 mg sodium, 57 g carb., 4 g fiber, 5 g pro.*

FAST FIX **Chicken Thighs with Shallots & Spinach**

This moist and tender chicken comes complete with its own vegetable side dish. The simple recipe creates an all-in-one supper in only 30 minutes.
—**GENNA JOHANNES** WRIGHTSTOWN, WI

START TO FINISH: 30 MIN.
MAKES: 6 SERVINGS

- 6 **boneless skinless chicken thighs (about 1½ pounds)**
- ½ **teaspoon seasoned salt**
- ½ **teaspoon pepper**
- 1½ **teaspoons olive oil**
- 4 **shallots, thinly sliced**
- ⅓ **cup white wine or reduced-sodium chicken broth**
- 1 **package (10 ounces) fresh spinach**
- ¼ **teaspoon salt**
- ¼ **cup fat-free sour cream**

1. Sprinkle chicken with seasoned salt and pepper. In a large nonstick skillet coated with cooking spray, heat the oil over medium heat. Add the chicken; cook 6 minutes on each side or until a thermometer reads 165°. Remove from pan; keep warm.
2. In same pan, cook and stir shallots until tender. Add wine; bring to a boil. Cook and stir until liquid is reduced by half. Add spinach and salt; cook and stir just until the spinach is wilted. Stir in sour cream; serve with chicken.
PER SERVING *225 cal., 10 g fat (2 g sat. fat), 77 mg chol., 338 mg sodium, 8 g carb., 1 g fiber, 24 g pro.* **Diabetic Exchanges:** *3 lean meat, 1½ fat, 1 vegetable.*

CHICKEN THIGHS WITH SHALLOTS & SPINACH

"For a light, cool lunch or dinner on a warm summer's day, it's hard to beat Orzo-Tuna Salad with Tomatoes. Wash it down with lemonade or iced tea."

—JENNI DISE PHOENIX, AZ

ORZO-TUNA SALAD WITH TOMATOES

FAST FIX ▸ Orzo-Tuna Salad with Tomatoes

START TO FINISH: 25 MIN.
MAKES: 4 SERVINGS

- ¾ cup uncooked whole wheat orzo pasta
- 4 large tomatoes, sliced
- 16 small fresh basil leaves
- 1 pouch (11 ounces) light tuna in water
- 1 cup cubed part-skim mozzarella cheese
- 3 tablespoons minced fresh basil
- 2 tablespoons olive oil
- 2 tablespoons balsamic vinegar
- ⅛ teaspoon salt
- ⅛ teaspoon pepper

1. Cook the orzo pasta according to the package directions. Arrange sliced tomatoes on a serving plate; top with the whole basil leaves.
2. Drain the orzo pasta; rinse with cold water and place in a large bowl. Add the tuna, mozzarella cheese and minced basil. In a small bowl, whisk the oil, balsamic vinegar, salt and pepper; drizzle over the pasta mixture and toss to combine. Spoon over the tomatoes.

PER SERVING *392 cal., 15 g fat (5 g sat. fat), 41 mg chol., 523 mg sodium, 31 g carb., 7 g fiber, 34 g pro.* **Diabetic Exchanges:** *4 lean meat, 1½ starch, 1½ fat, 1 vegetable.*

FAST FIX ▸ Saucy Pork Chop Skillet

With a delectable sauce, this pork chop skillet makes home-style food quick, convenient and delicious. I pair the saucy meat with brown rice, but you could also use whole grain noodles for a change of pace. Round out a healthier-for-you meal with a tossed green salad.

—**DONNA ROBERTS** MANHATTAN, KS

START TO FINISH: 30 MIN.
MAKES: 6 SERVINGS

- 3 cups instant brown rice
- 2 teaspoons canola oil
- 6 boneless pork loin chops (6 ounces each)
- 1 small onion, sliced
- 1 cup canned diced tomatoes
- 1 cup reduced-sodium beef broth
- 1 tablespoon dried parsley flakes
- ½ teaspoon salt
- ¼ teaspoon pepper
- ⅛ teaspoon dried basil
- ⅛ teaspoon dried oregano
- 2 tablespoons all-purpose flour
- ½ cup water

1. Cook rice according to the package directions. Meanwhile, in a large nonstick skillet coated with cooking spray, heat oil over medium-high heat. Brown the pork chops on both sides. Remove from the pan.
2. Cook and stir the onion in drippings over medium-high heat until tender. Stir in the tomatoes, broth, parsley and seasonings. Bring to a boil. Return the pork to pan. Reduce heat; simmer, covered, for 6-8 minutes or until a thermometer inserted into the pork reads 145°.
3. Remove the pork to a serving plate. Mix flour and water until smooth; stir into pan. Bring to a boil; cook and stir for 2 minutes or until thickened. Pour over pork; serve with rice.

PER SERVING *436 cal., 13 g fat (4 g sat. fat), 83 mg chol., 382 mg sodium, 39 g carb., 3 g fiber, 38 g pro.* **Diabetic Exchanges:** *5 lean meat, 2½ starch.*

SAUCY PORK CHOP SKILLET

FAST FIX
Shrimp & Chicken Sausage with Grits

START TO FINISH: 30 MIN.
MAKES: 5 SERVINGS

- 3 **cups water**
- 1 **cup quick-cooking grits**
- 4 **ounces reduced-fat cream cheese, cubed**
- 3 **fully cooked spicy chicken sausage links (3 ounces each), cut into ½-inch slices**
- 2 **teaspoons canola oil, divided**
- 2 **garlic cloves, minced**
- 2 **green onions, chopped, divided**
- 4 **teaspoons whole wheat flour**
- 1½ **cups chicken broth**
- ¼ **cup fat-free evaporated milk**
- 1 **pound uncooked medium shrimp, peeled and deveined**
- 1 **medium tomato, chopped**

1. In a large saucepan, bring water to a boil. Slowly stir in grits. Reduce heat;

cook and stir for 5-7 minutes or until thickened. Stir in the cream cheese until melted.

2. Meanwhile, in a large skillet, brown sausage in 1 teaspoon oil. Remove and keep warm.

3. In the same pan, heat remaining oil over medium-high heat. Add garlic and half of the green onions; cook and stir for 1 minute. Stir in the flour until blended; gradually whisk in chicken broth and milk. Bring to a boil, stirring constantly; cook and stir for 2 minutes or until thickened.

4. Stir in shrimp and sausage; cook for 3-5 minutes or until shrimp turn pink. Serve with grits; top with tomato and remaining green onion.

PER SERVING *367 cal., 13 g fat (5 g sat. fat), 161 mg chol., 810 mg sodium, 30 g carb., 2 g fiber, 31 g pro.* **Diabetic Exchanges:** *4 lean meat, 2 starch, ½ fat.*

HONEY LIME CHICKEN

Honey Lime Chicken

My grandfather used to grill this for our Thanksgiving dinner. I would pass up the turkey so I could eat more of his chicken!
—**ANN NISEWONDER** DALLAS, TX

PREP: 10 MIN. + MARINATING
GRILL: 10 MIN.
MAKES: 4 SERVINGS

- 4 **boneless skinless chicken breast halves (5 ounces each)**
- 1 **cup white wine**
- ½ **cup honey**
- 2 **tablespoons lime juice**
- ¼ **teaspoon ground ginger**
- ¼ **teaspoon garlic powder**
- ¼ **teaspoon salt**
- ¼ **teaspoon pepper**
  Hot cooked couscous, optional

1. Place chicken in a large resealable plastic bag. In a small bowl, whisk the white wine, honey, lime juice and ginger; add to chicken. Seal the bag and turn to coat. Refrigerate 2 hours, turning once.

2. Drain the chicken, discarding the marinade. Sprinkle chicken with garlic powder, salt and pepper.

3. Moisten a paper towel with cooking oil; using long-handled tongs, rub on grill rack to coat lightly. Grill chicken, covered, over medium heat or broil 4 in. from heat 5-6 minutes on each side or until a thermometer reads 165°. If desired, serve with couscous.

PER SERVING *186 cal., 3 g fat (1 g sat. fat), 78 mg chol., 216 mg sodium, 8 g carb., trace fiber, 29 g pro.* **Diabetic Exchanges:** *4 lean meat, ½ starch.*

"I'm originally from Tennessee and had never had shrimp and grits until I moved to South Carolina. I think my version is just as tasty but easier on the waistline."
—**ATHENA RUSSELL** FLORENCE, SC

SHRIMP & CHICKEN SAUSAGE WITH GRITS

Oven-Fried Chicken Drumsticks

Here's a great way to make drumsticks. Greek yogurt in the marinade makes them moist, and we all love the crispy coating.

—KIM WALLACE DENNISON, OH

PREP: 20 MIN. + MARINATING
BAKE: 40 MIN.
MAKES: 4 SERVINGS

- 1 cup fat-free plain Greek yogurt
- 1 tablespoon Dijon mustard
- 2 garlic cloves, minced
- 8 chicken drumsticks (4 ounces each), skin removed
- ½ cup whole wheat flour
- 1½ teaspoons paprika
- 1 teaspoon baking powder
- 1 teaspoon salt
- 1 teaspoon pepper
  Olive oil-flavored cooking spray

1. In a large resealable plastic bag, combine the plain yogurt, mustard and garlic. Add the chicken; seal the bag and turn to coat. Refrigerate 8 hours or overnight.
2. Preheat oven to 425°. In another plastic bag, mix the flour, paprika, baking powder, salt and pepper. Remove chicken from marinade and add, one piece at a time, to flour

mixture; close bag and shake to coat. Place on a wire rack over a baking sheet; spritz with cooking spray. Bake 40-45 minutes or until a thermometer reads 180°.
PER SERVING *227 cal., 7 g fat (1 g sat. fat), 81 mg chol., 498 mg sodium, 9 g carb., 1 g fiber, 31 g pro.* **Diabetic Exchanges:** *4 lean meat, ½ starch.*

Chicken in Tomato-Caper Sauce

When this colorful main course is on the menu, I add a side dish of pasta and a simple salad. If you don't have capers, substitute diced green olives.

—SHEMAINE ROHRBACH ALLENTOWN, PA

CHICKEN IN TOMATO-CAPER SAUCE

PREP: 20 MIN. • **COOK:** 15 MIN.
MAKES: 4 SERVINGS

- 4 boneless skinless chicken breast halves (6 ounces each)
- ¼ teaspoon pepper
- 2 tablespoons olive oil, divided
- 1 medium onion, chopped
- 3 garlic cloves, minced
- 2 cans (14½ ounces each) no-salt-added diced tomatoes, undrained
- 1 package (6 ounces) fresh baby spinach
- 2 tablespoons drained capers
- 2 tablespoons minced fresh basil or 2 teaspoons dried basil
- ¼ teaspoon cayenne pepper
- ½ cup shredded part-skim mozzarella cheese
- ½ cup grated Parmesan cheese

1. Pound chicken breasts with a meat mallet to ¼-in. thickness; sprinkle with pepper. In a large nonstick skillet, heat 1 tablespoon oil over medium heat. Brown chicken on both sides; remove from pan.
2. In same skillet, heat remaining oil over medium-high heat. Add onion; cook and stir until tender. Add garlic; cook 1 minute longer. Stir in tomatoes, spinach, capers, basil and cayenne. Return chicken to pan. Cook, covered, 8-10 minutes or until chicken is no longer pink.
3. Sprinkle with cheeses. Remove from heat; let stand, covered, until cheese is melted.
PER SERVING *392 cal., 16 g fat (5 g sat. fat), 111 mg chol., 545 mg sodium, 17 g carb., 5 g fiber, 45 g pro.* **Diabetic Exchanges:** *6 lean meat, 1 starch, 1 fat.*

OVEN-FRIED CHICKEN DRUMSTICKS

FAST FIX ▶ Shrimp Fajitas

I recently lost 50 pounds, and my husband lost 65. Now we're always searching for tasty ways to keep the weight off. With lots of spice, these seafood fajitas leave us satisfied.
—**CHARLENE CHAMBERS** ORMOND BEACH, FL

START TO FINISH: 30 MIN. • **MAKES:** 4 SERVINGS

- 1 **pound uncooked medium shrimp, peeled and deveined**
- 4 **tablespoons minced fresh cilantro, divided**
- 1 **tablespoon plus 2 teaspoons olive oil, divided**
- 3 **teaspoons Caribbean jerk seasoning**
- ⅛ **teaspoon chili powder**
- ⅛ **teaspoon ground cumin**
- 1 **cup (8 ounces) fat-free sour cream**
- 1 **large onion, halved and thinly sliced**
- 1 **medium sweet red pepper, cut into thin strips**
- 1 **medium green pepper, cut into thin strips**
- 8 **flour tortillas (6 inches), warmed**
- ½ **cup salsa**

1. In a large bowl, toss the shrimp with 2 tablespoons cilantro, 1 tablespoon oil and spices; let stand 10 minutes. Meanwhile, in a small bowl, mix the sour cream and remaining cilantro.
2. In a large nonstick skillet coated with cooking spray, heat 1 teaspoon oil over medium-high heat. Add the onion and peppers; cook and stir until crisp-tender. Remove from the pan.
3. In the same pan, heat remaining oil over medium-high heat. Add the shrimp; cook and stir until shrimp turn pink. Return the onion mixture to pan; heat through. Serve with tortillas, salsa and sour cream mixture.
PER SERVING *418 cal., 13 g fat (1 g sat. fat), 147 mg chol., 962 mg sodium, 44 g carb., 2 g fiber, 29 g pro.*

SHRIMP FAJITAS

MEDITERRANEAN GRILLED CHICKEN & GREENS

Mediterranean Grilled Chicken & Greens

Here's a hearty salad that has everything I'm looking for in a main course—it's easy to prepare, delicious and a healthier option. Marinate the chicken overnight for a flavor boost.
—**DIANE HALFERTY** CORPUS CHRISTI, TX

PREP: 15 MIN. + MARINATING • **GRILL:** 10 MIN. • **MAKES:** 4 SERVINGS

- ¼ **cup orange juice**
- 6 **garlic cloves, minced**
- 1 **tablespoon balsamic vinegar**
- 1½ **teaspoons dried thyme**
- ½ **teaspoon salt**
- 4 **boneless skinless chicken breast halves (5 ounces each)**
- 2 **packages (5 ounces each) spring mix salad greens**
- 2 **cups cherry tomatoes, halved**
- ½ **cup crumbled feta cheese**
- ¼ **cup pitted Greek olives, halved**
- ¼ **cup prepared vinaigrette**

1. In a large resealable plastic bag, combine the first five ingredients. Add the chicken; seal the bag and turn to coat. Refrigerate 8 hours or overnight.
2. Drain the chicken, discarding marinade. Moisten a paper towel with cooking oil; using long-handled tongs, rub on the grill rack to coat lightly. Grill chicken, covered, over medium heat or broil 4 in. from heat 5-6 minutes on each side or until a thermometer reads 165°.
3. In a large bowl, combine the salad greens, tomatoes, feta cheese and olives. Drizzle with vinaigrette; toss to coat. Slice chicken; serve with salad.
PER SERVING *282 calories, 11 g fat (3 g sat. fat), 86 mg chol., 717 mg sodium, 12 g carb., 3 g fiber, 33 g pro.* **Diabetic Exchanges** *4 lean meat, 2 vegetable, 1 fat.*

FAST FIX ▶ Speedy Chicken Marsala

START TO FINISH: 30 MIN. • **MAKES:** 4 SERVINGS

- 8 ounces uncooked whole wheat or multigrain angel hair pasta
- 4 boneless skinless chicken breast halves (5 ounces each)
- ¼ cup all-purpose flour
- 1 teaspoon lemon-pepper seasoning
- ½ teaspoon salt
- 2 tablespoons olive oil, divided
- 4 cups sliced fresh mushrooms
- 1 garlic clove, minced
- 1 cup dry Marsala wine

1. Cook the pasta according to the package directions. Pound the chicken with a meat mallet to ¼-in. thickness. In a large resealable plastic bag, mix the flour, lemon pepper and salt. Add the chicken, one piece at a time; close the bag and shake to coat.

2. In a large skillet, heat 1 tablespoon oil over medium heat. Add chicken; cook for 4-5 minutes on each side or until no longer pink. Remove from pan.

3. In the same skillet, heat the remaining oil over medium-high heat. Add the mushrooms; cook and stir until tender. Add the garlic; cook 1 minute longer. Add the Marsala wine; bring to a boil. Cook for 5-6 minutes or until the liquid is reduced by half, stirring to loosen browned bits from the pan. Return the chicken to the pan, turning to coat with the sauce; heat through.

4. Drain the pasta; serve with chicken mixture.

PER SERVING *493 cal., 11 g fat (2 g sat. fat), 78 mg chol., 279 mg sodium, 50 g carb., 7 g fiber, 40 g pro.*

"Chicken Marsala is one of my favorite dishes to order in restaurants. I came up with a version I can make quickly on a weeknight at home." —**TRISHA KRUSE** EAGLE, ID

SPEEDY CHICKEN MARSALA

PORK & POTATO SUPPER

FAST FIX ▶ Pork & Potato Supper

Meat-and-potato lovers will never suspect that this home-style supper is lower in fat and calories. After one taste, my family made sure I added it to our list of regular menus.
—**MACEY ALLEN** GREEN FOREST, AR

START TO FINISH: 30 MIN. • **MAKES:** 4 SERVINGS

- 2 tablespoons butter, divided
- 1 pork tenderloin (1 pound), cut into ¼-inch slices
- 1 cup sliced fresh mushrooms
- 2 garlic cloves, minced
- 8 small red potatoes, quartered
- 1 can (14½ ounces) reduced-sodium chicken broth, divided
- 2 teaspoons Worcestershire sauce
- ¼ teaspoon salt
- ¼ teaspoon pepper
- 2 tablespoons all-purpose flour
- 4 green onions, sliced

1. In a 12-in. skillet, heat 1 tablespoon butter over medium heat. Cook pork 2-4 minutes on each side or until tender. Remove from pan.

2. In same pan, heat remaining butter over medium-high heat. Add mushrooms; cook and stir until almost tender. Add garlic; cook 1 minute longer. Stir in potatoes, 1½ cups chicken broth, Worcestershire sauce, salt and pepper. Bring to a boil. Reduce heat; simmer, covered, 10-15 minutes or until potatoes are tender.

3. In a small bowl, mix the flour and remaining chicken broth until smooth. Stir into the mushroom mixture. Bring to a boil; cook and stir until sauce is thickened. Stir in green onions. Return pork to pan and heat through.

PER SERVING *282 cal., 10 g fat (5 g sat. fat), 78 mg chol., 565 mg sodium, 21 g carb., 2 g fiber, 27 g pro.* **Diabetic Exchanges:** *3 lean meat, 1½ fat, 1 starch.*

FAST FIX ▶ Open-Faced Roast Beef Sandwiches

Horseradish and the peppery mustard flavor of arugula bring a bit of zing to these open-faced beef sandwiches. You may want to fix a few extra because most people who eat one want another!
—**MARY PRICE** YOUNGSTOWN, OH

START TO FINISH: 15 MIN.
MAKES: 8 SERVINGS

- 1 pound sliced deli roast beef
- 8 slices ciabatta bread (½ inch thick)
- 2 cups fresh arugula
- 2 cups torn romaine
- 4 teaspoons olive oil
- 1 tablespoon lemon juice
- 1 tablespoon white wine vinegar
- 1½ teaspoons prepared horseradish

1. Place the roast beef on the ciabatta slices. In a large bowl, combine arugula and romaine.
2. In a small bowl, whisk remaining ingredients until blended. Drizzle over greens; toss to coat. Arrange over beef; serve immediately.
PER SERVING *150 calories, 5 g fat (1 g sat. fat), 32 mg chol., 422 mg sodium, 14 g carb., 1 g fiber, 14 g pro.* **Diabetic Exchanges:** *2 lean meat, 1 starch, ½ fat.*

OPEN-FACED ROAST BEEF SANDWICHES

"I threw Italian chicken sausage and vegetables together one night when I was trying to use up produce before going out of town. Now the recipe is a mainstay." —**ELIZABETH KELLEY** CHICAGO, IL

SAUSAGE & VEGETABLE SKILLET DINNER

FAST FIX ▶ Sausage & Vegetable Skillet Dinner

START TO FINISH: 30 MIN.
MAKES: 4 SERVINGS

- 1 tablespoon olive oil
- 1 package (12 ounces) fully cooked Italian chicken sausage links, cut into 1-inch pieces
- 1 large onion, chopped
- 3 garlic cloves, minced
- ¼ teaspoon crushed red pepper flakes
- 8 medium red potatoes (about 2 pounds), thinly sliced
- 1 package (10 ounces) frozen corn
- 1¼ cups vegetable broth
- ¼ teaspoon pepper
- 2 cups fresh baby spinach

1. In a 12-in. skillet, heat the oil over medium-high heat. Add the sausage and onion; cook and stir until sausage is browned and onion is tender. Add the garlic and pepper flakes; cook 1 minute longer.
2. Add the red potatoes, corn, vegetable broth and pepper; bring to a boil. Reduce heat; simmer, covered, 12-15 minutes or until the potatoes are tender. Add the spinach; cook just until wilted.
PER SERVING *413 calories, 11 g fat (3 g sat. fat), 65 mg chol., 804 mg sodium, 58 g carb., 7 g fiber, 22 g pro.*

SLOW COOKER ▶ Slow Cooker Split Pea Soup

Have some extra ham in the refrigerator? Make a delicious split pea soup. Just toss all of the ingredients into the slow cooker, turn it on, and dinner's done.
—**PAMELA CHAMBERS** WEST COLUMBIA, SC

PREP: 15 MIN. • **COOK:** 8 HOURS
MAKES: 8 SERVINGS

- 1 package (16 ounces) dried green split peas, rinsed
- 2 cups cubed fully cooked ham
- 1 large onion, chopped
- 1 cup julienned or chopped carrots
- 3 garlic cloves, minced
- ½ teaspoon dried rosemary, crushed
- ½ teaspoon dried thyme
- 1 carton (32 ounces) reduced-sodium chicken broth
- 2 cups water

In a 4- or 5-qt. slow cooker, combine all ingredients. Cover and cook on low for 8-10 hours or until peas are tender.
FREEZE OPTION *Freeze cooled soup in freezer containers. To use, thaw overnight in the refrigerator. Heat through in a saucepan over medium heat, stirring occasionally.*
PER SERVING *260 cal., 2 g fat (1 g sat. fat), 21 mg chol., 728 mg sodium, 39 g carb., 15 g fiber, 23 g pro.* **Diabetic Exchanges:** *2½ starch, 2 lean meat.*

Black Bean Turkey Enchiladas

My best friend and I created these. Freeze one pan for a quick meal another time.

—**HOLLY BABER** SEATTLE, WA

PREP: 35 MIN. • **BAKE:** 15 MIN.
MAKES: 14 SERVINGS

- 1¼ pounds lean ground turkey
- 1 small onion, chopped
- 1 teaspoon reduced-sodium taco seasoning
- ½ teaspoon ground cumin
- ¼ teaspoon pepper
- 1 package (8 ounces) reduced-fat cream cheese, cubed
- 1 cup (4 ounces) shredded Mexican cheese blend, divided
- 1 can (15 ounces) black beans, rinsed and drained
- 1½ cups frozen corn, thawed
- 1 can (14½ ounces) fire-roasted diced tomatoes, drained
- 2 cans (4 ounces each) chopped green chilies
- ¼ cup salsa
- 14 whole wheat tortillas (8 inches), warmed
- 2 cans (10 ounces each) enchilada sauce
  Minced fresh cilantro
- ¾ cup reduced-fat plain Greek yogurt

1. Preheat oven to 375°. In a large nonstick skillet, cook turkey, onion and seasonings over medium heat 6-8 minutes or until turkey is no longer pink and onion is tender. Stir in cream cheese and ½ cup Mexican cheese blend until melted. Stir in beans, corn, tomatoes, chilies and salsa.

2. Place ½ cup turkey mixture off center on each tortilla. Roll up and place seam side down in two 13-in. x 9-in. baking dishes coated with cooking spray. Top with the enchilada sauce; sprinkle with remaining cheese.

3. Bake, uncovered, at 375° for 15-20 minutes or until heated through. Sprinkle with the cilantro; serve with plain yogurt.

FREEZE OPTION *Cool unbaked casseroles; cover and freeze. To use, partially thaw in the refrigerator overnight. Remove 30 minutes before baking. Preheat oven to 375°. Bake casseroles as directed, increasing time to 20-25 minutes or until heated through and a thermometer inserted into center reads 165°.*

PER SERVING *343 cal., 13 g fat (5 g sat. fat), 51 mg chol., 795 mg sodium, 37 g carb., 5 g fiber, 19 g pro.* **Diabetic Exchanges:** *3 lean meat, 2½ starch.*

FAST FIX
Garden Quinoa Salad

This quinoa salad can be served hot or cold. Any leftovers are good the next day.

—**PATRICIA NIEH** PORTOLA VALLEY, CA

START TO FINISH: 30 MIN.
MAKES: 4 SERVINGS

- 1½ cups quinoa, rinsed and well drained
- 7 cups water, divided
- 1 pound fresh asparagus, cut into 2-inch pieces
- ½ pound fresh sugar snap peas
- ½ pound fresh green beans, trimmed
- 2 tablespoons olive oil
- 2 tablespoons lemon juice
- 2 tablespoons minced fresh parsley
- 1 teaspoon grated lemon peel
- ¾ teaspoon salt
- 1 cup cherry tomatoes, halved
- 3 tablespoons salted pumpkin seeds or pepitas

1. In a large saucepan, cook and stir the quinoa over medium-high heat 3-5 minutes or until toasted. Add 3 cups water; bring to a boil. Reduce the heat; simmer, covered, 12-15 minutes or until the liquid is absorbed. Transfer to a large bowl.

2. Meanwhile, in a large saucepan, bring 4 cups water to a boil. Add the asparagus and snap peas; cook, uncovered, 2-4 minutes or just until crisp-tender. Remove vegetables; immediately drop into ice water.

3. Return water to a boil. Add green beans; cook 3-4 minutes or until crisp-tender. Remove beans; drop into ice water. Drain vegetables; pat dry.

4. In a small bowl, whisk oil, lemon juice, parsley, lemon peel and salt. Add tomatoes and blanched vegetables to quinoa; drizzle with dressing and toss to combine. Top with pumpkin seeds.

PER SERVING *417 cal., 15 g fat (2 g sat. fat), 0 chol., 533 mg sodium, 58 g carb., 9 g fiber, 16 g pro.*

GARDEN QUINOA SALAD

BLACK BEAN TURKEY ENCHILADAS

MARINATED STEAK & PEPPER FAJITAS

FAST FIX # Broccoli & Cheese Potato Soup

If I don't have frozen broccoli on hand for my soup, I'll substitute frozen spinach or chopped carrots and celery.

—**MARY PRICE** YOUNGSTOWN, OH

START TO FINISH: 30 MIN.
MAKES: 3 SERVINGS

- 3 **cups cubed peeled potatoes**
- 1 **medium onion, chopped**
- 2 **garlic cloves, minced**
- 2 **cups reduced-sodium chicken broth**
- 1¾ **cups water**
- ¼ **teaspoon pepper**
- ⅛ **teaspoon salt**
- 3 **cups frozen broccoli florets**
- 3 **tablespoons all-purpose flour**
- ⅓ **cup fat-free milk**
- ½ **cup shredded reduced-fat sharp cheddar cheese**
  Minced fresh parsley

1. In a large saucepan, combine the first seven ingredients; bring to a boil. Reduce heat; simmer, covered, for 10-15 minutes or until potatoes are tender. Stir in broccoli; return to a boil.
2. In a small bowl, whisk the flour and milk until smooth; stir into the soup. Cook and stir for 2 minutes or until thickened. Remove from the heat; cool slightly.
3. Process in batches in a blender until smooth. Return to the pan; heat through. Sprinkle servings with cheese and parsley.
PER SERVING *262 cal., 4 g fat (3 g sat. fat), 14 mg chol., 636 mg sodium, 44 g carb., 5 g fiber, 14 g pro.* **Diabetic Exchanges:** *2 starch, 1 medium-fat meat, 1 vegetable.*

BROCCOLI & CHEESE POTATO SOUP

Marinated Steak & Pepper Fajitas

I think these are the best fajitas ever, and they're much healthier than the typically pan-fried versions served in restaurants. A homemade marinade gives the steak terrific flavor, and peppers bring a spicy kick. For a change of pace, use flatbreads in place of the whole wheat tortillas.

—**ERIN MICHNIACK** MANHATTAN, KS

PREP: 25 MIN. + MARINATING
GRILL: 20 MIN. • **MAKES:** 8 SERVINGS

- ½ **cup tequila or reduced-sodium beef broth**
- ½ **cup lime juice**
- 4 **garlic cloves, sliced**
- 1 **teaspoon grated lime peel**
- 1 **teaspoon chili powder**
- ¾ **teaspoon salt**
- ¾ **teaspoon pepper**
- 4 **poblano peppers, halved and seeded**
- 4 **jalapeno peppers, halved and seeded**
- 1 **large sweet onion, cut crosswise into ¾-inch-thick slices**
- 1½ **pounds beef skirt steaks or flank steak**
- 8 **whole wheat tortillas (8 inches), warmed**
- ½ **cup shredded Mexican cheese blend**

1. In a small bowl, whisk the first seven ingredients until blended. Divide marinade between two large resealable plastic bags. Add peppers and onion to one bag; seal bag and turn gently to coat. Cut skirt steaks in half and add to the second bag; seal bag and turn to coat. Refrigerate vegetables and beef 8 hours or overnight.
2. Drain the vegetables and beef, discarding the marinade. Grill onion and poblanos, covered, over medium heat 4-6 minutes on each side or until tender. Grill jalapenos 2-3 minutes on each side or until crisp-tender. Grill the steaks, covered, over medium heat 4-6 minutes on each side or until meat reaches the desired doneness (for medium-rare, a thermometer should read 145°; medium, 160°; well-done, 170°). Let steaks stand 5 minutes.
3. Cut peppers into strips; coarsely chop onion. Thinly slice steaks across the grain. Serve vegetables and beef on tortillas; top with cheese.
NOTE *Wear disposable gloves when cutting hot peppers; the oils can burn skin. Avoid touching your face.*
PER SERVING *375 calories, 14 g fat (5 g sat. fat), 56 mg chol., 325 mg sodium, 29 g carb., 4 g fiber, 29 g pro.* **Diabetic Exchanges** *3 lean meat, 1½ starch, 1 vegetable, 1 fat.*

TEXAS TABBOULEH

Texas Tabbouleh

I used to live in Texas and, after moving away, missed the classic Tex-Mex taste that was always such a big part of meals. To bring it back, I decided to create a dish that reminds me of pico de gallo. My tabbouleh goes over well with friends because it's so different from what they've had, and it's popular at parties, too.

—**TAMMY DAVIS** ARLINGTON, VA

PREP: 40 MIN. + CHILLING
MAKES: 10 SERVINGS

- 1 cup bulgur
- 2 cups boiling water
- 3 medium tomatoes
- 1 cup finely chopped red onion
- 2 green onions, thinly sliced
- ½ cup chopped sweet red pepper
- ½ cup chopped green pepper
- 2 jalapeno peppers, seeded and chopped
- ½ cup fresh cilantro leaves, chopped
- ¼ cup lime juice
- 3 tablespoons canola oil
- 2 garlic cloves, minced
- ¼ teaspoon salt
- ¼ teaspoon coarsely ground pepper
- 1 can (15 ounces) black beans, rinsed and drained
- 1 cup (4 ounces) crumbled queso fresco or feta cheese

1. Place bulgur in a large bowl; stir in boiling water. Let stand, covered, 30 minutes or until bulgur is tender and most of the liquid is absorbed. Drain well, pressing out any excess water. Cool completely.
2. Stir in the tomatoes, onions, peppers, cilantro, lime juice, oil and seasonings. Add the black beans and toss to combine. Refrigerate, covered, at least 30 minutes. Serve with the queso fresco.
NOTE *Wear disposable gloves when cutting hot peppers; the oils can burn skin. Avoid touching your face.*
PER SERVING *139 cal., 4 g fat (1 g sat. fat), 4 mg chol., 161 mg sodium, 21 g carb., 5 g fiber, 6 g pro.* **Diabetic Exchanges:** *1 starch, ½ fat.*

FAST FIX ▸
Snow Peas
& Beef Stir-Fry

START TO FINISH: 30 MIN.
MAKES: 6 SERVINGS

- ½ cup reduced-sodium soy sauce
- ½ cup sherry or water
- 2 tablespoons cornstarch
- 2 teaspoons sugar
- 2 tablespoons canola oil, divided
- 2 garlic cloves, minced
- 1 beef top sirloin steak (1½ pounds), thinly sliced
- ½ pound sliced fresh mushrooms
- 1 medium onion, cut into thin wedges
- 8 ounces fresh snow peas
  Hot cooked rice

1. In a small bowl, whisk soy sauce, sherry, cornstarch and sugar. Transfer ¼ cup mixture to a large bowl; stir in 1 tablespoon oil and garlic. Add beef; toss to coat. Let stand 15 minutes.
2. Heat a large skillet over medium-high heat. Add half of the beef mixture; stir-fry 1-2 minutes or until no longer pink. Remove from pan; repeat with remaining beef.
3. In same pan, heat the remaining oil over medium-high heat until hot. Add the mushrooms and onion; cook and stir until mushrooms are tender. Add the peas; cook 2-3 minutes longer or until crisp-tender.
4. Stir remaining soy sauce mixture and add to pan. Bring to a boil; cook and stir 1-2 minutes or until sauce is thickened. Return beef to pan; heat through. Serve with rice.
PER SERVING *265 cal., 9 g fat (2 g sat. fat), 46 mg chol., 12 g carb., 2 g fiber, 28 g pro.*

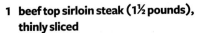

"Why settle for takeout food when you can enjoy this tastier, lighter stir-fry? For easier prep, warm up ready-to-serve brown rice in the microwave."
—**DONNA LINDECAMP** MORGANTON, NC

SNOW PEAS & BEEF STIR-FRY

CHICKEN PASTA SKILLET

FAST FIX ## Chicken Pasta Skillet

My husband is a fan of macaroni and cheese, but I wanted to serve a healthier dish. When I substituted whole wheat pasta and tossed in some chicken and veggies, he asked for seconds.
—**HEATHER McCLINTOCK** COLUMBUS, OH

START TO FINISH: 30 MIN. • **MAKES:** 6 SERVINGS

3 cups uncooked whole wheat spiral pasta
2 cups fresh broccoli florets
2 tablespoons plus 1 teaspoon all-purpose flour
1¼ cups reduced-sodium chicken broth
2 tablespoons butter
½ cup fat-free half-and-half cream
4 ounces reduced-fat process cheese (Velveeta), cubed
1 teaspoon garlic-herb seasoning blend
¼ teaspoon salt
2½ cups cubed cooked chicken breast
½ cup shredded cheddar cheese

1. In a large saucepan, cook pasta according to package directions, adding broccoli during the last 2 minutes of cooking; drain.
2. Meanwhile, in a small bowl, whisk the flour and chicken broth until smooth. In a large skillet, melt the butter over medium heat; stir in the broth mixture. Add half-and-half cream. Bring to a boil; cook and stir 1 minute or until thickened. Add the process cheese, seasoning blend and salt; stir until smooth.
3. Add chicken and pasta mixture; heat through, stirring occasionally. Remove from heat; sprinkle with cheddar cheese. Let stand, covered, 5-10 minutes or until the cheese is melted.
PER SERVING *335 cal., 11 g fat (6 g sat. fat), 72 mg chol., 671 mg sodium, 29 g carb., 4 g fiber, 29 g pro.* **Diabetic Exchanges:** *3 lean meat, 2 starch, 1 fat.*

FAST FIX ## Savory Tomato-Braised Tilapia

START TO FINISH: 30 MIN. • **MAKES:** 4 SERVINGS

4 tilapia fillets (6 ounces each)
¼ teaspoon seasoned salt
1 tablespoon lemon juice
2 tablespoons olive oil
1 small red onion, chopped
1 can (10 ounces) diced tomatoes and green chilies, undrained
¾ cup chopped roasted sweet red peppers
½ cup chicken broth
¼ cup tomato paste
1 teaspoon garlic powder
1 teaspoon dried oregano
Hot cooked pasta, optional

1. Sprinkle the tilapia fillets with the seasoned salt; drizzle with the lemon juice. In a large skillet, heat the oil over medium-high heat. Add the red onion; cook and stir until tender. Add the tomatoes, roasted peppers, chicken broth, tomato paste, garlic powder and oregano; cook and stir 2-3 minutes longer.
2. Place the fillets over the tomato mixture; cook, covered, 6-8 minutes or until fish flakes easily with a fork. If desired, serve with pasta.
PER SERVING *254 cal., 8 g fat (2 g sat. fat), 83 mg chol., 740 mg sodium, 10 g carb., 2 g fiber, 34 g pro.* **Diabetic Exchanges:** *5 lean meat, 1½ fat, 1 vegetable.*

"I shared this fish recipe with my bunco group, and now one of my friends makes it all the time."
—**NANCY SHIVELY** SHOREWOOD, IL

SAVORY TOMATO-BRAISED TILAPIA

SESAME CHICKEN NOODLE SALAD

Sesame Chicken Noodle Salad

Here's my "go-to" meal when I'm short on time. It's quick, easy and takes advantage of any leftover cooked chicken in the fridge. Use reduced-fat salad dressing to keep things lighter.

—**JESS APFE** BERKELEY, CA

PREP: 25 MIN. • **COOK:** 15 MIN. • **MAKES:** 4 SERVINGS

- 8 ounces uncooked whole wheat angel hair pasta
- 2 cups cubed cooked chicken breast
- 1½ cups coleslaw mix
- 1 can (11 ounces) mandarin oranges, drained
- 1 medium sweet red pepper, julienned
- 1 cup fresh sugar snap peas, trimmed and halved
- 3 green onions, chopped
- ¼ teaspoon salt
- ⅔ cup reduced-fat Asian toasted sesame salad dressing
- ¼ cup chopped salted peanuts

1. Cook the pasta according to the package directions.
2. In a large bowl, combine chicken, coleslaw mix, oranges, red pepper, snap peas and green onions; sprinkle with salt and toss to combine.
3. Drain the pasta and rinse in cold water. Add the pasta and dressing to chicken mixture; toss to coat. Sprinkle with salted peanuts.
PER SERVING *519 cal., 11 g fat (1 g sat. fat), 54 mg chol., 631 mg sodium, 72 g carb., 10 g fiber, 35 g pro.*

FAST FIX ▶ Thai Chicken Curry

START TO FINISH: 30 MIN. • **MAKES:** 4 SERVINGS

- 1 pound boneless skinless chicken breasts, cut into ½-inch cubes
- ½ teaspoon salt
- ¼ teaspoon pepper
- 1 tablespoon olive oil
- 6 green onions, thinly sliced
- 1 garlic clove, minced
- 2 tablespoons cornstarch
- 1½ cups chicken stock
- ¾ cup light coconut milk
- 1 tablespoon lime juice
- 1 teaspoon red curry paste
- 1 teaspoon reduced-sodium soy sauce
- 2 cups cooked brown rice
- ¼ cup finely shredded unsweetened coconut

1. Toss chicken with salt and pepper. In a large nonstick skillet, heat oil over medium-high heat. Add the chicken; cook and stir 2-3 minutes or until the outside surface of the chicken is no longer pink. Add green onions and garlic; cook 1 minute longer.
2. In a small bowl, mix cornstarch and stock until smooth; stir into pan. Add coconut milk, lime juice, curry paste and soy sauce. Bring to a boil. Reduce heat; simmer, uncovered, 5-6 minutes or until sauce is slightly thickened. Serve with rice; sprinkle with coconut.
NOTE *Look for unsweetened coconut in the baking or health food section.*
PER SERVING *358 cal., 13 g fat (6 g sat. fat), 63 mg chol., 635 mg sodium, 31 g carb., 3 g fiber, 28 g pro.* **Diabetic Exchanges:** *3 lean meat, 2 starch, 1½ fat.*

"While in New York, I fell in love with Thai food. My chicken curry is on the milder side."
—**COREY RUPP** GREENTOWN, PA

THAI CHICKEN CURRY

FAST FIX ▶ Tilapia Tacos

I absolutely love fish tacos and wanted to create a slimmed-down version. These fill the bill and are fast to fix, too.

—JADE PETERSON PORTLAND, OR

START TO FINISH: 30 MIN.
MAKES: 4 SERVINGS

- 1 egg
- 1 tablespoon fat-free milk
- ½ teaspoon green hot pepper sauce
- ½ cup cornmeal
- 2 tablespoons all-purpose flour
- ¼ teaspoon ground cumin
- ¼ teaspoon pepper
- 4 tilapia fillets (4 ounces each), cut lengthwise in half
- 4 teaspoons olive oil
- 1 can (15 ounces) Southwestern black beans
- 8 corn tortillas (6 inches), warmed
- 3 plum tomatoes, chopped
- 2 cups shredded cabbage
- ½ cup salsa verde
- ¼ cup minced fresh cilantro
- 1 medium lime, cut into 8 wedges

1. Preheat oven to 375°. In a shallow bowl, whisk the egg, milk and hot pepper sauce. In another shallow bowl, mix the cornmeal, flour, cumin and pepper. Dip the tilapia fillets in egg mixture, then in cornmeal mixture, patting to help coating adhere. Place on a baking sheet coated with cooking spray. Drizzle the tops with oil. Bake 15-20 minutes or until the fish flakes easily with a fork.

2. Meanwhile, place beans in a small saucepan; heat through over medium-low heat, stirring occasionally. Serve tilapia in tortillas; top with beans, tomatoes, cabbage, salsa verde and cilantro. Serve with lime wedges.

PER SERVING *438 cal., 9 g fat (2 g sat. fat), 87 mg chol., 567 mg sodium, 57 g carb., 12 g fiber, 34 g pro.*

Toffee Cheesecake Bars

Thanks to this creative recipe, cheesecake doesn't have to be off-limits when you're watching your diet. The bars are so good, they taste like an indulgence.

—EDIE DESPAIN LOGAN, UT

PREP: 25 MIN. • **BAKE:** 20 MIN. + CHILLING
MAKES: 2½ DOZEN

- 1 cup all-purpose flour
- ¾ cup confectioners' sugar
- ⅓ cup baking cocoa
- ⅛ teaspoon baking soda
- ½ cup cold butter
- 1 package (8 ounces) reduced-fat cream cheese
- 1 can (14 ounces) sweetened condensed milk
- 2 eggs, lightly beaten
- 1 teaspoon vanilla extract
- 1¼ cups milk chocolate English toffee bits, divided

1. In a small bowl, combine the flour, confectioners' sugar, cocoa and baking soda. Cut in the butter until mixture resembles coarse crumbs. Press onto the bottom of an ungreased 13-in. x 9-in. baking dish. Bake at 350° for 12-15 minutes or until set.

2. In a large bowl, beat cream cheese until fluffy. Add the milk, eggs and vanilla; beat until smooth. Stir in ¾ cup toffee bits. Pour over crust. Bake 18-22 minutes longer or until center is almost set.

3. Cool on a wire rack for 15 minutes. Sprinkle with remaining toffee bits; cool completely. Cover and refrigerate for 8 hours or overnight.

PER SERVING *169 cal., 9 g fat (5 g sat. fat), 39 mg chol., 120 mg sodium, 19 g carb., trace fiber, 3 g pro.* **Diabetic Exchanges:** *2 fat, 1 starch.*

TOFFEE CHEESECAKE BARS

TILAPIA TACOS

Banana Chip Cake

Here is my adaptation of Ben & Jerry's Chunky Monkey Ice Cream—my all-time favorite. The hardest part of making the cake is waiting for it to cool!

—**BARBARA PRYOR** MILFORD, MA

PREP: 25 MIN. • **BAKE:** 40 MIN. + COOLING
MAKES: 16 SERVINGS

- 1 package yellow cake mix (regular size)
- 1¼ cups water
- 3 eggs
- ½ cup unsweetened applesauce
- 2 medium bananas, mashed
- 1 cup miniature semisweet chocolate chips
- ½ cup chopped walnuts

1. In a large bowl, combine the cake mix, water, eggs and applesauce; beat on low speed for 30 seconds. Beat on medium for 2 minutes. Stir in the bananas, chips and walnuts.

2. Transfer to a 10-in. fluted tube pan coated with cooking spray and sprinkled with flour. Bake at 350° for 40-50 minutes or until a toothpick inserted near the center comes out clean. Cool for 10 minutes before removing from pan to a wire rack to cool completely.

PER SERVING *233 cal., 9 g fat (4 g sat. fat), 40 mg chol., 225 mg sodium, 38 g carb., 1 g fiber, 3 g pro.*

LEMON BLACKBERRY PARFAITS

BANANA CHIP CAKE

Lemon Blackberry Parfaits

Pair the tongue-tingling flavors of lemon and blackberries for luscious but light parfaits. Serve the desserts immediately if you like crisp graham crackers, or within 4 hours for a moister crumb.

—**AMBER NEEDHAM** BELLBROOK, OH

PREP: 25 MIN. + CHILLING
MAKES: 6 SERVINGS

- 3 eggs
- ½ cup plus ¼ cup sugar, divided
- ¾ cup lemon juice
- 1 tablespoon grated lemon peel
- 2 tablespoons butter
- 4 ounces fat-free cream cheese
- 1 cup plus 6 tablespoons reduced-fat whipped topping, divided
- 3 cups fresh blackberries
- 3 whole graham crackers, crushed

1. In a small heavy saucepan over medium heat, whisk the eggs, ½ cup sugar, lemon juice and lemon peel until blended. Add the butter; cook, whisking constantly, until the mixture is thickened and coats the back of a spoon. Transfer to a small bowl; cool. Cover and refrigerate until chilled.

2. In a small bowl, beat the cream cheese and remaining sugar until smooth. Fold in the lemon mixture and 1 cup whipped topping. Spoon half of the cream cheese mixture into six parfait glasses. Top with half of the blackberries and half of the cracker crumbs. Repeat the layers. Top with the remaining whipped topping. Serve immediately.

PER SERVING *292 cal., 9 g fat (5 g sat. fat), 117 mg chol., 213 mg sodium, 48 g carb., 4 g fiber, 8 g pro.*

NIKKI BARTON'S CHICKEN CORDON
BLEU PASTA AND SPINACH SALAD
WITH POPPY SEED DRESSING *PAGE 290*

Tasteful Get-Togethers

Bring everyone to the table with the complete meals in this chapter. From a tropical spread to an Italian feast, these **memorable menus** are perfect for Sunday dinner or any day at all.

MIKE SCHULZ'S RHUBARB-BLUEBERRY CRUMBLE *PAGE 289*

PAMELA VITTI KNOWLES' MANGO CHUTNEY PORK ROAST *PAGE 284*

NIKKI BARTON'S SPARKLING CIDER POUND CAKE *PAGE 291*

BIG DINNER, BIG FUN
BY KELLY ANDERSON

BALSAMIC BRAISED POT ROAST

POT ROAST DAY with my family conjures up all kinds of tender memories. Pot roast is one of those dishes that brought—and still brings—everyone to the table with a sense of togetherness. While we ate, we reminisced about Mom's birthday meals or the opening game of football season.

Crisp fall days in Kansas City when I was growing up meant huge family gatherings were on the horizon. Both my parents came from families with six siblings each. Can you imagine the holiday meals? Forty-five people crowded into one house—and each of us helped to make a dish. The spreads were unbelievable. But what I loved most were the days after Thanksgiving, when turkey leftovers seemed to be part of every meal.

When Sunday rolled around, we were tired of turkey, but we didn't want to lose the fun and warmth of communal meals. That's when someone would cook up that comfort food classic, pot roast.

Family—and, yes, this pot roast—stands the test of time. The days when everyone gathers to eat are truly happy days.

Balsamic Braised Pot Roast

I spent years altering and tweaking this recipe, an easy yet elegant way to prepare an inexpensive cut of meat. I knew it was a success when adults and children alike gobbled it up—and even the kids at my daughter's preschool asked for more!

—KELLY ANDERSON GLENDALE, CA

PREP: 30 MIN. • **BAKE:** 2½ HOURS
MAKES: 8 SERVINGS

- 1 **boneless beef chuck roast (3 to 4 pounds)**
- 1 **teaspoon salt**
- ½ **teaspoon pepper**
- 2 **tablespoons olive oil**
- 3 **celery ribs with leaves, cut into 2-inch pieces**
- 2 **medium carrots, cut into 1-inch pieces**
- 1 **medium onion, coarsely chopped**
- 3 **medium turnips, peeled and quartered**

- 1 **large sweet potato, peeled and cubed**
- 3 **garlic cloves, minced**
- 1 **cup dry red wine or beef broth**
- 1 **can (14½ ounces) beef broth**
- ½ **cup balsamic vinegar**
- 1 **bunch fresh thyme sprigs**
- 4 **fresh sage leaves**
- 2 **bay leaves**
- ¼ **cup cornstarch**
- ¼ **cup cold water**

1. Preheat oven to 325°. Sprinkle the roast with salt and pepper. In an ovenproof Dutch oven, heat oil over medium heat. Brown roast on all sides. Remove from pan.

2. Add celery, carrots and onion to the same pan; cook and stir until tender. Add turnips, sweet potato and garlic; cook 1 minute.

3. Add the wine, stirring to loosen browned bits from pan. Stir in broth, vinegar and herbs. Return roast to pan; bring to a boil. Cover and bake 2½ to 3 hours or until meat is tender.

4. Remove the beef and vegetables; keep warm. Discard the herbs from the cooking liquid; skim the fat. In a small bowl, mix the cornstarch and water until smooth; stir into the cooking liquid. Bring to a boil, stirring constantly; cook and stir 2 minutes or until thickened. Serve with pot roast and vegetables.

FAST FIX ▶ Romaine & Orange Salad with Lime Dressing

A tangy homemade dressing makes a bowful of romaine lettuce, red onion and mandarin oranges extra special.
—LINDA PALLOTTO MANTUA, OH

START TO FINISH: 15 MIN.
MAKES: 6 SERVINGS

- 2 **tablespoons olive oil**
- 1 **tablespoon lime juice**
- 1 **small garlic clove, minced**
- ¾ **teaspoon sugar**
- ⅛ **teaspoon salt**
- ⅛ **teaspoon grated lime peel**
- 6 **cups torn romaine**
- ½ **cup sliced red onion**
- 1 **can (11 ounces) mandarin oranges, drained**

In a bowl, whisk the first six ingredients. In a bowl, combine the romaine and onion. Drizzle with the dressing; toss to coat. Top with the oranges. Serve immediately.

Dill & Chive Peas

START TO FINISH: 10 MIN.
MAKES: 4 SERVINGS

- 1 **package (16 ounces) frozen peas**
- ¼ **cup snipped fresh dill**
- 2 **tablespoons minced fresh chives**
- 1 **tablespoon butter**
- 1 **teaspoon lemon-pepper seasoning**
- ¼ **teaspoon kosher salt**

Cook peas according to package directions. Stir in remaining ingredients; serve immediately.

"Growing my own vegetables and herbs inspires me to keep things fresh in the kitchen with dishes like Dill & Chive Peas."
—**TANNA RICHARD** CEDAR RAPIDS, IA

WHOLE WHEAT POTATO ROLLS

DILL & CHIVE PEAS

Whole Wheat Potato Rolls

Here's a yummy addition to just about any meal. Extra rolls freeze well, too.
—**DEVON VICKERS** GODDARD, KS

PREP: 30 MIN.+ RISING • **BAKE:** 10 MIN.
MAKES: 24 ROLLS

- 1 **package (¼ ounce) active dry yeast**
- 2 **cups warm water (110° to 115°)**
- ½ **cup sugar**
- ½ **cup canola oil**
- 2 **eggs**
- ⅓ **cup mashed potato flakes**
- 1½ **teaspoons salt**
- 2 **cups all-purpose flour**
- 4 **to 4¾ cups whole wheat flour**
- 2 **tablespoons butter, melted**
  Quick-cooking oats, optional

1. In a small bowl, dissolve yeast in warm water. In a large bowl, combine the sugar, oil, eggs, potato flakes, salt, yeast mixture, all-purpose flour and 2½ cups whole wheat flour. Beat until smooth. Stir in enough remaining whole wheat flour to form a soft dough (dough will be sticky).

2. Turn the dough onto a floured surface; knead until smooth and elastic, about 6-8 minutes. Place in a greased bowl, turning once to grease the top. Cover with plastic wrap and let rise in a warm place until doubled, about 1½ hours.

3. Punch down dough. Turn onto a lightly floured surface; divide and shape into 24 balls. Place 2 in. apart on greased baking sheets. Cover with kitchen towels; let rise in a warm place until doubled, about 30 minutes.

4. Preheat oven to 375°. Brush tops with melted butter; if desired, sprinkle with oats. Bake 9-11 minutes or until lightly browned. Serve warm.

IT TAKES FOUR LONG TABLES placed end to end to seat my entire extended family during the holidays. There are about four dozen of us, our plates heaped with wonderful food and the room bustling with chatter and laughter. It's loud and chaotic and I wouldn't trade it for anything in the world—not even when pets start nabbing food off the table.

Food has always been important in our family, one of the bonds that ties us together. I'm the oldest of five and had hardworking parents. By the time I was 10, my father had taught me to cook meals for the whole family. Now that I have my own family—husband Sean and 4-year-old daughter Colette—I'm trying to master cooking meals for a smaller group. I've become very good at freezing leftovers.

I love being part of a big family. You never have to look far to find a friend, and someone always has your back. For the rest of our lives, the highlight of the holidays will always be our noisy, fun and very merry family crowding together around one huge table loaded with food.

Beef Bolognese with Linguine

After a lot of tasting and tweaking, I finally came up with this recipe, which is based on a dish from an Italian restaurant where I worked. I serve the beefy linguine when I have a house full of holiday guests the Sunday before or after Christmas.

—CHRISTINE WENDLAND

BROWNS MILLS, NJ

PREP: 30 MIN. • **COOK:** 3½ HOURS
MAKES: 18 SERVINGS (1 CUP EACH)

- 3 **pounds lean ground beef (90% lean)**
- ⅓ **cup olive oil**
- 3 **medium onions, chopped**
- 3 **large carrots, chopped**
- 6 **celery ribs, chopped**
- 1 **can (12 ounces) tomato paste, divided**
- 9 **garlic cloves, sliced**
- 3 **tablespoons dried parsley flakes**
- 5 **teaspoons kosher salt**
- 3 **teaspoons dried basil**

SAVORY BISCUIT-BREADSTICKS
APPLE WALNUT SALAD
BEEF BOLOGNESE WITH LINGUINE

- 3 **teaspoons dried marjoram**
- 1½ **teaspoons coarsely ground pepper**
- ¼ **teaspoon crushed red pepper flakes**
- 1½ **cups dry red wine**
- 3 **cans (28 ounces each) diced tomatoes, undrained**
- 1½ **cups beef stock**
- 6 **bay leaves**
- 3 **cups 2% milk**
- ¾ **cup grated Parmesan cheese**
  Hot cooked linguine
  Additional grated Parmesan cheese, optional

1. In a stockpot, cook half of the beef over medium heat for 8-10 minutes or until no longer pink, breaking into crumbles. Remove beef with a slotted spoon; set aside. Pour off drippings. Repeat with remaining beef.

2. In the same stockpot, heat oil over medium heat. Add the onions, carrots and celery; cook and stir until tender. Stir in 1 cup tomato paste; cook and stir 3 minutes longer. Add the garlic, seasonings and beef.

3. Stir in wine. Bring mixture to a boil; cook until almost evaporated. Add the tomatoes, stock and bay leaves; return to a boil. Reduce heat; simmer sauce, uncovered, for 3 hours or until it reaches desired consistency, stirring in milk halfway through cooking.

4. Remove bay leaves. Stir in cheese and remaining tomato paste; heat through. Serve with linguine and, if desired, additional cheese.

Savory Biscuit-Breadsticks

Ordinary ingredients like refrigerated biscuits are fun to experiment with. Shape the dough into ropes and add a coating of Parmesan cheese, red pepper flakes and garlic to create yummy breadsticks.
—**BILLY HENSLEY** MOUNT CARMEL, TN

START TO FINISH: 20 MIN.
MAKES: 10 BREADSTICKS

- ½ cup grated Parmesan cheese
- 2 teaspoons dried minced garlic
- ¼ teaspoon crushed red pepper flakes
- 1 tube (12 ounces) refrigerated buttermilk biscuits
- 2 tablespoons olive oil

In a shallow bowl, mix the Parmesan cheese, garlic and red pepper flakes. Roll each biscuit into a 6-in. rope. Brush lightly with oil; roll in cheese mixture. Place on a greased baking sheet. Bake at 400° for 8-10 minutes or until golden brown.

FAST FIX
Apple Walnut Salad

This green salad gets autumn flair from dried cranberries, pumpkin seeds and chunks of apple. Toss in leftover turkey or chicken for a filling main course.
—**BJORG MARTIN** NOBLESVILLE, IN

START TO FINISH: 30 MIN.
MAKES: 12 SERVINGS (⅔ CUP DRESSING)

- ⅓ cup honey
- ¼ cup white balsamic vinegar
- 2 tablespoons olive or flaxseed oil
- 8 cups torn romaine
- 4 cups fresh baby spinach

TOPPINGS
- 6 slices sweet onion, quartered
- 1 cup cubed Jarlsberg or Swiss cheese
- 1 medium apple, chopped
- 1 cup coarsely chopped walnuts
- ½ cup salted pumpkin seeds or pepitas
- ¼ cup dried cranberries, optional

In a small bowl, whisk the honey, vinegar and oil; set aside. Just before serving, place romaine and spinach in a large bowl; drizzle with dressing and toss to coat. Sprinkle with toppings.

SLOW COOKER
Slow Cooker Chocolate Lava Cake

Everyone who tries this rich cake, warm from the slow cooker, falls in love with it.
—**LATONA DWYER** PALM BEACH GARDENS, FL

PREP: 15 MIN. • **COOK:** 3 HOURS
MAKES: 12 SERVINGS

- 1 package devil's food cake mix (regular size)
- 1⅓ cups water
- 3 eggs
- ⅓ cup canola oil
- 2 cups cold 2% milk
- 1 package (3.9 ounces) instant chocolate pudding mix
- 2 cups (12 ounces) semisweet chocolate chips

1. In a large bowl, combine the cake mix, water, eggs and oil; beat on low speed for 30 seconds. Beat on medium for 2 minutes. Transfer to a greased 4-qt. slow cooker.

2. In another bowl, whisk the milk and instant chocolate pudding mix for 2 minutes. Let stand for 2 minutes or until soft-set. Spoon over the cake batter; sprinkle with chocolate chips. Cover and cook on high for 3-4 hours or until a toothpick inserted in the cake portion comes out with moist crumbs. Serve warm.

SLOW COOKER CHOCOLATE LAVA CAKE

DELICIOUS TRADITIONS
BY PAMELA VITTI KNOWLES

MY HUSBAND GREW UP in Eleuthera, a Bahamian island of pink sand, where all of the family's cooking was done on an outdoor stove and baked goods were wrapped in banana leaves instead of being placed in pans.

I fell in love with Randy on a trip to Nassau, where my mom was living the summer I was 18. It was literally love at first sight; by Thanksgiving, we were a couple. The following October we married. That was 28 years ago. I took to the culture immediately, and we lived there 21 amazing years. Randy came from a huge family, and they all welcomed me in.

Food traditions are a big thing to Bahamians, and Randy's family was no exception. His mom, Lily Naomi Knowles, was famous for her cooking and her big heart. Everyone called her Momma.

Every Sunday after church we went to Momma's. She set out a feast of island specialties to feed not just her family, but also her neighborhood—anyone who was hungry. People came from all over, and she gave them the meal of their lives: johnnycake, baked macaroni and cheese, and the most incredible dessert, guava duff. She was a devout Christian and lived by that feed-the-hungry ethic. Although she passed away in 2006, her beautiful spirit lives on in her recipes, which I've handed down to my own two kids.

EAT SMART Mango Chutney Pork Roast

While traditional Bahamian pork is usually stewed or fried, this roast has traditional flavors and features the fruits and peppers that grew in our backyard.

—PAMELA VITTI KNOWLES
HENDERSONVILLE, NC

PREP: 15 MIN. • **BAKE:** 1 HOUR + STANDING
MAKES: 6 SERVINGS (2 CUPS CHUTNEY)

- 1 **tablespoon butter**
- 1 **boneless pork loin roast (2 to 3 pounds)**
- ½ **teaspoon each salt, pepper and ground ginger**

MANGO CHUTNEY

- 2 **medium mangoes, peeled and cubed**
- ¼ **cup finely chopped red onion**
- ¼ **cup finely chopped sweet red pepper**
- 1 **jalapeno pepper, seeded and minced**
- 2 **tablespoons white vinegar**
- 1 **tablespoon grated fresh gingerroot**
- ⅛ **teaspoon each salt, ground turmeric and ground cloves**

1. In a large skillet, heat the butter over medium-high heat. Brown the pork roast on all sides. Sprinkle with the salt, pepper and ginger.

2. Place the pork roast on a rack in a shallow roasting pan. Bake at 350° for 1 to 1½ hours or until a thermometer reads 145°. Remove roast from oven; tent with foil. Let stand for 10 minutes before slicing.

3. Meanwhile, in a large saucepan, combine all chutney ingredients. Cook, uncovered, over medium heat for 8-10 minutes to allow flavors to blend, stirring occasionally. Serve with pork.

PER SERVING *256 cal., 9 g fat (4 g sat. fat), 80 mg chol., 305 mg sodium, 13 g carb., 2 g fiber, 30 g pro.* ***Diabetic Exchanges:** 4 lean meat, 1 fruit, ½ fat.*

MANGO CHUTNEY PORK ROAST

Momma's Warm Potato Salad

FAST FIX

My husband's mother, who was known to all as Momma, made the absolute best potato salad. It's like a really good egg salad with potatoes in it.

—PAMELA VITTI KNOWLES
HENDERSONVILLE, NC

START TO FINISH: 25 MIN.
MAKES: 6 SERVINGS

- 3 medium Yukon Gold potatoes (about 1½ pounds), peeled and cubed
- 6 hard-cooked eggs, chopped
- 2 celery ribs, chopped
- 1 small onion, chopped
- ½ cup chopped green pepper
- ½ cup mayonnaise
- 2 tablespoons Dijon mustard
- ¾ teaspoon salt
- ½ teaspoon pepper
- ⅛ teaspoon hot pepper sauce

1. Place the potatoes in a large saucepan; add water to cover. Bring to a boil. Reduce heat; cook, uncovered, 10-15 minutes or until tender. Drain potatoes and place in a large bowl. Add eggs, celery, onion and green pepper.
2. In a small bowl, mix the remaining ingredients; add to potato mixture. Toss gently to coat. Serve warm. Cover and refrigerate leftovers.

MOMMA'S WARM POTATO SALAD

PINEAPPLE RUM PUNCH

Bahamian Peas & Rice

The No. 1 Bahamian dish, this hearty side with chunks of ham and bacon gets served along with two other starches—potato salad plus macaroni and cheese!

—PAMELA VITTI KNOWLES
HENDERSONVILLE, NC

PREP: 15 MIN. • **COOK:** 50 MIN.
MAKES: 14 SERVINGS

- 3 bacon strips, chopped
- 1 medium onion, chopped
- 1 celery rib, chopped
- ½ cup chopped green pepper
- 1 can (15 ounces) pigeon peas, drained
- 1 cup cubed fully cooked ham
- ¼ cup tomato paste
- 3 fresh thyme sprigs
- 1 teaspoon salt
- ½ teaspoon pepper
- 5½ cups water
- 1 can (13.66 ounces) coconut milk
- 3 cups uncooked brown rice

1. In a Dutch oven, cook the bacon over medium heat until crisp, stirring occasionally. Remove with a slotted spoon; drain on paper towels. Discard the drippings, reserving 1 tablespoon.
2. Add the onion, celery and green pepper to the bacon drippings; cook and stir over medium-high heat for 5-7 minutes or until tender. Stir in the pigeon peas, ham, tomato paste, thyme, salt and pepper.
3. Add the water, coconut milk and cooked bacon; bring to a boil. Stir in rice. Reduce heat; cover and simmer for 45-50 minutes or until rice is tender. Remove thyme sprigs.

FAST FIX

Pineapple Rum Punch

I came up with a tropical beverage using my favorite Bahamian juices. It's inspired by the popular Bahama Mama cocktail and Goombay Punch soft drink.

—PAMELA VITTI KNOWLES
HENDERSONVILLE, NC

PREP: 10 MIN. • **MAKES:** 12 SERVINGS

- 3½ cups unsweetened pineapple juice
- 1½ cups orange juice
- 1 cup coconut water
- 1 cup coconut rum
- 1 cup orange peach mango juice
- 1 cup dark rum
- ¼ cup Key lime juice
- 3 tablespoons Campari liqueur or grenadine syrup

In a pitcher, combine all ingredients. Serve over ice.

I'M 9 YEARS OLD and I love to cook. I started helping my mom, Peggy Roos, bake when I was 4. Now I make cupcakes whenever I can and other desserts, too. (The big mixer is awesome, and so is the smell of food when it's baking.)

I gave my mom a coupon book that I made, and one of the coupons was good for one special meal, cooked by me! She cashed it in on Mother's Day, so I picked out some recipes myself and made her an entire meal. I tried to keep her out of the kitchen while I was cooking so I could surprise her, but she did help light the grill. Because it was a special meal, I set the table and used our special serving platters.

The part I liked best was when my parents cleaned up, because I worked so hard that day making the meal. It took all afternoon! Because my mom makes so many yummy dinners for me, I really wanted to make one for her.

GRILLED SHRIMP SCAMPI

EAT SMART

Grilled Shrimp Scampi

My shrimp scampi is easy to make on the grill, and the homemade marinade goes together with just five ingredients. I serve the skewers over jasmine rice.

—**PEGGY ROOS** MINNEAPOLIS, MN

PREP: 15 MIN. + MARINATING
GRILL: 10 MIN. • **MAKES:** 6 SERVINGS

- 2 tablespoons olive oil
- 2 tablespoons lemon juice
- 3 garlic cloves, minced
- ¼ teaspoon salt
- ¼ teaspoon pepper
- 1½ pounds uncooked jumbo shrimp, peeled and deveined
  Hot cooked jasmine rice
  Minced fresh parsley

1. In a large bowl, whisk the first five ingredients. Add shrimp; toss to coat. Refrigerate, covered, 30 minutes.
2. Thread shrimp onto six metal or soaked wooden skewers. Grill, covered, over medium heat or broil 4 in. from heat 6-8 minutes or until shrimp turn pink, turning once. Serve with rice; sprinkle with parsley.

PER SERVING *118 cal., 4 g fat (1 g sat. fat), 138 mg chol., 184 mg sodium, 1 g carb., trace fiber, 18 g pro.* **Diabetic Exchanges:** *2 meat, ½ fat.*

FAST FIX

Layered Ranch Dip

You'll be the hero of snacktime when you set out this yummy ranch dip with a big bowl of chips. Everyone loves it!

—**PEGGY ROOS** MINNEAPOLIS, MN

START TO FINISH: 10 MIN.
MAKES: 8 SERVINGS

- 2 cups (16 ounces) sour cream
- 1 envelope ranch salad dressing mix
- 1 medium tomato, chopped
- 1 can (4 ounces) chopped green chilies, drained
- 1 can (2¼ ounces) sliced ripe olives, drained
- ¼ cup finely chopped red onion
- 1 cup (4 ounces) shredded Monterey Jack cheese
  Corn chips or tortilla chips

In a small bowl, mix the sour cream and ranch salad dressing mix; spread into a large shallow dish. Layer with the tomato, green chilies, olives, onion and cheese. Refrigerate until serving. Serve with chips.

Garden Potato Pancakes

Like potato pancakes? Try adding corn, cheese and bits of zucchini, onion and carrot for extra flavor and color.

—PEGGY ROOS MINNEAPOLIS, MN

PREP: 20 MIN. • **COOK:** 5 MIN./BATCH
MAKES: 12 PANCAKES

- 2 **medium zucchini, grated**
- 2 **eggs**
- ¼ **cup whole wheat flour**
- ½ **teaspoon salt**
- ¼ **teaspoon pepper**
- ¼ **teaspoon dried basil**
- 1 **large onion, finely chopped**
- 1 **medium potato, grated**
- 1 **medium carrot, grated**
- ⅓ **cup frozen corn, thawed**
- ¼ **cup shredded sharp white cheddar cheese**
  Oil for frying
  Cracked black pepper and sour cream, optional

1. In a strainer or colander, drain the zucchini, squeezing to remove the excess liquid. Pat dry. In a large bowl, whisk the eggs, flour, salt, pepper and basil until blended. Stir in the onion, potato, carrot, corn, white cheddar cheese and zucchini.

2. In an electric skillet, heat ¼ in. of oil to 375°. Working in batches, drop the vegetable mixture by ⅓ cupfuls into the oil; press to flatten slightly. Fry 2-3 minutes on each side or until golden brown. Drain on paper towels. If desired, sprinkle with cracked pepper and serve with sour cream.

RASPBERRY & WHITE CHOCOLATE CHEESECAKE

GARDEN POTATO PANCAKES

Raspberry & White Chocolate Cheesecake

Tangy red raspberries, decadent white chocolate and rich cheesecake—what a heavenly combination! It's a wonderful way to end a special meal.

—PEGGY ROOS MINNEAPOLIS, MN

PREP: 40 MIN.
BAKE: 1¾ HOURS + CHILLING
MAKES: 16 SERVINGS

- 1 **package (10 ounces) frozen sweetened raspberries, thawed**
- 1 **tablespoon cornstarch**

CRUST
- 1 **cup all-purpose flour**
- 2 **tablespoons sugar**
- ½ **cup cold butter**

FILLING
- 4 **packages (8 ounces each) cream cheese, softened**
- 1½ **cups sugar**
- 1¼ **cups heavy whipping cream**
- 2 **teaspoons vanilla extract**
- 2 **eggs, lightly beaten**
- 12 **ounces white baking chocolate, melted and cooled**

1. In a small saucepan, mix the raspberries and cornstarch until blended. Bring to a boil; cook and stir 1-2 minutes or until thickened. Press through a fine-mesh strainer into a bowl; discard seeds. Cool completely.

2. Preheat oven to 350°. Place a greased 9-in. springform pan (with 3-in. sides) on a double thickness of heavy-duty foil (about 18 in. square). Wrap foil securely around pan.

3. For crust, in a small bowl, mix flour and sugar. Cut in butter until crumbly. Press onto the bottom of the prepared pan. Place pan on a baking sheet. Bake 20-25 minutes or until golden brown. Cool on a wire rack. Reduce the oven setting to 325°.

4. For filling, in a large bowl, beat cream cheese and sugar until smooth. Beat in cream and vanilla. Add eggs; beat on low speed just until blended. Stir in cooled chocolate. Pour half of the mixture over crust. Spread with half of the raspberry puree. Top with remaining batter. Drop remaining puree by tablespoonfuls over top. Cut through batter with a knife to swirl.

5. Place the springform pan in a larger baking pan; add 1 in. of hot water to the larger pan. Bake 1¾ to 2 hours or until the edge of the cheesecake is set and golden. (The center of the cheesecake will jiggle when moved.) Remove the springform pan from the water bath. Cool cheesecake on a wire rack for 10 minutes. Loosen cheesecake from pan with a knife; remove foil. Cool 1 hour longer. Refrigerate overnight. Remove rim from pan.

SUMMER LOVING
BY MIKE SCHULZ

NOTHING MAKES A BOY closer to his father than growing up in a house filled with women. At least that was the case for me, the only son in a family with six daughters.

I loved getting one-on-one time with Dad. He was the main cook in our family, so I'd help chop veggies—all fresh from the garden—and endlessly stir pots of gravy so they wouldn't burn.

As a 10-year-old, I saw my duties expand when Dad started building the family a new house. He was generous with the number of nails he let me hammer!

Decades later, I've stayed close to family traditions. I'm the primary cook for my family and built our house. And just as my dad did with me, I take my six grandchidren—from my own houseful of daughters—under my wing and let them tinker alongside me in the kitchen.

They've helped me make everything from Key lime pie to manicotti. My dad loved experimenting with food, and he'd be happy to see us doing the same.

It's not only through cooking that I try to keep Dad's spirit alive. The things I do with my family are similar to what I did growing up. We play card games, walk on the beach on Lake Huron and have bonfires. I'm used to a packed house, so I enjoy it when they all visit. I end up making a lot of the foods my dad did because, conveniently, they feed a crowd. That's just how I like it.

FAUX POTATO SALAD
DAD'S LEMONY GRILLED CHICKEN

EAT SMART **FAST FIX** ▶ **Faux Potato Salad**

Does cauliflower work in potato salad? You bet—along with bits of carrot, green olives and other tasty surprises.
—**MIKE SCHULZ** TAWAS CITY, MI

START TO FINISH: 30 MIN. • **MAKES:** 8 SERVINGS

- 1 medium head cauliflower, broken into florets
- 1 medium carrot, chopped
- 2 hard-cooked eggs, chopped
- 4 green onions, chopped
- 1 celery rib, chopped
- ¼ cup pitted green olives, halved lengthwise
- ¼ cup thinly sliced radishes
- ¼ cup chopped dill pickle
- ¼ cup fat-free mayonnaise
- 1 tablespoon Dijon mustard
- ¼ teaspoon salt
- ⅛ teaspoon pepper

1. In a saucepan, bring 1 in. of water to a boil. Add cauliflower florets; cook, covered, 5-8 minutes or until tender. Drain and rinse in cold water. Pat dry and place in a large bowl. Add carrot, eggs, green onions, celery, olives, radishes and pickle.
2. In a small bowl, mix the remaining ingredients. Add to cauliflower mixture; toss to coat. Refrigerate until serving.
PER SERVING 61 cal., 2 g fat (trace sat. fat), 54 mg chol., 375 mg sodium, 7 g carb., 3 g fiber, 3 g pro. **Diabetic Exchanges:** 1 vegetable, ½ starch.

---

⑤INGREDIENTS
Dad's Lemony Grilled Chicken

A marinade featuring lemon juice, onions and garlic brings tangy flavor to this chicken. Fire up the grill and enjoy!
—**MIKE SCHULZ** TAWAS CITY, MI

PREP: 20 MIN. + MARINATING • **GRILL:** 30 MIN. • **MAKES:** 8 SERVINGS

- 1 cup olive oil
- ⅔ cup lemon juice
- 6 garlic cloves, minced
- 1 teaspoon salt
- ½ teaspoon pepper
- 2 medium onions, chopped
- 8 chicken drumsticks (2 pounds)
- 8 bone-in chicken thighs (2 pounds)

1. In a small bowl, whisk the first five ingredients until blended; stir in the onions. Pour 1½ cups marinade into a large resealable plastic bag. Add the chicken; seal bag and turn to coat. Refrigerate overnight. Cover and refrigerate remaining marinade.
2. Prepare grill for indirect heat. Drain chicken, discarding marinade in bag. Place chicken on grill rack, skin side up. Grill, covered, over indirect medium heat 15 minutes. Turn; grill 15-20 minutes longer or until a thermometer reads 180°, basting occasionally with reserved marinade.

Rhubarb-Blueberry Crumble

Rhubarb is often paired with strawberries, but blueberries give it a delightfully different and summery touch.

—MIKE SCHULZ TAWAS CITY, MI

PREP: 15 MIN. • **BAKE:** 40 MIN. • **MAKES:** 8 SERVINGS

- ⅔ **cup sugar**
- 2 **tablespoons cornstarch**
- ¼ **teaspoon salt**
- 3 **cups fresh blueberries**
- 3 **cups sliced fresh or frozen rhubarb, thawed**

TOPPING

- ¾ **cup biscuit/baking mix**
- ⅓ **cup sugar**
- ⅛ **teaspoon salt**
- ⅓ **cup cold unsalted butter, cubed**
- ½ **cup old-fashioned oats**
- ½ **cup chopped almonds**

1. Preheat oven to 375°. In a large bowl, mix the sugar, cornstarch and salt. Add blueberries and rhubarb; toss to coat. Transfer to a greased 8-in.-square baking dish.

2. For the topping, in a small bowl, mix the baking mix, sugar and salt. Cut in the butter until crumbly; stir in the oats and chopped almonds. Sprinkle over the filling. Bake 40-45 minutes or until the filling is bubbly and the topping is golden brown.

NOTE *If using frozen rhubarb, measure rhubarb while still frozen, then thaw completely. Drain in a colander, but do not press liquid out.*

RHUBARB-BLUEBERRY CRUMBLE

OUR BIG NIGHT IN
BY NIKKI BARTON

IF THERE WAS ONE THING everyone in my family loved to do when I was growing up, it was gathering around the table for Sunday dinner.

After a long week packed with school, sporting events and extracurricular activities, we knew this time was special. It was reserved for sitting down together, reconnecting and catching up over a wonderful meal.

Carrying on the tradition in my own family has proven to be a tremendous blessing. Both my husband and I are home on Sundays, and we have fun preparing dinner together. In fact, this simple activity has brought us closer. While our son and daughter are young, we want them to grasp the importance—and the fun—of eating together as a family.

During autumn, the welcoming aromas of cheesy casseroles baking in the oven and zesty soups simmering on the stove fill our home with comfort. And it seems that, more than in any other season, Sunday dinners in fall bring an added measure of warmth—not only to our tummies, but to our hearts.

Chicken Cordon Bleu Pasta

Facebook fans of my blog, Chef in Training, inspired me to fix this creamy pasta casserole using ingredients I had on hand. Success! I took the dish for another flavorful spin and added a bit of smoky bacon and toasted bread crumbs.

—**NIKKI BARTON** PROVIDENCE, UT

PREP: 25 MIN. • **BAKE:** 20 MIN. • **MAKES:** 6 SERVINGS

- 3 cups uncooked penne pasta
- 2 cups heavy whipping cream
- 1 package (8 ounces) cream cheese, softened and cubed
- 1½ cups (6 ounces) shredded Swiss cheese, divided
- ½ teaspoon onion powder
- ½ teaspoon garlic salt
- ¼ teaspoon pepper
- 3 cups sliced cooked chicken breast
- ¾ cup crumbled cooked bacon
- ¾ cup cubed fully cooked ham
- 3 tablespoons dry bread crumbs

1. Preheat oven to 350°. Cook pasta according to package directions for al dente; drain.
2. Meanwhile, in a large saucepan, heat the heavy whipping cream and cream cheese over medium heat until smooth, stirring occasionally. Stir in 1 cup cheese, onion powder, garlic salt and pepper until blended.
3. In a large bowl, combine chicken, bacon, ham and pasta. Add the sauce; toss to coat. Transfer to a greased 13x9-in. baking dish. Sprinkle with the remaining cheese; top with bread crumbs. Bake, uncovered, 18-22 minutes or until heated through.

SPINACH SALAD WITH POPPY SEED DRESSING
CHICKEN CORDON BLEU PASTA

FAST FIX ▶ ## Spinach Salad with Poppy Seed Dressing

Here's a family favorite I love bringing to parties. It makes a wonderful side dish or even a light lunch.

—**NIKKI BARTON** PROVIDENCE, UT

START TO FINISH: 25 MIN. • **MAKES:** 6 SERVINGS (1 CUP DRESSING)

- 4 cups fresh baby spinach
- 4 cups torn iceberg lettuce
- 1½ cups sliced fresh mushrooms
- ½ pound bacon strips, cooked and crumbled

DRESSING

- ¼ cup red wine vinegar
- ¼ cup chopped red onion
- 3 tablespoons sugar
- ¾ teaspoon salt
- ¼ teaspoon ground mustard
- ½ cup canola oil
- 1½ teaspoons poppy seeds

1. In a large bowl, combine spinach, lettuce, mushrooms and bacon. Place vinegar, onion, sugar, salt and mustard in blender. While processing, gradually add oil in a steady stream. Transfer to a bowl; stir in poppy seeds.
2. Divide salad among six plates; drizzle with dressing.

Sparkling Cider Pound Cake

Looking for an extra-special dessert for the autumn season? This homemade pound cake is incredible and reminds me of fall with every bite. Using sparkling apple cider in both the batter and the glaze gives it a refreshing, unique taste. Enjoy a piece after dinner, for brunch or with your afternoon tea.

—**NIKKI BARTON** PROVIDENCE, UT

PREP: 20 MIN. • **BAKE:** 40 MIN. + COOLING • **MAKES:** 12 SERVINGS

- ¾ cup butter, softened
- 1½ cups sugar
- 3 eggs
- 1½ cups all-purpose flour
- ¼ teaspoon baking powder
- ¼ teaspoon salt
- ½ cup sparkling apple cider

GLAZE
- ¾ cup confectioners' sugar
- 3 to 4 teaspoons sparkling apple cider

1. Preheat oven to 350°. Line bottom of a greased 9x5-in. loaf pan with parchment paper; grease paper.
2. In a large bowl, cream butter and sugar until light and fluffy. Add the eggs, one at a time, beating well after each addition. In another bowl, whisk flour, baking powder and salt; add to creamed mixture alternately with cider, beating well after each addition.
3. Transfer to prepared pan. Bake 40-50 minutes or until a toothpick inserted in center comes out clean. Cool in pan 10 minutes before removing to a wire rack to cool completely.
4. In a small bowl, mix glaze ingredients until smooth; spoon over top of cake, allowing it to flow over sides.

SPARKLING CIDER POUND CAKE

JUDY HERNKE'S
PEANUT BUTTER
MERINGUE PIE *PAGE 297*

Cooking School

Make your **kitchen time even easier** with helpful how-to's and tips from the *Taste of Home* Cooking School pros. **To learn more** about this program, visit *tasteofhome.com/Cooking-Schools*.

**DEB WILLIAMS'
FAVORITE CHILI
CHEESEBURGERS** PAGE 299

**BERNICE JANOWSKI'S
WHITE CHOCOLATE MOUSSE
CHERRY PIE** PAGE 302

**KAREN CAMBIOTTI'S
PUMPKIN AND SAUSAGE PENNE**
PAGE 301

Pretzel Time

Enjoy a big homemade twist or a delicious dessert using mini munchies from the store. These how-to's and tips make it easy. What's knot to love?

Soft Beer Pretzels

When it comes to great pairings of food and drink, I put pretzels and beer near the top of the list. That's why I combined them in this recipe. Try it when you're hosting a crowd to watch the big game on TV.

—ALYSSA WILHITE WHITEHOUSE, TX

SOFT BEER PRETZELS

PREP: 1 HOUR + RISING • **BAKE:** 10 MIN.
MAKES: 8 PRETZELS

- 1 **bottle (12 ounces) amber beer or nonalcoholic beer**
- 1 **package (¼ ounce) active dry yeast**
- 2 **tablespoons unsalted butter, melted**
- 2 **tablespoons sugar**
- 1½ **teaspoons salt**
- 4 **to 4½ cups all-purpose flour**
- 10 **cups water**
- ⅔ **cup baking soda**

TOPPING
- 1 **egg yolk**
- 1 **tablespoon water**
  Coarse salt

1. In a small saucepan, heat the beer to 110°-115°; remove from the heat. Stir in the yeast until dissolved. In a large bowl, combine the butter, sugar, 1½ teaspoons salt, yeast mixture and 3 cups flour; beat on medium speed until smooth. Stir in enough remaining flour to form a soft dough (dough will be sticky).

2. Turn the dough onto a floured surface; knead until smooth and elastic, about 6-8 minutes. Place in a greased bowl, turning once to grease the top. Cover with plastic wrap and let rise in a warm place until doubled, about 1 hour.

3. Preheat oven to 425°. Punch dough down. Turn onto a lightly floured surface; divide and shape into eight balls. Roll each into a 14-in. rope; twist into a pretzel shape.

4. In a Dutch oven, bring water and baking soda to a boil. Drop pretzels, two at a time, into boiling water. Cook 30 seconds. Remove with a slotted spoon; drain well on paper towels.

5. Place the pretzels 2 in. apart on greased baking sheets. In a small bowl, whisk the egg yolk and water; brush over pretzels. Sprinkle with coarse salt. Bake 10-12 minutes or until golden brown. Remove from the pans to a wire rack to cool.

TO MAKE PRETZEL ROLLS *Divide and shape into eight balls. Roll each into a 14-in. rope. Starting at one end of rope, loosely wrap dough around itself to form a coil. Tuck end under; pinch to seal. Boil, top and bake as directed.*

TO MAKE PRETZEL BITES *Divide and shape into eight balls; roll each into a 12-in. rope. Cut each rope into 1-in. pieces. Boil and top as directed; bake at 400° for 6-8 minutes or until golden brown. Makes 8 dozen.*

TO FREEZE *Place cooled pretzels in resealable plastic freezer bags. Store in freezer. To use, thaw at room temperature or microwave on high 20-30 seconds or until heated through.*

PICK A SHAPE

Inch by inch, homemade pretzels are a cinch. Make a rope of dough 14 inches long for traditional pretzels, 14 inches for rolls and 12 inches for bites.

Chocolate-Peanut Butter Crunch Bars

Here's my sweet-salty twist on the usual Rice Krispies squares. I add toppings of creamy peanut butter and rich chocolate, then sprinkle on pretzels and peanuts. It's a great change of pace.

—SHERRI MELOTIK OAK CREEK, WI

PREP: 20 MIN. + CHILLING
MAKES: 3 DOZEN

- 3 cups miniature pretzels, coarsely chopped
- 10 tablespoons butter, divided
- 1 package (10½ ounces) miniature marshmallows
- 3 cups Rice Krispies
- ½ cup light corn syrup, divided
- ¾ cup peanut butter chips
- 1 cup (6 ounces) semisweet chocolate chips
- ¼ cup dry roasted peanuts, chopped

1. Reserve ⅓ cup chopped pretzels. In a large microwave-safe bowl, microwave 6 tablespoons butter on high for 45-60 seconds or until melted. Stir in the miniature marshmallows; cook 1 to 1½ minutes or until the marshmallows are melted, stirring every 30 seconds. Stir in Rice Krispies and the remaining chopped pretzels. Immediately press into a greased 13x9-in. baking pan.

2. In another microwave-safe bowl, combine 2 tablespoons butter and ¼ cup light corn syrup. Microwave, uncovered, on high for 45-60 seconds or until the butter is melted, stirring once. Add peanut butter chips; cook 30-40 seconds or until the chips are melted, stirring once. Spread over the Rice Krispies layer.

3. In a microwave-safe bowl, combine the remaining corn syrup and remaining butter. Cook on high for 45-60 seconds or until butter is melted, stirring once. Add chocolate chips; cook 30-40 seconds longer or until chips are melted, stirring once. Spread over top.

4. Sprinkle with peanuts and reserved pretzels; press down gently. Cover and refrigerate 30 minutes or until set. Cut into bars. Store in airtight containers.

NOTE *This recipe was tested in a 1,100-watt microwave.*

CHOCOLATE-PEANUT BUTTER CRUNCH BARS

THE TASTY 10

Pretzel Dipping
Here's what fellow cooks dip into:

1 Hummus
Blend it with chopped Greek olives, crumbled low-fat feta cheese and some lemon zest.
—CHARLENE SHERMAN
FORT LAUDERDALE, FL

2 Caramelized onion dip
Caramelize sweet onions, let them cool and add them to a mixture of sour cream and mayo. Salt and pepper to taste.
—KRISTIN CLAUSS BURKHARDT
WAYNE, PA

3 Maple glaze
Stir enough milk and maple syrup into confectioners' sugar to form a dipping sauce, then add diced cooked bacon.
—BILL HILBISH
COEUR D'ALENE, ID

4 Beer dip
Combine cream cheese, Hidden Valley ranch dressing, cheddar cheese, beer and a splash of milk.
—VICKI DUNSIRN JUNGEN
GREENVILLE, WI

5 Raspberry mustard
Mix equal parts honey, raspberry preserves and whole-grain Dijon.
—JENNIFER BAKER
CONCORD, NC

6 My own pretzel dip
I mix 8 oz. homemade hot green salsa and 8 oz. very finely shredded cheddar, then stir in mayo until the dip has the right consistency.
—BARB WHITE PFAFF LIBBY, MT

7 Buffalo-style sour cream
Add as much Frank's RedHot sauce as you can handle to a container of sour cream.
—RACHEL ROWLSON COLDWATER, MI

8 Jalapeno cheese sauce
Cook and stir 1 minced garlic clove in 1 Tbsp. melted butter for 1 minute in a saucepan over medium heat. Stir in 1 Tbsp. flour and cook 2 minutes. Whisk in ¾ cup whole milk and bring just to a boil. Remove from the heat and stir in 1 cup finely shredded cheddar cheese, 1 finely chopped seeded jalapeno pepper, a couple of dashes crushed red pepper flakes and salt to taste.
—QUILA CUMMINS BRIGHT
SPOKANE, WA

9 Guacamole
Homemade can't be beat.
—DIANA LICCKETTO SCARAMUZZI
MOUNT EPHRAIM, NJ

10 Chocolate ice cream!
—SUZI GOLDSBURY
WICHITA, KS

Meringue Magic

Whip up a meringue that kisses the sky with a little help from our Cooking School pros.

FLORIDA CITRUS MERINGUE PIE

"Thanks to the tangy burst that comes from an orange and lemon, Florida Citrus Meringue Pie has tongue-tingling fruit flavor. The fluffy, light-as-air top layer is the perfect contrast."

—**BARBARA CARLUCCI** ORANGE PARK, FL

Florida Citrus Meringue Pie

PREP: 30 MIN. • **BAKE:** 15 MIN. + CHILLING
MAKES: 8 SERVINGS

- Pastry for single-crust pie (9 inches)
- 1 cup sugar
- 5 tablespoons cornstarch
- ½ teaspoon salt
- 1 cup water
- 1 cup orange juice
- 4 egg yolks
- ½ cup lemon juice
- 2 tablespoons butter
- 1 teaspoon grated lemon peel
- 1 teaspoon grated orange peel

MERINGUE
- 4 egg whites
- 1 teaspoon vanilla extract
- ¼ teaspoon cream of tartar
- ½ cup sugar

1. Preheat oven to 450°. On a lightly floured surface, roll pastry dough to a ⅛-in.-thick circle; transfer to a 9-in. pie plate. Trim pastry to ½ in. beyond rim of plate; flute edge. Line unpricked pastry with a double thickness of foil. Fill with pie weights, dried beans or uncooked rice.

2. Bake 8-10 minutes or until bottom is lightly browned. Remove foil and weights; bake 5-8 minutes longer or until golden brown. Cool on a wire rack. Reduce oven setting to 350°.

3. Meanwhile, in a large saucepan, mix sugar, cornstarch and salt. Whisk in water and orange juice. Cook and stir over medium-high heat until thickened and bubbly. Reduce heat to low; cook and stir 2 minutes longer (mixture will be thick). Remove from heat.

4. In a small bowl, whisk a small amount of hot mixture into yolks; return all to pan, whisking constantly. Bring to a gentle boil; cook and stir for 2 minutes. Remove from heat. Gently stir in lemon juice, butter and peels.

5. For meringue, in a large bowl, beat egg whites with vanilla and cream of tartar on medium speed until foamy. Gradually add the sugar, 1 tablespoon at a time, beating on high after each addition until dissolved. Continue beating the whites until soft glossy peaks form.

6. Transfer hot filling to crust. Spread meringue over filling, sealing to edge of crust; swirl top with the back of a spoon.

7. Bake for 13-16 minutes or until the meringue is golden brown. Cool on a wire rack; serve pie within 2 hours. Refrigerate leftovers.

PASTRY FOR SINGLE-CRUST PIE (9 INCHES) *Combine 1¼ cups all-purpose flour and ¼ tsp. salt; cut in ½ cup cold butter until crumbly. Gradually add 3-5 Tbsp. ice water, tossing with a fork until dough holds together when pressed. Wrap in plastic wrap and refrigerate 1 hour.*

Separate Your Eggs

If you are among the home cooks suffering from separation anxiety when it comes to eggs, take the advice of Cooking School Pro Cheryl Cohen from Dover, Ohio. Rule No. 1? Egg yolk contains fat—and even a speck of it in your whites will prevent them from whipping to a foam.

- If you don't have an egg separator, use tools you already have on hand, such as a slotted spoon or a funnel. Allow the egg white to run through while the spoon or funnel catches the yolk.

- If, despite your best efforts, you still end up with a small speck of egg yolk in your bowl, remove it with a clean spoon. It can be tempting to remove bits of yolk with your finger, but resist the urge. Your skin has oils on it that will deflate the meringue.

top tips

....
Separate the egg whites and yolks while they are cold—it's easier. But before you beat the whites, let them stand at room temperature for a bit.
....
Beat in the sugar 1 tablespoon at a time so that it dissolves completely, producing a silky-smooth meringue.
....
Choose a dry day to do your baking. Meringues absorb moisture on humid days and become limp or sticky.
....
For picture-perfect peaks and swirls in your meringue, touch an offset spatula to the meringue before baking, then quickly lift. Repeat.

Peanut Butter Meringue Pie

My sons clamor for this peanut butter pie. My mom found the recipe in a magazine for farmers' wives years ago, and now I'm teaching our daughters-in-law to make it.
—**JUDY HERNKE** MUNDELEIN, IL

PREP: 45 MIN. + CHILLING
BAKE: 15 MIN. + COOLING
MAKES: 8 SERVINGS

Pastry for single-crust pie (9 inches)
- ¾ cup confectioners' sugar
- ½ cup creamy peanut butter
- ⅔ cup sugar
- 3 tablespoons cornstarch
- 2 tablespoons all-purpose flour
- Dash salt
- 3 cups 2% milk
- 3 egg yolks
- 2 tablespoons butter
- 1 teaspoon vanilla extract

MERINGUE
- 3 egg whites
- Dash cream of tartar
- ¼ cup sugar

PEANUT BUTTER MERINGUE PIE

1. Roll out pastry to fit a 9-in. pie plate. Transfer the pastry to pie plate. Trim pastry to ½ in. beyond edge of plate; flute edges. Line unpricked pastry with a double thickness of heavy-duty foil. Fill with dried beans, uncooked rice or pie weights.

2. Bake at 450° for 8 minutes. Remove the foil and weights; bake 5-7 minutes longer or until lightly browned. Cool on a wire rack.

3. Meanwhile, in a small bowl, beat the confectioners' sugar and peanut butter until crumbly, about 2 minutes. Set aside.

4. In a large heavy saucepan, combine the sugar, cornstarch, flour and salt. Stir in milk until smooth. Cook and stir over medium-high heat until mixture is thickened and bubbly. Reduce heat; cook and stir 2 minutes longer.

5. Remove from the heat. Stir a small amount of hot mixture into egg yolks; return all to pan, stirring constantly. Bring to a gentle boil; cook and stir 2 minutes longer. Remove from the heat. Stir in butter and vanilla.

6. Sprinkle 1 cup of the peanut butter mixture over the crust. Pour the hot filling over the top.

7. In a large bowl, beat the egg whites and cream of tartar on medium speed until soft peaks form. Gradually beat in the sugar, 1 tablespoon at a time, on high until stiff glossy peaks form and the sugar is dissolved. Spread evenly over the hot filling, sealing the edges to the crust. Sprinkle with the remaining peanut butter mixture.

8. Bake at 350° for 12-15 minutes or until meringue is golden brown. Cool on a wire rack for 1 hour. Refrigerate for at least 4 hours before serving. Store leftovers in the refrigerator.
NOTE *Let pie weights cool before storing. Beans and rice may be reused as pie weights, but not for cooking.*

PRETTY PEAKS

A fluffy mountain of meringue starts with a clean bowl, says Cooking School Pro Karen Davis of Stuart, Iowa. Stainless steel or glass works best. Plastic is more likely to have an oily residue.

❶ Beat egg whites with an electric mixer on medium speed until the peaks curl down when you lift the beaters up. This is soft-peak stage.

❷ For stiff peaks, continue beating on high until the volume increases and the mixture thickens. Lift the beaters; the peaks should stand straight. If you tilt the bowl, the mixture should not slide.

Best of the Burgers

Give beef patties the right stuff for an exceptional cookout.

BURGER SECRETS

1 I add Worcestershire sauce, minced garlic and a bit of ranch dressing to my ground meat mix. It makes for one happy husband!
—**HEATHER SHORE** TAMAQUA, PA

2 Butter and toast the buns. Stuff the patty with sauteed onion, fresh jalapeno, cooked bacon bits and cheese. Cook it on a hot gril—and never, ever smoosh it down with a spatula!
—**CAMI CASEY** HEREFORD, TX

3 It's Greek to me! I mix chopped red onion, Greek seasoning and some crumbled feta cheese into ground beef or turkey. Grill the patties, then pile on marinated cucumber and red onion, tzatziki sauce and even more feta.
—**KRISTIE PLATT MAGILL** PENDLETON, OR

4 My family loves to top off our grilled turkey burgers with my homemade guacamole. And don't forget the green chilies, pepper jack cheese and bacon. After one of these, I have my hubby's heart in my hand!
—**BECCA TRUDELL** HENDERSON, NV

5 I call this the ultimate pretzel burger. Serve a sirloin burger on a soft pretzel bun; top it with a fried egg, bacon slices, lettuce, sharp cheddar, pickles, spicy mustard and ketchup.
—**BETH CHABOT** MACOMB, MI

"When these standouts are on the menu, I never have to call my family to the table twice. Get a jump start and stuff the patties ahead of time, then grill later."
—**JOYCE GUTH** MOHNTON, PA

Mushroom-Stuffed Cheeseburgers

PREP: 30 MIN. • **GRILL:** 10 MIN.
MAKES: 8 SERVINGS

- 2 **bacon strips, finely chopped**
- 2 **cups chopped fresh mushrooms**
- ¼ **cup chopped onion**
- ¼ **cup chopped sweet red pepper**
- ¼ **cup chopped green pepper**
- 2 **pounds lean ground beef (90% lean)**
- 2 **tablespoons steak sauce**
- ½ **teaspoon seasoned salt**
- 4 **slices provolone cheese, halved**
- 8 **kaiser rolls, split**

1. In a large skillet, cook the bacon over medium heat until crisp, stirring occasionally. Remove with a slotted spoon; drain on paper towels. Cook and stir the mushrooms, onion and peppers in the bacon drippings until tender. Using slotted spoon, remove to a small bowl; cool completely. Stir in the bacon.

2. In a large bowl, combine the beef, steak sauce and seasoned salt, mixing lightly but thoroughly. Shape into 16 thin patties. Top eight of the patties with cheese, folding over the cheese to fit within ¾ inch of the edge. Spread with the mushroom mixture. Top with the remaining patties, pressing edges to enclose filling.

3. Grill the burgers, uncovered, over medium-high heat or broil 4 in. from heat 5-6 minutes on each side or until a thermometer inserted in the meat portion reads 160°. Serve on rolls.

FAST FIX ▶ Favorite Chili Cheeseburgers

I like to experiment when fixing burgers, and loading them with sharp cheddar makes them absolutely delicious. When I want lighter fare, I use a mixture of lean ground beef and ground turkey.

—**DEB WILLIAMS** PEORIA, AZ

START TO FINISH: 20 MIN.
MAKES: 4 SERVINGS

- 1 **pound ground beef**
- 2 **tablespoons chili sauce**
- 1 **tablespoon chili powder**
- ½ **cup shredded cheddar cheese**
- 4 **hamburger-size pretzel buns or hamburger buns, split**
- ½ **cup nacho cheese sauce, warmed**

1. In a large bowl, combine the beef, chili sauce and powder, mixing lightly but thoroughly. Shape into eight ¼-in.-thick patties. Place 2 tablespoons cheese onto the center of each of four patties. Top with remaining patties; press edges firmly to seal.

2. Grill the burgers, covered, over medium heat or broil 4 in. from heat 4-6 minutes on each side or until a thermometer reads 160°. Serve on buns with cheese sauce.

FAVORITE CHILI CHEESEBURGERS

"Pack a little heat with fresh jalapeno and pepper jack cheese."
—**JAMIE DUNN** OWASSO, OK

top tips

FROM THE COOKING SCHOOL PROS

"Combine ripe tomatoes, a bit of basil and fresh mozzarella for a Caprese burger."
—**DANA ELLIOTT** DANVILLE, IN

"The classic Greek pairing of spinach and feta creates the alpha and the omega of stuffed burgers."
—**KRISTI LARSON** BOUNTIFUL, UT

BURGER DELUXE

Sometimes a little hamburger helper—in the form of an expert's advice—is just what you need to ensure burger success. Here are Cooking School Pro Guy Klinzing's tips for making perfect patties.

- Stay loose! The less you handle the patty, the more tender the cooked burger will be.
- Cook stuffed burgers over medium heat. If the fire is too hot, the outside burns and the inside remains uncooked.
- For an extra-melty filling, choose a cheese that melts quickly and smoothly, such as American or Muenster.
- Resist the urge to flatten your burger patties with a spatula as they cook. You'll press out those precious flavorful juices.
- Allow the cooked burgers to rest a few minutes before serving.

Great Pumpkin

Reach for cooking pumpkins—smaller and sweeter than those used for jack-o'-lanterns. Then follow these steps for amazing fall treats.

Walnut-Streusel Pumpkin Pie

I'm a fan of streusel topping, cream cheese and pumpkin pie, so I combined them in one dessert recipe. It's one of my first choices when I need a standout treat for a holiday or other special occasion.
—**DEBORAH PAULSON** DEER PARK, WA

PREP: 25 MIN. • **BAKE:** 65 MIN. + COOLING
MAKES: 10 SERVINGS

        Pastry for single-crust pie
          (9 inches)
  1   **can (15 ounces) pure pumpkin or**
        1¾ cups fresh pumpkin puree
  1   **can (14 ounces) sweetened**
        condensed milk
  ½   **cup sugar**
  ½   **cup packed dark brown sugar**
  2   **eggs**
  1   **tablespoon all-purpose flour**
  ½   **teaspoon salt**
  1½ **teaspoons ground cinnamon**
  ½   **teaspoon ground nutmeg**
  ¼   **teaspoon ground ginger**
CREAM CHEESE FILLING
  1   **package (8 ounces) cream cheese,**
        softened
  ¼   **cup sugar**
  ½   **teaspoon vanilla extract**
  1   **egg, lightly beaten**
TOPPING
  ¼   **cup old-fashioned oats**
  ¼   **cup packed dark brown sugar**
  2   **tablespoons all-purpose flour**
  ¼   **teaspoon ground cinnamon**
  ¼   **teaspoon ground nutmeg**
  2   **tablespoons cold butter, cubed**
  ¼   **cup chopped walnuts**

1. Line a 9-in. deep-dish pie plate with the pie pastry; trim and flute the edge. Refrigerate while preparing the filling. In a large bowl, beat the pumpkin, sweetened condensed milk, sugars, eggs, flour, salt and spices until blended; transfer to crust.
2. In another bowl, beat the cream cheese, sugar and vanilla until smooth. Add the egg; beat on low speed just until combined. Spoon evenly over pumpkin layer.
3. In a small bowl, combine the first five topping ingredients; cut in butter until crumbly. Stir in walnuts; sprinkle over the filling. Cover the edge with foil to prevent overbrowning.
4. Bake at 400° for 15 minutes. Reduce the heat to 350°; bake 50-60 minutes longer or until a knife inserted near the center comes out clean.
5. Remove foil. Cool on a wire rack. Serve within 2 hours or refrigerate, covered, until cold.

WALNUT-STREUSEL PUMPKIN PIE

Pumpkin and Sausage Penne

My Italian father-in-law used to swear he'd eat pasta only with red sauce. But when I prepared this main course, he changed his mind!

—**KAREN CAMBIOTTI** STROUDSBURG, PA

START TO FINISH: 30 MIN.
MAKES: 2 SERVINGS

- ¾ cup uncooked penne pasta
- 2 Italian sausage links, casings removed
- ½ cup chopped sweet onion
- 1 garlic clove, minced
- 1 teaspoon olive oil
- ⅓ cup white wine or chicken broth
- 1 bay leaf
- ¾ cup chicken broth
- ⅓ cup canned pumpkin or fresh pumpkin puree
- 3 teaspoons minced fresh sage, divided
- ⅛ teaspoon each salt, pepper and ground cinnamon
  Dash ground nutmeg
- 3 tablespoons half-and-half cream
- 2 tablespoons shredded Romano cheese

PUMPKIN AND
SAUSAGE PENNE

1. Cook pasta according to package directions. Meanwhile, in a large skillet, cook sausage over medium heat until no longer pink, breaking into crumbles. Remove with a slotted spoon; drain on paper towels. Discard drippings, reserving 1 teaspoon.
2. Cook and stir onion and garlic in oil and reserved drippings over medium-high heat until tender. Add wine and bay leaf. Bring to a boil; cook until

liquid is reduced by half. Stir in broth, pumpkin, 1½ teaspoons sage and remaining seasonings; cook 1 minute longer. Add the cream and sausage; heat through. Remove bay leaf.
3. Drain pasta; transfer to a large bowl. Add sausage mixture; toss to coat. Sprinkle with cheese and remaining sage.

MAKE YOUR OWN PUMPKIN PUREE

1¾ CUPS PUREE = ONE 15-OZ. CAN PUMPKIN

❶ Select a cooking pumpkin (about 4-6 lbs.); wash and dry. With a small serrated or heavy knife, remove the top of the pumpkin. Use a sawing motion to cut the pumpkin into 4 quarters. Scrape out all of the seeds and stringy pulp.
❷ Place the pumpkin, flesh side down, on a 15x10x1-in. baking pan. Bake at 350° for 45-60 minutes or until a fork inserted into the skin comes out easily.

❸ Scoop out the flesh, add a few chunks at a time to a food processor and process until smooth.
❹ Place the puree in a large strainer lined with 4 pieces of cheesecloth or 1 large coffee filter. Place the strainer over a large bowl; cover and refrigerate for 8 hours. Remove the pumpkin from the strainer and discard the liquid. The puree is ready to use or freeze for up to one year.

Chocolate Curls

Finish your special desserts with a fancy flourish of decadence.

White Chocolate Mousse Cherry Pie

What do you get when you top a cookie crust with a cherry-almond filling and light-as-air mousse? Pure bliss!

—**BERNICE JANOWSKI** STEVENS POINT, WI

PREP: 1 HOUR • **BAKE:** 15 MIN. + CHILLING
MAKES: 8-10 SERVINGS

- 14 **Oreo cookies**
- ¾ **cup chopped macadamia nuts**
- 2 **tablespoons butter, melted**

FILLING
- 1 **tablespoon cornstarch**
- 2 **tablespoons water**
- 1 **can (21 ounces) cherry pie filling**
- ½ **teaspoon almond extract**

WHITE CHOCOLATE MOUSSE
- 1 **envelope unflavored gelatin**
- 3 **cups heavy whipping cream, divided**
- ¼ **cup sugar**
- ¼ **teaspoon almond extract**
- 1 **cup cold 2% milk**
- 1 **package (3.3 ounces) instant white chocolate pudding mix**
  Chocolate syrup and curls, optional

1. In a food processor, combine cookies and nuts; cover and process until cookies are finely chopped. Add butter; cover and pulse until mixture resembles coarse crumbs.

2. Press the mixture onto the bottom and up the sides of an ungreased 9-in. deep-dish pie plate. Bake at 350° for 8-10 minutes or until set. Cool on a wire rack.

3. For the filling, combine cornstarch and water in a small saucepan until smooth. Stir in the cherry pie filling. Bring mixture to a boil; cook and stir for 1 minute or until slightly thickened. Remove from the heat; stir in extract. Cool completely.

4. For mousse, in a small saucepan, sprinkle gelatin over ½ cup cream; let stand for 1 minute. Heat over low heat, stirring until gelatin is completely dissolved. Remove from the heat.

5. In a large bowl, beat remaining cream until it begins to thicken. Add the sugar and extract; beat until soft peaks form. Gradually beat in gelatin mixture. In a large bowl, whisk the milk and pudding mix for 2 minutes (mixture will be thick). Fold whipped cream mixture into the pudding. Refrigerate until slightly firm, about 30 minutes.

6. Spread cooled filling into crust; top with mousse. Refrigerate for 2 hours or until firm. Garnish with chocolate syrup and curls if desired.

WHITE CHOCOLATE MOUSSE CHERRY PIE

COCONUT-FILLED CHOCOLATE CUPCAKES

1. For the filling, place the egg white and salt in a small bowl; let stand at room temperature for 30 minutes. Combine the coconut and flour; set aside. Beat the egg white on medium speed until soft peaks form. Gradually add the sugar, beating on high until glossy peaks form and the sugar is dissolved. Gradually fold in the coconut mixture, about ¼ cup at a time; set aside.

2. In a large bowl, cream shortening and sugar until light and fluffy. Add eggs and vanilla; mix well. Combine the flour, cocoa, salt and baking soda; add to creamed mixture alternately with the buttermilk and water. Fill paper-lined muffin cups half full. Drop the filling by teaspoonfuls into the center of each cupcake. Cover filling with 2 tablespoons batter.

3. Bake at 350° for 18-22 minutes or until a toothpick inserted in the cake portion comes out clean. Cool for 10 minutes before removing from pans to wire racks to cool completely.

4. For the glaze, in a small saucepan, combine the sugar and milk. Bring to a boil, stirring constantly. Remove from the heat; stir in the shortening and chocolate chips until melted. Beat until thickened. Spread over cupcakes and garnish with toasted coconut and chocolate curls.

Coconut-Filled Chocolate Cupcakes

If you're nuts about chocolate and coconut, this is definitely the cupcake for you. The chocolate ganache is so tempting, you just might end up with a shortage when it's time to frost!

—**LUANN KLINK** FROSTBURG, MD

PREP: 45 MIN. + STANDING
BAKE: 20 MIN. + COOLING
MAKES: 26 CUPCAKES

- 1 **egg white**
   Dash salt
- 1 **cup flaked coconut**
- 1 **tablespoon all-purpose flour**
- 2 **tablespoons sugar**

BATTER

- ⅔ **cup shortening**
- 1½ **cups sugar**
- 2 **eggs**
- 1 **teaspoon vanilla extract**
- 2½ **cups all-purpose flour**
- ½ **cup baking cocoa**
- 1 **teaspoon salt**
- ¾ **teaspoon baking soda**
- 1 **cup buttermilk**
- ½ **cup water**

GLAZE

- 2 **cups sugar**
- ½ **cup milk**
- ½ **cup shortening**
- 1 **cup (6 ounces) semisweet chocolate chips**
   Toasted coconut and chocolate curls

CHOCOLATE CURLS

For the best chocolate curls, you'll need room-temperature chocolate bars and a little bit of practice. Follow the helpful how-to's below when you want to top off desserts with curly curls or long curls of chocolate delight.

CANDY BAR METHOD Grab a king-size chocolate bar and a vegetable peeler and "peel" off curls. Keep a backup candy bar handy to use when one bar softens in your hand. Place curls on the dessert with a toothpick.

MELTED METHOD Melt ½ cup chopped milk or white chocolate or candy coating in a microwave-safe bowl. Stir until smooth. Spread the melted chocolate thinly (about ⅛ inch thick) on plastic wrap or waxed paper. Let the chocolate stand until almost set but not completely hard. Gently roll up the plastic wrap, jelly-roll style. Place it in refrigerator for 5 minutes or until the chocolate is completely hard. Unroll the chocolate and break it into shards.

General Recipe Index

This handy index lists every recipe by food category, major ingredient and/or cooking method, so you can easily locate recipes to suit your needs.

✓ *Recipe includes Nutrition Facts*

Pumpkin Harvest Beef Stew, 39
Spring-Thyme Chicken Stew, 263

STRAWBERRIES

Brown-Sugar Salmon with Strawberries, 236
Dutch Baked Pancake with Strawberry-Almond Compote, 148
Glazed Fruit Medley, 27
Lemon-Berry Ice Cream Pie, 115
Rhubarb Fool with Strawberries, 125
Strawberries & Cream Torte, 229
✓Strawberry-Hazelnut Meringue Shortcakes, 127
Strawberry Lemonade Smoothie, 16
Strawberry Walnut Torte, 189
✓Sunny Strawberry & Cantaloupe Salad, 24

STUFFING

Pork Chops with Corn Bread Stuffing, 236
Roast Turkey with Sausage-Cabbage Stuffing, 203

SWEET POTATOES

Apple & Pecan Stuffed Sweet Potatoes, 54
✓My Underground Vegetable Salad, 24
Pumpkin Harvest Beef Stew, 39
Roasted Kielbasa & Vegetables, 64
Roasted Potatoes with Garlic Butter, 188
Sweet Potato & Chickpea Salad, 29
Sweet Potato Crostini, 8
Sweet Potato Hummus, 194
Sweet Potato Pancakes with Cinnamon Cream, 155
Tempting Teriyaki Chicken Stew, 172

TACOS, ENCHILADAS & BURRITOS

Black Bean Turkey Enchiladas, 271
Chicken Burritos, 61
Garlic Beef Enchiladas, 60
Tilapia Tacos, 276

TOMATOES

✓Basil Corn & Tomato Bake, 48
Beer Brat Chili, 154
✓Bruschetta Chicken, 72
Chicken in Tomato-Caper Sauce, 267
Chili-Rubbed Steak & Bread Salad, 26
Connie's Tortellini Salad, 160
✓Creamy Tomato Tortellini with Sausage, 255
Fire-Roasted Tomato Soup, 252
Fresh Corn & Arugula Salad, 25
✓Fresh Corn & Tomato Fettuccine, 169
Garden Quinoa Salad, 271
Garlicky Beef & Tomatoes with Pasta, 257

✓Green Beans with Bacon and Tomatoes, 55
Grilled Havarti & Mushrooms, 249
✓Grilled Vegetable Orzo Salad, 20
Harvest Salad with Cherry Vinaigrette, 227
Haunted Antipasto Salad, 195
Herb & Sun-Dried Tomato Muffins, 80
Hero Pasta Salad, 23
Homemade Antipasto Salad, 23
✓Italian Fresh Vegetable Salad, 158
Mediterranean Grilled Chicken & Greens, 268
✓Mediterranean Vegetable Pitas, 34
✓My Underground Vegetable Salad, 24
Orzo-Tuna Salad with Tomatoes, 265
Pizza-Flavored Pasta Sauce, 75
Pizza Macaroni & Cheese, 77
✓Rainbow Vegetable Skillet, 170
Roasted Tomato Soup with Fresh Basil, 45
Savory Tomato-Braised Tilapia, 274
Simple Tomato Soup, 38
Slow & Easy Minestrone, 168
✓Spicy Cowboy Chili, 157
Spicy Gazpacho Salad, 30
Sun-Dried Tomato Focaccia, 88
Taco Corn Bread Casserole, 65
Texas Tabbouleh, 273
Tomato-Basil Grilled Cheese, 249
Tomato Pie, 57
Tomato, Sausage & Cheddar Bread Pudding, 154
✓Tomatoes with Buttermilk Vinaigrette, 192
✓Tuscan-Style Roasted Asparagus, 189
Worth Every Penne, 178

TORTILLAS

Black Bean Turkey Enchiladas, 271
Candy Corn Quesadillas, 198
Fiesta Turkey Tortilla Soup, 252
Flying Bat Pizzas, 195
Garlic Beef Enchiladas, 60
Indian-Spiced Chickpea Wraps, 261
Marinated Steak & Pepper Fajitas, 272
✓Mustache Tortilla Cutouts, 38
Shrimp Fajitas, 268
Shrimp Fried Rice Quesadillas, 180
Tilapia Tacos, 276
Wasabi Beef Fajitas, 179

TURKEY, TURKEY BACON & TURKEY SAUSAGE

Bacon Breakfast Cups, 146
✓Black Bean 'n' Pumpkin Chili, 42
Black Bean Turkey Enchiladas, 271
Carolina Crab Boil, 71
✓Cincinnati-Style Chili, 41

Cottage Pie, 69
Fiesta Turkey Tortilla Soup, 252
Green Bean Casserole Stuffed Mushrooms, 9
Hearty Turkey & Feta Sandwich, 261
Loaded Baked Potato Dip, 17
Momma's Turkey Stew with Dumplings, 179
Portobello Pasta Bake, 239
Roast Turkey with Sausage-Cabbage Stuffing, 203
Turkey-Cranberry Minis, 8
Turkey Sage Sausage Patties, 149
Turkey Sausage Pizza, 262
✓Turkey Verde Lettuce Wraps, 245
Turkey Wild Rice Soup, 36
White Chili, 37

VEGETABLES (also see specific kinds)

Autumn Vegetable Mash, 162
✓Chicken & Vegetable Curry Couscous, 254
Crunchy Vegetable Salad, 176
✓Faux Potato Salad, 288
✓Garden Bow Tie Salad, 22
Garden Potato Pancakes, 287
Quick Shepherd's Pie, 246
✓Rainbow Vegetable Skillet, 170
Slow & Easy Minestrone, 168
✓Veg Jambalaya, 234

YEAST BREADS

Candy Cane Rolls, 213
Russian Krendl Bread, 212
Sun-Dried Tomato Focaccia, 88

ZUCCHINI

Brunch Strata, 144
Chocolate Zucchini Cake, 120
Connie's Tortellini Salad, 160
✓Five-Cheese Jumbo Shells, 68
✓Grilled Vegetable Orzo Salad, 20
✓Italian Fresh Vegetable Salad, 158
Roasted Kielbasa & Vegetables, 64
Summer Vegetable Cobbler, 60
Zucchini Nut Bread, 83

Alphabetical Recipe Index

This handy index lists every recipe in alphabetical order so you can easily find your favorites.

✓ Recipe includes Nutrition Facts